Dynamics Reported

Expositions in Dynamical Systems

Dynamical Systems are a rapidly developing field with a strong impact on applications. Dynamics Reported is a series of books of a new type. Its principal goal is to make available current topics, new ideas and techniques. Each volume contains about four or five articles of up to 60 pages. Great emphasis is put on an excellent presentation, well suited for advanced courses, seminars etc. such that the material becomes accessible to beginning graduate students. To explain the core of a new method contributions will treat *examples* rather than general theories, they will describe *typical results* rather than the most sophisticated ones. Theorems are accompanied by *carefully written proofs*. The presentation is as *self-contained* as possible.

Authors will receive 5 copies of the volume containing their contributions. These will be split among multiple authors.

Authors are encouraged to prepare their manuscripts in Plain TEX or LATEX. Detailed information and macro packages are available via the Managing Editors.

Manuscripts and correspondence should be addressed to the Managing Editors:

C. K. R. T. Jones
Division of Applied Mathematics
Brown University
Providence, Rhode Island 02912
USA
e-Mail: ckrtj@cfm.brown.edu

U. Kirchgraber
Mathematics
Swiss Federal Institute
of Technology (ETH)
CH-8092 Zürich, Switzerland
e-Mail: kirchgra@math.ethz.ch

H. O. Walther
Mathematics
Ludwig-Maximilians University
W-8000 Munich
Federal Republic of Germany
e-Mail: Hans-Otto.Walther
@mathematik.
uni-muenchen.dbp.de

C. K. R. T. Jones   U. Kirchgraber   H. O. Walther
(Managing Editors)

Dynamics Reported

Expositions in Dynamical Systems

New Series: Volume 1

With Contributions of
R. Bielawski, H. W. Broer, R. H. Cushman, L. Gorniewicz,
G. Iooss, A. F. Ivanov, M. Levi, S. Plaskacz, A. N. Sharkovsky,
A. Vanderbauwhede, G. Vegter

 Springer-Verlag
Berlin Heidelberg New York
London Paris Tokyo
Hong Kong Barcelona
Budapest

ISBN 3-540-54193-4 Springer-Verlag Berlin Heidelberg New York
ISBN 0-387-54193-4 Springer-Verlag New York Berlin Heidelberg

Library of Congress Cataloging-in-Publication Data
Dynamics reported: expositions in dynamical systems / C. K. R. T. Jones, U. Kirchgraber, H. O. Walther,
managing editors; with contributions of R. Bielawski . . . [et al.].   p.   cm.
ISBN 3-540-54193-4 (Springer-Verlag Berlin Heidelberg New York: alk. paper).
ISBN 0-387-54193-4 (Springer-Verlag New York Berlin Heidelberg: alk. paper)
1. Differentiable dynamical systems. I. Kirchgraber, Urs, 1945- . II. Walther, Hans-Otto.
III. Bielawsi, R.   QA614.8.D96 1991 003'.85-dc20 91-23213 CIP

© Springer-Verlag Berlin Heidelberg 1992
Printed in the United States of America

Typesetting: Springer T$_E$X in-house system
41/3140-5 4 3 2 1 0 – Printed on acid-free paper

Preface

DYNAMICS REPORTED reports on recent developments in dynamical systems.

Dynamical systems of course originated from ordinary differential equations. Today, dynamical systems cover a much larger area, including dynamical processes described by functional and integral equations, by partial and stochastic differential equations, etc. Dynamical systems have involved remarkably in recent years. A wealth of new phenomena, new ideas and new techniques are proving to be of considerable interest to scientists in rather different fields. It is not surprising that thousands of publications on the theory itself and on its various applications are appearing.

DYNAMICS REPORTED presents carefully written articles on major subjects in dynamical systems and their applications, addressed not only to specialists but also to a broader range of readers including graduate students. Topics are advanced, while detailed exposition of ideas, restriction to *typical* results – rather than the *most general* ones – and, last but not least, lucid proofs help to gain the utmost degree of clarity.

It is hoped, that *DYNAMICS REPORTED* will be useful for those entering the field and will stimulate an exchange of ideas among those working in dynamical systems.

Summer 1991

Christopher K.R.T Jones
Urs Kirchgraber
Hans-Otto Walther

Managing Editors

Table of Contents

On Littlewood's Counterexample of Unbounded Motions in Superquadratic Potentials

Mark Levi

Center Manifold Theory in Infinite Dimensions

A. Vanderbauwhede, G. Iooss

Oscillations in Singularly Perturbed Delay Equations

A.F. Ivanov, A.N. Sharkovsky

Topological Approach to Differential Inclusions on Closed Subsets of $\mathbb{R}^n$

R. Bielawski, L. Górniewicz, S. Plaskacz

Bifurcational Aspects of Parametric Resonance

H.W. Broer
G. Vegter

Abstract. *Generic nonlinear oscillators with parametric forcing are considered near resonance. This can be seen as a case-study in the bifurcation theory of Hamiltonian systems with or without certain discrete symmetries. In the analysis, among other things, structure preserving normal form or averaging techniques are used, as well as equivariant singularity theory and theory of flat perturbations.*

1. Setting of the Problem

a. Introduction

This paper is concerned with a parametrically forced oscillator, i.e. an oscillator with periodically varying coefficients, near resonance. There exists a vast amount of literature on this subject, especially on the linear case which involves differential equations of Mathieu-type. The present study deals with the nonlinear problem, localized near a central equilibrium solution of the free oscillator. In particular the branching off of certain subharmonic periodic solutions is studied, and more general bifurcational aspects of this.

The motivating example is the pendulum near its lower equilibrium, the length of which is varied periodically with small amplitude. Both this amplitude and the length of the pendulum then are considered as parameters of the problem. However, the present approach asks for a somewhat more general set-up. In our setting both the potential function, near a minimum, and the periodic parametric forcing will be chosen in a more or less arbitrary way. In fact, while restricting to this *universe* of function-pairs, the bifurcation problem is studied from the generic point of view. This means that our interest is with phenomena that are persistent under small perturbation of these functions. In this universe we shall distinguish two sub-universes determined by reflectional symmetries of the functions.

As a consequence this study restricts to the Hamiltonian context, while certain reversibilities are optional. A question is whether genericity in the above restricted sense also leads to persistence in this wider, i.e. general Hamiltonian, setting. It will be shown that to a large extent this is indeed the case.

On the other hand, we deal with small perturbations of autonomous, or time-independent, systems that are degenerate in the more general context and this leads to some discrepancy between the two kinds of genericity.

A more precise and formal introduction of these contexts will be given in part c of this section, see below.

Our approach is the following. We first give a more elaborate sketch of our problem using the classical example of the pendulum near its lower equilibrium.

Next we introduce our more general class of systems. We start out by applying a normal form procedure leading to an approximation that is time-independent, or autonomous, to any order. This procedure respects the symplectic structure as well as the reversibilities involved, due to an appropriate formulation in Liealgebra terms. Thus, up to flat "perturbation" terms, the problem reduces to the investigation of an autonomous Hamiltonian system on the plane, which may or may not display certain discrete symmetries. The main ingredient of this reduced analysis is equivariant singularity theory. At the end we discuss the possible effects of the re-incorporation of the flat terms.

b. The Parametrically Forced Pendulum, Motivation

To illustrate our ideas we briefly describe the planar (mathematical) pendulum with parametric forcing. For more details e.g. compare [Sto,MS,Ar1(§25)]. The free pendulum has the following equation of motion:

$$\ddot{x} = -\omega^2 \sin x,$$

$x \in \mathbb{R}$, where $\omega > 0$ is a parameter of the system. (To be precise $\omega = \sqrt{g/l}$, where l is the length of the pendulum and g the gravitational acceleration.) In the parametric forcing we let ω vary periodically with time (for example by varying the length l periodically). For instance we may take

$$\omega(t)^2 = \omega_0^2(1 + \varepsilon \cos \Omega t).$$

where ε and ω_0/Ω are parameters of the system. Rescaling t to Ωt then yields the following equation of motion:

$$\ddot{x} + (\alpha^2 + \beta \cos t) \sin x = 0, \tag{1}$$

with the parameters $\alpha = \omega_0/\Omega$ and $\beta = \varepsilon\alpha^2$.

We consider the 2π-periodic solution $x = \dot{x} = 0$. The stability of this solution can be studied by the linearization

$$\ddot{x} + (\alpha^2 + \beta \cos t)x = 0, \tag{2}$$

the so-called Mathieu-equation. In fact, if $P_{\alpha,\beta} : (\mathbb{R}^2, 0) \to (\mathbb{R}^2, 0)$ is the Poincaré (period) mapping of the forced pendulum (1), then its derivative $D_{(0,0)}P_{\alpha,\beta}$ at $(x, \dot{x}) = (0, 0)$ is the analogous mapping of the linearization (2). It is well known, e.g. again compare [Ar1(§25)] and also see below, that $P_{\alpha,\beta}$ is (orientation- and) area-preserving, whence $D_{(0,0)}P_{\alpha,\beta} \in Sl(2, \mathbb{R})$. So if $\lambda_{\alpha,\beta}^j$ $(j = 1, 2)$ are the eigenvalues of $D_{(0,0)}P_{\alpha,\beta}$, then for their product one has $\lambda^1_{\alpha,\beta} \cdot \lambda^2_{\alpha,\beta} = 1$. From this it follows that either both eigenvalues are on the complex unit circle, forming a complex-conjugate pair, or that both eigenvalues are real. The case when the eigenvalues lie on the intersection of the unit circle and the real line, i.e. where $\lambda^1_{\alpha,\beta} = \lambda^2_{\alpha,\beta} = \pm 1$, is called parabolic. Away from this parabolic case, the case when the eigenvalues lie on the unit circle is called *elliptic* (stable) while the case where the eigenvalues are real is called *hyperbolic* (unstable). In the (α, β)-plane this gives rise to the following well-known picture, e.g. compare [MS,Sto,Ar1(§25)].

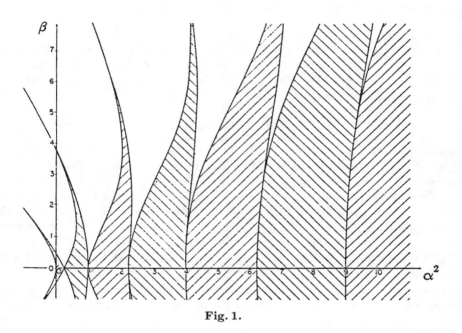

Fig. 1.

The shaded regions form the elliptic case, while their boundaries correspond to the parabolic case. The remaining part of the (α, β)-plane forms the hyperbolic case. The non-shaded regions are *tongues* emanating from the points $(\alpha, \beta) = (k/2, 0)$, where the order of contact of the boundary curves at the α-axis equals k $(k = 1, 2, \ldots)$; in particular, for $k = 1$ these boundary curves in the parameter plane meet transversally at $(\alpha, \beta) = (k/2, 0)$. These, and related phenomena are usually referred to as *parametric resonance*. For similar resonance tongues in other contexts also compare e.g. [Ar2,3,4].

Clearly at these boundary curves the dynamics near the trivial 2π-periodic solution $x = \dot{x} = 0$ changes and therefore the above picture can be viewed as part of a *bifurcation diagram*. A general problem is to describe the dynamics of the forced pendulum (1) in a neighbourhood of the parameter points $(\alpha, \beta) =$

$(k/2,0)$, $k = 1,2,3,\ldots$ in the parameter plane, focussing on the bifurcations. A question then is whether the corresponding (local) 2-parameter families are "generic" in the sense that certain features of their dynamics are persistent under small perturbations of these families. Also, if this would not be the case, one could try to "stabilize" the system by the introduction of extra parameters. As said before here it is important to specify the class of dynamical systems to work i.e. to perturb in. We'll see that that the wider the class, the more complicated the bifurcation diagram in the parameter plane, and the simpler the (secondary) bifurcations that occur.

c. Setting of the Problem, Outline of the Method

Although the above questions motivate our research, for the moment they are too ambitious; this in particular holds for a general analysis concerning the tongues emanating from $(\alpha, \beta) = (k/2, 0)$ with $k \geq 2$, the boundaries of which do not meet transversally. What we shall do instead is consider a more general parametrically forced oscillator

$$\ddot{x} + (\alpha^2 + \beta p(t))V'(x) = 0, \qquad (3)$$

with $p(t + 2\pi) \equiv p(t)$, $V(x) = \frac{1}{2}x^2 + O(x^3)$ as $x \to 0$. Moreover we shall pose generic conditions on the functions p and V. Notice that the pendulum case considered before corresponds to $p(t) = \cos t$ and $V(x) = 1 - \cos x$. Again we consider the 2π-periodic solution $x = \dot{x} = 0$ and its linear type which can be studied via the linearization $\ddot{x} + (\alpha^2 + \beta p(t))x = 0$: a generalization of the Mathieu-equation (2). As before in the (α, β)-parameter plane one sees hyperbolic resonance tongues emanating from the points $(\alpha, \beta) = (k/2, 0), k = 1,2,3,\ldots$.

In the following we'll restrict our attention to a fixed k and study the 2-parameter family (3) for (α, β) near $(k/2, 0)$. Our main interest is with the dynamics related to the (sub-)harmonic periodic solutions suggested by the normal linear part (i.e. by the Floquet-exponents) of the trivial 2π-periodic solution. In the case of odd k, in this way, we'll meet *period-doubling*. In relation to this we consider the k-th Fourier coefficient $a_k = (2\pi)^{-1} \int_0^{2\pi} p(t)e^{-ikt}dt$ of the function p. According to [Ar2] – also see below – the parabolic boundary curves of the k-th tongue in the parameter plane meet transversally at the apex $(\alpha, \beta) = (k/2, 0)$ if and only if $a_k \neq 0$, which is a generic condition. Most of the time we shall assume this condition to hold, so we mainly consider tongues with transverse boundary curves. Clearly, if one wishes to unfold "nontransverse tongues" in a generic way, extra parameters are needed.

As said before our bifurcation analysis restricts to the universe of the function-pairs (p, V), with the forcing p and potential V as above. Our (structural) stability results relate to this universe, which is included in a wider Hamiltonian universe. We shall also consider the question to what extent the families (3) are stable in this wider context. As a special case we sometimes also work under the assumption that the function p is even, i.e. that $p(-t) \equiv p(t)$. Then the systems (3) are time-reversible. This reversibility can (and below will) be phrased in terms of a certain $\mathbb{Z}_2$-symmetry. As a subcase of this one also may incorporate the assumption that V is even, i.e. that $V(-x) \equiv V(x)$, which yields another $\mathbb{Z}_2$-symmetry. At the end we give a remark on the case when small dissipation is included.

Now let us briefly describe how this paper is organized. In §2 we give a normal form theory for the periodic solution $x = \dot{x} = 0$. We work in the generalized phase space $\mathbb{R}^2 \times \mathbb{R}/(2\pi\mathbb{Z})$, with coordinates $(x, \dot{x})$ and $t(mod\,2\pi)$, or in a suitable covering space of this. Here the covering mapping is the so-called Van der Pol transformation, suggested by the normal linear behaviour of our periodic solution in the parameter point $(\alpha, \beta) = (k/2, 0)$. The deckgroup of this covering induces a (discrete) symmetry which, in the above special cases is compatible with the symmetries at hand. This is a geometric and convenient tool for the analysis of the subharmonics corresponding to the resonances at hand, also compare [Ar2,3(p.311),Ar4(Ch.7,§4)]. In fact in our specific case we only meet a nontrivial deckgroup in the case of odd k: this turns out to correspond to the flip or period doubling of the Poincaré mapping.

On the covering space we get a normal form by averaging-out the time-dependence to arbitrarily high order, both in the variables $(x, \dot{x})$ and in the parameters. We'll formulate the normal form theory in Liealgebra terms, implying that the normal form transformations respect the structures present in each case. E.g. compare [Ste,Ta1,2,Br1,4,Mee,BT,BBH,Ar3,4], for more references see below, although these methods at least go back to [Po1,2,Bi]. One could carry out the analysis on the time-dependent Hamilton functions with their Poisson brackets, but instead we'll remain in the world of vector fields with its Lie brackets. In this way it is easier to adjust the analysis and computations e.g. in case one wishes to incorporate dissipation. Thus, up to flat terms, the problem reduces to the investigation of *certain* families of (equivariant) Hamilton functions on the plane, viz. to the singularity theory of these. Analogous methods in [Sa1,Ar4] are used to investigate a less degenerate case of resonance, for general background also compare [Mey1,2]. In e.g. [Dui,Mee] the Moser-Weinstein method is used to obtain a similar reduction to singularity theory of functions. A related method, the Lyapunov-Schmidt reduction, is used in [Va].

Next in §3, using the proof of §2 as a computational device, we compute the 4-jets corresponding to our present case by a twofold averaging.

Subsequently, in §4, we study the *sufficiency* of these 4-jets in the class of planar C^∞-functions, i.e. in howfar higher order terms really can be disregarded. Here, among other things, we use equivariant singularity theory as developed by e.g. [Po,Ri,GS,GSM,GSS]. It turns out that sufficiency holds in some, but not in all cases. In these degenerate cases a machine-assisted threefold averaging might provide us with "generic" higher order terms? Also, by choosing nearby parameter points $(\alpha, \beta) = (p/q, 0)$ as new reference points, we apply the same method in order to investigate higher order subharmonics.

Finally, in §5 we come upon some dynamical conclusions. Here our treatment is a little more sketchy; for motivation we refer to relevant analogous places in the literature. The planar Hamilton functions obtained by the normal form procedure provide us with so-called integrable approximations of the Poincaré mappings. One question is which dynamical phenomena of these are persistent for infinitely flat nonintegrable perturbations. We discuss both the persistence of quasi-periodic circles and of the (sub-) harmonic closed orbits and their stable and unstable manifolds. For a similar local study in this conservative setting e.g. compare [Br2,BB]. We also touch the point of the flatness of transverse homo- and heteroclinic behaviour (entailing chaotic dynamics), e.g. compare [BV,BT]. Finally we'll discuss the contrast between the linear and the nonlinear case in terms of (Lyapunov-) stability and a perpetual adiabatic invariant.

Acknowledgements

The authors like to thank Robert Roussarie for his great help in the computations of §4. Also they thank Richard Cushman, Stephan van Gils, Jan-Cees van der Meer, James Montaldi and Jan Sanders for their helpful comments, moreover they are indebted to Peter Fiddelaers for checking the normal form computations by machine and to Rense Posthumus for helping with the graphics. Finally the first author acknowledges hospitality to the University of Dijon and to the Limburgs Universitair Centrum of Diepenbeek where parts of this paper were prepared.

2. A Normal Form Theory

a. Preliminaries

Consider the parametrically forced oscillator (3)

$$\ddot{x} + (\alpha^2 + \beta p(t))V'(x) = 0$$

with $p(t + 2\pi) \equiv p(t)$ and $V(x) = \frac{1}{2}x^2 + O(x^3)$ as $x \to 0$. As the (generalized) phase space we take $\mathbb{R} \times \mathbb{R} \times \mathbb{R}/(2\pi\mathbb{Z})$ with coordinates x, y and $t(mod\, 2\pi)$, where $y := \dot{x}$. Here we obtain a vector field $X = X^{\alpha,\beta}(x, y, t)$ given by

$$X^{\alpha,\beta}(x, y, t) = y\frac{\partial}{\partial x} - (\alpha^2 + \beta p(t))V'(x)\frac{\partial}{\partial y} + \frac{\partial}{\partial t}.$$

This vector field is Hamiltonian with Hamilton function

$$H_{\alpha,\beta}(x, y, t) = \frac{1}{2}y^2 + (\alpha^2 + \beta p(t))V(x).$$

In the case where p is even, i.e. where $p(-t) \equiv p(t)$, the vector field X is time-reversible. This means that if the involution $R : \mathbb{R}^2 \times \mathbb{R}/(2\pi\mathbb{Z}) \to \mathbb{R}^2 \times \mathbb{R}/(2\pi\mathbb{Z})$ is given by $R(x, y, t) := (x, -y, -t)$, then $R_*(X) = -X$. (In that case R takes integral curves into integral curves reversing the time-parametrization.) If moreover $V(-x) \equiv V(x)$ and the involution $I : \mathbb{R}^2 \times \mathbb{R}/(2\pi\mathbb{Z}) \to \mathbb{R}^2 \times \mathbb{R}/(2\pi\mathbb{Z})$ is defined by $I(x, y, t) := (-x, y, -t)$, then also $I_*(X) = -X$.

We shall make use of the Poincaré (period or return) mapping

$$P_{\alpha,\beta} : (\mathbb{R}^2, 0) \to (\mathbb{R}^2, 0),$$

defined by the relation

$$X_{2\pi}^{\alpha,\beta}(x,y,0) = (P_{\alpha,\beta}(x,y),2\pi).$$

Here $X_t^{\alpha,\beta}$ denotes the time t flow of the vector field $X^{\alpha,\beta}$. By Stokes' theorem it follows that $P_{\alpha,\beta}$ is area preserving.

Recall that we consider parameter points (α,β) near $(\alpha_0,\beta_0) := (k/2,0)$, for some fixed $k = 1,2,3,\ldots$. For notational convenience we next introduce the complex variable $z := y + i\alpha_0 x$, identifying $\mathbb{R}^2$ and $\mathbb{C}$. A calculation then shows that so X becomes the system

$$\begin{cases} \dot{z} = i\alpha_0 z - ((\alpha^2 - \alpha_0^2) + \beta p(t))V'(x) - \alpha_0^2(V'(x) - x) \\ \dot{t} = 1. \end{cases} \qquad (4)$$

b. Subharmonics: A Covering Space and Discrete Symmetry

First, more in general, we consider a vector field X on $\mathbb{C} \times \mathbb{R}/(2\pi\mathbb{Z})$ of the (system) form

$$\begin{cases} \dot{z} = f(z,\bar{z},t) \\ \dot{t} = 1. \end{cases} \qquad (5)$$

If P is the corresponding Poincaré mapping, the periodic points of P of period $q \geq 1$ correspond to subharmonic periodic solutions of X of period $2\pi q$. In our case $f(0,0,t) \equiv 0$, which implies that always $z = 0$ is a fixed point of P corresponding to a 2π-periodic solution. Then, if $z \neq 0$ is any other periodic point of P one easily defines a rotation number for z. If z has prime period q and rotation number p/q, the corresponding periodic solution in the phase space forms a $p : q$ torus knot. In order to study this we consider the q-sheeted covering

$$\Pi : \mathbb{C} \times \mathbb{R}/(2\pi q\mathbb{Z}) \to \mathbb{C} \times \mathbb{R}/(2\pi\mathbb{Z}),$$
$$(\zeta,t) \mapsto (\zeta e^{itp/q}, t(mod\,2\pi)). \qquad (6)$$

The corresponding group $\mathcal{D}$ of decktransformations is generated by

$$(\zeta,t) \mapsto (\zeta e^{2\pi ip/q}, t - 2\pi), \qquad (7)$$

which means that $\Pi \circ T = \Pi$ for all $T \in \mathcal{D}$. Notice that $\mathcal{D}$ is cyclic of order q. Now the vector field X can be lifted to a vector field $\tilde{X}$ on $\mathbb{C} \times \mathbb{R}/(2\pi q\mathbb{Z})$, which means that $\Pi_*(\tilde{X}) = X$. Moreover $\tilde{X}$ is $\mathcal{D}$-equivariant, which means that $T_*(\tilde{X}) = \tilde{X}$ for all $T \in \mathcal{D}$. (In fact all of this also holds for arbitrary vector fields on $\mathbb{C} \times \mathbb{R}/(2\pi\mathbb{Z})$ and the $\mathcal{D}$-equivariant vectorfields on $\mathbb{C} \times \mathbb{R}/(2\pi q\mathbb{Z})$ are precisely the lifts of those.)

Let $\tilde{P} : \mathbb{C} \to \mathbb{C}$ be the Poincaré mapping of $\tilde{X}$, generated by its $2\pi q$-flow. Then fixed points of $\tilde{P}$, by Π, correspond to periodic points of P of period q and the above considerations apply. Observe that the covering of a closed X-orbit by closed $\tilde{X}$-orbits can be of various types. One possibility is the connected covering by one $\tilde{X}$-orbit, projecting down q to 1. Another possibility is that the X-orbit is covered by q different $\tilde{X}$-orbits, all mapped onto each other by the elements of $\mathcal{D}$ and each of which projects down 1 to 1. Moreover observe the following. If, as in our case, the vector field X is Hamiltonian, this Hamiltonian character is inherited by the lift $\tilde{X}$. Indeed if X has a Hamilton function H, then a lift $\tilde{H}$ of H is a Hamilton function for $\tilde{X}$. This is related to the fact that for t fixed the planar map $\zeta \mapsto z = \zeta e^{itp/q}$ is orientation- and area-preserving. Notice that the lift $\tilde{H}$ also is $\mathcal{D}$-equivariant, i.e. that $\tilde{H} \circ T = \tilde{H}$ for all $T \in \mathcal{D}$.

As said before our interest is with the dynamics near the periodic solution $z = 0$, related to the (sub-)harmonics suggested by the normal linear part $\dot{z} = i\alpha_0 z$, $(i = 1)$. The covering map Π then exactly is the so-called Van der Pol transformation of the trivial 2π-periodic solution $z = 0$, e.g. compare [Ha(p.198),GH(p.173)]. In fact we take $p/q = k/2$, with $gcd(p,q) = 1$. So $q = 2$ if k is odd, while $q = 1$ if k is even. Notice that for k odd subharmonics of period 4π may occur: as announced earlier in our bifurcation problem this is going to correspond to period-doubling.

In the picture below we sketched the possible coverings of the closed orbits in the case $k = 1$. The central circle of the Möbius-strip has a connected 2:1 covering, while its boundary has a disconnected covering where each component projects down diffeomorphically.

Finally we remark that it is easily seen that in the cases where p or both p and V are even, similar to R and I there exist involutions $\tilde{R}$ and $\tilde{I}$ on the covering space with $\tilde{R} * (\tilde{X}) = -\tilde{X}$ and $\tilde{I} * (\tilde{X}) = -\tilde{X}$ respectively.

c. The Normal Form

Again we start with a slightly more general situation. Let X be a family of vector fields on $\mathbb{C} \times \mathbb{R}/(2\pi\mathbb{Z})$ of the form (5)

$$\begin{cases} \dot{z} = f(z, \bar{z}, t, \mu) \\ \dot{t} = 1. \end{cases}$$

Here μ is an r-dimensional parameter for some $r \geq 1$. Let us assume that $f(0, 0, t, \mu) \equiv 0$, then for all μ we have the 2π-periodic solution $z = 0$. We next assume that for $\mu = 0$ the Floquet exponent of this solution is ip/q, for some $p \in \mathbb{Z}$, $q \in \mathbb{N}$ with $gcd(p,q) = 1$. (Notice that this is equivalent to saying that the Poincaré mapping of X at $z = 0$, $\mu = 0$ has the derivative $e^{2\pi ip/q}$.) By the Floquet theory, cf. [Ha], we then may assume that X has the form

$$\begin{cases} \dot{z} = i\dfrac{p}{q}z + O(z^2 + |\mu|^2) \\ \dot{t} = 1 \end{cases}$$

as $z^2 + |\mu|^2 \to 0$, uniform in t. Compare our special case (4). Now consider the covering (6), which happens to be the Van der Pol transformation, as said before. By this we may lift X to $\tilde{X}$, a vector field on $\mathbb{C} \times \mathbb{R}/(2\pi q\mathbb{Z})$, which is of the form

$$\begin{cases} \dot{\zeta} = O(\zeta^2 + |\mu|^2) \\ \dot{t} = 1 \end{cases} \tag{8}$$

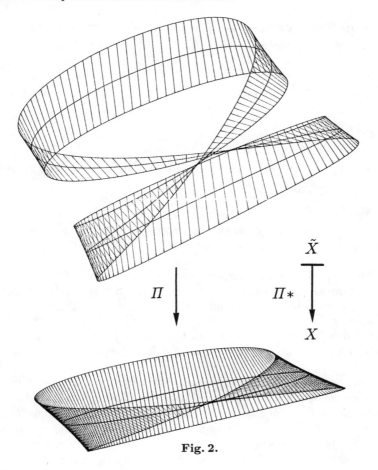

Fig. 2.

as $\zeta^2 + |\mu|^2 \to 0$, uniformly in t. We recall that $\tilde{X}$ then *automatically* is equivariant with respect to the deckgroup $\mathcal{D}$ of the covering.

We now give a normal form for the lift $\tilde{X}$. In fact, by near-identity transformations of the form

$$\Psi : \mathbb{C} \times \mathbb{R}/(2\pi q\mathbb{Z}) \to \mathbb{C} \times \mathbb{R}/(2\pi q\mathbb{Z}),$$
$$(\zeta, t) \mapsto (\zeta + w(\zeta, \bar{\zeta}, t, \mu), t) \tag{9}$$

we "simplify" $\tilde{X}$ successively to any order in $\zeta^2 + |\mu|^2$; here the transformations are tangent to the identity of the appropriate order such that they can't spoil previously achieved simplifications. In the present setting *simple* means *autonomous*: we average-out the time-dependence. It is important that the structures we work in are preserved by these coordinate changes. Therefore we wish them to be canonical and to commute with the decktransformations and the other discrete symmetries at hand. To be precise we have

Normal Form Theorem. *Let* $n = 1, 2, 3, 4, \ldots$ *be given. Then there exists a canonical $\mathcal{D}$-equivariant transformation Ψ as in (9), such that*

$$\Psi * (\tilde{X}) = \tilde{\mathcal{N}} + \tilde{\mathcal{Z}},$$

with $\tilde{\mathcal{Z}}(\zeta, t, \mu) = O((\zeta^2 + |\mu|^2)^{(n+1)/2})$ *as* $\zeta^2 + |\mu|^2 \to 0$, *uniformly in* t, *where $\tilde{\mathcal{N}}$ has the autonomous form*

$$\tilde{\mathcal{N}}^\mu(\zeta, t) = N^\mu(\zeta) + \frac{\partial}{\partial t}.$$

Here $N = \{N^\mu\}$ is a family of vector fields on the ζ-plane that are Hamiltonian and $\mathbb{Z}_q$-equivariant.

Remark. Here by $\mathbb{Z}_q$ we mean the group of planar rotations over the angles $2\pi l/q$, $1 \leq l \leq q$, around the origin. The corresponding equivariance is what $\mathcal{D}$-equivariance induces on autonomous systems.

Proof. An appropriate language for structure-preserving formal normal forms is that of graded or filtered Liealgebras, e.g. compare [Ste,Ta2,Br1,Mee] for such a theory near equilibrium points and [BBH,Br4] for an analogue near quasi-periodic invariant tori. A completely similar theory exists near periodic solutions; for simplicity however we here restrict to the case at hand. In the next section this proof will be used as a device for an explicit computation of a *3rd* order normal form.

To be more precise we start from the Liealgebra of r-parameter families of $\mathcal{D}$-equivariant, volume-preserving vector fields on the phase space $\mathbb{R}^2 \times \mathbb{R}/(2\pi q\mathbb{Z})$. For the sake of convenience the coordinates are called η, ξ and $t(mod\, 2\pi q)$ and the parameter is called μ. (Later on we shall see that $\zeta = \eta + i\alpha_0 \xi$ or $\zeta = \eta + i\xi$.) Also it is convenient to regard such a family of vector fields as a *vertical* vector field on $\mathbb{R}^2 \times \mathbb{R}/(2\pi q\mathbb{Z}) \times \mathbb{R}^r$. We then consider the associated Liealgebra of formal power series in (ξ, η, μ), the coefficients being $2\pi q$-periodic in t. A general element has the form

$$Y(\xi, \eta, \mu, t) = K(\xi, \eta, \mu, t)\frac{\partial}{\partial \xi} + L(\xi, \eta, \mu, t)\frac{\partial}{\partial \eta} + M(\xi, \eta, \mu, t)\frac{\partial}{\partial t},$$

with vanishing divergence and $\mathcal{D}$-symmetry, where K, L and M are C^∞-functions, respectively formal power series. Our main interest is with elements Y where $M \equiv 1$: they correspond to our time-dependent Hamiltonian, $\mathcal{D}$-equivariant case.

In fact our lifted vector field $\tilde{X}$ exactly is of this form. The *idea* of the present approach now is the following. We apply induction with respect to the degree n, adjusting the Taylor series step by step. So assuming that normalization up to degree $n - 1$ has been accomplished, we must find a transformation Ψ that normalizes the terms of degree n. This map Ψ will be infinitesimally generated by a vector field Y as above, in this case with $M \equiv 0$. In fact its flow $\Psi := Y_1$ over time 1 will be a transformation as desired. In this way all the structure we work in is preserved: Firstly the transformation Ψ, being generated by Y, preserves the volume and $\mathbb{Z}_q$-symmetry. Notice that in the t-direction Ψ acts as the identity-map. Therefore, secondly, the transformed vector field $\Psi * (\tilde{X})$ again is both time-dependent Hamiltonian (i.e. volume-preserving with $M \equiv 1$) and $\mathcal{D}$-equivariant. Compare the references at the beginning of this proof.

To be explicit we define a *gradation* of the formal Liealgebra by introducing the subsets $\mathcal{H}_n$, $n \geq 1$, as follows: $\mathcal{H}_n$ consists of exactly those elements Y, where the coefficients K, L and M are homogeneous polynomials in (ξ, η, μ), with $degr\,(K) = degr\,(L) = n$ and $degr\,(M) = n - 1$. (The choice of n and $n - 1$ is forced by the fact that we deal with a Liealgebra.)

Now, as a member of $\mathcal{H}_1$, consider the vector field $S = \frac{\partial}{\partial t}$ and its adjoint action $ad\,S$, defined via the Liebrackets by $ad\,S(Y) = [S, Y]$. It is easy to see that

$$ad\,S(Y) = \frac{\partial K}{\partial t} \frac{\partial}{\partial \xi} + \frac{\partial L}{\partial t} \frac{\partial}{\partial \eta} + \frac{\partial M}{\partial t} \frac{\partial}{\partial t}.$$

Therefore $ad\,S$ for all $n \geq 1$ induces a map $\mathcal{H}_n \to \mathcal{H}_n$, which we also denote by $ad\,S$. This last map for all n is semisimple, implying a direct sum splitting

$$\mathcal{H}_n = \mathcal{A}_n \oplus \mathcal{T}_n.$$

Here $\mathcal{A}_n := \operatorname{Ker} ad\,S$ consists of all $Y \in \mathcal{H}_n$ that are t-independent, while $\mathcal{T}_n$ contains exactly those $Y \in \mathcal{H}_n$ for which the $2\pi q$-average

$$\hat{Y} := \frac{1}{2\pi q} \int_0^{2\pi q} Y(.,t)\,dt$$

vanishes. In fact we claim that $\mathcal{T}_n = \operatorname{Im} ad\,S$. Indeed, for a given $B = P\frac{\partial}{\partial \xi} + Q\frac{\partial}{\partial \eta} + R\frac{\partial}{\partial t}$ with $\hat{B} = 0$ and for $Y = K\frac{\partial}{\partial \xi} + L\frac{\partial}{\partial \eta} + M\frac{\partial}{\partial t}$ the equation $ad\,S(Y) = B$ is equivalent to

$$\frac{\partial K}{\partial t} = P, \quad \frac{\partial L}{\partial t} = Q, \quad \frac{\partial M}{\partial t} = R.$$

Since $\hat{P} = \hat{Q} = \hat{R} = 0$, we can integrate within the class of $2\pi q$-periodic functions, the solution Y being unique if we also require $\hat{Y} = 0$. More generally, for a given $X \in \mathcal{H}_n$, the equation

$$ad\,S(Y) + G = X$$

has a uniquely determined solution by requiring that $G = \hat{X}$ and $\hat{Y} = 0$.

As said before the normal form for our vector field $\tilde{X}$ amounts to an inductive adjustment of its Taylor series with respect to $(\zeta, \bar{\zeta}, \mu)$ or, equivalently, (ξ, η, μ). In terms of the above we consider the homogeneous n-th order part of this Taylor series as an element of $\mathcal{H}_n, n \geq 1$. At the n-th step, by a structure preserving diffeomorphism (9) we transform the corresponding part into $\operatorname{Ker} ad\,S$, thereby making the coefficients t-independent.

First, for $n = 1$ there is nothing to prove, compare (8).

Second, for $n \geq 2$ assume that

$$\tilde{X} = S + G^2 + G^3 + \cdots + G^{n-1} + X^n + O((\xi^2 + \eta^2 + \mu^2)^{(n+1)/2}),$$

where $S = \frac{\partial}{\partial t}$, with $G^k \in \operatorname{Ker} ad S \subset \mathcal{H}_k$, $2 \leq k \leq n-1$ and $X^n \in \mathcal{H}_n$. Also $\tilde{X} - S$ has no $\frac{\partial}{\partial t}$-component (i.e. $\tilde{X}$ has the form Y with $M \equiv 1$). In other words: $\tilde{X}$ is in normal form up to order $n-1$. For any $Y \in \mathcal{H}_n$ we now consider the flow Y_s over time s and define $\tilde{X}^s := (Y_s) * \tilde{X}$. We then have that $\frac{\partial}{\partial s}\tilde{X}^s = [\tilde{X}^s, Y]$ and therefore, by Taylor's formula,

$$\tilde{X}^1 = \tilde{X} + [\tilde{X}, Y] + O((\xi^2 + \eta^2 + \mu^2)^{(n+1)/2})$$
$$= S + G^2 + G^3 + \cdots + G^{n-1} + X^n + [S, Y] + O((\xi^2 + \eta^2 + \mu^2)^{(n+1)/2}).$$

Then, solving the equation $X^n + [S, Y] = G^n$, or

$$ad S(Y) - G^n = -X^n,$$

with $G^n = \hat{X}^n \in \operatorname{Ker} ad S$ and Y as before, the vector field is normalized up to order n:

$$\Psi = Y_1 \quad \text{and}$$
$$\Psi_*(\tilde{X}) = S + G^2 + G^3 + \cdots + G^{n-1} + G^n + O((\xi^2 + \eta^2 + \mu^2)^{(n+1)/2}),$$

as required. $\square$

The above normal form for the lifted vector field $\tilde{X}$ along its closed orbit $\zeta = 0$, by construction, projects down, thereby giving a similar normal form for the vector field X along its closed orbit $z = 0$. Moreover we so also obtain a local normal form for the Poincaré mapping P of X at $z = 0$ which we shall explore now. For simplicity we assume that $\tilde{X}$ itself already is on n-th order normal form, i.e. as $\Psi_*(\tilde{X})$ in the conclusion of the theorem.

To be more explicit, as before let $P : \mathbb{C} \to \mathbb{C}$ denote the Poincaré mapping of X, generated by the 2π-flow $X_{2\pi}$. From the above theorem we find a relation between P and the planar 2π-flow $N_{2\pi}$. First by $J : \mathbb{C} \to \mathbb{C}$ let's denote the rotation $z \mapsto z e^{2\pi i p/q}$. Clearly then $J_*(N) = N$. Now we claim that

Corollary. *Let n, P, J and N be as above. Then*

$$P = J \circ N_{2\pi} + O((z^2 + |\mu|^2)^{(n+1)/2}),$$

as $z^2 + |\mu|^2 \to 0$, uniformly in t.

Proof. We directly compute

$$(P(z), 2\pi) = X_{2\pi}(z, 0) = X_{2\pi}(\Pi(z, 0)) = \Pi(\tilde{X}_{2\pi}(z, 0))$$
$$= \Pi(\tilde{N}_{2\pi}(z, 0)) + O((z^2 + |\mu|^2)^{(n+1)/2})$$
$$= \Pi(N_{2\pi}(z), 2\pi) + O((z^2 + |\mu|^2)^{(n+1)/2})$$
$$= ((J \circ N_{2\pi})(z), 2\pi) + O((z^2 + |\mu|^2)^{(n+1)/2}),$$

where, for simplicity, the parameters are suppressed. $\square$

This $\mathbb{Z}q$-symmetry in the local normal form of diffeomorphisms is known to hold in many different, both conservative and dissipative settings, e.g. compare [Mo1,Ta1,Ar2,3]. In fact the above Liealgebra proof also applies in these settings, compare [Ta1,Br1].

The point here is that the Poincaré mapping can be expressed in terms of the planar vector field N (and the rotation J) and that our normal form theorem gives an explicit computing device for N, cf. §3. This gives the possibility of an approximate description of the dynamics by giving pictures of the phase-portraits of N, cf. §§4,5.

Remarks. (i). In our case where $p/q = k/2$ the normalizing transformations in the relevant cases can be chosen to commute with the involutions $\tilde{R}$ and $\tilde{I}$ as well. In the corresponding cases the Hamiltonian of the vector field N then exhibits an "extra" $\mathbb{Z}_2$- respectively $\mathbb{Z}_2 \oplus \mathbb{Z}_2$-equivariance; for details see the end of the next section. This directly follows from our Liealgebra approach, which encompasses the preservation of these discrete symmetries.

(ii). The normal form transformation at the n-th induction step has the form $\Psi = Y_{-1}$, with $Y \in \mathcal{H}_n$, with $\hat{Y} = 0$. As before we write $Y = K\frac{\partial}{\partial \xi} + L\frac{\partial}{\partial \eta}$, then $\Psi = id - (K, L) + O((\xi^2 + \eta^2 + \mu^2)^{(n+1)/2})$. Let's explore this a bit further writing the n-th order part $G^n + B^n$ in the complex system form $\dot{\zeta} = f_n(\zeta, \bar{\zeta}, t, \mu)$, using that $\zeta = \eta + i\xi$. In that case G^n corresponds to $\dot{\zeta} = \hat{f}_n(\zeta, \bar{\zeta}, \mu)$ and B^n to $\dot{\zeta} = f_n(\zeta, \bar{\zeta}, t, \mu) - \hat{f}_n(\zeta, \bar{\zeta}, \mu)$, where $\hat{\ }$ again takes the $2\pi q$-time average. From this we see that $\frac{\partial}{\partial t}(L + iK) = f_n - \hat{f}_n$. Therefore, in terms of (9),

$$
w(\zeta, \bar{\zeta}, t, \mu) = \int_0^t (\hat{f}_n(\zeta, \bar{\zeta}, \mu) - f_n(\zeta, \bar{\zeta}, s, \mu))\, ds + \Delta(\zeta, \bar{\zeta}, \mu)
$$
$$
+ O((\xi^2 + \eta^2 + \mu^2)^{(n+1)/2}),
\tag{10}
$$

where Δ is the correction term serving to get $\hat{w} = O((\xi^2 + \eta^2 + \mu^2)^{(n+1)/2})$.

Observe that similar results would follow from the theory of averaging, e.g. compare [BM,Ha,GH,SV,Mu], for the remark on the fact that we can get the average $\hat{w} = 0$ also compare [Sa2]. One could say that the above is a model theorem for averaging in Liealgebra terms;

(iii). A normal form for the vector field X along the orbit $z = 0$ also can be obtained without going to the covering space, compare [CW,Io,BBH,Br4]. In fact the above proof applies with S replaced by $S = \partial/\partial t + i\alpha_0(z\partial/\partial z - \bar{z}\partial/\partial \bar{z})$.

(iv). If the above theorem is applied *ad infinitum* the vector field $\tilde{X}$ is made formally autonomous, since the normal form transformations are tangent to the identity mapping of the appropriate order. In the C^∞-setting a t-periodic version of Borel's theorem, cf. [Na], applied on the level of Hamilton- and generating functions then gives an approximation $\tilde{X} = \tilde{N} + \mathcal{F}$ with $\tilde{N}$ autonomous and $\mathcal{F}$ infinitely flat at $(\zeta, \mu) = (0, 0)$. Moreover both $\tilde{N}$ and $\mathcal{F}$ then are Hamiltonian and equivariant with respect to the discrete symmetry groups at hand. For similar arguments compare [Br1,BT].

We end this section with an observation on the normal form $\tilde{\mathcal{N}} + \tilde{\mathcal{Z}}$ for $\beta = 0$ in our specific case of a forced oscillator. Here we take $\mu = (\beta, \delta)$, with $\delta := \alpha^2 - \alpha_0^2$ a *detuning* parameter. Since for $\beta = 0$ the right-hand side of (4) does not depend on t the lifted vector field $\tilde{X}$ then gets the form

$$\begin{cases} \dot{\zeta} = e^{-i\alpha_0 t} F(\zeta e^{i\alpha_0 t}, \bar{\zeta} e^{-i\alpha_0 t}, \delta) \\ (\dot{t} = 1), \end{cases}$$

where F is real-valued and t-independent. This implies that $\tilde{X}$ for $\beta = 0$ is equivariant with respect to the $SO(2, \mathbb{R})$-action

$$R : SO(2, \mathbb{R}) \times \mathbb{C} \times \mathbb{R}/(2\pi q\mathbb{Z}) \to \mathbb{C} \times \mathbb{R}/(2\pi q\mathbb{Z}).$$
$$(\phi, \zeta, t) \mapsto R_\phi(\zeta, t) := (\zeta e^{i\alpha_0 \phi}, t - \phi),$$

where we identify $SO(2, \mathbb{R})$ with $\mathbb{R}/(2\pi q\mathbb{Z})$ in the obvious way. Since our normal form transformations keep the parameters fixed, and since this $SO(2, \mathbb{R})$-symmetry also is a Liealgebra-restriction, this symmetry is inherited by the normal form. This implies that for $\beta = 0$ both $\tilde{\mathcal{N}}$ and $\tilde{\mathcal{Z}}$ automatically are $SO(2, \mathbb{R})$-equivariant. For the normalized part $N^{0,\delta}$ this yields the form

$$\dot{\zeta} = \sum_{j=1}^{[n/2]} i a_j(\delta) \zeta^j \bar{\zeta}^{j-1}$$

where the coefficients a_j are real-valued since N is Hamiltonian. In fact $a_j(\delta)$ is a real polynomial in δ of degree $n - 2j - 1$, $1 \le j \le [n/2]$.

3. Computation of a Third-Order Normal Form

We now return to our special case (4), of which we wish to obtain a third order normal form, following the recipe of the previous section. So we are given a vector field X

$$\begin{cases} \dot{z} = i\alpha_0 z - ((\alpha^2 - \alpha_0^2) + \beta p(t))V'(x) - \alpha_0^2(V'(x) - x) \\ (\dot{t} = 1), \end{cases}$$

with $(z, t) \in \mathbb{C} \times \mathbb{R}/(2\pi\mathbb{Z})$ and where $z = \dot{x} + i\alpha_0 x$. We recall that $\alpha_0 = k/2$ for some fixed $k \in \mathbb{N}$ and that we consider (α, β) near $(\alpha_0, 0)$.

As before let $\delta := \alpha^2 - \alpha_0^2$ be a detuning parameter and let's put $\mu = (\beta, \delta)$. Also we specify the following Taylor- and Fourier expansions:

$$V(x) = \frac{1}{2}x^2 + \frac{1}{3}cx^3 + \frac{1}{4}dx^4 + O(x^5) \quad \text{as} \quad x \to 0, \tag{11a}$$

$$p(t) = \sum_{n=-\infty}^{\infty} a_n e^{int}. \tag{11b}$$

Notice that $a_{-n} = \bar{a}_n$, since p is real valued.

Then, by the Van der Pol transformation (6) we pass to the covering space $\mathbb{C} \times \mathbb{R}/(2\pi q\mathbb{Z})$ where $p/q = k/2$ with $gcd(p, q) = 1$ (so where $q = 2$ or $q = 1$ depending on whether k is odd respectively even). On this covering space we have the lift $\tilde{X}$ of X which, as a special case of (8), has the ($2\pi q$-time periodic) form

$$\begin{cases} \dot{\zeta} = f_2(\zeta, \bar{\zeta}, t, \mu) + f_3(\zeta, \bar{\zeta}, t, \mu) + O((\zeta^2 + |\mu|^2)^2) \\ (\dot{t} = 1), \end{cases} \tag{12}$$

with f_2 and f_3 homogeneous of degree 2 respectively 3 in ζ and $\bar{\zeta}$ and μ. Recall that $z = \zeta e^{i\alpha_0 t}$ whence $\dot{\zeta} = (\dot{z} - i\alpha_0 z)e^{-i\alpha_0 t}$. From this we get the following explicit expressions for f_2 and f_3:

$$f_2(\zeta, \bar{\zeta}, t, \mu) = \frac{i}{2\alpha_0} \left(\delta + \beta \sum a_n e^{int} \right) (\zeta - \bar{\zeta} e^{-2i\alpha_0 t})$$
$$+ \frac{c}{4}(\zeta^2 e^{i\alpha_0 t} - 2\zeta\bar{\zeta} e^{-i\alpha_0 t} + \bar{\zeta}^2 e^{-3i\alpha_0 t}) \tag{13a}$$

and

$$f_3(\zeta, \bar{\zeta}, t, \mu) = \frac{c}{4\alpha_0^2} \left(\delta + \beta \sum a_n e^{int} \right) (\zeta^2 e^{i\alpha_0 t} - 2\zeta\bar{\zeta} e^{-i\alpha_0 t} + \bar{\zeta}^2 e^{-3i\alpha_0 t})$$
$$- \frac{id}{8\alpha_0}(\zeta^3 e^{2i\alpha_0 t} - 3\zeta^2\bar{\zeta} + 3\zeta\bar{\zeta}^2 e^{-2i\alpha_0 t} - \bar{\zeta}^3 e^{-4i\alpha_0 t}). \tag{13b}$$

We also compute the $2\pi q$-time averages

$$\hat{f}_2(\zeta, \bar{\zeta}, \mu) = \frac{i}{2\alpha_0}((\delta + \beta a_0)\zeta - \beta a_k \bar{\zeta}) \tag{14a}$$

and

$$\hat{f}_3(\zeta, \bar{\zeta}, \mu) = \frac{3id}{8\alpha_0}\zeta^2\bar{\zeta} + \beta Q_1(\zeta, \bar{\zeta}, \mu), \tag{14b}$$

where

$$Q_1(\zeta, \bar{\zeta}, \mu) = \begin{cases} 0 & \text{if } k \text{ is odd} \\ \dfrac{c}{4\alpha_0^2}(a_{-l}\zeta^2 - 2a_l\zeta\bar{\zeta} + a_{3l}\bar{\zeta}^2) & \text{if } k = 2l. \end{cases}$$

Following the induction steps of the proof in the previous section we begin normalizing the second order terms. Since after that we'll also normalize the third order terms we need to have a good knowledge of the second order part of the normal form transformation.

A brief computation shows that in the present case formula (10) reads

$$w(\zeta, \bar{\zeta}, t, \mu) = -\frac{1}{2\alpha_0} \left(\beta \sum_{n \neq 0} \frac{a_n}{n} e^{int} \zeta + \left(\frac{\delta}{k} e^{-ikt} - \beta \sum_{n \neq k} \frac{a_n}{n-k} e^{i(n-k)t} \right) \bar{\zeta} \right)$$
$$+ \frac{ic}{4\alpha_0} \left(e^{i\alpha_0 t}\zeta^2 + 2e^{-i\alpha_0 t}\zeta\bar{\zeta} - \frac{1}{3}e^{-3i\alpha_0 t}\bar{\zeta}^2 \right) + O((\zeta^2 + |\mu|^2)^{3/2}). \tag{15}$$

As in the above proof, for simplicity again using the letter z for the new complex variable, we put

$$z = \zeta + w(\zeta, \bar{\zeta}, t, \mu), \tag{16}$$

and conclude that

$$\begin{aligned}
\dot{z} &= \dot{\zeta} + \partial w/\partial \zeta\, \dot{\zeta} + \partial w/\partial \bar{\zeta}\, \dot{\bar{\zeta}} + \partial w/\partial t \\
&= \hat{f}_2(\zeta, \bar{\zeta}, \mu) + (f_3 + \partial w/\partial \zeta\, f_2 + \partial w/\partial \bar{\zeta}\, \bar{f}_2)(\zeta, \bar{\zeta}, t, \mu) \\
&\quad + O((\zeta^2 + |\mu|^2)^2),
\end{aligned} \tag{17}$$

In order to express (17) in the $(z, \bar{z}, t, \mu)$-coordinates we realize that, by (16), $\zeta = z - w(z, \bar{z}, t, \mu) + O((z^2 + |\mu|^2)^{3/2})$.

Of course the second order terms in (17) are as predicted in the normal form theorem. Our main interest now is with the third order part which, in the next step, also will be normalized to its $2\pi q$-time average. So all we have to do is compute this average.

As a first contribution one has

$$\begin{aligned}
\mathrm{Av}\{f_2(\zeta, \bar{\zeta}, \mu)\}(z, \bar{z}, \mu) &= \frac{1}{2\pi q} \int_0^{2\pi q} \hat{f}_2(\zeta(z, \bar{z}, s, \mu), \bar{\zeta}(z, \bar{z}, s, \mu), \mu)\, ds \\
&= \hat{f}_2(z, \bar{z}, \mu) + O((z^2 + |\mu|^2)^2),
\end{aligned} \tag{18}$$

where here and in the sequel $\mathrm{Av}\{h\}$ is synonymous to $\hat{h}$. In this computation we used that $\hat{f}_2$, by (14a), is linear in ζ and $\bar{\zeta}$ and that the $2\pi q$-time average of w vanishes.

We next compute the remaining part of (17). First of all one directly obtains from (15) that

$$(\partial w/\partial \zeta)(\zeta, \bar{\zeta}, t, \mu) = -\frac{\beta}{2\alpha_0} \sum_{n \neq 0} \frac{a_n}{n} e^{int} + \frac{ic}{2\alpha_0}(e^{i\alpha_0 t}\zeta + e^{-i\alpha_0 t}\bar{\zeta}) + O(\zeta^2 + |\mu|^2),$$

and

$$\begin{aligned}
(\partial w/\partial \bar{\zeta})(\zeta, \bar{\zeta}, t, \mu) ={}& -\frac{1}{2\alpha_0}\left(\frac{\delta}{k} e^{-ikt} - \beta \sum_{n \neq k} \frac{a_n}{n-k} e^{i(n-k)t} \right) \\
& + \frac{ic}{2\alpha_0}\left(e^{-i\alpha_0 t}\zeta - \frac{1}{3} e^{-3i\alpha_0 t}\bar{\zeta} \right) + O(\zeta^2 + |\mu|^2),
\end{aligned}$$

which, with some effort, gives

$$\begin{aligned}
\mathrm{Av}\{(\partial w/\partial \zeta\, f_2)\}(z, \bar{z}, \mu) ={}& \frac{i\beta}{k^2} L_1(\mu)\bar{z} + \beta Q_2(z, \bar{z}, \mu) \\
& - \frac{ic^2}{8\alpha_0} z^2 \bar{z} + O((z^2 + |\mu|^2)^2),
\end{aligned} \tag{19a}$$

and

$$\begin{aligned}
\mathrm{Av}\{(\partial w/\partial \bar{\zeta}\, \bar{f}_2)\}(z, \bar{z}, \mu) ={}& \frac{i}{k^2}((L_2(\delta)\delta + L_3(\mu)\beta)z + \beta L_4(\mu)\bar{z}) + \beta Q_3(z, \bar{z}, \mu) \\
& - \frac{7ic^2}{24\alpha_0} z^2 \bar{z} + O((z^2 + |\mu|^2)^2).
\end{aligned} \tag{19b}$$

Here $L_1, L_2, L_3,$ and L_4 are given by

$$L_1(\mu) = \delta \frac{a_k}{k} + \beta \sum_{m \neq 0} \frac{a_m a_{k-m}}{m}, \qquad L_2(\delta) = -\frac{\delta}{k},$$

$$L_3(\mu) = -2\delta \frac{a_0}{k} + \beta \sum_{m \neq k} \frac{|a_m|^2}{m - k}, \qquad L_4(\mu) = \delta \frac{a_k}{k} - \beta \sum_{m \neq 0} \frac{a_{m+k} \bar{a}_m}{m}.$$

Moreover we have for the cubic terms Q_2 and Q_3:

$$Q_2(z, \bar{z}, \mu) = \begin{cases} 0 & \text{if } k \text{ is odd} \\ \dfrac{c}{8l^2}(-a_{-l}z^2 + 2a_l z\bar{z} + \dfrac{5}{3}a_{3l}\bar{z}^2) & \text{if } k = 2l, \end{cases}$$

and

$$Q_3(z, \bar{z}, \mu) = \begin{cases} 0 & \text{if } k \text{ is odd} \\ \dfrac{c}{24l^2}(-7a_{-l}z^2 + 14a_l z\bar{z} + a_{3l}\bar{z}^2) & \text{if } k = 2l. \end{cases}$$

Finally we abbreviate

$$E_2(\mu) = \frac{1}{k}(\delta + \beta a_0) + \frac{1}{k^2}(\delta L_2(\delta) + \beta L_3(\mu)), \tag{20a}$$

$$\Phi_1(\mu) = -\frac{a_k}{k} + \frac{1}{k^2}(L_1(\mu) + L_4(\mu)), \tag{20b}$$

$$Q = Q_1 + Q_2 + Q_3, \tag{20c}$$

then $E_2(\mu)$ is real-valued, while $\Phi_1(\mu)$ is complex-valued. Moreover Q now reads

$$Q(z, \bar{z}) = \begin{cases} 0 & \text{if } k \text{ is odd} \\ \dfrac{c}{6l^2}(-a_{-l}z^2 + 2a_l z\bar{z} + 3a_{3l}\bar{z}^2) & \text{if } k = 2l. \end{cases} \tag{21}$$

Combining (14), (18), (19), (20) and (21) from (17) we obtain the desired third order normal form which we again denote by $\tilde{X}$ and the corresponding Hamilton function by $\tilde{H}$. In this complex notation the relation between $\tilde{X}$ and $\tilde{H}$ is given via a small digression into Wirtinger calculus. In fact, putting $z = y + i\alpha_0 x$ one sees that

$$\partial/\partial y = \partial/\partial z + \partial/\partial \bar{z}, \quad \partial/\partial x = i\alpha_0(\partial/\partial z - \partial/\partial \bar{z}).$$

From this it follows that the expression

$$\tilde{X}^\mu(x, y, t) = \partial \tilde{H}/\partial y(x, y, t, \mu) \frac{\partial}{\partial x} - \partial \tilde{H}/\partial x(x, y, t, \mu) \frac{\partial}{\partial y} + \frac{\partial}{\partial t}$$

gives the complex system form $\dot{z} = 2i\alpha_0 \partial \tilde{H}/\partial \bar{z}$, $(\dot{t} = 1)$.

We summarize our results in

Proposition. *Let $\tilde{H}$ be normalized as above. Then $\tilde{H}$ is given by*

$$\tilde{H}(z, \bar{z}, t, \mu) = \frac{1}{k} E(\mu)|z|^2 + \frac{\beta}{k} \text{Re}\,(\Phi(\mu)\bar{z}^2) + \beta K(z, \bar{z}) + \frac{A}{2k}|z|^4 \qquad (22a)$$
$$+ R(z, \bar{z}, t, \mu)$$

where $A = \frac{9d-10c^2}{12k}$, $E = E_2 + O(|\mu|^3)$ is real-valued, $\Phi = \Phi_1 + O(|\mu|^2)$ and where K has the form

$$K(z, \bar{z}) = \begin{cases} 0 & \text{if } k \text{ is odd} \\ \frac{c}{6l^3}(\text{Im}\,(a_l z\bar{z}^2) + \text{Im}\,(a_{3l}\bar{z}^3)) & \text{if } k = 2l, \end{cases} \qquad (22b)$$

and where finally the remainder R has the form

$$R(z, \bar{z}, t, \mu) = |z|^6 R_1(|z|) + \delta|z|^4 R_2(|z|, \delta) \qquad (22c)$$
$$+ \beta O(|z|^3(|z|^2 + |\mu|^2)^{1/2}) + r(z, \bar{z}, t, \mu)$$

as $z^2 + |\mu|^2 \to 0$, uniform in t. Here R_1 and R_2 are real-valued functions, defined near $0 \in \mathbb{R}$ and $(0,0) \in \mathbb{R}^2$ respectively, while r is infinitely flat at $(z, \bar{z}, \mu) = (0,0,0)$, uniform in t.

Proof. We apply the normal form procedure to infinite order, also using the Borel theorem, cf. the end of §2c. This yields the form

$$\dot{z} = 2i\alpha_0 \partial\tilde{H}/\partial\bar{z}, \quad (\dot{t} = 1),$$

with

$$\partial\tilde{H}/\partial\bar{z}(z, \bar{z}, t, \mu) = \frac{1}{k}E(\mu)z + \frac{\beta}{k}\Phi(\mu)\bar{z} + \frac{\beta}{ik}Q(z, \bar{z}) + \frac{A}{k}z^2\bar{z} + \text{hot},$$

which, by suitable integration, yields the real-valued form (22). To obtain the remainder (22c) we use that for $\beta = 0$ the normal form is $SO(2, \mathbb{R})$-symmetric. $\square$

Remarks. (*i*). A short computation shows that K as a homogeneous 3rd degree real-valued polynomial is completely "arbitrary", i.e. by variation of the Fourier-coefficients a_l and a_{3l} we can get any such polynomial.

(*ii*). Next we study the effects of the various discrete symmetries on the normalized 4th order part of $\tilde{H}$. First of all in the case of odd k we have for the deckgroup $\mathcal{D}$ that $\mathcal{D} \cong \mathbb{Z}_2$, meaning that the normalized 4th order part of $\tilde{H}$ is equivariant with respect to the involution $-id : (x, y) \mapsto (-x, -y)$. Below we shall refer loosely to this as one of the $\mathbb{Z}_2$-symmetric cases.

Then let's consider the cases with $\tilde{R}$- or $\tilde{R}$- and $\tilde{I}$-reversibility. First, if we only have that $p(-t) \equiv p(t)$, i.e. if we are in the $\tilde{R}$-reversible case, then the normalized, 4th order part of $\tilde{H}$ is equivariant with respect to the involution $(x, y) \mapsto (x, -y)$. This means that this part of $\tilde{H}$ is a function of x and y^2, which implies that $\text{Im}\,\Phi = 0$ and $\text{Im}\,a_l = \text{Im}\,a_{3l} = 0$. (In fact by the evenness of p all Fourier-coefficients a_n are real!) This case also will be referred to as one of the $\mathbb{Z}_2$-symmetric cases. If, second, also $V(-x) \equiv V(x)$, we moreover have $\tilde{I}$-

reversibility, which here amounts to equivariance with respect to the involution $(x, y) \mapsto (-x, y)$. In that case the normalized, 4th order part of $\tilde{H}$ is a function of x^2 and y^2, implying that $\operatorname{Im} \Phi = 0$ while $K \equiv 0$, c.q. $Q \equiv 0$. (Notice that in the case of odd k the $\tilde{I}$-reversibility gives no further restrictions on the normal form, since then the discrete symmetries are interdependent.) This case below will be referred to as the $\mathbb{Z}_2 \oplus \mathbb{Z}_2$-symmetric case.

4. The Planar Hamilton Function

a. Introduction

First consider the setting of the end of §2c, where the t-dependence has been averaged out to infinite order. Up to flat "perturbation" terms we then work with planar Hamilton functions of class C^∞. The functions can be subject to the various discrete symmetries we saw before. In the previous section we determined a normal form for the 4-jet of these functions. In the present section we study these 4-jets and investigate in how far they are sufficient for the corresponding functions. In particular we try to classify modulo smooth local left-right equivalence, preserving the possible symmetries and to obtain as complete as possible descriptions of the bifurcations. Recall that a left-right equivalence consists of parameter-dependent changes of coordinates, both in domain and range, together with a reparametrization.

Pictures will be incorporated showing the relevant level sets of the functions i.e. the phase portraits of the corresponding planar vector fields, again cf. §2c. Of course, by abandoning the symplectic (or canonical) setting, we lose information on the exact time-parametrization of the integral curves, although the sense of this parametrization still can be preserved.

We mainly work under the generic condition that $a_k \neq 0$, but also some remarks will be made on the case where $a_k = 0$.

As long as we only deal with planar (i.e. t-independent) functions we can simplify the normal form (22) further writing $z = y + i\tilde{x}$, so with a scaling $\tilde{x} = \alpha_0 x$. Notice that for the vector field this corresponds to a time-scaling. Denoting the function by H in stead of $\tilde{H}$ we get from (22a,b)

$$H(z, \bar{z}, \mu) = \frac{1}{2}E(\mu)|z|^2 + \frac{1}{2}\beta \operatorname{Re}\left(\Phi(\mu)\bar{z}^2\right) + \beta P_3(z, \bar{z}) + \frac{1}{4}A|z|^4 + hot(|z|, |\mu|) \quad (23)$$

with P_3 some arbitrary real-valued and homogeneous polynomial of degree 3 and where the *higher order terms*, apart from the flat t-dependent term, are as in (22c).

In the equivariant cases H is as mentioned at the end of the previous section. We here discuss the effects on the polynomial P_3. In the case of odd k and in the case where there is $\mathbb{Z}_2 \oplus \mathbb{Z}_2$-symmetry we have $P_3 \equiv 0$. In the case of even k with only $\mathbb{Z}_2$-symmetry P_3 has the form

$$P_3(x, y) = B_0 x^3 + B_2 x y^2,$$

with B_0 and B_2 arbitrary real constants.

b. The Type of the Origin as a Singularity, Part of the Bifurcation Diagram

Our first aim is to study the bifurcation diagram governing the type of the origin $z = 0$ as a singularity of the function H. This is the present equivalent of the diagram in Fig. 1, cf. §1b, corresponding to the Mathieu equation. Clearly the type of $z = 0$ is first of all determined by the coefficients E and Φ. In fact one easily shows that for $E^2 \neq \beta^2|\Phi|^2$ the singularity is nondegenerate (or Morse): a saddle for $E^2 < \beta^2|\Phi|^2$ and a maximum or minimum for $E^2 > \beta^2|\Phi|^2$. This corresponds to the hyperbolic respectively the elliptic cases referred to in §§1a,b. The boundary $E^2 = \beta^2|\Phi|^2$ corresponds to the parabolic case.

In order to study the shape of this boundary we start reconsidering the linear functions L_1, L_2, L_3 and L_4 of the parameter $\mu = (\beta, \delta)$. Splitting off the dependence on the Fourier-coefficient a_k we get

$$L_1(\mu) = \frac{1}{k}\left((\delta + \beta a_0)a_k - \frac{1}{2}\beta a_{2k}\bar{a}_k\right) + \beta \sum_{m \neq -k, 0, k, 2k} \frac{a_m a_{k-m}}{m},$$

$$L_2(\delta) = -\frac{\delta}{k},$$

$$L_3(\mu) = -2\delta\frac{a_0}{k} - \frac{1}{2}\beta\frac{|a_k|^2}{k} + \beta \sum_{|m| \neq k} \frac{|a_m|^2}{m - k},$$

$$L_4(\mu) = \frac{1}{k}\left((\delta + \beta a_0)a_k - \frac{1}{2}\beta a_{2k}\bar{a}_k\right) - \beta \sum_{m \neq -2k, -k, 0, k} \frac{a_{m+k}\bar{a}_m}{m}.$$

Substitution of this in (20) gives

$$E_2(\mu) = \frac{1}{k}(\delta + \beta a_0) - \frac{1}{k^3}\left(\delta^2 + 2\beta\delta a_0 + \frac{1}{2}\beta^2|a_k|^2\right) + \beta^2 B,$$

$$\Phi_1(\mu) = -\frac{k^2 - 2(\delta + \beta a_0)}{k^3}a_k - \frac{\beta a_{2k}}{k^3}\bar{a}_k + \beta\Theta.$$

Here B and Θ are a real respectively a complex constant, independent of a_k. (We recall that in the reversible cases Φ, Φ_1, a_k and Θ are real.)

Next we reparametrize $(\beta, \delta) \mapsto (\beta, \varepsilon)$, where $\varepsilon := \delta + \beta a_0$. Then E_2 and Φ_1 rewrite to

$$E_2(\mu) = \frac{1}{k^3}(k^2\varepsilon - \varepsilon^2 + \beta^2(a_0^2 - \frac{1}{2}|a_k|^2)) + \beta^2 B,$$

$$\Phi_1(\mu) = \frac{1}{k^3}((k^2 - 2\varepsilon)a_k - \beta a_{2k}\bar{a}_k) + \beta\Theta,$$

where we now put $\mu = (\beta, \varepsilon)$.

Then the equation $E_2^2 = \beta^2|\Phi_1|^2$ gives us the lower order terms of the boundary curve of the k-th tongue. In fact we get for $a_k \neq 0$:

$$\varepsilon = \pm|a_k|\beta + O(\beta^2)$$

and for $a_k = 0$:

$$\varepsilon = \left(-\left(kB + \left(\frac{a_0}{k}\right)^2\right) \pm k|\Theta|\right)\beta|\beta| + O(\beta^3),$$

as $\beta \to 0$, which for $\Theta \neq 0$ gives the following pictures.

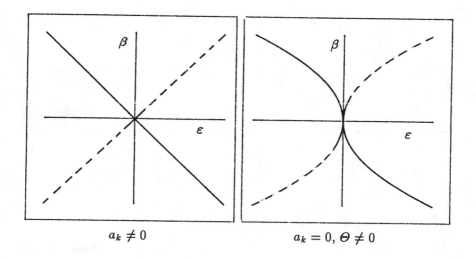

$$a_k \neq 0 \qquad\qquad a_k = 0,\ \Theta \neq 0$$

Fig. 3.

We see that the boundary consists of two curves, for $a_k \neq 0$ meeting transversally at $\mu = 0$, while for $a_k = 0$ they are tangent, though for $\Theta \neq 0$ only to 1st order. Compare [Ar2] and Fig. 1 in §1b.

We end these considerations by studying further intersections of the two boundary-curves $E = \pm\beta|\Phi|$. In work of Chillingworth and Afsharnejad [Af] a similar investigation is carried out. Further intersections are given by the equations

$$E = 0 \quad \text{and} \quad \Phi = 0.$$

In the general case Φ is complex, suggesting that further intersections are a codimension 3 phenomenon, which probably won't occur in our 2-parameter family. In the reversible cases, however, Φ is real. Then this phenomenon has codimension 2 and further intersections do occur. In fact the above equations now rewrite to

$$\varepsilon = O(\beta^2) \quad \text{as} \quad \beta \to 0 \quad \text{and} \quad \beta = -\frac{k^2 a_k}{a_{2k}a_k + k^3\Theta} + O(\varepsilon) \quad \text{as} \quad \varepsilon \to 0$$

respectively, assuming that $\Theta \neq 0$. So we see that for such an intersection to occur for $\beta \neq 0$ it is needed that a_k is sufficiently close to 0. Below, in the lefthand picture we sketched the boundary-curves for this case.

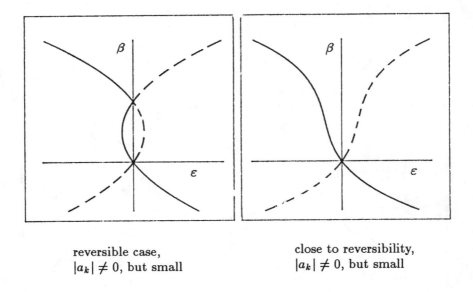

reversible case,   close to reversibility,
$|a_k| \neq 0$, but small $|a_k| \neq 0$, but small

Fig. 4.

In the righthand picture we sketched what is expected to happen when we perturb away from reversibility. So we conjecture that the reversible cases are not generic in the general one.

c. Bifurcations in the Case $a_k \neq 0$

In this subsection we shall consider the planar Hamiltonian family $H_\mu :=$ $H(.,.,\mu)$ of the form (23) in more detail. In particular we study the bifurcations of H_μ occurring as $\mu = (\beta, \varepsilon)$ ranges over a neighbourhood of 0 in $\mathbb{R}^2$. Here $\varepsilon = \delta + \beta a_0$ as in subsection b. It is easy to check that the reparametrization $(\beta, \delta) \mapsto (\beta, \varepsilon)$ does not change the form of the higher order terms (22c), provided that δ is replaced by ε.

Our first interest is with bifurcations of one of the following two types: Either at $\mu \in \mathbb{R}^2$ the function H_μ near the origin of $\mathbb{R}^2$ has a degenerate singularity, or near the origin are two nondegenerate singularities of index 1, i.e saddle points, whose level sets coincide. The latter case corresponds to a homo- or hetero-clinic orbit in the planar vector field. It turns out that generically these phenomena are the only ones to happen outside some arbitrarily small wedge-like neighbourhood of the line $\beta = 0$ minus the origin $(\beta, \varepsilon) = (0, 0)$.

Second we consider the behaviour near this line, i.e. in such a, sufficiently small, wedge-like neighbourhood. From the last remark of §2 we recall that for $\beta = 0$ the family (23) is rotationally symmetric. As we shall see below this entails whole circles filled with singular points. We shall discuss the way in which singularities, relevant for our study, branch off from this degeneracy.

c1. The Singularity-Theory Approach

We begin with the following observation. The family (23) may be considered as a 2-parameter unfolding of $H_0(z, \bar{z}) = \frac{1}{4}A|z|^4 + O(|z|^5)$. This function H_0 moreover is rotationally symmetric, cf. the final remark of §2. According to e.g. [Gi(p.109)] it therefore has infinite codimension. Hence the 2-parameter family (23) in the general setting of planar functions could never be a stable unfolding of H_0. However, since we work in a special class of functions the stability problem becomes easier: we only have to consider certain perturbations. In fact there is a restrictive form of stability that applies here and that we shall explain now. First it means that the family (23) is stable under smooth local left-right equivalences provided that we consider neighbourhoods of $\mu = 0$ in $\mathbb{R}^2$ minus an arbitrarily narrow punctured wedge containing the line $\beta = 0$. In these restricted neighbourhoods of $(z, \mu) = (0, 0)$ the family (23) generically only undergoes bifurcations of the types described in an earlier paragraph. The non-zero singularities and their possibly connecting level-sets all occur at a characteristic distance $\sqrt{|\beta|}$ from $z = 0$.

Second the present stability notion is concerned with a sufficiently narrow wedge shaped neighbourhood of the line $\beta = 0$. Here we have at least topological local stability within our degenerate class of functions. Now the non-zero singularities and their possibly connecting level-sets occur at a characteristic distance $\sqrt{|\varepsilon|}$ from $z = 0$.

Finally these two approaches can be matched so to obtain local topological equivalences between nearby families. In that sense our family of functions is structurally stable and our resonance bifurcation has codimension 2. The remainder of part c1 is devoted to an elaboration of this stability-notion and to a qualitative description of all generic bifurcations in the present case where the Fourier-coefficient a_k does not vanish.

To this end we shall perform a sequence of smooth changes of coordinates that bring the family (23) into a polynomial normal form of degree 4. These transformations depend smoothly on the parameter μ in a restricted neighbourhood of the point $(z, \mu) = (0, 0)$, i.e. with a narrow punctured wedge around the line $\beta = 0$ deleted. While constructing this sequence sufficient open conditions on the coefficients of (23) are introduced. We thus obtain

- Structural stability of these restriced families under smooth left-right equivalence;
- A complete description of the bifurcations of the family (23) for μ ranging over such a restricted neighbourhood.

The first step in this sequence is a normalization of the quadratic part of (23). Second we scale the parameters according to $\varepsilon = \bar{\varepsilon}\beta$. Thus a restricted neighbourhood of (0,0) in the (β, ε)-plane of the form $|\varepsilon| \leq C|\beta|$ corresponds a full neighbourhood of the line segment $\{0\} \times [-C, C]$ in the $(\beta, \bar{\varepsilon})$-plane. An appropriate scaling of the (x, y)-variables then guarantees that the $(\beta, \bar{\varepsilon})$-parametrized family (23) can be seen as a small perturbation of its 4-jet. The third step is a smooth change of coordinates eliminating the terms of degree at least 5. We generate this transformation infinitesimally, using a homotopy method that is well known in the theory of singularities. Compare [Gi,Ma].

We now briefly explain how this works. So suppose our goal is to bring a family of functions $H^0_\mu(x, y)$ into a "normal form" $H^1_\mu(x, y)$. We begin performing a transformation in the range $\mathbb{R}$ that maps the singular levels of H^0_μ to the corresponding ones of H^1_μ. Next we consider the homotopy $\mathcal{H}_\mu$ between H^0_μ and H^1_μ defined by

$$\mathcal{H}_\mu(x, y, t) := (1 - t)H^0_\mu(x, y) + tH^1_\mu(x, y).$$

We subsequently try to find a family of vector fields Y_μ of the form

$$Y_\mu(x, y, t) = \xi_\mu(x, y, t)\frac{\partial}{\partial x} + \eta_\mu(x, y, t)\frac{\partial}{\partial y} + \frac{\partial}{\partial t},$$

satisfying the Infinitesimal Stability Condition:

$$Y_\mu \mathcal{H}_\mu \equiv 0,$$

where the juxtaposition denotes taking the directional derivative. This last equation can be solved locally in x, y, μ and t using the Malgrange-Mather Preparation Theorem, cf. [Ma]. We begin the construction of the family Y_μ in a neighbourhood of the most degenerate singularities, subsequently determining the solutions in neighbourhoods of the Morse-singularities respectively the regular points. Due to the linearity of the Infinitesimal Stability Condition these local solutions can be glued together to obtain a more global infinitesimal solution, also to be denoted by Y_μ. The time 1 flow $\Psi_\mu := Y_{\mu,1}$ of Y_μ then is a right-equivalence between H^0_μ and H^1_μ.

The details of this approach are contained in the subsections c11, c12 and c13, below.

c11. Normalization of the Quadratic Part

For μ in a neighbourhood of $(0,0)$ in $\mathbb{R}^2$ we shall put the part of (23) that is quadratic in $(z, \bar{z})$ on a diagonal form. First notice that in our symmetric cases we already have a diagonal form, since then $\operatorname{Im} \Phi(\mu) = 0$. Otherwise, in the case where $a_k \neq 0$, by just rotating over the angle $\frac{1}{2}\operatorname{Arg} \Phi(\mu)$, we also can diagonalize this quadratic part to

$$E(\mu)|z|^2 - \beta|\Phi(\mu)|\operatorname{Re} z^2.$$

Here it is used that $\Phi(0,0) = -a_k/k \neq 0$, cf. (20b), implying that this angle near $(0,0)$ depends smoothly on μ. Notice that this rotation does not change the Hamiltonian character, nor the rotationally symmetric terms of the Hamiltonian. In particular the third degree polynomial P_3 remains arbitrary in the case of even k, while the rotational symmetry for $\beta = 0$ is not affected. Notice that also the $\mathbb{Z}_2$-symmetry occurring for odd k is not affected, since $-id$ commutes with the above rotation.

Next we locally reparametrize $\mu \mapsto \tilde{\mu}(\mu)$, with component-functions $\tilde{\mu} = (\tilde{\beta}, \tilde{\varepsilon})$, where

$$\tilde{\beta}(\mu) := \beta |\Phi(\mu)|^{-1} \quad \text{and} \quad \tilde{\varepsilon}(\mu) := E(\mu)|\Phi(\mu)|^{-2}.$$

Since, again by (20b), $\Phi(0,0) \neq 0$ and $E(\mu) = \varepsilon/k + O(|\mu|^2)$ as $\mu \to 0$, this defines a diffeomorphism near $\mu = (0,0)$. Its local inverse will be denoted by $\tilde{\mu} \mapsto \mu(\tilde{\mu})$. Using the abbreviation $\tilde{\Phi} := \Phi(\mu(\tilde{\mu}))$ we see that the function $\tilde{H}(z, \bar{z}, \tilde{\mu})$, defined by

$$\tilde{H}(z, \bar{z}, \tilde{\mu}) := |\tilde{\Phi}|^{-4} H(|\tilde{\Phi}|z, |\tilde{\Phi}|\bar{z}, \mu(\tilde{\mu})),$$

satisfies

$$\tilde{H}(z, \bar{z}, \tilde{\mu}) = \tilde{\varepsilon}|z|^2 - \tilde{\beta}\operatorname{Re} z^2 + \tilde{\beta}P_3(z, \bar{z}) + \frac{1}{4}A|z|^4 + hot,$$

where the higher order terms are as in (22c). Deleting all tildas and passing to real coordinates (x, y) with $z = y + ix$ our family of functions (23) then is brought into the form

$$H_\mu(x, y) = \varepsilon(x^2 + y^2) + \beta(x^2 - y^2) + \beta P_3(x, y) + \frac{1}{4}A(x^2 + y^2) + hot, \quad (24)$$

where again the higher order terms are as in (22c).

c12. Further Reduction

In view of the stability problems mentioned above, we now delete an arbitrarily small wedge from the parameter plane, which contains the line $\beta = 0$.

In fact, since in this setting the boundary of the resonance tongue of part a has the form $\varepsilon = \pm\beta + O(\beta^2)$, we restrict to the region of parameters $\mu = (\beta, \varepsilon)$, satisfying

$$|\varepsilon| \leq C|\beta|, \quad \beta \geq 0 \tag{25}$$

for some arbitrary constant $C > 1$. Next we study the position of the singular points of the family H_μ in this region.

4.1. Lemma. *There exist constants $c_1 > 0$ and $\beta_1 > 0$ and a neighbourhood U of $(0,0)$ in $\mathbb{R}^2$, such that for $|\varepsilon| \leq C|\beta|$ and $|\beta| \leq |\beta_1|$ any singular point in U of H_μ, given by (24), satisfies $(x^2 + y^2)^{1/2} \leq c_1|\beta|^{1/2}$.*

Proof. (Compare e.g. [CH(Chs.6,7)].) Suppose that the conclusion does not hold. Then there are sequences $(\mu_n, x_n, y_n) \to (0, 0, 0)$ as $n \to \infty$, such that both

(i) (x_n, y_n) is a singular point of H_{μ_n}, and
(ii) $\beta_n/r_n^2 \to 0$ as $n \to \infty$.

Here $r_n^2 := x_n^2 + y_n^2$. Since by (25) one has $|\varepsilon_n| \leq C|\beta_n|$, it follows that also $\varepsilon_n/r_n^2 \to 0$ as $n \to \infty$. Using (24) we find from the fact that $\partial H_{\mu_n}/\partial y(x_n, y_n) = 0$ that

$$0 = 2\frac{\varepsilon_n - \beta_n}{r_n^2}\frac{y_n}{r_n} + \frac{\beta_n}{r_n}\frac{\partial P_3}{\partial y}\left(\frac{x_n}{r_n}, \frac{y_n}{r_n}\right) + A\frac{y_n}{r_n} + R_n,$$

where, from (22c), it is directly seen that

$$R_n = O(r_n)^2 + \frac{\beta_n}{r_n}O((r_n^2 + \beta_n^2 + \varepsilon_n^2)^{\frac{1}{2}}) + O(\varepsilon_n),$$

implying that $\varepsilon_n \to 0$ as $n \to \infty$. Since $\partial P_3 / \partial y(\frac{x_n}{r_n}, \frac{y_n}{r_n})$ is bounded we conclude that $y_n/r_n \to 0$ as $n \to \infty$.

One similarly proves that $x_n/r_n \to 0$ as $n \to \infty$. Since $(x_n/r_n)^2 + (y_n/r_n)^2 = 1$ we so arrive at a contradiction, which proves the lemma.   □

Since in the present context our interest is with the singular points of H_μ, the above lemma suggests the following scaling

$$\varepsilon = \beta\bar{\varepsilon}, \quad x = \beta^{\frac{1}{2}}\bar{x}, \quad y = \beta^{\frac{1}{2}}\bar{y}, \quad H = \beta^2\bar{H} \tag{26}$$

Again deleting all bars from (24) and (25) we obtain the family of Hamiltonians

$$H_\mu(x,y) = \varepsilon(x^2 + y^2) + (x^2 - y^2) + \beta^{1/2}P_3(x,y) + \frac{1}{4}A(x^2+y^2)^2 \\ + \beta R(x,y,\varepsilon,\beta). \tag{27}$$

From (22c) it follows that

$$R(x,y,\varepsilon,\beta) = (x^2 + y^2)^{3/2}R_1(x,y,\varepsilon,\beta),$$

with $R_1(x,y,\varepsilon,\beta) \le c(x^2 + y^2 + \varepsilon^2 + \beta^2)^{\frac{1}{2}}$ for some positive constant c, when $|\beta|$ is sufficiently small, $|\varepsilon| \le C$ and (x,y) ranges over some compact neighbourhood of the origin. In the sequel we sometimes need this rather detailed expression for R. In other cases, however, it is sufficient to know that $R = O(1)$ as $\beta \to 0$, uniform in (x,y,ε).

Replacing $\nu := \beta^{1/2}$ from (27) we get as a "polynomial" normal form

$$H_\mu(x,y) = \varepsilon(x^2 + y^2) + (x^2 - y^2) + \nu P_3(x,y) + \frac{1}{4}A(x^2+y^2)^2 \\ + \nu^2 R(x,y,\varepsilon,\nu^2). \tag{28}$$

From now on we write $\mu := (\varepsilon, \nu)$.

We next turn to the polynomial P_3. Recall that $P_3 \equiv 0$ if k is odd or if there is a $\mathbb{Z}_2 \oplus \mathbb{Z}_2$-symmetry. We shall say that P_3 is a *general polynomial* if it is of either of the following two forms:

$B_0x^3 + B_1x^2y + B_2xy^2 + B_3y^3$, with $B_0 \neq 0 \neq B_3$, in the case where k is even and there is no further symmetry, or

$B_0x^3 + B_2xy^2$, with $B_0 \neq 0$, in the case where k is even and there is $\mathbb{Z}_2$-symmetry.

We then have as the main result of this section

4.2. Proposition. *Suppose that $P_3(x,y) = B_0 x^3 + B_1 x^2 y + B_2 xy^2 + B_3 y^3$ is a general polynomial and suppose that $A \neq 0$. Then there is a neighbourhood U of $(0,0)$ in $\mathbb{R}^2$ and a constant $\nu_0 > 0$, such that on the set $U \times [-C, C] \times [-\nu_0, \nu_0] \subset \mathbb{R}^2 \times \mathbb{R}^2$ the family (28) is smoothly left-right equivalent to the family*

$$H_\mu^0(x,y) = \varepsilon(x^2 + y^2) + (x^2 - y^2) + \nu N_3(x,y) + \frac{1}{4}A(x^2 + y^2)^2, \qquad (29)$$

where $N_3(x,y) = B_0 x^3 + B_3 y^3$. Moreover if (28) has any of the $\mathbb{Z}_2$-symmetries or the $\mathbb{Z}_2 \oplus \mathbb{Z}_2$-symmetry, this symmetry can be preserved by the 2-parameter family of diffeomorphisms on $\mathbb{R}^2$ that realizes the "right" part of the left-right equivalence.

Proof. We first give a proof in the case of even k and in the absence of symmetry. Subsequently we indicate how to modify this proof for the equivariant cases.

I. k is even, no symmetry: Our proof consists of three steps.
1. Construction of the left-right equivalence on neighbourhoods $U_\pm$ of $(x, y, \varepsilon, \nu) = (0, 0, \pm 1, 0)$. Here we cope with the degenerate singularities, occurring near the apexes $(\varepsilon, \nu) = (\pm 1, 0)$ of the resonance tongues.
2. Extension of the left-right equivalence to the singular set

$$\Sigma(H) := \{(x, y, \mu) \in \mathbb{R}^4 \,|\, \partial H/\partial x(x, y, \mu) = \partial H/\partial y(x, y, \mu) = 0\}.$$

3. Extension of the left-right equivalence to a full neighbourhood of $\Sigma(H)$ in $\mathbb{R}^4$.

Step 1. Consider the point $(x_0, y_0, \varepsilon_0, \nu_0) = (0, 0, 1, 0)$. We first split off the non-degenerate part of the 2-jet of H, thus restricting to a 1-dimensional manifold on which a 2-parameter family of Hamiltonian functions is defined. This family turns out to be stable, even under right-equivalence, implying that our equivalence can be constructed on a neighbourhood of $(x_0, y_0, \varepsilon_0, \nu_0) = (0, 0, 1, 0)$ in $\mathbb{R}^4$.

In order to perform the splitting we derive from (28) that

$$\partial H_\mu / \partial x(x, y) = 2(\varepsilon + 1)x + \nu \partial P_3 / \partial x(x, y) + Ax(x^2 + y^2) + \nu^2 \frac{\partial R}{\partial x},$$

with R as in (28). Therefore $\partial^2 H/\partial x^2(x_0, y_0, \varepsilon_0, \nu_0) = 4 \neq 0$, so the equation

$$\partial H/\partial x(x, y, \varepsilon, \nu) = 0$$

can be solved for x, yielding a function $x = f(y, \varepsilon, \nu)$ satisfying

$$f(y, \varepsilon, \nu) = -\frac{\nu(B_2 + O(\nu))}{2(\varepsilon + 1)} y^2 + O(y^3)$$

as $y \to 0$, uniformly as $\mu = (\varepsilon, \nu)$ ranges over a compact neighbourhood of $\mu_0 = (\varepsilon_0, \nu_0)$ in $\mathbb{R}^2$. Hence

$$H(f(y, \mu) + \xi, y, \mu) = K(y, \mu) + \xi^2 R(\xi, y, \mu)$$

with $K(y,\mu) := H(f(y,\mu),y,\mu)$ and $R(x_0,y_0,\mu_0) = \frac{1}{2}\partial^2 H/\partial x^2(x_0,y_0,\mu_0) = 2$.

Let Ψ be the composition of the local diffeomorphism

$$(x,y,\mu) \mapsto (x + f(y,\mu),y,\mu)$$

and the inverse of

$$(\xi,y,\mu) \mapsto (\xi\sqrt{R(\xi,y,\mu)},y,\mu),$$

then

$$(H \circ \Psi)(x,y,\mu) = x^2 + K(y,\mu).$$

Elaborating the expression for K we find

$$K(y,\mu) = (\varepsilon - 1)y^2 + \nu(B_3 + O(\nu))y^3 + \frac{1}{4}Ay^4 + \nu O(y^4).$$

It is this 2-parameter family of functions we wish to establish stability of. To do this is a more or less standard application of the Malgrange-Mather Preparation Theorem, cf. [Ma(pp.178,179)]. We now recall some of the corresponding details.

Let $\mathcal{E}_1$ denote the ring of germs at 0 of funtions $(\mathbb{R},0) \to (\mathbb{R},0)$. Its maximal ideal m consists of those germs f for which $f(0) = 0$. Notice that $f \in \mathrm{m}^2$ if and only if $f(0) = 0$ and $f'(0) = 0$. If $f_1,f_2,\ldots,f_k$ are elements of $\mathcal{E}_1$ then $\mathbb{R}\{f_1,\ldots,f_k\}$ denotes the real vector space generated by $f_1,f_2,\ldots,f_k$. Similarly $\mathrm{m}\{f_1,\ldots,f_k\}$ is the $\mathcal{E}_1$-module generated by these functions.

For the family K one easily verifies that

$$\mathrm{m}^2 \subset \mathrm{m}\left\{\frac{\partial K}{\partial y}\Big|_{\mathbb{R}\times\{\mu_0\}}\right\} + \mathbb{R}\left\{\frac{\partial K}{\partial\varepsilon}\Big|_{\mathbb{R}\times\{\mu_0\}}, \frac{\partial K}{\partial\nu}\Big|_{\mathbb{R}\times\{\mu_0\}}\right\}. \qquad (30)$$

Application of the Malgrange-Mather Preparation Theorem now yields that the family K is a stable unfolding of the function $K|_{\mathbb{R}\times\{\mu_0\}}$ *within* the class of functions that, together with their first derivative, vanish at $0 \in \mathbb{R}$.

Similarly one finds that the 2-parameter family K^0_μ, defined by

$$K^0_\mu(y,\mu) := (\varepsilon - 1)y^2 + \nu B_3 y^3 + \frac{1}{4}Ay^4,$$

is a stable unfolding of $K^0_{\mu_0}$, within the same class of functions.

Then a standard argument from the theory of singularities of functions finally shows that K is right-equivalent to K^0.

Therefore the family H near (x_0,y_0,μ_0) is right-equivalent to $K^0_\mu(y) + x^2$. One similarly shows that the family H^0 near (x_0,y_0,μ_0) is right-equivalent to $K^0_\mu(y) + x^2$.

In an analogous way one proves that on a neighbourhood of $(0,0,-1,0)$ both H and H^0 are right-equivalent to $(\varepsilon + 1)x^2 + \nu B_0 x^3 + \frac{1}{4}Ax^4 - 2y^2$.

This finishes step 1.

Step 2. Next, by left-right equivalences, we modify the family H in such a way that for each value of μ in the relevant parameter region the singular levels of the normal form coincide with those of this modification. This enables us to construct the left-right equivalence in step 3, essentially by matching local solutions.

So now we look for diffeomorphisms

$$\Psi_1 : \mathbb{R}^2 \times \mathbb{R}^2 \to \mathbb{R}^2 \times \mathbb{R}^2 \quad \text{and} \quad \Psi_2 : \mathbb{R} \times \mathbb{R}^2 \to \mathbb{R} \times \mathbb{R}^2$$

of the respective forms

$$\Psi_1(x,y,\mu) = (\psi_1(x,y,\mu), \phi(\mu)), \Psi_2(t,\mu) = (\psi_2(t,\mu), \phi(\mu)), \tag{31}$$

such that

(i) $\Psi_2 \circ \bar{H} \circ \Psi_1|_{\Sigma(H^0)} = \bar{H}^0|_{\Sigma(H^0)}$;
(ii) Ψ_1 and Ψ_2 are the identity map on $U_\pm$ and $\bar{H}(U_\pm)$ respectively;
(iii) For all $(x_0, y_0, \mu_0) \in \Sigma(H^0)$ the derivative $D_{(x_0,y_0)}\Psi_{1,\mu_0}$ is the identity map.

Here $\bar{H} : \mathbb{R}^2 \times \mathbb{R}^2 \to \mathbb{R} \times \mathbb{R}^2$ is defined by $\bar{H}(x,y,\mu) := (H(x,y,\mu), \mu)$, while $\bar{H}^0$ is defined analogously. In order to establish (i), (ii) and (iii) we observe the following:

> If (x,y) is a degenerate singular point of H_μ for ν sufficiently small and $|\varepsilon| \le C$, then $(x,y,\mu) \in U_- \cup U_+$. $\tag{32}$

For a constant $\nu_1 > 0$ sufficiently small the set $\Sigma(H) \cap \{\nu = \nu_1\}$ is depicted schematically in the figure below. From now on we assume that $A < 0$, the case where $A > 0$ is completely similar.

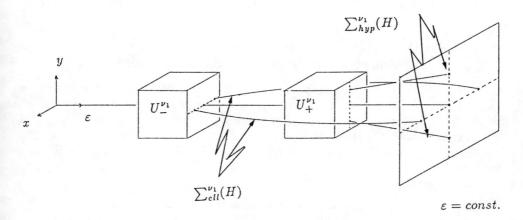

Fig. 5.

As a consequence of (32) the set $\Sigma(H)$ intersected with the complement of $U_+ \cup U_-$ is a codimension 2 manifold that intersects each of the planes $\varepsilon = \varepsilon_1$, $\nu = \nu_1$ transversally.

For ϕ we take any extension of the reparametrization on $U_\pm$ coming from the equivalences constructed in step 1, the single condition to be imposed on ϕ being that $\phi(\{\nu = 0\}) \subset \{\nu = 0\}$: ϕ should map the region $\nu \geq 0$ into itself.

Next for $\varepsilon > \varepsilon_1 > -1$ consider the set $\Sigma_{ell}(H)$, consisting of those points (x, y, μ) for which (x, y) is an elliptic singular point of H_μ, different from $(0, 0)$. For this parameter-region the elliptic singular points of H_μ are of the form $(x_\pm(\varepsilon, 0), y_\pm(\varepsilon, 0))$, with

$$(x_\pm(\varepsilon, 0), y_\pm(\varepsilon, 0)) = (\pm\sqrt{-2(\varepsilon + 1)/A}, 0),$$

as easily follows from (28).

Putting $H_\pm(\mu) := H_\mu(x_\pm(\mu), y_\pm(\mu))$, it is not hard to check that

$$\partial H_+/\partial\nu(\varepsilon, 0) \neq \partial H_-/\partial\nu(\varepsilon, 0) \tag{33a}$$

$$H_+(\varepsilon, 0) = H_-(\varepsilon, 0). \tag{33b}$$

These same properties hold for H^0.

Let $\pi : \mathbb{R}^4 \to \mathbb{R}^2$ be the projection $(x, y, \mu) \mapsto \mu$, then we finally observe that for all $\mu \in \pi(U_+)$

$$H_\pm(\mu) \notin H(U_\pm), \tag{34}$$

with the same property for H^0.

Now to finish this construction, in view of (33), (34) we claim that there are diffeomorphisms Ψ_1 and Ψ_2 of the form (31), defined on a neighbourhood of $\Sigma(H^0) \subset \mathbb{R}^4$ and on a neighbourhood of its image $\bar{H}(\Sigma(H^0)) \subset \mathbb{R} \times \mathbb{R}^2$ such that ψ_1 maps the singular points of H_μ^0 onto those of $H_{\phi(\mu)}$ and ψ_2 maps the singular level sets of H_μ^0 onto the corresponding level sets of $H_{\phi(\mu)}$. Denoting the elliptic singular points of H_μ^0 by $(x_\pm^0(\mu), y_\pm^0(\mu))$ we express this more formally by

$$\psi_1(x_\pm^0(\mu), y_\pm^0(\mu), \mu) = (x_\pm(\phi(\mu)), y_\pm(\phi(\mu))) \tag{35a}$$

$$H^0(x_\pm^0(\mu), y_\pm^0(\mu), \mu) = \psi_2(H(x_\pm(\phi(\mu)), y_\pm(\phi(\mu)), \mu), \mu). \tag{35b}$$

Condition (35a) is easy to satisfy. As far as (35b) is concerned the conditions (33) guarantee that we can use interpolation on the image space $\mathbb{R}$ in order to establish this. Moreover condition (34) ensures that such a definition of ψ_2 is not in conflict with the choice in step 1.

The extension of Ψ_1 and Ψ_2 to a full neighbourhood of $\Sigma(H^0)$ in $\mathbb{R}^2 \times \mathbb{R}$ is analogous.

This ends step 2.

Step 3. In order to finish our construction we first extend Ψ_1 and Ψ_2 to all of $\mathbb{R}^2 \times \mathbb{R}^2$ and $\mathbb{R}^2 \times \mathbb{R}$ respectively. Notice that $\Psi_2 \circ \bar{H} \circ \Psi_1$ need not be equal to $\bar{H}^0$ globally. Let us denote $\bar{H}^1 := \Psi_2 \circ \bar{H} \circ \Psi_1$, then $\bar{H}^1$ has the form $\bar{H}^1(x, y, \mu) = (H^1(x, y, \mu), \mu)$.

We now shall construct a left-right equivalence using a standard homotopy method, cf. [Ma]. To this purpose for $0 \leq t \leq 1$ we take

$$\mathcal{H}(x, y, \mu, t) := (1 - t)H^0(x, y, \mu) + tH^1(x, y, \mu) \tag{36}$$

and then have

4.3. Lemma. *There exists a vector field* Y *of the form*

$$Y(x, y, \mu, t) = \xi(x, y, \mu, t)\frac{\partial}{\partial x} + \eta(x, y, \mu, t)\frac{\partial}{\partial y} + \frac{\partial}{\partial t},$$

defined on a neighbourhood of $DT := \{(0, 0, \delta, 0, t) | -C \leq \delta \leq C \text{ and } 0 \leq t \leq 1\}$, *such that* $Y\mathcal{H} \equiv 0$.

Proof of the Lemma. In order to solve the equation $Y\mathcal{H} \equiv 0$ for Y, we first determine local solutions using singularity theory of functions. In the sequel $\mathcal{E}_2, \mathcal{E}_3$ and $\mathcal{E}_{2,3}$ respectively denote the rings of germs of functions $\mathbb{R}^2 \to \mathbb{R}$, $\mathbb{R}^3 \to \mathbb{R}$, and $\mathbb{R}^2 \times \mathbb{R}^3 \to \mathbb{R}$ at some fixed point (x_0, y_0), (μ_0, t_0) and (x_0, y_0, μ_0, t_0) respectively. From the context it will be obvious which point is meant.

1. On $U_\pm \times [0, 1]$ we take $\xi \equiv 0$ and $\eta \equiv 0$, since H^0 and H^1 coincide on these sets, cf. step 1.

2. If we abbreviate $\mathcal{H}_t(x, y, \mu) := \mathcal{H}(x, y, \mu, t)$ then observe that $\Sigma(\mathcal{H}_t) = \Sigma(\mathcal{H}_0)$ for all $0 \leq t \leq 1$. For all $(x_0, y_0, \mu_0) \in \Sigma(\mathcal{H}_{t_0}) \backslash (U_- \cup U_+)$ we know that (x_0, y_0) is a nondegenerate singular point of $\mathcal{H}|_{\mathbb{R}^2 \times \{(\mu_0, t_0)\}}$. Indeed, as a consequence of condition (iii) imposed on Ψ in step 1, we see that

$$\partial^2 \mathcal{H}/\partial x^2(x_0, y_0, \mu_0, t_0) = ((1 - t_0) + t_0 a)\partial^2 H^0/\partial x^2(x_0, y_0, \mu_0, t_0)$$

where a is the derivative with respect to the first variable of the map ψ_2 at the point $(H^0(x_0, y_0, \mu_0), \mu_0)$. In particular we have that $a > 0$.

A similar expression can be derived for the other second order derivatives of $\mathcal{H}$ at the point (x_0, y_0, μ_0, t_0). This proves that (x_0, y_0) is a nondegenerate singular point of $\mathcal{H}|_{\mathbb{R}^2 \times \{(\mu_0, t_0)\}}$, and hence that

$$\mathcal{E}_2 \subset \mathcal{E}_2 \left\{ \frac{\partial \mathcal{H}}{\partial x}\Big|_{\mathbb{R}^2 \times \{(\mu_0, t_0)\}}, \frac{\partial \mathcal{H}}{\partial y}\Big|_{\mathbb{R}^2 \times \{(\mu_0, t_0)\}} \right\} + \mathbb{R}.$$

Another application of the Malgrange-Mather Preparation Theorem, cf. [Ma (pp. 178, 179)], now yields that

$$\mathcal{E}_{2,3} \subset \mathcal{E}_{2,3} \left\{ \frac{\partial \mathcal{H}}{\partial x}, \frac{\partial \mathcal{H}}{\partial y} \right\} + \mathcal{E}_3.$$

Hence there exist germs $\xi, \eta \in \mathcal{E}_{2,3}$ and $\zeta \in \mathcal{E}_3$ such that

$$-\frac{\partial \mathcal{H}}{\partial t} = \xi\frac{\partial \mathcal{H}}{\partial x} + \eta\frac{\partial \mathcal{H}}{\partial y} + \zeta.$$

Since $\frac{\partial \mathcal{H}}{\partial t} = H^1 - H^0$ vanishes on $\Sigma(\mathcal{H}_t)$, cf. step 2, we see that $\zeta \equiv 0$, i.e. that $Y\mathcal{H} \equiv 0$ is solvable near any point of $\Sigma(\mathcal{H}_t)$.

3. The equation $Y\mathcal{H} \equiv 0$ obviously is solvable near regular points of $\mathcal{H}$.

Given these local solutions we take a partition of unity in order to patch them together to a global solution Y on a full neighbourhood of the set DT. Notice that here we use the compactness of DT. □

To finish the proof of Proposition 4.2 we now show that the time-evolution of the vector field Y can be used to construct a right-equivalence between H^1 and H^0. Let Y_t be the time t map of Y, then $Y\mathcal{H} \equiv 0$ implies that $\mathcal{H} \circ Y_t = \mathcal{H}$. Obviously Y_t is of the form

$$Y_t(x, y, \mu, t_0) = (\tilde{Y}(x, y, \mu, t), t + t_0)$$

for some mapping $\tilde{Y} : \mathbb{R}^2 \times \mathbb{R}^3 \to \mathbb{R}^2 \times \mathbb{R}^3$. Taking

$$\tilde{\Psi}(x, y, \mu) := \tilde{Y}(x, y, \mu, 1)$$

we see that $H^1 \circ \tilde{\Psi} = H^0$.

This concludes our construction of a global left-right equivalence between H and H^0 in the case of even k and in the absence of symmetry.

II. The symmetric cases: We briefly retrace our steps under I for the cases in which H has one of the $\mathbb{Z}_2$-symmetries or the $\mathbb{Z}_2 \oplus \mathbb{Z}_2$-symmetry. For similar considerations we refer to e.g. [GS, GSM, GSS].

Step 1. The splitting transformation Ψ by its construction is equivariant, since the Implicit Function Theorem gives "equivariant solutions of equivariant equations."

Subsequently the equivalence of the families K and K^0 is established using the $\mathbb{Z}_2$- or $\mathbb{Z}_2 \oplus \mathbb{Z}_2$- equivariant version of the Malgrange-Mather Preparation Theorem for functions of one variable, cf. [Po].

Step 2. The construction of Ψ_1 and Ψ_2 in this step obviously is adaptable to the equivariant case, since then the sets $\Sigma(H)$ and $\Sigma(H^0)$ are invariant.

Step 3. Again using equivariant versions of the Malgrange-Mather Preparation Theorem we obtain an equivariant solution Y of the equation $Y\mathcal{H} \equiv 0$. Hence the time-evolution of Y is equivariant as well.

This finishes the construction of a left-right equivalence in the presence of symmetry and hence the proof of our proposition. □

c13. Bifurcation Diagram for the Family H^0

Finally we direct our attention to the bifurcation diagram of the normal form H^0 as obtained in Proposition 4.2, for parameter points $\mu = (\varepsilon, \nu)$ ranging over the set $[-C, C] \times [-\nu_0, \nu_0]$. From the beginning of this part recall that bifurcations correspond to the occurrence of one of the following two situations:

(*i*) H^0_μ has a degenerate singular point in the bounded neighbourhood U of $(x, y) = (0, 0)$ in $\mathbb{R}^2$.

(*ii*) H^0_μ has two hyperbolic singular points connected by the corresponding singular level set. The associated vector field then has a heteroclinic orbit.

The Case of Even k With no Symmetry

We first consider the case of even k in the absence of symmetry, i.e. the most general case. Here the polynomial N_3 has the form $N_3(x,y) = B_0 x^3 + B_3 y^3$ with $B_0 \neq 0 \neq B_3$. Application of the scaling

$$x = |A|^{-\frac{1}{2}} \bar{x}, \quad y = |A|^{-\frac{1}{2}} \bar{y}, \quad \nu = |A|^{\frac{1}{2}} B_0^{-1} \bar{\nu}, \quad H^0 = |A|^{-1} \bar{H}^0$$

and, as before, omitting the bars again, yields the family of functions

$$H_\mu^0(x,y) = \varepsilon(x^2 + y^2) + (x^2 - y^2) + \nu(x^3 + by^3) + \frac{1}{4}\sigma(x^2 + y^2)^2, \qquad (37)$$

with $b = B_3 B_0^{-1}$ and $\sigma = \text{sign} A$. Without damage to generality we may restrict to the case

$$b > 0 \quad \text{and} \quad \sigma = -1,$$

since the remaining cases are completely similar.

Singular Points of H^0

From (37) it directly follows that the equations

$$\frac{\partial H^0}{\partial x} = 0, \quad \frac{\partial H^0}{\partial y} = 0$$

giving the singularities of H^0, are equivalent to the disjunction of the following systems of equations

$$x = 0, \quad y = 0; \qquad (38a)$$
$$x = 0, \quad 2(\varepsilon - 1) + 3\nu by - y^2 = 0; \qquad (38b)$$
$$y = 0, \quad 2(\varepsilon + 1) + 3\nu x - x^2 = 0; \qquad (38c)$$
$$2(\varepsilon + 1) + 3\nu x - (x^2 + y^2) = 0, \quad 2(\varepsilon - 1) + 3\nu by - (x^2 + y^2) = 0. \quad (38d)$$

Notice that (38b) yields two singular points $(0, y_\pm(\mu))$ with $y_- < y_+$, provided that $9b^2\nu^2 + 8(\varepsilon - 1) > 0$. Similarly (38c) yields two singular points $(x_\pm(\mu), 0)$ with $x_- < x_+$, provided that $9\nu^2 + 8(\varepsilon + 1) > 0$. Finally (38d) implies that $3\nu(by - x) = 4$, which rules out solutions in a bounded neighbourhood of $(0,0)$ for $|\nu|$ sufficiently small.

Also we observe that $(x,y) = (0,0)$ is a solution of

(38b) if and only if $\varepsilon = 1$ (the right tongue-boundary),
(38c) if and only if $\varepsilon = -1$ (the left tongue-boundary).

These observations lead to the subdivision of the range $-C \leq \varepsilon \leq C$, $-\nu_0 \leq \nu \leq \nu_0$ into five regions, each of which is a connected component of the range of parameters with only nondegenerate singular points. Checking the Hessian determinant at each of these singular points one easily derives the type of each of them. The results of this computation are listed in the table below.

	Region	Singular Points
I.	$-C \leq \varepsilon < -1 - \frac{9}{8}\nu^2$	elliptic: $(0,0)$
II.	$-1 - \frac{9}{8}\nu^2 < \varepsilon < -1$	elliptic: $(0,0)$ and $(x_+,0)$ hyperbolic: $(x_-,0)$
III.	$-1 < \varepsilon < 1 - \frac{9}{8}b^2\nu^2$	elliptic: $(x_-,0)$ and $(x_+,0)$ hyperbolic: $(0,0)$
IV.	$1 - \frac{9}{8}b^2\nu^2 < \varepsilon < 1$	elliptic: $(x_-,0)$, $(x_+,0)$ and $(0,y_-)$ hyperbolic: $(0,0)$ and $(0,y_+)$
V.	$1 < \varepsilon \leq C$	elliptic: $(x_-,0)$, $(x_+,0)$ and $(0,0)$ hyperbolic: $(0,y_-)$ and $(0,y_+)$

Heteroclinic Orbits Associated to H^0

Inspection of the above table reveals that heteroclinic orbits don't occur in any of the parameter-regions I, II or III. Denoting $h_\pm(\mu) := H^0_\mu(0, y_\pm(\mu), \mu)$ we observe that a heteroclinic orbit occurs for parameter points μ belonging to

region IV if and only if $h_+(\mu) = 0$;
region V if and only if $h_+(\mu) = h_-(\mu)$.

4.4. Lemma.
(i) For μ in region IV:

$$h_+(\mu) < 0 \text{ if } \varepsilon < 1 - b^2\nu^2;$$
$$h_+(\mu) = 0 \text{ if } \varepsilon = 1 - b^2\nu^2;$$
$$h_+(\mu) > 0 \text{ if } \varepsilon > 1 - b^2\nu^2.$$

(ii) For μ in region V:

$$h_+(\mu) > h_-(\mu).$$

Proof. Using (38b) we find

$$h_\pm(\mu) = (\varepsilon - 1)y_\pm^2 + \nu b y_\pm^3 - \frac{1}{4}y_\pm^4$$

$$= (\varepsilon - 1)y_\pm^2 + \nu b y_\pm^3 - \frac{1}{4}y_\pm^2(2(\varepsilon - 1) + 3\nu b y_\pm),$$

i.e.

$$h_\pm(\mu) = \frac{1}{2}(\varepsilon - 1)y_\pm^2 + \frac{1}{4}\nu b y_\pm^3. \tag{39}$$

Therefore, using the explicit form of y_+ obtained from (38b), we get

$$h_\pm(\mu) = y_\pm^2 \left\{ \frac{1}{2}(\varepsilon - 1) + \frac{3}{8}\nu^2 b^2 \pm \frac{1}{8}\nu b \sqrt{9\nu^2 b^2 + 8(\varepsilon - 1)} \right\},$$

from which the first part of the lemma easily follows.

In order to prove the second part we observe that

$$h_+(\mu) - h_-(\mu) = \frac{1}{2}(\varepsilon - 1)(y_+^2 - y_-^2) + \frac{1}{4}\nu b(y_+^3 - y_-^3)$$

$$= \frac{1}{2}(y_+ - y_-)\{(\varepsilon - 1)(y_+ + y_-) + \frac{1}{2}\nu b(y_+^2 + y_+y_- + y_-^2)\}.$$

From (38b) it follows that $y_+ + y_- = 3b\nu$ and $y_+y_- = -2(\varepsilon - 1)$. Hence $y_+^2 + y_+y_- + y_-^2 = (y_+ + y_-)^2 - y_+y_- = 9b^2\nu^2 + 2(\varepsilon - 1)$. Therefore

$$h_+(\mu) - h_-(\mu) = \frac{1}{2}(y_+ - y_-)\{4(\varepsilon - 1) + \frac{9}{2}b^2\nu^2\}b\nu. \tag{40}$$

Since $\varepsilon > 1$ and $y_- < y_+$, for μ in the region V the second part of the lemma is a direct consequence of (40).   □

The curve $\varepsilon = 1 - b^2\nu^2$ subdivides the region IV into two subregions, cf. the bifurcation diagram in Fig. 6. Since $H^0(x, y, \mu)$ is negative for $x^2 + y^2$ sufficiently large, the preceeding analysis, summarized in the above table and in Lemma 4.4, yields the qualitative information depicted in the rest of Fig. 6.

These phase-portraits can be interpreted as follows. The 2π evolution of some planar vector field corresponding to it is conjugate to an integrable approximation of the Poincaré mapping P of our original vector field X of the form (4).

The central singularity at $\mu = 0$ is the degenerate maximum $-\frac{1}{4}(x^2 + y^2)^2$, the phase portrait of which looks like picture 1. Away from the central singularity the following secondary local bifurcations occur:

Picture	Normal Form $H(x, y) = \frac{1}{2}y^2 + V(x)$	Name
2, 6	$V_\mu(x) = x^3 - \mu x$	saddle-node/fold
4, 10	$V_\mu(x) = x^3 - \mu x^2$	exchange/fold

The second of these is generic since the origin always is singular. Moreover picture 8 shows a heteroclinic bifurcation. Notice that the roman numbers of the regions in the above table concerning the singularities correspond to the present numbers as follows:

I corresponds to 1;   II corresponds to 3;
III corresponds to 5;   IV corresponds to 7, 8 and 9;
V corresponds to 11.

Remark. How to obtain bifurcation diagram and phase portraits for $\beta < 0$? One directly shows that the bifurcation diagram is obtained by reflection of the part for $\beta > 0$ in the ε-axis. The phase portraits then are given by reflecting

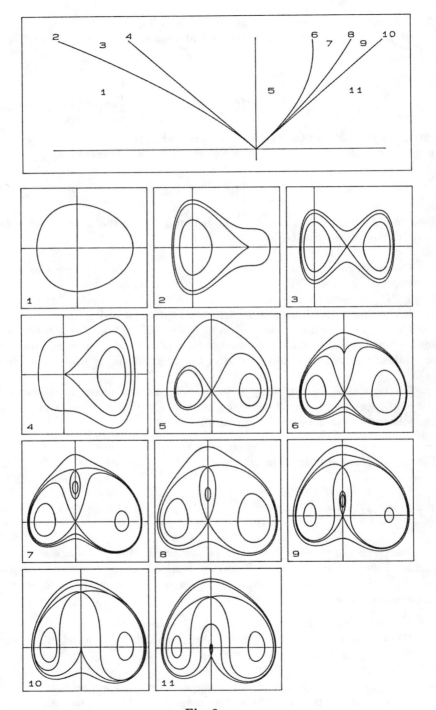

Fig. 6.

the corresponding ones for $\beta > 0$ in the diagonal $y = x$. In fact if the scaling transformation (26) is replaced by

$$\varepsilon = -\beta\bar{\varepsilon}, \quad x = (-\beta)^{\frac{1}{2}}\bar{y}, \quad y = (-\beta)^{\frac{1}{2}}\bar{x}, \quad H = \beta^2\bar{H} \text{ writing } \nu := -(-\beta)^{\frac{1}{2}},$$

then, in stead of (28), we get

$$\begin{aligned} H_\mu(x,y) = {} & \varepsilon(x^2 + y^2) + (x^2 - y^2) + \nu P_3(y,x) + \frac{1}{4}A(x^2 + y^2)^2 \\ & + \nu^2 R(y,x,\varepsilon,\nu^2). \end{aligned}$$

Evidently this statement also applies for the special cases below.

The Case of Even k with $\mathbb{Z}_2$-symmetry

Now, cf. Proposition 4.2, we have that $N_3(x,y) = B_0 x^3$ and hence we are in the case $b = 0$ of the preceding analysis. For simplicity we again restrict to the case $A < 0$.

Therefore region IV collapses into the right tongue-boundary. For μ in region V, the singular points $(0, y_-)$ and $(0, y_+)$ are mapped onto each other by the involution R_0. Thus they lie in the same level set of H^0: the symmetry here forces a heteroclinic orbit to be stable.

The phase portraits associated to the various parameter regimes are depicted in Fig. 7. The dynamical interpretation of the pictures is as in Fig. 6.

Away from the central singularity the following local bifurcations occur:

Picture	Normal form $H(x,y) = \frac{1}{2}y^2 + V(x)$	Name
2	$V_\mu(x) = x^3 - \mu x$	saddle-node/fold
4	$V_\mu(x) = x^3 - \mu x^2$	exchange/fold
6	$V_\mu(x) = x^4 - \mu x^2$	double-node/cusp (equivariant)

Here the last case is generic by $\mathbb{Z}_2$-symmetry. The comment on the exchange is as under Fig. 6. The translation of the roman region numbering to the present one is almost as before.

The Cases of Even k with $\mathbb{Z}_2 \oplus \mathbb{Z}_2$-Symmetry and of Odd k

Here always N_3 identically vanishes, giving for H^0 the simple form

$$H_\mu^0(x,y) = \varepsilon(x^2 + y^2) + (x^2 - y^2) + \frac{1}{4}A(x^2 + y^2)^2.$$

Notice that also the dependence on ν has disappeared. The qualitative information now is depicted in Fig. 8. Again the symmetry forces heteroclinic orbits to be stable. For even k the dynamical interpretation of the pictures is as in Figs. 6

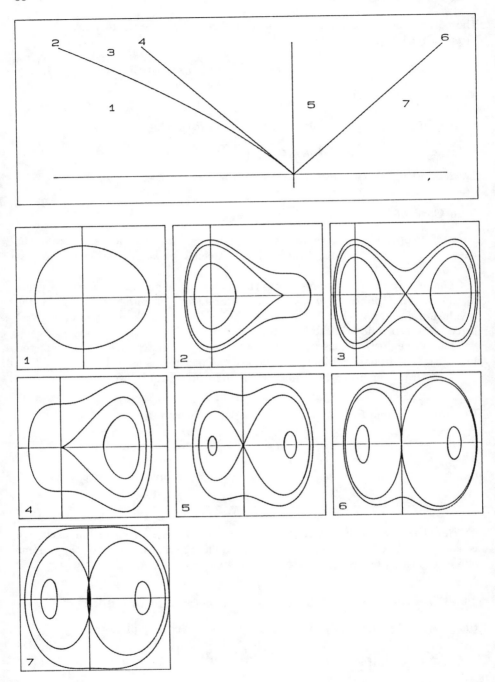

Fig. 7.

Picture	Normal form $H(x,y) = \frac{1}{2}y^2 + V(x)$	Name
2	$V_\mu(x) = x^4 - \mu x^2$	double-node/cusp (equivariant)
4	$V_\mu(x) = -x^4 - \mu x^2$	double-saddle/cusp (equivariant)

and 7. For odd k the integrable approximation of the Poincaré mapping P is obtained from the phase portrait by composing the 2π map of a corresponding vector field with $-id$. In particular the nontrivial equilibria of the phase portraits are periodic points of P of period 2. It is this case where the period-doubling- or flip-bifurcation occurs.

The period doubling for odd k occurs along the lines 2 and 4. Again these cases are generic by symmetry.

Remarks. (i) Due to the scaling (26) the preceeding analysis only holds on neighbourhoods of $(x,y) = (0,0)$ of the asymptotic size $\sqrt{\beta}$ as $\beta \to 0$. Given a wedge-like restriction (25) on the parameters, however, one can extend the equivalences to a full neighbourhood of $(x,y,\beta,\varepsilon) = (0,0,0,0)$. The proof of this is straightforward, using the fact that for $A \neq 0$ the functions (or rather their additive inverses) are proper, while further away from $(x,y) = (0,0)$ all their level curves are circular. (Also compare lemma 4.1.) A simple way to extend the equivalences uses the gradients of the functions.

(ii) Let us for a while return to the pendulum (1), which is a $\mathbb{Z}_2 \oplus \mathbb{Z}_2$-symmetric case. So the analysis of the generic tongues is contained in Fig. 8. For the forcing term we have $p(t) = \cos t$, so only the first tongue ($k = 1$) is generic, all others are degenerate.

An interesting question concerns the stabilization of the upper equilibrium of the pendulum, i.e. where it stands upright. To this end consider the second order equation (3)

$$\ddot{x} + (\alpha^2 + \beta p(t))V'(x) = 0,$$

this time with $V(x) = -\frac{1}{2}x^2 + O(x^3)$ as $x \to 0$. The methods of the present paper apply to this situation, now for (α, β) near $(0,0)$.

c2. Near the Line $\beta = 0$

We again turn to the family (24)

$$H_\mu(x,y) = \varepsilon(x^2 + y^2) + \beta(x^2 - y^2) + \beta P_3(x,y) + \frac{1}{4}A(x^2 + y^2)^2 + hot.$$

We now are interested in the dynamics for parameter values near the line $\beta = 0$. In fact we'll consider wedge-shaped neighbourhoods of the punctured line with the origin $(\varepsilon, \beta) = (0,0)$ deleted. First we claim that, analogous to Lemma 4.1 we have the following. If the parameters vary over a wedge-like neighbourhood

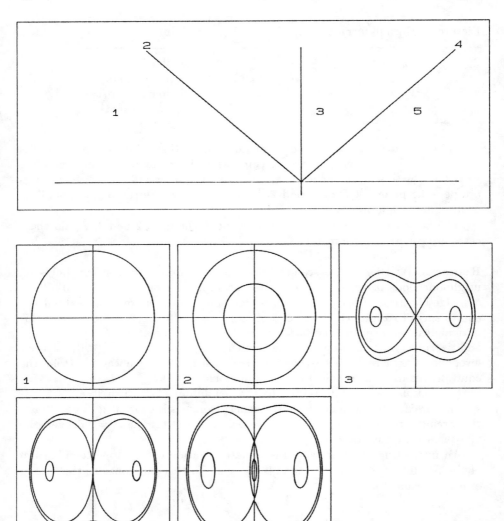

Fig. 8.

$|\beta| < C|\varepsilon|$, with $|\varepsilon|$ small, any singularity of (24) occurs at a distance $O(\sqrt{|\varepsilon|})$ from the origin $(x, y) = (0, 0)$.

Again restricting to the case $A < 0$, the only interesting case occurs for $\varepsilon > 0$. The above considerations then suggest the following scaling, complementary to (26):

$$\beta = \varepsilon\bar{\beta}, \quad x = \varepsilon^{\frac{1}{2}}\bar{x}, \quad y = \varepsilon^{\frac{1}{2}}\bar{y}, \quad H = \varepsilon^2\bar{H}. \tag{41}$$

Here the point $(\bar{x}, \bar{y})$ varies on some compact neighbourhood of $(0, 0)$ while both the parameters ε and $|\bar{\beta}|$ will be chosen sufficiently small. This means that, unscaled, we consider wedge-like neighbourhoods $|\beta| < C|\varepsilon|$ with small C, i.e. with a small opening angle, and with $|\varepsilon|$ small.

Deleting all bars again we so obtain

$$H_\mu(x, y) = x^2 + y^2 + \frac{1}{4}A(x^2 + y^2)^2 + (x^2 + y^2)^2 O_S(\varepsilon^{\frac{1}{2}})$$
$$+ \beta\{x^2 - y^2 + O(\varepsilon^{\frac{1}{2}}(x^2 + y^2)^{3/2})\}$$

where the restterm $O_S(\varepsilon^{\frac{1}{2}})$ is an $O(\varepsilon^{\frac{1}{2}})$-term with circular symmetry, cf. the Proposition of §3.

Since our interest is with singular points of H_μ away from the origin of the phase plane we blow up by passing to polar coordinates, putting: $x = \rho\cos\theta$ and $y = \rho\sin\theta$. Thus we get as a function of ρ and θ:

$$H_\mu(\rho\cos\theta, \rho\sin\theta) = \rho^2 + \frac{1}{4}A\rho^4 + \rho^4 O_S(\varepsilon^{\frac{1}{2}}) + \beta\{\rho^2(\cos^2\theta - \sin^2\theta) + \rho^3 O(\varepsilon^{\frac{1}{2}})\}.$$

Our singular points are given by the equations

$$\frac{\partial H_\mu}{\partial\rho}(\rho\cos\theta, \rho\sin\theta) = 0, \quad \frac{\partial H_\mu}{\partial\theta}(\rho\cos\theta, \rho\sin\theta) = 0,$$

yielding

$$2\rho + A\rho^3 + \rho^3 O_S(\varepsilon^{\frac{1}{2}}) + \rho^2 O(\beta) = 0 \quad \text{and} \quad \beta\{\rho^2\sin 2\theta + \rho^3 O(\varepsilon^{\frac{1}{2}})\} = 0,$$

with smooth families of solutions $\rho = \rho_m(\varepsilon, \beta)$, $\theta = \theta_m(\varepsilon, \beta)$ for $m = 0, 1, 2, 3$ given by

$$\rho_m^2(\varepsilon, \beta) = -2/A + hot(\varepsilon^{\frac{1}{2}}, \beta) \quad \text{and} \quad \theta_m(\varepsilon, \beta) = m\pi/2 + hot(\varepsilon^{\frac{1}{2}}, \beta).$$

So for each value of the parameters ε and β with both $\varepsilon > 0$ and $|\beta| > 0$ sufficiently small there are exactly four singular points, labeled by m, two of them lying near the x-axis and the other two near the y-axis. For $\beta = 0$ the circle with radius $\rho_m(\varepsilon, 0)$ is completely filled with singularities.

We wish to study how the type of these four families of singularities $\rho = \rho_m(\varepsilon, \beta)$, $\theta = \theta_m(\varepsilon, \beta)$ changes when the parameter β passes through zero. In order to do this we compute the sign of their Hessian determinants. We recall that for nonvanishing determinant we have a nondegenerate (or Morse) singularity: A positive sign corresponds to an elliptic singularity (maximum or minimum), a negative sign to a hyperbolic one (saddle point).

After some calculations we get in the point $(\rho_m(\varepsilon, \beta)\cos\theta_m(\varepsilon, \beta), \rho_m(\varepsilon, \beta)\sin\theta_m(\varepsilon, \beta), \varepsilon, \beta)$

$$\frac{\partial^2 H_\mu}{\partial \rho^2}(-) = \frac{1}{2} + 3A\rho_m^2(\varepsilon,\beta) + hot(\varepsilon^{\frac{1}{2}},\beta) = -1 + hot(\varepsilon^{\frac{1}{2}},\beta),$$

$$\frac{\partial^2 H_\mu}{\partial \theta^2}(-) = \beta\{4\rho_m^2(\varepsilon,\beta)\cos 2\theta_m(\varepsilon,\beta) + O(\varepsilon^{\frac{1}{2}})\}$$

$$= \begin{cases} -2\beta/A + \beta hot(\varepsilon^{\frac{1}{2}},\beta), & \text{for } m = 0,2,\ldots, \\ 2\beta/A + \beta hot(\varepsilon^{\frac{1}{2}},\beta), & \text{for } m = 1,3,\ldots. \end{cases}$$

$$\frac{\partial^2 H_\mu}{\partial \rho \partial \theta}(-) = \beta hot(\varepsilon^{\frac{1}{2}},\beta).$$

For the Hessian determinant we then have for sufficiently small $e > 0$ and $|\beta| > 0$ that

$$\text{sign det} \begin{bmatrix} -1 + hot(\varepsilon^{\frac{1}{2}},\beta) & \beta hot(\varepsilon^{\frac{1}{2}},\beta) \\ \beta hot(\varepsilon^{\frac{1}{2}},\beta) & \pm 2\beta/A + \beta hot(\varepsilon^{\frac{1}{2}},\beta) \end{bmatrix} = (-1)^{m-1}\text{sign}\beta,$$

Here we use that $A < 0$. We conclude the following

4.5. Proposition. *For the smooth families of singularities* $\rho = \rho_m(\varepsilon,\beta)$, $\theta = \theta_m(\varepsilon,\beta)$, $m = 0,1,2,3$, *the following holds: For* $\varepsilon > 0$ *and* $|\beta| > 0$ *both sufficiently small, all singularities are nondegenerate. Moreover for each family the type changes with the sign of* β.

In particular, when β *changes from negative to positive the singularities near the x-axis pass from elliptic to hyperbolic and vice versa for the singularities near the y-axis.*

In Fig. 9 we summarized this qualitative information, for a case with symmetry. In the following such a change of type of a Morse singularity through a circle filled with singularities we'll call a *Birkhoff-bifurcation*. In the more general setting of planar functions this is a very degenerate phenomenon, also see the beginning of subsection c1. The above proposition however says that in the present universe, where only the functions p and V (forcing and potential) are involved, the Birkhoff-bifurcation is a generic phenomenon.

In fact in this universe we even have a form of structural stability:

4.6. Corollary. *For positive constants* C *and* ε_0, *in the parameter plane consider the wedge* $|\beta| < C|\varepsilon|$, $|\varepsilon| < \varepsilon_0$. *For* C *and* ε_0 *sufficiently small the family of planar Hamiltonians* (24), *parametrized over this wedge, is structurally stable in the present universe, where the classification is modulo topological right-equivalence.*

Proof. The proof we have in mind is straightforward, since the singularities for $\beta \neq 0$ are of Morse-type and the levels of the saddles in the nonsymmetric case are distinct, provided that the third order term is a *general polynomial* in the sense of subsection c13.

In fact, taking two nearby planar families of the form (24), the search is for a parameter-dependent homeomorphism of the plane that maps the singularities and the level sets of one family to corresponding ones of the other.

In view of the above genericity assumptions for $\beta \neq 0$ one directly constructs the family of homeomorphisms between the singularities and their level sets, depending continuously on the parameters. The limit for $\beta = 0$ of this family of homeomorphisms maps the singular circles onto each other. Finally extension to the nonsingular level sets is obvious.   □

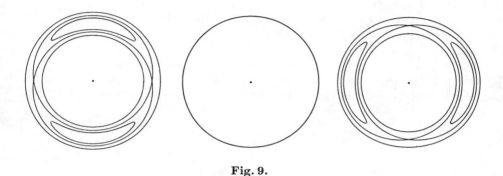

Fig. 9.

Remarks. (i) Due to the scaling (41), the above construction yields a topological equivalence on a shrinking neighbourhood of the origin in the (x, y)-plane. At the end of subsection c1 we discussed extension of the equivalences to full neighbourhoods of the origin, given a wedge-like restriction. In the present case such an extension of the topological equivalences also is possible, where now we have to stay near the ε-axis. The argument runs as before.

(ii) We observe that the restriction (25) in the parameter plane deals with arbitrarily wide wedges around the β-axis while presently we need to restrict to sufficiently narrow wedges around the ε-axis, compare the remarks following (41). An obvious question then is whether for two nearby families the equivalences found on the two wedges can be glued together so giving one *topological* equivalence between them on a full neighbourhood of $(x, y, \varepsilon, \beta) = (0, 0, 0, 0)$. This question can be answered affirmatively, so in that sense our family of functions is structurally stable and our bifurcation has codimension 2. Again one may ask what remains of this statement when working with *smooth* equivalences ...

d. Some Remarks on a Case of Small a_k

In this subsection we consider the case where for the value of k under consideration the Fourier-coefficient a_k is small, i.e. near 0. From subsection b we recall that for vanishing a_k the boundaries of the k-th resonance tongue are tangent at the point $(\alpha, \beta) = (k/2, 0)$. From this we see that for a bifurcational analysis of this case more parameters are needed: in particular a_k itself might naturally be included as a parameter.

In stead of doing this systematically we indicate why the polynomial

$$\frac{1}{2} E_2(\mu)|z|^2 + \frac{1}{2}\beta \mathrm{Re}\left(\Phi_1(\mu)\bar{z}^2\right) + \beta P_3(z, \bar{z}) + \frac{1}{4} A|z|^4 \tag{42}$$

corresponding to the 4-jet of (23) is not sufficient. In our considerations we restrict to the reversible case with odd k, where this "degeneracy" of (42) is most likely. From the above subsection b we recall that

$$E_2(\mu) = \frac{1}{k^3}(k^2\varepsilon - \varepsilon^2 + \beta^2(a_0^2 - \frac{1}{2}k|a_k|^2)) + \beta^2 B,$$

$$\Phi_1(\mu) = \frac{1}{k^3}((k^2 - 2\varepsilon)a_k - \frac{1}{2}\beta a_{2k}\bar{a}_k) + \beta\Theta,$$

where now Φ_1, a_k, Θ, etc. are real. The constants B and Θ are independent of a_k. Also we recall that $P_3(z, \bar{z}) \equiv 0$ for our case of odd k. As we saw at the end of subsection b, for small $|a_k| \neq 0$ the boundary curves of the k-th resonance tongue, for $\beta \neq 0$, have an extra point of intersection. In this case the phase portraits of (42) gives rise to the diagram of Fig. 10, which also is interesting for its own sake. Here we assume that $\Theta \neq 0$. In particular, for simplicity, we restrict to the case $\Theta > 0$. Also, as before, we take $A < 0$.

First recall that for $a_k \neq 0$ the part around the point $(\beta, \varepsilon) = (0, 0)$ is "known" from the above. The whole picture, however, doesn't look persistent for addition of higher order terms, let alone structurally stable. To illustrate this let's consider the dynamics near the line $\Phi = 0$. At first sight a Birkhoff-bifurcation seems to occur, comparable to what happens along the line $\beta = 0$, see c2, above. For $\Phi = 0$ our polynomial (42) has the form

$$\frac{1}{2} E_2(\mu)(x^2 + y^2) + \frac{1}{4} A(x^2 + y^2)^2, \tag{43}$$

where $\mu = (\beta, \varepsilon)$ parametrizes the line $\Phi = 0$. We see that this form is $SO(2, \mathbb{R})$-symmetric, which gives rise to circles completely filled with singular points, compare the situation for $\beta = 0$ as described in subsection c2. However, unlike there, in the present case there is no reason for an $SO(2, \mathbb{R})$-symmetry in the higher order terms. This means that addition of higher order terms, even when generated by the special form of our equations, in general probably will break this symmetry and produce more "complicated" pictures, where the circles of singular points fall apart into finitely many. So we conjecture that in this sense (42) is not sufficient.

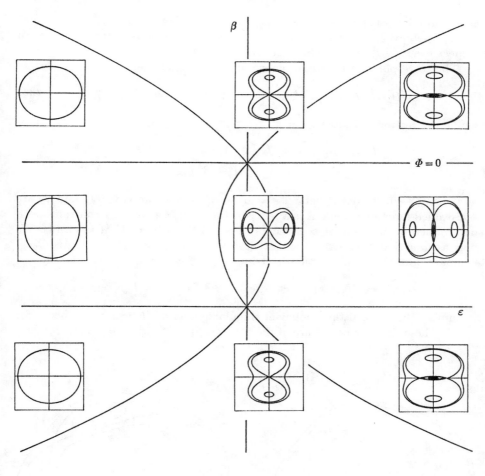

Fig. 10.

e. Nearby Higher Order Subharmonics

Higher order subharmonic solutions may occur, branching off from the trivial
solution $z = 0$ when in the parameter plane we have $\beta = 0$ and α passes through
rationals near $k/2$. These subharmonics can be studied using the same method
as before.

So let us start with a vector field X of the form (4). For $\alpha_0 = p/q$ near
$k/2$ we first apply the normal form procedure of §§2,3. Here we take p and q
with $gcd(p,q) = 1$ and $q \geq 5$ where this last condition is easily fulfilled by
taking α_0 sufficiently close to $k/2$. Again as in §2 we lift to the q-sheeted cov-

ering, obtaining a family $\tilde{X} = \tilde{X}^{\alpha,\beta}(z, \bar{z}, t)$ that is Hamiltonian, $\mathbb{Z}_q$-equivariant, $SO(2, \mathbb{R})$-equivariant for $\beta = 0$ and autonomous up to terms that are flat with respect to (z, α, β) in the point $(0, \alpha_0, 0) \in \mathbb{C} \times \mathbb{R} \times \mathbb{R}$.

The corresponding family of planar functions looks like

$$H_{\beta,\varepsilon}(z, \bar{z}) = \varepsilon |z|^2 + A |z|^4 + \beta \mathrm{Re}\,(\Theta \bar{z}^q) + R(z, \bar{z}, \beta, \varepsilon), \qquad (44)$$

where the restterm R has the form

$$\begin{aligned} R(z, \bar{z}, \beta, \varepsilon) = {} & |z|^6 f_1(|z|, \varepsilon) + \beta |z|^4 f_2(|z|, \varepsilon) \\ & + \beta O((|z|^2 + \beta^2 + \varepsilon^2)^{(q/2)+1}), \end{aligned}$$

as $(z, \beta, \varepsilon) \to 0$. Here, as before, $\varepsilon = \alpha^2 - \alpha_0^2 + \beta a_0$. Moreover f_1 and f_2 are real-valued functions, while A is a real constant and Θ a complex constant, both determined by the Fourier coefficients of p and the q-jet of V at 0, cf. (4). We may assume that Θ is real as well, otherwise we rotate over an angle $(\mathrm{Arg}\,\Theta)/q$, compare part c11 of this section. Putting $z = re^{i\phi}$ we obtain for our family

$$H(re^{i\phi}, re^{-i\phi}, \beta, \varepsilon) = \varepsilon r^2 + A r^4 + \beta \Theta r^q \cos q\phi + R(r, \phi, \beta, \varepsilon).$$

Assuming that $A < 0$ the nontrivial singular points of H near $r = 0$ occur for $\varepsilon > 0$. These singular points are of the form $(r, \phi) = (r_m, \phi_m)$, $0 \le m < 2q$, with

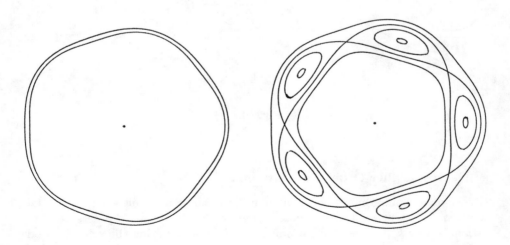

Fig. 11.

$$(r_m, \phi_m) = \left(\sqrt{-\varepsilon/2A} + O(\beta^2), \frac{m\pi}{2q} + O(\beta) \right),$$

uniformly for $\beta \to 0$, provided that $0 \leq \varepsilon \leq C\beta^2$ for some arbitrary constant $C > 0$. One easily checks that the Hessian determinant of H at the singular point (r_m, ϕ_m) has the same sign as $\Theta \cos(q\phi_m)$. Hence the singular points are elliptic for even m and hyperbolic for odd m, while they all occur at the asymptotic distance $\sqrt{-\varepsilon/2A}$ from the origin $z = 0$. Compare Fig. 11. For similar pictures e.g. see [Ar3,4,Dui]. Clearly in the dynamics this corresponds to subharmonic solutions of order q.

In the parameter plane consider the curve with equation $\varepsilon = 0$, that in the (α, β)-variables has the form $\alpha = p/q - \frac{1}{2}a_0\beta + O(\beta^2)$. We see that this curve is the left boundary of a parameter region where these subharmonics occur. Following the procedure of this section one could give a more complete bifurcational analysis of (44). In particular one would expect Birkhoff bifurcations to occur when trespassing the line $\beta = 0$, in which the elliptic singularities become hyperbolic and *vice versa*. Compare the above subsection c2.

5. Dynamical Conclusions

In §4 we classified integrable approximations of the family of Poincaré mappings $\{P_\mu\}_\mu$ governing our dynamics. Here integrability has to be understood in the sense of [BT]: a diffeomorphism is integrable if it can be embedded in a flow. In this section we'll discuss the effect of perturbations that are infinitely flat (i.e. vanish to all orders) in both z and μ. Compare e.g. [Br1,Br2,BB,BV,BT,HMS,FS]. The main questions are: What integrable dynamical phenomena are persistent for these perturbations? Does nonintegrable dynamics occur? We shall not go into all details here, but instead refer to relevant places in the literature. A rigourous investigation of the present case still will require some effort.

At the end of this section we briefly discuss a number of subjects: The discrepancy between the linear case and our nonlinear case in terms of Lyapunov stability and a perpetual adiabatic invariant. Also we'll give a remark concerning the dissipative case.

a. (Sub-) harmonics and Their Invariant Manifolds

The periodic points of period 1 and 2 found in the integrable systems of §4 as well as those of higher period (§4e) all are persistent for flat perturbations while moreover their linear types do not change. Also the bifurcation lines related to this type may be deformed slightly: the order of contact with the lines in the integrable case is infinite. This is a direct consequence of the Implicit Function Theorem, e.g. see [Ca,CH].

The invariant manifolds will be deformed slightly, but it is to be expected that after the perturbation the homo- and hetero-clinic connections will not

persist in the simple, integrable way. In general there will be no coincidence of
the corresponding stable and unstable manifolds. This expectation is based on a
result, compare [Ro], saying that generically these manifolds only have transverse
intersections. As is well known, e.g. see [Mo1,2,Ar4], this transversality would
give rise to chaotic dynamics. In Fig. 12 we depicted the difference between
integrable and transverse homoclinic behaviour, also compare [Ar1,3,4]. In the
transverse case it is said that "the separatrices split."

One problem however is that our perturbations are special, whence it is not
sure that, say for $\beta \neq 0$, we would be in this general case. This sensitivity of
genericity for the context we already met in §4.

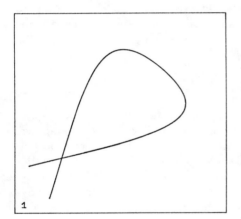
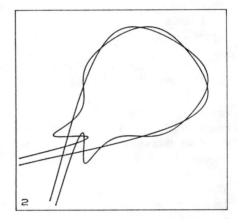

Fig. 12.

Another problem is the *flatness* of the transversality phenomenon, meaning
that it can be annihilated by perturbations that are (infinitely) flat in z and μ.
This is a consequence of the normal form theorem of §2. Such flat perturbations
are arbitrary small in the C^∞-topology. Hence we see that the families $\{P_\mu\}_\mu$,
with integrable behaviour in some neighbourhood of $(z, \mu) = (0, 0)$, are dense.
This implies that the family of Poincaré mappings probably is not finitely determined by any finite jet at $(z, \mu) = (0, 0)$. A *fortiori* we conclude that this
family then is not structurally stable. This lack of structural stability is familiar
in Hamiltonian systems of more than one degree of freedom.

Also the "tangle" corresponding to transversality only could in a neighbourhood of the unperturbed loop, which is flat in μ. In this sense our (sub-) harmonics can only be generators of tiny areas with chaotic dynamics. For more

details on this subject of flatness we refer to e.g. [BV,BT]. One method to positively detect such transversal "tangle" involves Melnikov functions, e.g. see [GH]. In our case these functions necessarily also will be flat. Following the ideas of [HMS,FS], and assuming real analyticity, one might be able to get a better hold of this flatness of the Melnikov function, particularly proving it to be exponential.

Another familiar point concerning the flatness is the following. Let us compare the settings of §4e and of the earlier part of §4. In the earlier part, which contains the main analysis of this paper, we use a Hamilton function corresponding to the normal form of the family $\{P_\mu\}_\mu$ at the point $(z, \alpha, \beta) = (0, k/2, 0)$ for integer k. In subsection e we do the same using the normal form at the point $(z, \alpha, \beta) = (0, p/q, 0)$ for p/q near $k/2$.

We notice that the two approaches reveal different things, each of them only "sees" the (sub-)harmonics and their invariant manifolds, as suggested by the corresponding Floquet parts $\dot{z} = i\alpha_0 z$, where $\alpha_0 = k/2$, or $\alpha_0 = p/q$ respectively. In each case all other (sub-)harmonic phenomena turn out to be flat. Of course if we would choose a nearby irrational α_0 the normal form would be the rotationally symmetric Birkhoff normal form, implying that in that setting all (sub-)harmonic phenomena are flat.

b. Quasi-Periodic Invariant Circles

As is known from KAM-theory, e.g. see [Ar1,3,4,Mo2,Pö], the integrable behaviour is generally preserved when restricting to the invariant circles with quasi-periodic dynamics, i.e. where the corresponding rotation number is strongly irrational (or diophantine). In fact, in general such an invariant circle is only slightly deformed by the flat perturbation, while the whole collection of these perturbed circles is a diffeomorphic image of the collection in the integrable case. Here the general considerations apply for each fixed value of the parameters. As a consequence the union of quasi-periodic circles generally has positive measure.

Of course in this local situation one has to check whether the precise requirements of KAM-theory are fulfilled, for examples of this in the conservative setting see e.g. [Br2,BB]. One point is the twist-condition, saying that the rotation numbers vary sufficiently for each value of the parameters. Generically, by an analyticity argument, we know that this condition is satisfied almost everywhere. Another point then is to control the size of the perturbation, where both the twist and the diophantine condition play a rôle. Problems occur near places where the rotation number has a critical value. Then a more precise study of the Hamiltonian family (23) is needed.

Near the elliptic points the situation is known, e.g. compare [Pö], the elliptic points are density points of quasi-periodic circles. This means that the relative measure of those circles, related to shrinking neighbourhoods of these points, tends to 1. For a general discussion of this also see [BHT(§7c)].

By the Poincaré-Birkhoff Fixed Point Theorem, see [Bi,Mo1], in between the quasi-periodic circles subharmonics exist with all intermediate rotation numbers. Of course the subharmonics found in §4e are part of this collection. A question is whether the full dynamical complexity of [BT] does occur here. This would mean that arbitrary numbers of subharmonics of a given high period exist near the quasi-periodic circles.

c. Miscellaneous Remarks

We begin comparing the nonlinear case that is the subject of this paper with the corresponding linear case. As we saw in §1b this linear equation reads

$$\ddot{x} + (\alpha^2 + \beta p(t))x = 0$$

which for $p(t) = \cos t$ reduces to the Mathieu equation (2). The corresponding Poincaré mapping is an element of the linear group $Sl(2, \mathbb{R})$. Its dynamics is Lyapunov-stable in the elliptic case and unstable in the hyperbolic case, as is well known. In the parabolic cases for $\beta \neq 0$ the Poincaré mapping is similar to $\begin{bmatrix} \pm 1 & 1 \\ 0 & \pm 1 \end{bmatrix}$ again implying instability. In [Le] the stability in the elliptic case also is related to adiabatic invariants. For definitions e.g. compare [Ar1,3,4].

In the nonlinear case, stability is invoked by the higher order terms. In fact, the origin $(x, \dot{x}) = (0,0)$, for parameter points near the tongue point $(\alpha, \beta) = (k/2, 0)$, now is enclosed by quasi-periodic invariant circles of an asymptotic radius $\sqrt{|\beta| + |\alpha - \alpha_0|}$, as directly follows from the considerations of §§4,5b. This implies Lyapunov stability for parameter points near the tongue point. We can express this stability in terms of an adiabatic invariant, as we shall sketch now. In fact it follows from the considerations mentioned above that near this tongue point the radius $|z|$, as in the normal form (22,23), is a perpetual adiabatic invariant, where the variation of $|z|$ is of order $\sqrt{|\beta| + |\alpha - \alpha_0|}$. This implies that the "unperturbed" energy H, with parameter values $\beta = 0$ and $\alpha = \alpha_0$ near the tongue point also is a perpetual adiabatic invariant.

We end this section with a remark on the dissipative case. Forced oscillations with dissipation have been studied by many people, both in generic settings, e.g. see [Ar3,Ta1], and in specific case studies, e.g. compare [ABP,Mc,Med,Mc,Sm]. In the present case, which is somewhere in between, we propose a perturbation analysis from the Hamiltonian setting, cf. [Ca].

References

[ABP] F.T. Arechi, R. Badii, A. Politi, Generalized multistability in a nonlinear dynamical system, Preprint Instituto Nazionale di Ottica, 1986

[Af]   Z. Afsharnejad, Bifurcation geometry of Mathieu's equation, Indian J. Pure Appl. Math., **17**, (1986)

[Ar1] V.I. Arnol'd, Mathematical methods of classical mechanics, Springer, 1980

[Ar2] V.I. Arnol'd, Loss of stability of self-oscillations close to resonance and versal deformations of equivariant vector fields, Funct. Anal. Appl. **11**, no. 2, (1977), 1–10

[Ar3] V.I. Arnol'd, Geometrical methods in the theory of ordinary differential equations, Springer, 1983

[Ar4]   V.I. Arnol'd, Dynamical systems III, Springer, 1988

[BB]   B.L.J. Braaksma, H.W. Broer, Quasi-periodic flow near a codimension one singularity of a divergence free vector field in dimension four. In: Bifurcation, théorie ergodique et applications (Dijon, 1981), Astérisque, **98–99**, (1982), 74–142

[BBH]   B.L.J. Braaksma, H.W. Broer, G.B. Huitema, Toward a quasi-periodic bifurcation theory, Mem. AMS. **83**, 421, (1990), 83–167

[BHT]   H.W. Broer, G.B. Huitema, F. Takens, Unfoldings of quasi-periodic tori, Mem. AMS. **83**, 421, (1990), 1–82

[Bi]   G.D. Birkhoff, Dynamical systems, AMS Publications, 1927

[BM]   N.N. Bogoljubov, Yu.A. Mitropolskii, Asymptotic methods in the theory of nonlinear oscillations, Gordon and Breach, 1961

[Br1]   H.W. Broer, Formal normal forms for vector fields and some consequences for bifurcations in the volume preserving case. In: Dynamical systems and turbulence, Warwick, 1980 (eds. D. Rand, L.-S. Young), LNM 898, Springer, (1981), 54–74

[Br2]   H.W. Broer, Quasi-periodic flow near a codimension one singularity of a divergence free vector field in dimension three. In: Dynamical systems and turbulence, Warwick, 1980 (eds. D. Rand, L.-S. Young), LNM 898, Springer, (1981), 75–89

[Br3]   H.W. Broer, Quasi-periodicity in local bifurcation theory. In: Bifurcation theory, mechanics and physics (eds. C.P. Bruter, A. Aragnol, A. Lichnérowicz), Reidel, (1983), 177–208. (Reprint from Nieuw Arch. Wisk. (4), vol. **1**, (1983), 1–32)

[Br4]   H.W. Broer, On some quasi-periodic bifurcations, Delft Progress Report **12**, (1988), 79–96

[BT]   H.W. Broer, F. Takens, Formally symmetric normal forms and genericity, Dynamics Reported **2**, (1989), 39–59

[BV]   H.W. Broer, G. Vegter, Subordinate Sil'nikov bifurcations near some singularities of vector fields having low codimension, Ergod. Th & Dynam Sys. **4**, (1984), 509–525

[Ca]   J. Carr, Applications of centre manifold theory. Springer Applied Math. Sciences **35**, 1981

[CH]   S.-N. Chow, J.K. Hale, Methods of bifurcation theory, Springer, 1982

[CW]   S.-N. Chow, D. Wang, Normal forms of codimension 2 bifurcating orbits, in Multiparameter bifurcation theory, (eds. M. Golubitsky and J. Guckenheimer), AMS, 1985

[Dui]   J.J. Duistermaat, Bifurcations of periodic solutions near equilibrium points of Hamiltonian systems. In: Bifurcation theory and applications, Montecatini 1983, (ed. L. Salvadori), LNM 1057, Springer, (1984), 55–105

[FS]   E. Fontich, C. Simó, The splitting of separatrices for analytic diffeomorphisms, Ergod. Th & Dynam Sys. 10, (1990), 295–318

[GH]   J. Guckenheimer, P. Holmes, Nonlinear oscillations, dynamical systems, and bifurcations of vector fields, Springer, 1983

[Gi]   C.G. Gibson, Singular points of smooth mappings, Pitman 1979

[GS]   M. Golubitsky, D.G. Schaefer, Singularities and groups in bifurcation theory, Appl. Math. Sc. **51**, Springer, 1985

[GSM]   M. Golubitsky, I. Stewart, Generic bifurcation of Hamiltonian systems with symmetry (with an appendix by J.E. Marsden), Physica **24D**, (1987), 391–405

[GSS]   M. Golubitsky, I. Stewart, D.G. Schaefer, Singularities and groups in bifurca-
         tion theory. Vol. II. Appl. Math. Sc. **69**, Springer, 1988

[Ha]   J.K. Hale, Ordinary differential equations, Wiley & Sons, 1969; Krieger, 1980

[HMS]   P. Holmes, J.E. Marsden, J. Scheurle, Exponentially small splittings of separa-
         trices with applications to KAM-theory and degenerate bifurcations, Contem-
         porary Mathematics **81**, (1988), 213–244

[Io]   G. Iooss, Global characterization of the normal form for a vector field near a
         closed orbit, J. Diff. Eq. **76**, no. 1, (1988),47–76

[Le]   M. Levi, Adiabatic invariants of the linear Hamiltonian systems with periodic
         coefficients, J. Diff. Eq. **42**, no. 1, (1981), 47–71

[Ma]   J. Martinet, Singularités des fonctions et applications différentiables, Mono-
         grafias de Matemática da PUC/Rio de Janeiro, N.1, 1977

[Mc]   J.B. McLaughlin, Period-doubling bifurcations and chaotic motion for a para-
         metrically forced pendulum, J. Stat. Phys. **24**, no. 2, (1981), 375–388

[Med]   M. Medved, On generic bifurcations of second order ordinary differential equa-
         tions near closed orbits, Astérisque **50**, (1977), 293–297

[Mee]   J.C. van der Meer, The Hamiltonian Hopf bifurcation, LNM 1160, (1985),
         Springer

[Mey1]   K. Meyer, Generic bifurcations of periodic points, Trans. Am. Math. Soc. **149**,
         (1970), 95–107

[Mey2]   K. Meyer, Generic bifurcations in Hamiltonian systems. In Dynamical Systems-
         Warwick 1974, LNM 468, Springer (1975), 62–70

[Mo1]   J.K. Moser, Lectures on Hamiltonian systems, Mem. AMS **81**, 1968

[Mo2]   J.K. Moser, Stable and random motions in dynamical systems, with special
         emphasis on celestial mechanics, Princeton University Press, 1973

[MS]   J. Meixner, F.W. Schäfke, Mathieusche Funktionen und Sphäroidfunktionen,
         Springer, 1954

[Mu]   J. Murdock, Qualitative theory of nonlinear resonance by averaging and dy-
         namical systems methods, Dynamics Reported **1**, (1988), 91–172

[Na]   R. Narasimhan, Analysis of real and complex manifolds, North-Holland, 1968

[Po]   V. Poènaru, Singularités C^∞ en présence de symmetrie, LNM 510, Springer,
         1976

[Po1]   H. Poincaré, Thèse, Oeuvres 1, (1879), LIX–CXXIX, Gauthier-Villars, 1928

[Po2]   H. Poincaré, Les méthodes nouvelles de la mécanique céleste II, Dover, 1957

[Pö]   J. Pöschel, Integrability of Hamiltonian systems on Cantor sets, Comm. Pure
         Appl. Math. **35**, (1982), 653–696

[Ri]   R.J. Rimmer, Generic bifurcations for involutary area preserving maps, Mem.
         AMS **41**, no. 272, 1983

[Ro]   R.C. Robinson, Generic properties of conservative systems I, II, Amer. J. Math.
         92, (1970), 562–603, 897–906

[Sa1]   J.A. Sanders, Are higher order resonances really interesting? Celestial Mech.
         16, no. 4, (1977), 421–440

[Sa2]   J.A. Sanders, Second quantization and averaging: Fermi resonance, J. Chem.
         Phys. **74**, (1981), 5733–5736

[Sm]   H.L. Smith, On the small oscillations of the periodic Rayleigh equation, Quart.
         Appl. Math. **44**, (1986), no. 2, 223–247

[Ste]   S. Sternberg, Finite Liegroups and the formal aspects of dynamical systems, J.
         Math. Mech. **10**, (1961), 451–474

[Sto]   J.J. Stoker, Nonlinear vibrations, Interscience New York, 1950

[SV]   J.A. Sanders, F. Verhulst, Averaging methods in nonlinear dynamical systems, Appl. Math. Sc. **59**, Springer, 1985

[Ta1]   F. Takens, Forced oscillations and bifurcations. In: Applications of Global Analysis I, Comm. Math. Inst. University of Utrecht **3**, (1974), 1–59

[Ta2]   F. Takens, Singularities of vector fields, Publ. Math. IHES **43**, (1974), 48–100

[Va]   A. Vanderbauwhede, Subharmonic branching in reversible systems, Preprint Université de Nice, 1989

A Survey of Normalization Techniques Applied to Perturbed Keplerian Systems

Richard H. Cushman

Mathematics Institute, Rijksuniversiteit Utrecht, Budapestlaan 6,
3508TA Utrecht, The Netherlands

Abstract: *This article is a survey of the use of normal form techniques in the study of Hamiltonian perturbations of the two body problem in three space. We treat the following examples in some detail: the quadratic Zeeman effect, orbiting dust, a three dimensional lunar problem, and the main problem of artificial satellite theory.*

1. Introduction

This paper discusses the use of normal form for analyzing Hamiltonian systems which are small perturbations of the Kepler Hamiltonian. Recall that the Kepler Hamiltonian describes the motion of two bodies in three space under mutual gravitational attraction. The basic idea of normal form theory is to construct a change of coordinates, which preserves the Hamiltonian form of the equations of motion, so that up to some finite order in the perturbation parameter the Hamiltonian in the new coordinates *commutes* with the flow of the Kepler Hamiltonian. Truncating the transformed Hamiltonian at the order at which it is in normal form gives a normalized Hamiltonian which has the Kepler Hamiltonian as an additional integral. This integral expresses the fact the the normalized Hamiltonian has an extra symmetry which we call the Keplerian symmetry.

To remove the Keplerian symmetry of the normalized Hamiltonian, we use the reduction theorem of Marsden and Weinstein [1], and obtain a two degree of freedom Hamiltonian system on the reduced phase space of all bounded Keplerian orbits of a fixed (negative) energy. Quite surprisingly, in the orbiting dust and lunar problems (see §2), the reduced Hamiltonian can be brought into normal form once again. Because the coordinate change giving the truncated normal form commutes with rotation about the z-axis, the normal form of the reduced Hamiltonian has an integral which corresponds to the z-component of angular momentum. The quadratic Zeeman effect and artificial satellite problems (see §2.1 and §2.5) already have an axial symmetry. Thus the second normalization is not needed. Again we try to use the reduction process this time to remove the axial symmetry of the normalized Hamiltonian. But the axial symmetry has fixed points. Therefore we can *not* apply the reduction theorem of Marsden and Weinstein for those values of the z-component of angular momentum whose level set contain a fixed point. To carry out reduction for *all* values of the z-component of the angular momentum, we need a recent result of Arms, Gotay, and Cushman [2]. Performing this reduction gives rise to a one degree of freedom Hamiltonian on a second reduced phase space which is *not* always a smooth manifold. The critical points of the second reduced Hamiltonian on the second reduced phase space are the relative equlibria of the twice normalized truncated Hamiltonian system. In this paper we give a complete description of the relative equilibria for the second order normal form of the quadratic Zeeman effect, orbiting dust, lunar and artificial satellite problems.

We sum up what we have accomplished. After two applications of normalization and truncation, we have obtained a Liouville integrable Hamiltonian system [3]. In some sense this integrable system approximates the original Hamiltonian system. Of course, we do not expect the original system to be completely integrable. What we do expect, though, is that the relative equilibria of the integrable approximation lie close to solutions of the original Hamiltonian system of the same type. In particular, if a relative equilibrium is (quasi)periodic, then nearby there is a (quasi)periodic solution of the original Hamiltonian system which has the same number of frequencies as the relative equilibrium. Actually more should be true: the families of invariant manifolds formed by the relative equilibria should be present in the original Hamiltonian system. A precise form of this conjecture has been proved in [4], [5] and [6] for relative equilibria near an equibrium point of a resonant two degree of freedom Hamiltonian system. For relative equilibria of a perturbed three dimensional Keplerian problem, the persistence of the relative equilibria families is completely open.

Throughout the rest of this paper we will use standard facts about Hamiltonian mechanics which can be found in [3] or [7].

Acknowledgment

I would like to thank Dr. Eugene Lerman of the University of Utrecht and Dr. J.-C. van der Meer of the Technical University of Eindhoven for critically reading this paper. While writing a first draft of this paper, the author was supported by a visiting scholar award at the University of Calgary.

2. Perturbed Keplerian Systems

2.1 Basic Definitions

We now get down to business by defining the class of perturbed Hamiltonian systems which we will treat.

Let $\mathbf{R}^3 - \{0\} \subseteq \mathbf{R}^3$ be the space of positions with coordinates (ξ). On $\mathbf{R}^3$ put the Euclidean innerproduct $\langle\,,\,\rangle$ with induced norm $|\,|$. The tangent space $T_0\mathbf{R}^3 = \left(\mathbf{R}^3 - \{0\}\right) \times \mathbf{R}^3$ of $\mathbf{R}^3 - \{0\}$ is the space of positions and velocities with coordinates (ξ, η). On $T_0\mathbf{R}^3 \subseteq T\mathbf{R}^3$ we have a symplectic form which is the restriction of the standard symplectic form ω on $T\mathbf{R}^3$. A classical mechanical system on $(T_0\mathbf{R}^3, \omega)$ is given by a smooth function

$$H : T_0\mathbf{R}^3 \longrightarrow \mathbf{R},$$

called the *Hamiltonian*. The dynamics of the system $(T_0\mathbf{R}^3, \omega, H)$ are the solutions of the differential equation

$$\dot{\xi} = \frac{\partial H}{\partial \eta}$$
$$\dot{\eta} = -\frac{\partial H}{\partial \xi}$$

which are called *Hamilton's equations*. In other words, solutions of Hamilton's equations are the integral curves of the Hamiltonian vectorfield X_H on $T_0\mathbf{R}^3$.

Example 1. The Hamiltonian describing the motion of two bodies in $\mathbf{R}^3$ under the influence of gravity is the *Kepler Hamiltonian*

$$H_0 : T_0\mathbf{R}^3 \longrightarrow \mathbf{R} : (\xi, \eta) \longrightarrow \frac{1}{2}|\eta|^2 - \frac{\mu}{|\xi|}. \tag{1}$$

Here one of the bodies is fixed at the origin. The corresponding Hamiltonian vectorfield X_{H_0} is

$$\frac{d\xi}{dt} = \eta$$
$$\frac{d\eta}{dt} = -\mu\frac{\xi}{|\xi|^3}. \qquad \qquad \square$$

By a *perturbation of the Kepler Hamiltonian H_0* we mean a Hamiltonian

$$H = H_0 + \varepsilon H_1 + \varepsilon^2 H_2 + \cdots \tag{2}$$

which is a formal power series in ε with coefficients H_i, $i \geq 0$ which are smooth functions on $T_0\mathbf{R}^3$.

To illustrate our discussion of normalization of a perturbed Keplerian system we will treat the following examples: the quadratic Zeeman effect, orbiting dust, a three dimensional lunar problem, and the main problem of artificial satellite theory.

2.2 The Quadratic Zeeman Effect

The quadratic Zeeman effect is the peturbed Keplerian system

$$H = H_0 + \varepsilon^2 H_2$$

where the perturbation is

$$H_2(\xi, \eta) = \frac{1}{2}(\xi_1^2 + \xi_2^2). \tag{3}$$

The flow of the Hamiltonian vectorfield of H gives the motion of an electron in a classical hydrogen atom which is subjected to a uniform magnetic field. This field is sufficiently strong so that terms in the square of the Lamour frequency ε have to be considered. The Hamiltonian H comes from
  (i) adding the quadratic term $\frac{1}{2}\varepsilon^2|e_3 \times x|^2$ to the Hamiltonian

$$K(x, y) = \frac{1}{2}|y|^2 - \frac{\mu}{|x|} - \varepsilon\langle e_3, x \times y\rangle, \tag{4}$$

which describes the classical Zeeman effect, and then
  (ii) introducing rotating coordinates

$$(x, y) = (R_{\varepsilon t}\xi, R_{\varepsilon t}\eta), \tag{5}$$

where R_s is a rotation about the ξ_3-axis in $\mathbf{R}^3$ through an angle s. For more background about the physical model see [8].

The recent surge of interest in the quadratic Zeeman effect apparently comes from the observation of Zimmerman [9] that H has an additional approximate symmetry. In [10] Solovév computes an approximate integral to first order which expresses this symmetry. There have been several attempts [11,12] to analyze the dynamics of the ground state of the quadratic Zeeman effect. The ground state is a family of invariant varieties X_H which are made up of orbits lying in a fixed plane parallel to the magnetic field and passing through the center of attraction of the electric field of the hydrogen atom. Using techniques of singular reduction [2,13] the ground state was sucessfully analyzed in [14] (see §6.2).

2.3 Orbiting Dust

The problem of orbiting dust is described by the perturbed Keplerian system

$$H = H_0 + \varepsilon H_1$$

where the perturbation is given by

$$H_1(\xi, \eta) = -m(\xi_1\eta_2 - \xi_2\eta_1) + a\xi_1. \tag{6}$$

Consider the time dependent Hamiltonian

$$K(x, y, t) = \frac{1}{2}|y|^2 - \frac{\mu}{|x|} + \varepsilon a(x_1 \cos \varepsilon m t + x_2 \sin \varepsilon m t)$$

which describes the motion of dust under the influence of a radial radiation pressure of magnitude εa which is moving in circle in the x_1–x_2 plane with angular velocity εm. The Hamiltonian H is obtained from K by changing to rotating coordinates

$$(x, y) = (R_{\varepsilon m t}\xi, R_{\varepsilon m t}\eta)$$

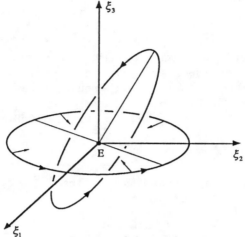

Figure 1. Orbiting dust

which co-rotate with the source of radiation. For more details about the physical model see [15]. When $m = 0$, H is the Hamiltonian describing the classical Stark effect.

In [12] Deprit gave an analysis of the first order normal form of H. In [16] van der Meer and Cushman computed the second order normal form and analyzed the resulting relative equilibria. This was the first paper to apply normalization *twice* to the study of a perturbed Keplerian system.

2.4 A Lunar Problem

The lunar problem is described by the perturbed Keplerian system

$$H = H_0 + \varepsilon H_1 + \varepsilon^2 H_2$$

where the perturbation is given by

$$H_1(\xi, \eta) = -(\xi_1 \eta_2 - \xi_2 \eta_1) \tag{7}$$

and

$$H_2(\xi, \eta) = -\frac{1}{2}(1 - \nu)(3\xi_1^2 - |\xi|^2). \tag{8}$$

The Hamiltonian H comes from the *three* dimensional restricted three body problem for large values of the Jacobi constant.

In more detail, the three dimensional restricted three body problem is the following. Let S, E, M be the sun, earth, and moon, respectively, with masses $1 - \nu, \nu$ and 0, respectively. Furthermore, suppose that S and E move uniformly in circles in the ξ_1–ξ_2 plane about their center of mass which is at the origin (see figure 2). It follows from Newton's law of gravitation that the motion of M is

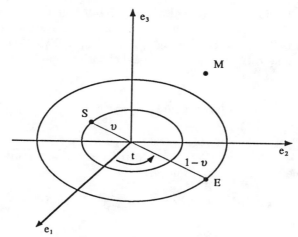

Figure 2. The lunar problem

described by the Hamiltonian

$$F = \frac{1}{2}|y|^2 - \frac{\nu}{|x - (1 - \nu)(\cos t, \sin t, 0)|} - \frac{1 - \nu}{|x + \nu(\cos t, \sin t, 0)|}.$$

Changing to rotating coordinates

$$(x, y) = (R_t \tilde{q}, R_t p),$$

which fixes the position of S and E at $\nu e_1 = (\nu, 0, 0)$ and $(1 - \nu)e_1 = (1 - \nu, 0, 0)$, respectively, the Hamiltonian F becomes

$$L = \frac{1}{2}|p|^2 - (\tilde{q}_1 p_2 - \tilde{q}_2 p_1) - \frac{\nu}{|\tilde{q} - (1 - \nu)e_1|} - \frac{(1 - \nu)}{|\tilde{q} + \nu e_1|}. \tag{9}$$

Shifting the position of E to the origin by setting

$$q = \tilde{q} - (1 - \nu)e_1,$$

L becomes

$$\mathcal{K}(q, p) = \frac{1}{2}|p|^2 - (q_1 p_2 - q_2 p_1) - (1 - \nu)p_2 - \frac{\nu}{|q|} - \frac{1 - \nu}{|q + e_1|}. \tag{10}$$

The Hamiltonian

$$K(q, p) = \frac{1}{2}|p|^2 - (q_1 p_2 - q_2 p_1) + (1 - \nu)(1 - q_1) - \frac{\nu}{|q|} - \frac{1 - \nu}{|q + e_1|} \tag{11}$$

and the Hamiltonian $\mathcal{K}$ have flows on $T_0 \mathbf{R}^3$ whose projection on $\mathbf{R}^3 - \{0\}$ are the same. This is easily checked by eliminating p from Hamilton's equations for $X_{\mathcal{K}}$ and X_K. If the value of K (the Jacobi constant) is very large and negative, then the motion of M is restricted to lie in a Hill region about S, E or infinity as can be verified using (11). We will assume that M moves in the Hill region around E and that the value of K is so large and negative that this region is contained in the ball $|q| < 1$. Expanding $|q + e_1|^{-1}$ in a Taylor series in q about zero up through quadratic terms and then substituting the resulting expression into (11) gives

$$K(q,p) = \frac{1}{2}|p|^2 - \frac{\nu}{|q|} - (q_1 p_2 - q_2 p_1) - (1 - \nu)(3q_1{}^2 - |q|^2) + O(|q|^3). \quad (12)$$

We wish to study the flow of X_K on the level surface $K = -\frac{1}{2}\delta^{-2}$ where δ is very small and positive. To bring (12) into the form of a perturbed Keplerian system we rescale the variables as follows:

$$q = \nu\delta^2\xi, \;\; p = \delta\eta, \;\; K = \delta^{-2}H, \;\; t = \delta^2\tau.$$

Then (12) becomes

$$H(\xi,\eta) = \frac{1}{2}|\eta|^2 - \frac{1}{|\xi|} - \varepsilon(\xi_1\eta_2 - \xi_2\eta_1) - \frac{1}{2}\varepsilon^2(1 - \nu)(3\xi_1^2 - |\xi|^2)$$
$$+ O(\nu^{-\frac{1}{3}}\varepsilon^{\frac{8}{3}}) \quad (13)$$

where $\varepsilon = \nu\delta^3$.

In Conley [17] one can find a treatment of the planar version of the lunar problem (see also [18]). The three dimensional lunar problem was treated by Kummer in [19] using a novel technique of regularization and normalization. The precise relationship between Kummer's techniques and the ones discussed in this paper is not clear at present.

2.5 The Artificial Satellite

The main problem of artificial satellite theory is described by the perturbed Keplerian system

$$H = H_0 + \varepsilon H_1$$

where

$$H_1(\xi,\eta) = \frac{\mu\alpha}{|\xi|^3}\left(\xi_3^2 - \frac{1}{2}(\xi_1^2 + \xi_2^2)\right). \quad (14)$$

The Hamiltonian H models the motion of an artificial satellite about an axially symmetric earth which is slightly oblate. The perturbation H_1 is the second term in the expansion of the geopotential in spherical harmonics. Here α is the equatorial radius of the earth and ε is its oblateness. See Brouwer [21] for more details about the physical model.

Calculating and analyzing the normal form of the main problem of artificial satellite theory has a long history. In 1953 Orlov [22] obtained the first order normal form by averaging over bounded Keplerian orbits. From this normal form he deduced the existence of certain nearly circular orbits for every inclination i except one: namely, where $cos^2 i = \frac{1}{5}$. What happens at this inclination became

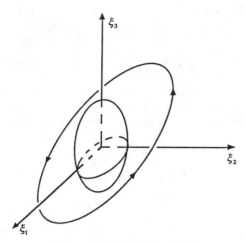

Figure 3. Artificial satellite

the problem of the *critical inclination*. It was not until 1959 that Brouwer [21] succeeded in computing the second order normal form of the main problem. Unfortunately Brouwer's analysis of his normal form did not permit him to see that he had solved the problem of the critical inclination. Its first solution was given in 1966 by Eckstein, Shi and Kevorkian [23] using the non-Hamiltonian method of matched asymptotic expansions. In 1983 Cushman [24] carried out a global geometric analysis of Brouwer's Hamiltonian using a technique which is now called singular reduction. The bifurcation giving rise to the critical inclination is described in [25] (see §6.4 and also [26]).

3. Normal Form: Theory

3.1 Regularization

Before we can apply the technique of normal form to a peturbed Keplerian system, we must eliminate the incompleteness of the flow of the Kepler Hamiltonian. This is caused by the second body reaching the origin in finite time, that is, colliding with the first body. Such collisions happen when the angular momentum $\xi \times \eta$ equals 0. To complete the flow we follow the regularization process of Moser [27]. This process changes the phase space from $T_0 \mathbf{R}^3$ to $T(S^3 - np)$, the tangent bundle of the three sphere $S^3 \subseteq \mathbf{R}^4$ minus the north pole: $np = (0, 0, 0, 1)$, and the Hamiltonian from a perturbation of the Kepler Hamiltonian to a perturbation of the Hamiltonian for geodesics on S^3.

In more detail, the *regularization process* is carried out in the following three steps. First, introduce a new time scale s by

$$\frac{ds}{dt} = \frac{k}{|\xi|}$$

and then define a new Hamiltonian

$$K(\xi, \eta) = \frac{|\xi|}{k}\left(H(\xi, \eta) + \frac{1}{2}k^2\right) + \frac{\mu}{k}$$

where H is the perturbed Keplerian system (2..2). Next, restrict (ξ, η) to lie in the level set $K^{-1}(\ell)$, $\ell = \frac{\mu}{k}$, $k > 0$. This level set corresponds to the level set $H^{-1}(-\frac{1}{2}k^2)$. Since the value of H is negative, for small values of ε the value of H_0 is negative. Hence we are treating perturbations of *bounded* Keplerian orbits. The reason for restricting to the level set $K^{-1}(\ell)$ is that the equations of motion for K are

$$\frac{d\xi}{ds} = \frac{|\xi|}{k}\frac{\partial H}{\partial \eta}$$

$$\frac{d\eta}{ds} = -\frac{|\xi|}{k}\frac{\partial H}{\partial \xi},$$

which are a time rescaling of Hamilton's equations for H. Finally, compose K with Moser's mapping

$$\mathcal{M} : T(S^3 - np) \subseteq T\mathbf{R}^4 \longrightarrow T_0\mathbf{R}^3 : (q, p) \longrightarrow (\xi, \eta)$$

where for $i = 1, 2, 3$

$$\xi_i = -\frac{1}{k}(p_i + q_i p_4 - p_i q_4)$$

$$= -\frac{1}{k}(p_i + S_{i4}),$$

$$\eta_i = \frac{kq_i}{1 - q_4}.$$

The mapping $\mathcal{M}$ is the composition of the tangent of stereographic projection from the north pole of S^3 and the map $(\xi, \eta) \longrightarrow (-\eta, \xi)$, which interchanges positions and velocities. The reason why $\mathcal{M}$ works is Hamilton's theorem which states that the velocity vectors during one period of an elliptical Keplerian orbit trace out a circle (see [28]). This completes the regularization process.

After carrying out the above regularization process on a perturbed Keplerian system, we obtain a Hamiltonian

$$G(q, p) = G_0(p) + \varepsilon G_1(q, p) + \varepsilon^2 G_2(q, p) + \cdots \tag{1}$$

which is a perturbation of the geodesic Hamiltonian

$$G_0(p) = |p|. \tag{2}$$

The flow of X_{G_0} is the *geodesic flow* on

$$T^+ S^3 = \{(q, p) \in T\mathbf{R}^4 | |q|^2 = 1, \langle q, p \rangle = 0, p \neq 0\},$$

the tangent bundle of the three sphere with the zero section omitted. We must remove the zero section to insure that G_0 is smooth. Thus G is *defined on*

$$T^+(S^3 - np) = \{(q, p) \in T\mathbf{R}^4 | |q|^2 = 1, q \neq (0, 0, 0, 1), \langle q, p \rangle = 0, p \neq 0\},$$

which has a symplectic form induced from the standard symplectic form on $T\mathbf{R}^4$.

In our examples, performing the regularization process gives

$$G_1 = 0, \tag{3}$$

$$G_2 = \frac{1}{2k^4}|p|(1-q_4)\left(p_1^2 + p_2^2 + 2(p_1 S_{14} + p_2 S_{24}) + S_{14}^2 + S_{24}^2\right) \tag{4}$$

for the quadratic Zeeman effect;

$$G_1 = -\frac{m}{k^2}(1-q_4)|p|(q_1 p_2 - q_2 p_1) - \frac{a}{k^3}(1-q_4)|p|p_1$$
$$\qquad -\frac{a}{k^3}(1-q_4)|p|(q_1 p_4 - q_4 p_1) \tag{5}$$

$$G_2 = 0 \tag{6}$$

for the orbiting dust; and

$$G_1 = -\frac{1}{k}|p|(1-q_4)(q_1 p_2 - q_2 p_1), \tag{7}$$

$$G_2 = -\frac{1}{2}\frac{(1-\nu)}{k^3}|p|\Big[3p_1^2 + 6(q_1 p_4 - q_4 p_1)(1-q_4)p_1$$
$$\qquad + 3(q_1 p_4 - q_4 p_1)^2(1-q_4) - |p|^2 + 3|p|^2(1-q_4)q_4$$
$$\qquad - 3q_4 p_1^2 + |p|^2 q_4^3\Big] \tag{8}$$

for the lunar problem.

Observe that in these three problems the Hamiltonian function G extends to a smooth function defined on *all* of $T^+ S^3$. Analytically speaking, we have regularized the flow of the perturbed Kepler Hamiltonian vectorfield X_H. The technical reason why G extends is that the lowest order term in the perturbation is linear in the velocities. In the artificial satellite problem G does *not* extend to a smooth function on $T^+ S^3$. This accounts for some of its extra difficulties.

3.2 Lie Series and Normal Form

Before trying to bring the Hamiltonian G into normal form, we discuss an abstract version of normal form. The basic mathematical structure needed in normal form theory is that of a Poisson algebra [29], which is defined in the following way. Let V be a smooth manifold and let $\mathcal{F}(V)$ be the vector space of formal power series in ε with coefficients which are in $C^\infty(V)$. We call $\mathcal{F}(V)$ the space of *smooth formal power series*. The triple $(\mathcal{F}(V), \cdot, \{\ ,\ \})$ is a *formal Poisson algebra* if $(\mathcal{F}(V), \cdot)$ is a real associative commutative algebra with unit, $(\mathcal{F}(V), \{\ ,\ \})$ is a real Lie algebra, and for every $f, g, h \in \mathcal{F}(V)$

$$\{f, g \cdot h\} = \{f, g\} \cdot h + g \cdot \{f, h\}. \tag{9}$$

Another way of stating (9) is that the linear map

$$ad_f : \mathcal{F}(V) \longrightarrow \mathcal{F}(V) : g \longrightarrow \{f, g\}$$

is a derivation on $(\mathcal{F}(V), \cdot)$. Thus ad_f can be identified with a *formal vectorfield* X_f on V which is called the *Hamiltonian vectorfield associated to* f. Here are two examples of formal Poisson algebras.

Example 2. Let (V, ω) be a smooth symplectic manifold. For $v \in V$ let

$$f(v) = \sum_{i=0}^{\infty} f_i(v)\varepsilon^i \text{ and } g(v) = \sum_{i=0}^{\infty} g_i(v)\varepsilon^i,$$

where $f_i, g_i \in C^{\infty}(V)$. Then for $f, g \in \mathcal{F}(V)$ define $\cdot$ by

$$(f \cdot g)(v) = \sum_{i=0}^{\infty} \Big(\big(\sum_{j+k=i} f_j(v)g_k(v) \big) \Big) \varepsilon^i$$

and $\{\ , \ \}$ by

$$\{f, g\}(v) = \sum_{i=0}^{\infty} \Big(\sum_{j+k=i} \{f_j, g_k\} \Big) \varepsilon^i$$

where for $f_j, g_k \in C^{\infty}(V)$

$$\{f_j, g_k\}(v) = \omega(v)(X_{f_j}(v), X_{g_k}(v)). \qquad \square$$

Example 3. Let $(\mathcal{G}, [\ , \ ])$ be a finite dimensional real Lie algebra with Lie bracket $[\ , \ ]$. On $\mathcal{F}(\mathcal{G}^*)$ define $\cdot$ and $\{\ , \ \}$ as in example 1, where for $f_j, g_k \in C^{\infty}(\mathcal{G}^*)$

$$\{f_j, g_k\}(\mu) = \mu\Big([df_j(\mu), dg_k(\mu)] \Big) \text{ for every } \mu \in \mathcal{G}^*. \qquad \square$$

Returning to the theory of Poisson algebras, once we have identified ad_f with the formal vectorfield X_f on V, an obvious question is: what is the formal flow of X_f? Consider the formal power series

$$\varphi_{\varepsilon}^f = exp(\varepsilon\, ad_f) = \sum_{n=0}^{\infty} \frac{\varepsilon^n}{n!} ad_f^n \qquad (10)$$

which is called the *Lie series* of f (see [30], [31]). Some properties of Lie series are given in

Lemma 3..1

i. *The formal flow of X_f is given by the mapping* $\varepsilon \longrightarrow \varphi_{\varepsilon}^f$.

ii. *For every fixed ε, the mapping φ_{ε}^f is an automorphism of the formal Poisson algebra, that is, for every $g, h \in \mathcal{F}(V)$*

$$\varphi_{\varepsilon}^f(g \cdot h) = \Big(\varphi_{\varepsilon}^f)(g) \Big) \Big(\varphi_{\varepsilon}^f(h) \Big) \qquad (11)$$

and

$$\varphi_{\varepsilon}^f(\{g, h\}) = \{\varphi_{\varepsilon}^f(g), \varphi_{\varepsilon}^f(h)\}. \qquad (12)$$

iii. *The mapping $\varepsilon \longrightarrow \varphi_{\varepsilon}^f$ is a one parameter group of automorphisms of the formal Poisson algebra.*

Proof. To prove (ii) we will show that (12) holds. The proof of (11) is essentially the same and is omitted. Since ad_f is a derivation on $(\mathcal{F}(V), \{\ ,\ \})$, applying Leibniz rule gives

$$\frac{\varepsilon^n}{n!} ad_f^n \{g, h\} = \sum_{k=0}^{n} \{\frac{\varepsilon^k}{k!} ad_f^k g, \frac{\varepsilon^{n-k}}{(n-k)!} ad_f^{n-k} h\}.$$

Summing both sides over $n \geq 0$ and using (10) gives (12).

The proof of (iii) goes as follows. For every $g \in \mathcal{F}(V)$,

$$\varphi_\varepsilon^f \circ \varphi_\eta^f(g) = \sum_{n=0}^{\infty} \frac{\varepsilon^n}{n!} ad_f^n \Big(\sum_{m=0}^{\infty} \frac{\eta^m}{m!} ad_f^m g \Big)$$

$$= \sum_{n,m=0}^{\infty} \frac{\varepsilon^n}{n!} \frac{\eta^m}{m!} ad_f^{n+m} g$$

$$= \sum_{k=0}^{\infty} \frac{(\varepsilon + \eta)^k}{k!} ad_f^k g$$

$$= \varphi_{\varepsilon+\eta}^f(g). \tag{13}$$

To show that (i) holds we differentiate (13) and obtain

$$\frac{d}{d\eta} \varphi_\eta^f(g) = \frac{d}{d\varepsilon}\Big|_{\varepsilon=0} \varphi_{\varepsilon+\eta}^f(g) = \frac{d}{d\varepsilon}\Big|_{\varepsilon=0} \varphi_\varepsilon^f \Big(\varphi_\eta^f(g) \Big)$$

$$= \frac{d}{d\varepsilon}\Big|_{\varepsilon=0} \sum_{n=0}^{\infty} \frac{\varepsilon^n}{n!} ad_f^n \Big(\varphi_\eta^f(g) \Big)$$

$$= ad_f \Big(\varphi_\eta^f(g) \Big) = X_f \Big(\varphi_\eta^f(g) \Big).$$

which established the assertions of the lemma.   □

For $f \in \mathcal{F}(V)$ we say that X_f has *periodic flow* if there is a positive smooth function T on V such that for every $v \in V$ and every $g \in \mathcal{F}(V)$, $\Big(\varphi_{T(v)}^f(g) \Big)(v) = g(v)$. Note that T is not necessarily the minimal period of an integral curve of X_f. Now we define the notion of normal form. Suppose that

$$H = H_0 + \varepsilon H_1 + \varepsilon^2 H_2 + \cdots$$

is a smooth formal power series and that X_{H_0} has a periodic flow. Then H is in *normal form* with respect to H_0 if

$$\{H_0, H_i\} = 0 \ \text{for all}\ i \geq 0. \tag{14}$$

If (14) holds for all i, $1 \leq i \leq n$, then we say that H is in *normal form up to terms of order n*.

A problem remains: given H, how do we find its normal form? The answer
to to use formal coordinate changes of the form φ_ε^f. Let $g = (g_1, \ldots, g_n)$ be a set
of local coordinates on V where g_i is a smooth function on V. Then

$$(\varphi_\varepsilon^f)^*(g) = (g_1 \circ \varphi_\varepsilon^f, \ldots, g_n \circ \varphi_\varepsilon^f)$$

are new *formal coordinates* on V. The next lemma, which is the basic property
of Lie series, shows how H changes under a formal change of coordinates.

Lemma 3..2 *Let* $H, F \in \mathcal{F}(V)$. *If* φ_ε^f *is the flow of* X_f, *then*

$$(\varphi_\varepsilon^F)^* H = exp(\varepsilon \, ad_F)H.$$

Proof. Let g be a set of local coordinates on V. Then

$$(\varphi_\varepsilon^F)^* H(g) = H(\varphi_\varepsilon^F(g))$$

$$= \sum_{n=0}^{\infty} \frac{1}{n!} \frac{d^n}{d^n \varepsilon}\bigg|_{\varepsilon=0} H(\varphi_\varepsilon^F(g))\varepsilon^n. \tag{15}$$

Since $\varphi_{\eta+\varepsilon}^F = \varphi_\eta^F \circ \varphi_\varepsilon^F$,

$$\frac{d}{d\varepsilon}(\varphi_\varepsilon^F)^* H = (\varphi_\varepsilon^F)^* \left(\frac{d}{d\eta}\bigg|_{\eta=0} (\varphi_\eta^F)^* H \right) = (\varphi_\varepsilon^F)^*(ad_F H).$$

Therefore by induction,

$$\frac{d^n}{d\varepsilon^n}(\varphi_\varepsilon^F)^* H = (\varphi_\varepsilon^F)^*(ad_F^n H)$$

which substituted into (15) proves the lemma. $\square$

To compute the normal form we need the following splitting property of
ad_{H_0}.

Lemma 3..3 *If* X_{H_0} *has periodic flow on* V, *then*

$$C^\infty(V) = ker \, ad_{H_0} \oplus im \, ad_{H_0}.$$

Proof. The idea of the proof is to decompose $f \in C^\infty(V)$ as

$$f = \overline{f} + (f - \overline{f})$$

where $\overline{f}$ is the average of f over the orbits of X_{H_0}, that is,

$$\overline{f} = \frac{1}{T} \int_0^T (\varphi_t^{H_0})^* f \, dt. \tag{16}$$

To finish the proof we must show that $g = f - \overline{f}$ lies in the image of ad_{H_0}. Note
that $\overline{g} = 0$. A straightforward argument shows that the equation $ad_{H_0} G = g$ is
solved by

$$G = \frac{1}{T} \int_0^T t(\varphi_t^{H_0})^* g \, dt. \tag{17}$$

For more details see [13]. ☐

To find the normal form of H to first order we carry out the following process. By lemma 3.2 we have

$$exp(\varepsilon\, ad_{G_1})H = H_0 + \varepsilon(H_1 + ad_{G_1}H_0) + O(\varepsilon^3) \qquad (18)$$

where $G_1 \in \mathcal{F}(V)$ is to be determined. Because Poisson bracket is skew symmetric, the first order terms in (18) may be rewritten as $-ad_{H_0}G_1 + H_1$. By lemma 3.3, we may write $H_1 = \overline{H_1} + H_1'$ where $H_1' \in im\, ad_{H_0}$ and $\overline{H_1} \in ker\, ad_{H_0}$. Using (17) we find a G_1 so that $ad_{H_0}G_1 = H_1'$. With this choice of G_1, equation (18) reads

$$exp(\varepsilon\, ad_{G_1})H = H_0 + \varepsilon\overline{H_1} + O(\varepsilon^2), \qquad (19)$$

which is the first order normal form of H since $\overline{H_1} \in ker\, ad_{H_0}$.

To find the second order normal form, just repeat the above argument on the terms in ε^2 of (19). For more details see [32], [33].

3.3 Constrained Normal Form

In trying to apply the above normalization algorithm to perturbations of the geodesic Hamiltonian on T^+S^3 we run into the difficulty of computing the requisite Poisson brackets on T^+S^3. Rather than using special coordinate charts, we prefer to work globally in Euclidean space. This requires that we discuss constrained Hamiltonian systems (see [34] and [35]).

Let $M \subseteq \mathbf{R}^{2n}$ be a smooth submanifold defined by

$$F_1 = 0, \ldots, F_{2r} = 0 \qquad (20)$$

with the additional property that the $2r \times 2r$ matrix, whose $(i, j)^{th}$ entry is $\{F_i, F_j\}(m)$, is invertible for all $m \in M$. Here $\{\,,\,\}$ is the standard Poisson bracket on $(\mathbf{R}^{2n}, \omega)$. Then $(M, \omega|M)$ is a symplectic manifold called the *constraint*.

Example 4. The manifold $TS^3 \subseteq T\mathbf{R}^4$ defined by

$$F_1(q,p) = |q|^2 - 1 = 0 \text{ and } F_2(q,p) = \langle q, p \rangle = 0 \qquad (21)$$

is a constraint, since

$$\{F_1, F_2\}(q,p) = 2\langle q, q \rangle = 2$$

for every $(q,p) \in TS^3$ implies that the 2×2 matrix $(\{F_i, F_j\}|T^+S^3) =$

$$\begin{pmatrix} 0 & +2 \\ -2 & 0 \end{pmatrix}$$

is invertible. Therefore $(TS^3, \omega|TS^3)$ is a symplectic submanifold of $(T\mathbf{R}^4, \omega)$. Since T^+S^3 is an open subset of TS^3, T^+S^3 is also a symplectic manifold. ☐

On $C^\infty(M)$ define a Poisson bracket $\{\,,\,\}_M$ by setting

$$\{f,g\}_M(m) = \omega(m)\Big(X_f(m), X_g(m)\Big) \tag{22}$$

for all $m \in M$, where $f, g \in C^\infty(M)$. Here X_f is the Hamiltonian vectorfield *on* M associated to f, that is, for every $v_m \in T_m M$

$$df(m)v_m = \omega(m)(X_f(m), v_m).$$

What we want to do is to construct smooth functions F^* and G^* on $\mathbf{R}^{2n}$, which are extensions of f and g, so that

$$\{f,g\}_M = \{F^*, G^*\}|M. \tag{23}$$

Here $F^*|M = f$ and $G^*|M = g$. To start with, let F be an arbitary smooth extension of f to $\mathbf{R}^{2n}$. Such an extension exists by the Whitney extension theorem, because M is a closed subset of $\mathbf{R}^{2n}$. Next we would like to use the right hand side of (22) to compute $\{\,,\,\}_M$. This we can not do right away because $X_F|M$ is not necessarily a vectorfield on M for the simple reason that M is not necessarily an invariant manifold of X_F. To correct this, we modify F. Let

$$F^* = F + \sum_{i=1}^{2r} \alpha_i F_i \tag{24}$$

and choose $\alpha_i \in C^\infty(\mathbf{R}^{2n})$ so that

$$\{F^*, F_j\}|M = 0 \ \text{ for all } 1 \le j \le 2r. \tag{25}$$

Note that (25) states that M is an invariant manifold of X_{F^*}. The following argument shows that the functions α_i exist. Substituting (24) into (25) gives

$$-\{F, F_j\}(m) = \sum_{i=1}^{2r} \alpha_j(m)\{F_i, F_j\}(m) \tag{26}$$

for every $m \in M$. Since M is a constraint, the mapping

$$M \longrightarrow Gl_{2r}(\mathbf{R}) : m \longrightarrow \Big(\{F_i, F_j\}(m)\Big)$$

is smooth. Thus we can solve (26) to obtain $\alpha_j \in C^\infty(M)$ for $1 \le j \le 2r$. Applying the Whitney extension theorem gives functions $\alpha_j \in C^\infty(\mathbf{R}^{2n})$ for $1 \le j \le 2r$. By construction, M is an invariant manifold of X_{F^*}. Therefore $X_{F^*}|M = X_{F^*|M} = X_f$ and similarly $X_{G^*}|M = X_g$. Hence for every $m \in M$,

$$\begin{aligned}
\{F^*, G^*\}(m) &= \omega(m)\Big(X_{F^*}(m), X_{G^*}(m)\Big) \\
&= \omega(m)\Big(X_f(m), X_g(m)\Big) \\
&= \{f, g\}_M
\end{aligned}$$

which is what we wanted to show.

Example 4 (continued). For $F \in C^{\infty}(T\mathbf{R}^4)$ let

$$F^* = F - \frac{1}{2}\{F, F_2\}F_1 + \frac{1}{2}\{F, F_1\}F_2$$

where $TS^3 \subseteq T\mathbf{R}^4$ is defined by $F_1 = 0$ and $F_2 = 0$ (21). Then a Poisson bracket $\{\ ,\ \}_{TS^3}$ on $C^{\infty}(TS^3)$ is given by

$$\{F|TS^3, G|TS^3\}_{TS^3} = \{F^*, G^*\}|TS^3. \qquad \square$$

Returning to discussing normal form, suppose that

$$H = H_0 + \varepsilon H_1 + \cdots$$

is a smooth formal power series on $\mathbf{R}^{2n}$ where X_{H_0} has a *periodic flow* which leaves the constraint $M \subseteq \mathbf{R}^{2n}$ *invariant*. We want to bring H into normal form using symplectic coordinate changes on $(\mathbf{R}^{2n}, \omega)$ which map M into itself. This process we call *constrained normalization*. As a first step in computing the constrained normal form of H, we forget about the constraint M and find a smooth function G_1 which brings H into normal form up to first order in ε. In other words, we solve

$$ad_{H_0}G_1 = H_1' = H_1 - \overline{H_1},$$

using lemma 3.3. Since M is not necessarily an invariant manifold of X_{G_1}, the change of coordinates $\varphi_{\varepsilon}^{G_1}$, which brings H into first order normal form, does not necessarily map M into itself. Therefore we must modify G_1. We try G_1^*. Then

$$ad_{H_0}G_1^* = ad_{H_0}G_1 + ad_{H_0}\left(\sum_{i=1}^{2r}\alpha_i F_i\right)$$

$$= ad_{H_0}G_1 + \sum_{i=1}^{2r}(ad_{H_0}\alpha_i)F_i + \sum_{i=1}^{2r}\alpha_i(ad_{H_0}F_i)$$

$$= ad_{H_0}G_1 - I_1$$

$$= H_1 - (\overline{H_1} + I_1).$$

Because
$\quad$ (i) $F_1 = 0, \ldots, F_{2}r = 0$ on M
and
$\quad$ (ii) M being an invariant manifold of X_{H_0} implies that $(ad_{H_0}F_i)|M = 0$
$\qquad$ for $1 \leq i \leq 2r$,
it follows that $I_1|M = 0$. Therefore

$$exp(\varepsilon\, ad_{G_1^*})H = H_0 + \varepsilon(\overline{H_1} + I_1) + \cdots.$$

Repeating this process gives

$$\mathcal{H} = H_0 + \varepsilon(\mathcal{H}_1 + I_1) + \varepsilon^2(\mathcal{H}_2 + I_2) + \cdots$$

where

$$\{H_0, \mathcal{H}_j\} = 0 \text{ and } I_j|M = 0 \text{ for all } j \geq 1.$$

Note that on M, $\mathcal{H}|M$ is in normal form, that is,

$$\{H_0|M, \mathcal{H}_j|M\}_M = 0 \text{ for all } j \geq 1.$$

4. Normal Form: Practice

In this section we apply the theory of constrained normal form to perturbations of the geodesic Hamiltonian G_0 on T^+S^3 of the form

$$G(q,p) = G_0(p) + \varepsilon G_1(q,p) + \varepsilon^2 G_2(q,p).$$

Recall that $G_0(p) = |p|$.

4.1 Extension to a Constrained System

To see G as a Hamiltonian system on $(T\mathbf{R}^4, \omega)$ constrained to $(T^+S^3, \omega|T^+S^3)$ we extend G_0 to the Hamiltonian

$$H_0(q,p) = \sqrt{|q|^2|p|^2 - \langle q,p \rangle^2}. \tag{1}$$

H_0 is smooth on the open symplectic submanifold $N = T\mathbf{R}^4 - \{H_0 = 0\}$ of $(T\mathbf{R}^4, \omega)$. It is easy to see that in the quadratic Zeeman effect, orbiting dust and lunar problems the functions G_1 and G_2 given by (3..3)–(3..8), extend to smooth functions H_1 and H_2, respectively, on N. In the artificial satellite problem we must remove all the points on T^+S^3 which lie on orbits of the geodesic flow which pass through the north pole of S^3. Thus we delete all points which lie on geodesics with zero angular momentum. In other words, we have to cut out the cone

$$C_6 = \{(q,p) \in T\mathbf{R}^4 | \sum_{1 \leq i < j \leq 3} (q_i p_j - q_j p_i)^2\} = 0$$

from N.

Before we can apply the constrained normalization procedure to the extended Hamiltonian

$$H = H_0 + \varepsilon H_1 + \varepsilon^2 H_2 \tag{2}$$

we need to know some properties of the vectorfield X_{H_0}. They are given in the following lemma (see [16] and [20]).

Lemma 4..1

   i. $H_0|T^+S^3 = |p|$.

   ii. T^+S^3 is an invariant manifold of X_{H_0}.

   iii. The flow $\varphi_t^{H_0}$ of X_{H_0} on $T\mathbf{R}^4$ is

$$\varphi_t^{H_0}(q,p) = \begin{pmatrix} -\frac{\langle q,p\rangle}{H_0}\sin 2t + \cos 2t & \frac{|q|^2}{H_0}\sin 2t \\ \frac{|p|^2}{H_0}\sin 2t & -\frac{\langle q,p\rangle}{H_0}\sin 2t + \cos 2t \end{pmatrix} \begin{pmatrix} q \\ p \end{pmatrix}$$

which is periodic of period π.

   iv. Let $f \in C^\infty(N)$. If $f|T^+S^3$ is an integral of $X_{H_0|T^+S^3}$, then f is the restriction to T^+S^3 of a smooth function of

$$S_{ij} = q_i p_j - q_j p_i, \quad 1 \le i,j \le 4.$$

in $T\mathbf{R}^4$. Note that

$$|p| = \sqrt{\sum_{1 \le i < j \le 4} S_{ij}^2}$$

is a smooth function on T^+S^3.

4.2 Normal Form for the Quadratic Zeeman Effect

We now compute the constrained normal form for the Hamiltonian

$$H(\xi,\eta) = \frac{1}{2}|\eta|^2 - \frac{\mu}{|\xi|} + \frac{1}{2}\varepsilon^2(\xi_1^2 + \xi_2^2)$$

of the quadratic Zeeman effect (see §2.2). After regularizing and extending (see §3.1 and §4.1) we obtain the Hamiltonian

$$H(q,p) = H_0(q,p) + \varepsilon^2 H_2(q,p) \tag{3}$$

on N where

$$H_0(q,p) = \sqrt{|q|^2|p|^2 - \langle q,p\rangle^2},$$

$$H_2(q,p) = \frac{1}{2k^4}|p|(1 - q_4)\Big(p_1^2 + p_2^2 + 2(p_1 S_{14} + p_2 S_{24})$$

$$+ S_{14}^2 + S_{24}^2 \Big). \tag{4}$$

Applying the constrained normal form algorithm (see §3.3), we find that the normal form of H up to order two is

$$\hat{\mathcal{H}} = H_0 + \varepsilon^2 \overline{H_2}$$

restricted to T^+S^3.

   To compute the average $\overline{H_2}$ of the Hamiltonian H_2 over the orbits of X_{H_0}, we use the following facts.

Fact 1. Let $f, g \in C^\infty(N)$. We say that $f \simeq g$ if and only if

$$(f - g)|T^+S^3 = 0.$$

If $f \simeq g$, then $\overline{f} \simeq \overline{g}$, because T^+S^3 is an invariant manifold of X_{H_0}.

Fact 2. The functions $|q|^2$, $|p|^2$, $\langle q, p \rangle$, $S_{ij} = q_i p_j - q_j p_i$ for $1 \leq i < j \leq 4$ are equal to their average, because they are integrals of X_{H_0}.

Fact 3. All odd degree monomials in the components of q and p have zero average.

Fact 4. $2\overline{q_i p_j} \simeq S_{ij}$ and $2\overline{p_i^2} \simeq \sum_{\ell=1}^{4} S_{\ell i}^2$.

From these facts, it follows that

$$\overline{H_2} = \frac{1}{2k^4} |p| \left(\overline{p_1^2} + \overline{p_2^2} + S_{14}^2 + S_{24}^2 - 2\overline{q_4 p_1} S_{14} - 2\overline{q_4 p_2} S_{24} \right)$$
$$\simeq \frac{1}{2k^4} |p| \left(2S_{12}^2 + (S_{12}^2 + S_{23}^2) + 5(S_{14}^2 + S_{24}^2) \right).$$

Hence the constrained normal form of the quadratic Zeeman effect up to order two is

$$\hat{\mathcal{H}} = |p| + \varepsilon^2 \frac{1}{2k^4} |p| \left(2S_{12}^2 + (S_{12}^2 + S_{23}^2) + 5(S_{14}^2 + S_{24}^2) \right) \tag{5}$$

restricted to $T^+S^3 \cap \{|p| = \ell\}$.

4.3 Other Examples of Constrained Normal Form

Let

$$H = H_0 + \varepsilon H_1 + \varepsilon^2 H_2 + \cdots$$

be a smooth formal power series on N, which restricts to a perturbation of the geodesic Hamiltonian on T^+S^3. Putting H into constrained normal form up to second order and then truncating gives a normalized Hamiltonian

$$\hat{\mathcal{H}} = |p| + \varepsilon \hat{\mathcal{H}}_1 + \varepsilon^2 \hat{\mathcal{H}}_2 \tag{6}$$

on T^+S^3 where $\hat{\mathcal{H}}_j$ is a smooth function of $|p|$ and S_{ij} for $j = 1, 2$.

Below we give the second order constrained normal form for the lunar, orbiting dust, and artificial satellite problems. The details of the calculations leading to these normal forms are given in [16] and [20] and are not repeated here.

For the orbiting dust problem the second order normal form on $H_0^{-1}(\ell) \cap T^+ S^3$ is

$$|p| = \frac{\mu}{k} = \ell,$$

$$\hat{\mathcal{H}}_1 = -\frac{m}{k^2}|p|S_{12} - \frac{3a}{2k^3}|p|S_{14},$$

$$\hat{\mathcal{H}}_2 = -\frac{17}{32}\frac{a^2}{k^6}|p|^3 - (\frac{m^3}{4k^4} + \frac{am}{8k^5})|p|S_{12}^2 + \frac{am}{4k^5}|p|S_{23}S_{34}$$
$$- \frac{51}{32}\frac{a^2}{k^6}|p|S_{14}^2 + \frac{9}{32}\frac{a^2}{k^6}S_{23}^2 - \frac{13}{8}\frac{am}{k^5}|p|S_{12}S_{14}. \tag{7}$$

For the lunar problem the second order normal form on $H_0^{-1}(\frac{1}{k}) \cap T^+ S^3$ is

$$|p| = \frac{1}{k},$$

$$\hat{\mathcal{H}}_1 = -\frac{1}{k}|p|S_{12},$$

$$\hat{\mathcal{H}}_2 = -3\frac{(1-\nu)}{k^3}|p|S_{14}^2 + \frac{1}{2}\frac{(1-\nu)}{k^3}|p|^3 + \frac{1}{4k^2}|p|S_{12}^2$$
$$+ \frac{3}{4}\frac{(1-\nu)}{k^3}|p|(S_{14}^2 + S_{24}^2 + S_{34}^2)$$
$$- \frac{3}{4}\frac{(1-\nu)}{k^3}|p|(S_{12}^2 + S_{13}^2 + S_{14}^2)$$
$$- \frac{1}{8k^2}(\frac{1}{2} + \frac{1}{|p|})S_{12}^2(S_{14}^2 + S_{24}^2 + S_{34}^2). \tag{8}$$

For the artificial satellite problem the second order normal form on $H_0(L) \cap T^+ S^3$ is

$$|p| = L,$$

$$\hat{\mathcal{H}}_1 = \frac{\mu^4 \alpha^2}{L^3 G^3}(\frac{1}{2} - \frac{3}{4}s^2)$$

$$\hat{\mathcal{H}}_2 = \frac{1}{2}\frac{\mu^6 \alpha^4}{L^3 G^7}\left[P(s^2, G) - 2m_{2,0}^*(s^2)(es \sin g)^2 \right] \tag{9}$$

where

$$P(s^2, G) = (-\frac{15}{8} + \frac{81}{16}s^2 - \frac{195}{64}s^4) + \frac{G}{L}(-\frac{3}{4} + \frac{9}{4}s^2 - \frac{27}{16}s^4)$$
$$+ \frac{G^2}{L^2}(\frac{3}{8} - \frac{27}{16}s^2 + \frac{75}{64}s^4),$$

$$m_{2,0}^*(s^2) = \frac{21}{16} - \frac{45}{32}s^2 \tag{10}$$

and

$$4G^2 = (x_1 + y_1)^2 + (x_2 + y_2)^2 + (x_3 + y_3)^2$$
$$4G^2 s^2 = (x_2 + y_2)^2 + (x_3 + y_3)^2$$
$$2Les \sin g = x_1 - y_1$$

where

$$x_1 = S_{12} + S_{34} \qquad y_1 = S_{12} - S_{34}$$
$$x_2 = S_{13} - S_{24} \qquad y_2 = S_{13} + S_{24}$$
$$x_3 = S_{23} + S_{14} \qquad y_3 = S_{23} - S_{14}.$$

4.4 Normalizaton of the Reduced Hamiltonian

Because the truncated Hamiltonian $\hat{\mathcal{H}}$ given by (6) is in normal form, the function $|p|$ is an integral of $X_{\mathcal{H}}$. Therefore $\hat{\mathcal{H}}$ is invariant under the S^1 action on T^+S^3 given by the flow of $X_{|p|}$, which is the geodesic flow on T^+S^3. Since the geodesic flow has *no* fixed points, we may use the reduction theorem of Marsden and Weinstein to remove the *Keplerian symmetry* from $\hat{\mathcal{H}}$. Note that the flow of the Kepler vectorfield on a negative energy level set in $T_0\mathbf{R}^3$ is *not* complete and hence does *not* define an S^1 action on this energy level set. Thus we must regularize before we can reduce the Keplerian symmetry of a normalized Hamiltonian system. After reduction, we obtain a Hamiltonian of two degrees of freedom.

Analytically we carry out reduction of the Kepler symmetry as follows. (For the geometric meaning of the reduction process see §5.1). First, fix the value of $|p|$, say at $\ell = \frac{\mu}{k}$. Then drop all constants from the resulting Hamiltonian. Next rescale time by setting $s = \frac{1}{\varepsilon}t$. We obtain the truncated reduced Hamiltonian

$$\tilde{\mathcal{H}}_\ell = \hat{\mathcal{H}}_1 + \varepsilon\hat{\mathcal{H}}_2, \tag{11}$$

which is a smooth function of S_{ij}, $1 \le i < j \le 4$.

Now we want to normalize the reduced Hamiltonian $\tilde{\mathcal{H}}_\ell$. To do this we need a Poisson algebra. Let $\mathcal{S}$ be a vector space with coordinates (S_{ij}) for $1 \le i < j \le 4$. As quadratic functions $q_i p_j - q_j p_i$ on $(T\mathbf{R}^4, \omega)$, the S_{ij} are closed under Poisson bracket (see table 1).

$\{A, B\}$	S_{12}	S_{13}	S_{14}	S_{23}	S_{24}	S_{34}	B
S_{12}	0	S_{23}	S_{24}	$-S_{13}$	$-S_{14}$	0	
S_{13}	$-S_{23}$	0	S_{34}	S_{12}	0	$-S_{14}$	
S_{14}	$-S_{24}$	$-S_{34}$	0	0	S_{12}	S_{13}	
S_{23}	S_{13}	$-S_{12}$	0	0	S_{34}	$-S_{24}$	
S_{24}	S_{14}	0	$-S_{12}$	$-S_{34}$	0	S_{23}	
S_{34}	0	S_{14}	$-S_{13}$	S_{24}	$-S_{23}$	0	
A							

Table 1. Poisson brackets

Therefore $(\mathcal{S}, \{\,,\,\})$ is a Lie algebra, which is isomorphic to $so(4)$. Consequently the space $\mathcal{F}(\mathcal{S})$ of smooth formal power series on $\mathcal{S}$ is a Poisson algebra $(\mathcal{F}(\mathcal{S}), \cdot, \{\,,\,\})$ (see example 3, §3.2).

To proceed further, we suppose that

$$\hat{\mathcal{H}}_1 = \alpha_0 S_{12}.\tag{12}$$

Then the Hamiltonian vectorfield $X_{\hat{\mathcal{H}}_1} = \alpha_0\, ad_{S_{12}}$ is linear and has

$$\alpha_0 \left(\begin{array}{ccc|ccc} 0 & 0 & 0 & & & \\ 0 & 0 & -1 & & & \\ 0 & 1 & 0 & & & \\ \hline & & & 0 & 0 & 0 \\ & & & 0 & 0 & -1 \\ & & & 0 & 1 & 0 \end{array}\right)\tag{13}$$

as its matrix with respect to the basis $\{S_{12}, S_{13}, S_{23}, S_{34}, -S_{24}, S_{14}\}$ of $\mathcal{S}$. Hence the flow of $X_{\hat{\mathcal{H}}_1}$ is periodic of period $2\pi/\alpha_0$. Using the process described in §3.2, we can bring the truncated reduced Hamiltonian $\tilde{\mathcal{H}}_\ell$ (11) into normal form.

Actually this normalizing process is the same as finding the normal form of $\tilde{\mathcal{H}}_\ell$ constrained to the manifold P_ℓ defined by

$$C_1 = \sum_{1\leq i<j\leq 4} S_{ij}^2 - \ell^2 = 0 \text{ and } C_2 = S_{12}S_{34} - S_{13}S_{24} + S_{14}S_{23} = 0.$$

The reason for this is that P_ℓ is defined by *Casimirs*, that is, for every $S \in \mathcal{F}(\mathcal{S})$, $\{C_1, S\} = 0$ and $\{C_2, S\} = 0$. Therefore P_ℓ is invariant under the flow of X_S for every $S \in \mathcal{F}(\mathcal{S})$; in particular for $X_{S_{12}}$. Hence *no* adjustment needs to be made in the coordinate changes to compute the constrained normal form as in §3.3. In §5.1 we show that P_ℓ is the phase space obtained after reducing the Keplerian symmetry.

Normalizing the reduced Hamiltonian $\tilde{\mathcal{H}}_\ell$ gives a Hamiltonian H_ℓ whose terms lie in $ker\, ad_{S_{12}}$. An easy calculation shows that the subalgebra $ker\, ad_{S_{12}}$ of $\mathcal{F}(\mathcal{S})$ is generated by

$$\begin{aligned} \sigma_1 &= S_{12} & \sigma_4 &= S_{34} \\ \sigma_2 &= S_{14}^2 + S_{24}^2 & \sigma_5 &= S_{13}S_{14} + S_{23}S_{24} \\ \sigma_3 &= S_{13}^2 + S_{23}^2 & \sigma_6 &= S_{13}S_{24} - S_{14}S_{23}. \end{aligned}\tag{14}$$

Hence the truncated normalized reduced Hamiltonian is

$$H_\ell = H_\ell(\sigma) = \mathcal{H}_1 + \varepsilon\mathcal{H}_2 = \alpha_0 S_{12} + \varepsilon\mathcal{H}_2(\sigma).\tag{15}$$

Example 5. In the lunar problem we see from (8) that

$$\mathcal{H}_1 = -\frac{1}{k^2}S_{12}\tag{16}$$

Averaging $\tilde{\mathcal{H}}_\ell$ (11) over the orbits of $X_{S_{12}}$ gives

$$\begin{aligned} \mathcal{H}_2 &= \alpha_1 S_{12}^2 + \alpha_2(S_{14}^2 + S_{24}^2) + \alpha_3(S_{13}^2 + S_{23}^2) \\ &\quad + \alpha_4 S_{34}^2 + \alpha_5 S_{12}^2(S_{14}^2 + S_{24}^2) + \alpha_6 S_{12}^2 S_{34}^2 \end{aligned}\tag{17}$$

where

$$\alpha_1 = \frac{1}{4k^3} - \frac{3}{4}\frac{(1-\nu)}{k^4}$$

$$\alpha_2 = -\frac{2}{3}\frac{(1-\nu)}{k^3} + \frac{3}{8}\frac{(1-\nu)}{k^4}$$

$$\alpha_3 = -\frac{3}{8}\frac{(1-\nu)}{k^4}$$

$$\alpha_4 = \frac{3}{4}\frac{(1-\nu)}{k^4}$$

$$\alpha_5 = -\frac{1}{8k^2}\left(\frac{1}{2} + k\right)$$

$$\alpha_6 = \frac{1}{8k^2}\left(\frac{1}{2} + k\right). \quad \Box \tag{18}$$

Example 6. In the orbiting dust problem we see from (7) that

$$\hat{\mathcal{H}}_1 = \gamma_1 S_{12} + \gamma_2 S_{14} \tag{19}$$

where

$$\gamma_1 = -\frac{m\ell}{k^2} \text{ and } \gamma_2 = -\frac{3a\ell}{k^3}.$$

Clearly $\hat{\mathcal{H}}_1$ is not of the form $\alpha_0 S_{12}$. However, we can apply the mapping $exp\,\lambda\,ad_S$ to bring $\hat{\mathcal{H}}_1$ into the required form. Using table 1 we see that $ad_{S_{24}} S_{12} = S_{14}$ and $ad_{S_{24}} S_{14} = -S_{12}$. Therefore

$$\mathcal{H}_1 = (exp\,\lambda\,ad_{S_{24}})\hat{\mathcal{H}}_1$$

$$= -\ell\left(\frac{m}{k^2}\cos\lambda - \frac{2}{3}\frac{a}{k^3}\sin\lambda\right)S_{12} - \ell\left(\frac{m}{k^2}\sin\lambda + \frac{3}{2}\frac{a}{k^3}\cos\lambda\right)S_{14}.$$

Choosing $\lambda = tan^{-1}\left(-\frac{3a}{2mk}\right)$ and $\alpha_0 = \sqrt{\left(\frac{m^2}{k^4} + \frac{9a^2}{4k^6}\right)}$ gives

$$\mathcal{H}_1 = -\ell\alpha_0 S_{12}. \tag{20}$$

Applying $exp\,\lambda ad_{S_{24}}$ to (11) and then averaging over the orbits of $X_{S_{12}}$ gives

$$\mathcal{H}_2 = \alpha_1 S_{12}^2 + \alpha_2(S_{14}^2 + S_{24}^2) + \alpha_3(S_{13}^2 + S_{23}^2)$$

$$+\alpha_4 S_{34}^2 + \alpha_5(S_{13}S_{14} + S_{23}S_{24}) \tag{21}$$

where

$$\alpha_1 = -\frac{\ell}{\alpha_0{}^2}\left(\frac{1}{4}\frac{m^5}{k^8} + \frac{1}{3}\frac{am^3}{k^9} - \frac{39}{16}\frac{a^2m^2}{k^{10}}\right)$$

$$\alpha_2 = -\frac{\ell}{\alpha_0{}^2}\left(\frac{9}{32}\frac{a^2}{k^{10}} + \frac{129}{64}\frac{a^2m^2}{k^{10}} + \frac{3}{8}\frac{am}{k^{11}}\right)$$

$$\alpha_3 = -\frac{\ell}{\alpha_0{}^2}\frac{3}{64}\frac{a^2m^2}{k^{10}}$$

$$\alpha_4 = -\frac{\ell}{\alpha_0{}^2}\frac{21}{36}\frac{a^2m^2}{k^{10}}$$

$$\alpha_5 = -\frac{\ell}{\alpha_0{}^2}\left(\frac{1}{8}\frac{am^3}{k^9} - \frac{9}{128}\frac{a^3m}{k^{11}}\right). \tag{22}$$

4.5 Normal Form and Symmetry

In the quadratic Zeeman effect, the normalized reduced Hamiltonian truncated at second order is

$$H_\ell = \varepsilon^2 \frac{\ell}{2k^4} \mathcal{H}_2 \tag{23}$$

where

$$\mathcal{H}_2 = 2S_{12}^2 + (S_{13}^2 + S_{23}^2) + 5(S_{14}^2 + S_{24}^2). \tag{24}$$

Because the lowest order terms in H_ℓ are quadratic, we *can not* normalize H_ℓ. However, from (24) we see that $\mathcal{H}_2$ lies in $ker\, ad_{S_{12}}$. Therefore S_{12} is an integral of H_ℓ, just as in the lunar and orbiting dust problems after normalizing the reduced Hamiltonian. Consequently H_ℓ is invariant under the S^1 action generated by the flow of $X_{S_{12}}$. This symmetry of H_ℓ comes from the fact the the original Hamiltonian (2..3) is invariant under the axial symmetry

$$\varphi : S^1 \times T_0\mathbf{R}^3 \longrightarrow T_0\mathbf{R}^3 : t, (\xi, \eta) \longrightarrow (R_t\xi, R_t\eta)$$

where

$$R_t = \begin{pmatrix} \cos t & -\sin t & 0 \\ \sin t & \cos t & 0 \\ 0 & 0 & 1 \end{pmatrix}.$$

Under the regularization and extension process of §4.1, the axial symmetry φ becomes a symmetry of the constrained Hamiltonian H (3) given by the S^1 action

$$\Phi : S^1 \times T\mathbf{R}^4 \longrightarrow T\mathbf{R}^4 : t, (q, p) \longrightarrow (\mathcal{R}_t q, \mathcal{R}_t p) \tag{25}$$

where

$$\mathcal{R}_t = \begin{pmatrix} \cos t & -\sin t & 0 & 0 \\ \sin t & \cos t & 0 & 0 \\ 0 & 0 & 1 & 0 \\ 0 & 0 & 0 & 1 \end{pmatrix}.$$

Because Φ is also a symmetry of H_0, which is the zeroth order term of the constrained Hamiltonian H, Φ_t and averaging over the flow of X_{H_0} commute. Consequently, Φ is a symmetry of the truncated normalized Hamiltonian $\hat{\mathcal{H}}$ (5). A straightforward calculation shows that Φ induces an S^1 action on $\mathcal{S}$ given by

$$\begin{aligned}
&\Phi_t^* S_{12} = S_{12} &&\Phi_t^* S_{34} = S_{34} \\
&\Phi_t^* S_{13} = \cos t\, S_{13} - \sin t\, S_{23} &&\Phi_t^*(-S_{24}) = \cos t(-S_{24}) - \sin t\, S_{14} \\
&\Phi_t^* S_{23} = \sin t\, S_{13} + \cos t\, S_{23} &&\Phi_t^* S_{14} = \sin t(-S_{24}) + \cos t\, S_{14} \; .
\end{aligned} \tag{26}$$

which has infinitesimal generator $X_{S_{12}}$ since

$$\left. \frac{d}{dt} \Phi_t^* \right|_{t=0} = X_{S_{12}}$$

(see (13)). Therefore the truncated normalized reduced Hamiltonian H_ℓ (24) is invariant under the flow of $X_{S_{12}}$.

A straightforward verification shows that the truncated normalized Hamiltonian of the artificial satellite problem (9) is also invariant under the flow of $X_{S_{12}}$. Because the original Hamiltonian (2..14) is invariant under the axial symmetry φ, one suspects that this is the origin of the symmetry of the normalized Hamiltonian. The following two lemmas justify this suspicion. They show that both the ordinary and constrained normalizing processes preserve every symmetry of the Hamiltonian which is also a symmetry of the Kepler Hamiltonian.

To handle symmetries in ordinary and constrained normalization we use the following set up. Let

$$H = H_0 + \varepsilon H_1 + \varepsilon^2 H_2 + \cdots$$

be a smooth formal power series in the Poisson algebra $(\mathcal{F}(V), \cdot, \{\ ,\ \})$ and suppose that X_{H_0} has a periodic flow $\varphi_t^{H_0}$. Let $\mathbf{G}$ be a Lie group acting on V by $\Phi : \mathbf{G} \times V \longrightarrow V$. Suppose that the $\mathbf{G}$-action Φ is *Poisson*, that is, for every $g \in \mathbf{G}$,

$$\Phi_g^* : \mathcal{F}(V) \longrightarrow \mathcal{F}(V) : f \longrightarrow f \circ \Phi_g$$

is an automorphism of the Poisson algebra $(\mathcal{F}(V), \cdot, \{\ ,\ \})$. We prove

Lemma 4..2 *Let Φ be a Poisson action of a Lie group $\mathbf{G}$ on $(\mathcal{F}(V), \cdot, \{\ ,\ \})$ which preserves H and H_0, that is, for every $g \in \mathbf{G}$, $\Phi_g^* H = H$ and $\Phi_g^* H_0 = H_0$. Then Φ preserves the normal form of H.*

Proof. A careful inspection of the normalizing process of §3.2 shows that it is enough to demonstrate that at each step only terms which are preserved by the action of Φ are added to the Hamiltonian. Thus it is enough to show that for every $F \in C^\infty(V)$ preserved by Φ, there is a solution $G \in C^\infty(V)$ of

$$ad_{H_0} G = F \tag{27}$$

which is preserved by Φ. Choose

$$G = \frac{1}{T} \int_0^T t(\varphi_t^{H_0})^* F \, dt.$$

From lemma 3.3 it follows that G is a solution of (27). We now show that G is preserved by Φ. Since $\Phi_g^* H_0 = H_0$ and since Φ_g^* is a Poisson algebra automorphism, for every $f \in \mathcal{F}(V)$ we have

$$\Phi_g^*(\{H_0, f\}) = \{\Phi_g^* H_0, \Phi_g^* f\} = \{H_0, \Phi_g^* f\}.$$

Consequently,

$$\Phi_g^* \circ ad_{H_0} = ad_{H_0} \circ \Phi_g^*$$

on $\mathcal{F}(V)$. Hence Φ_g^* commutes with the flow of X_{H_0} on $\mathcal{F}(V)$, that is, for every $f \in \mathcal{F}(V)$

$$\Phi_g^* \left((\varphi_t^{H_0})^* f \right) = (\varphi_t^{H_0})^* (\Phi_g^* f) \tag{28}$$

for every $g \in \mathbf{G}$. Therefore

$$
\begin{aligned}
\Phi_g^* G &= \frac{1}{T} \int_0^T t \Phi_g^* (\varphi_t^{H_0})^* F \, dt \\
&= \frac{1}{T} \int_0^T t (\varphi_t^{H_0})^* \Phi_g^* F \, dt \quad \text{using (28)} \\
&= G \quad \text{since } \Phi_g^* F = F.
\end{aligned}
$$

In other words, G is preserved by Φ, which is what we wanted to show. $\square$

To handle symmetries in constrained normalization we need to impose additional conditions of the Poisson action Φ. We assume that the group $\mathbf{G}$ is compact and the constraint M is invariant under Φ. With these extra hypotheses we prove

Lemma 4..3 *Let Φ be a Poisson action of a compact Lie group $\mathbf{G}$ on the Poisson algebra $(\mathcal{F}(\mathbf{R}^{2n}), \cdot, \{\,,\,\})$ which leaves the constraint $M \subseteq \mathbf{R}^{2n}$ invariant and preserves both H and H_0. If X_{H_0} has a periodic flow which leaves M invariant, then Φ preserves the constrained normal form of H.*

Proof. A careful look at the constrained normalization process of §3.3 shows that it is enough to demonstrate that at each step of the normalizing process, the modification

$$
G^* = G + \sum_{i=1}^{2r} \alpha_i F_i \tag{29}
$$

of a smooth Φ_g^*-invariant function G can be chosen to be Φ_g^*-invariant on M. Since M is invariant under Φ and is defined by $F_1 = F_2 = \cdots F_{2r} = 0$, each F_i is Φ-invariant. The function $\alpha_i \in C^\infty(M)$ exists by the argument establishing (29). Since $\mathbf{G}$ is compact, we can average α_i over $\mathbf{G}$ before extending it to a smooth function on $\mathbf{R}^{2n}$. Therefore the flow of X_{G^*} leaves M invariant and commutes with the action Φ *on M*. This is what we wanted to show. $\square$

Example 4 (continued). For the S^1 action Φ defined by (25), the modification

$$
G^* = G - \frac{1}{2}\{G, F_2\}F_1 + \frac{1}{2}\{G, F_1\}F_2
$$

of the Φ-invariant function G on $T^+ S^3$ need not be averaged over the orbits of Φ on $T^+ S^3$, because the functions $\alpha_1 = -\frac{1}{2}$ and $\alpha_2 = \frac{1}{2}$ are constant. Thus the constrained normal form of a regularized, extended perturbed Keplerian system with an axial symmetry also has an axial symmetry Φ. Hence the reduced normalized Hamiltonian is invariant under the flow of $X_{S_{12}}$. $\square$

5. Reduction to One Degree of Freedom

In this section we carry out the reduction of the twice normalized truncated Hamiltonian (4..6) to a one degree of freedom system. The reduction process proceeds geometrically by stages and is carried out using invariant theory. First we construct the reduced phase space P_ℓ for the Keplerian symmetry and then the reduced phase space $P_{\ell,c}$ for the axial symmetry.

5.1 Reduction of the Keplerian Symmetry

On T^+S^3 the flow of the geodesic vectorfield X_{G_0} generates an S^1 action which has no fixed points. Therefore we may apply the reduction theorem of Marsden and Weinstein [1] to obtain the reduced phase space $P_\ell = G_0(\ell)/S^1$ for the Keplerian symmetry. Every point of P_ℓ corresponds to a unique orbit of X_{G_0} of energy ℓ.

Unfortunately the reduction theorem gives no information how to construct P_ℓ. To do this we use invariant theory (see [2,36,24,37,16] for other applications of this technique). From lemma 4.1(iv) we know that the algebra of polynomials on T^+S^3 which are invariant under the flow of X_{G_0} is generated by the polynomials

$$S_{ij} = q_i p_j - q_j p_i$$

for $1 \leq i < j \leq 4$, where (q,p) are coordinates on $T\mathbf{R}^4$ (see [13]). An easy calculation shows that the S_{ij} satisfy the relation

$$S_{12}S_{34} - S_{13}S_{24} + S_{14}S_{23} = 0. \tag{1}$$

On the energy level $G_0^{-1}(\ell)$, the invariant polynomials also satisfy

$$\sum_{1 \leq i < j \leq 4} S_{ij}^2 = \ell^2. \tag{2}$$

The relations (1) and (2) define a smooth algebraic variety $\widetilde{G}_{2,4}$, which is diffeomorphic to $S_\ell^2 \times S_\ell^2 \subseteq \mathbf{R}^3 \times \mathbf{R}^3$:

$$x_1^2 + x_2^2 + x_3^2 = \ell^2 \text{ and } y_1^2 + y_2^2 + y_3^2 = \ell^2 \tag{3}$$

by the diffeomorphism ψ:

$$
\begin{array}{ll}
x_1 = S_{12} + S_{34} & y_1 = S_{12} - S_{34} \\
x_2 = S_{13} - S_{24} & y_2 = S_{13} + S_{24} \\
x_3 = S_{23} + S_{14} & y_3 = S_{23} - S_{14}.
\end{array}
\tag{4}
$$

The mapping ψ is a well known isomorphism between the Lie algebras $(so(4), [\,,\,])$ and $(so(3) \times so(3), [\,,\,])$. We would like to know that $S_\ell^2 \times S_\ell^2$ is unique. This is the principal result of

Lemma 5..1 *Any polynomial relation among the generators of the algebra of polynomials on $T^+S^3 \cap G_0^{-1}(\ell)$ which are invariant under the geodesic flow is a consequence of the relations given by (3).*

Proof. The proof requires a long detour into the provinces of algebraic geometry. The details are given in appendix 1. □

To show that $\widetilde{G}_{2,4}$ is the reduced space P_ℓ, we look at the mapping

$$\varrho : T^+S^3 \longrightarrow \bigwedge\nolimits^2(\mathbf{R}^4) : (q,p) \longrightarrow q \wedge p = \sum_{1 \le i < j \le 4} S_{ij}\, e_i \wedge e_j.$$

Here $\{e_1, \ldots, e_4\}$ is the standard basis of $\mathbf{R}^4$ and $\{e_i \wedge e_j\}$, $1 \le i < j \le 4$ is the standard basis of $\bigwedge^2(\mathbf{R}^4)$, the space of 2-vectors on $\mathbf{R}^4$. Geometrically, ϱ is the mapping which assigns to a geodesic on T^+S^3 with initial condition (q,p) the oriented two plane $q \wedge p$ in $\mathbf{R}^4$ spanned by q and p (see figure 4). Since the Plücker coordinates (S_{ij}) of $q \wedge p$ are integrals of X_{G_0}, the two plane $q \wedge p$ is invariant under the geodesic flow. Hence every geodesic is contained in a two plane given by a decomposable 2-vector, that is, an element of $\bigwedge^2(\mathbf{R}^4)$ which can be written as the exterior product of two vectors in $\mathbf{R}^4$. For $(q,p) \in T^+S^3$, neither q nor p are zero or linearly dependent. Thus the image of ϱ is contained in the set of *nonzero* decomposable 2-vectors $D^*_{2,4}$.

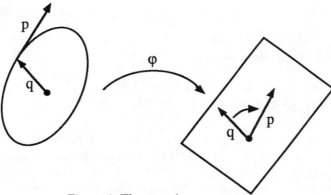

Figure 4. The mapping ϱ

The following argument shows that $D^*_{2,4}$ is defined by (1). Let $q,p \in \mathbf{R}^4$ and set $[i,j] = det \begin{pmatrix} q_i & q_j \\ p_i & p_j \end{pmatrix}$. Define an $(\mathbf{R}^2)^*$-valued trilinear mapping L on $\mathbf{R}^2$ by

$$L\left(\begin{pmatrix} q_i \\ p_i \end{pmatrix}, \begin{pmatrix} q_j \\ p_j \end{pmatrix}, \begin{pmatrix} q_k \\ p_k \end{pmatrix} \right) \begin{pmatrix} q_\ell \\ p_\ell \end{pmatrix} = [i,j][k,\ell] + [i,k][j,\ell] + [i,\ell][j,k].$$

Then it is straightforward to verify that L is skew symmetric, that is, $L \in \bigwedge^3 \mathbf{R}^2 \otimes (\mathbf{R}^2)^*$. But $\bigwedge^3 \mathbf{R}^2 = 0$. Therefore $L = 0$. Consequently the Plücker coodinates S_{ij} of every decomposable 2-vector satisfy (1). Suppose that (S_{ij}) for $1 \leq i < j \leq 4$ is a nonzero vector whose components satisfy (1). Then for some k, ℓ with $1 \leq k < \ell \leq 4$, $S_{\ell k} \neq 0$. By reordering the basis of $\mathbf{R}^4$, we may assume that $S_{12} \neq 0$. A short calculation shows that the Plücker coordinates of

$$(S_{12}, 0, -S_{23}, -S_{24}) \wedge \frac{1}{S_{12}}(0, S_{12}, S_{13}, S_{14})$$

are S_{ij}. Thus $D^*_{2,4}$ is defined by (1).

Let $T^\ell S^3$ be the space of all tangent vectors to S^3 of length $\ell > 0$, that is,

$$T^\ell S^3 = \{(q, p) \in T\mathbf{R}^4 |\, |q|^2 = 1,\, \langle q, p \rangle = 0,\, |p|^2 = \ell^2\}. \tag{5}$$

Restricting the map ϱ to $T^\ell S^3$ gives a mapping

$$\varrho_1 : T^\ell S^3 \longrightarrow \widetilde{G}_{2,4} : (q, p) \longrightarrow S = (S_{ij}), \tag{6}$$

because of the identity

$$\sum_{1 \leq i < j \leq 4} (q_i p_j - q_j p_i)^2 = |q|^2 |p|^2 - \langle q, p \rangle^2.$$

After this preparation we prove

Proposition 5..1 *The reduced space $P_\ell = G_0^{-1}(\ell)/S^1$ is the space $\widetilde{G}_{2,4}$ of oriented two planes in $\mathbf{R}^4$, and the reduction mapping is ϱ_1.*

Proof. To show that $\widetilde{G}_{2,4}$ is the reduced space P_ℓ, we must demonstrate that over every $S \in \widetilde{G}_{2,4}$ the fiber $\varrho_1^{-1}(S)$ of the reduction mapping is a single orbit of X_{G_0}. From (5) it follows that $T^\ell S^3$ is the set of ordered pairs of orthogonal vectors in $\mathbf{R}^4$ with the first vector having length 1 and the second vector length ℓ. Therefore $\varrho_1^{-1}(S)$ is the set of ordered orthogonal bases of the two plane with Plücker coordinates (S_{ij}). Moreover, the first basis vector has length 1 and the second length ℓ. Since $SO(2, \mathbf{R})$ acts transitively on this set of orthogonal bases, $\varrho_1^{-1}(S)$ is diffeomorphic to S^1 and hence consists of a single X_{G_0} orbit. This proves the proposition. $\qquad \square$

The mapping

$$r_1 : T^\ell S^3 \longrightarrow S^2_\ell \times S^2_\ell : (q, p) \longrightarrow \psi \circ \varrho_1(q, p) = (x, y), \tag{7}$$

where $\psi : \widetilde{G}_{2,4} \longrightarrow S^2_\ell \times S^2_\ell$ is the diffeomorphism given in (4), may also be considered a reduction mapping which removes the Keplerian symmetry. The next proposition gives some geometric properties of the mapping r_1.

Proposition 5..2

(*i*). r_1 is $(SO(4, \mathbf{R}), SO(3, \mathbf{R}) \times SO(3, \mathbf{R}))$ equivariant. In other words, if $A \in SO(4, \mathbf{R})$, then there are $B(A_1), B(A_2) \in SO(3, \mathbf{R})$ such that

$$r_1(Aq, Ap) = (B(A_1)x, B(A_2)y)$$

where $r_1(q, p) = (x, y)$. Moreover, the mapping

$$SO(4, \mathbf{R}) \longrightarrow SO(3, \mathbf{R}) \times SO(3, \mathbf{R}) : A \longrightarrow (B(A_1), B(A_2))$$

is a group homomorphism.

(*ii*). The mapping r_1 is a submersion.

(*iii*). Let $i : S^3 \longrightarrow S^2_\ell \times S^2_\ell$ be a smooth embedding of S^3 into $S^2_\ell \times S^2_\ell$. Then the fiber bundle $R_1 : r_1^{-1}(i(S^3)) \longrightarrow i(S^3)$ obtained by restricting the mapping r_1 to $r_1^{-1}(i(S^3))$ is a product bundle, that is, $r_1^{-1}(i(S^3))$ is diffeomorphic to $S^3 \times S^1$.

Proof.

The proof of (*i*) is deferred to appendix 2.

The proof of (*ii*) makes heavy use of the equivariance of r_1. It goes as follows. Since $SO(4, \mathbf{R})$ acts transitively on $T^\ell S^3$, it suffices to show that the differential of r_1 is surjective at one point in $T^\ell S^3$. Choose this point to be $\ell(e_2, e_3)$. Let F_{ij} be the skew symmetric 4×4 matrix with 1 in the $(i, j)^{th}$ entry, -1 in the (j, i)th entry, and 0 in the other entries. Then $\{F_{ij}\}$ for $1 \leq i < j \leq 4$ is a basis of $so(4, \mathbf{R})$. The curve

$$\Gamma_{ij} : t \longrightarrow \ell\Big((exp \, tF_{ij})e_2, (exp \, tF_{ij})e_3 \Big)$$

represents a tangent vector to $T^\ell S^3$ at $\ell(e_2, e_3)$. Thus the curve

$$\gamma_{ij} : t \longrightarrow r_1\Big(\Gamma_{ij}(t) \Big)$$

represents a tangent vector to $S^2_\ell \times S^2_\ell$ at $(x, y) = (0, 0, \ell, 0, 0, \ell)$. But the curves

$$t \longrightarrow \gamma_{12}(t) = \ell(0, \sin t, \cos t, 0, \sin t, \cos t)$$
$$t \longrightarrow \gamma_{34}(t) = \ell(0, \sin t, \cos t, 0, -\sin t, \cos t)$$
$$t \longrightarrow \gamma_{13}(t) = \ell(-\sin t, 0, \cos t, -\sin t, 0, \cos t)$$
$$t \longrightarrow \gamma_{24}(t) = \ell(\sin t, 0, \cos t, \sin t, 0, \cos t)$$

represent linearly independent vectors in $T_{(x,y)}(S^2_\ell \times S^2_\ell)$. Consequently, the mapping r_1 is a submersion. This completes the proof of (*ii*).

The proof of (*iii*) make use of facts about the classification of sphere bundles over spheres, which can be found in [38]. We know that an S^1 bundle over a three sphere S^3 is classified up to isomorphism by the homotopy class of the map from an equatorial two sphere S^2 of S^3 into the group $Diff^+(S^1)$ of orientation preserving diffeomorphisms of the fiber S^1. But $Diff^+(S^1)$ is homotopy equivalent to S^1, and every continuous map of S^2 onto S^1 is homotopic to a constant map. Therefore the bundle R_1 is a product bundle. This completes the proof of (*iii*). $\square$

5.2 Reduction of the Axial Symmetry

To construct the reduced space $P_{\ell,c}$ coming from the axial symmetry, we must know the flow of the vectorfield $X_{S_{12}}$ on $P_\ell = S_\ell^2 \times S_\ell^2$ explicitly. From the definition of the variables (x, y) in terms of S_{ij} (see (4)) and table 1 (see §4.4), a short calculation shows that the matrix of $ad_{S_{12}} = X_{S_{12}}$ with respect to the standard basis of $\mathbf{R}^3 \times \mathbf{R}^3$ is

$$
\left(
\begin{array}{ccc|ccc}
0 & 0 & 0 & & & \\
0 & 0 & -1 & & & \\
0 & 1 & 0 & & & \\
\hline
& & & 0 & 0 & 0 \\
& & & 0 & 0 & -1 \\
& & & 0 & 1 & 0
\end{array}
\right).
$$

Hence the flow of $X_{S_{12}}$ on $\mathbf{R}^3 \times \mathbf{R}^3$ is

$$
t, (x, y) \longrightarrow (\mathbf{R}_t x, \mathbf{R}_t y) \tag{8}
$$

where

$$
\mathbf{R}_t = \begin{pmatrix} 1 & 0 & 0 \\ 0 & \cos t & -\sin t \\ 0 & \sin t & \cos t \end{pmatrix}.
$$

Since $S_\ell^2 \times S_\ell^2$ is an invariant manifold of $X_{S_{12}}$, the mapping (8) induces a flow Φ on $S_\ell^2 \times S_\ell^2$, which has S_{12} as its momentum mapping. Therefore

$$
M_{\ell,c} = S_{12}^{-1}(c) \cap (S_\ell^2 \times S_\ell^2)
$$

is an invariant manifold of $X_{S_{12}}$. If $|c| > \ell$, then $M_{\ell,c} = \emptyset$ because $S_{12} = \frac{1}{2}(x_1 + y_1)$ while $|x_1| \leq \ell$ and $|y_1| \leq \ell$. From now on we will assume that $|c| \leq \ell$.

The flow Φ defines an S^1 action on $M_{\ell,c}$ which has fixed points:

$$
\pm\ell(1, 0, 0, 1, 0, 0)
$$

when $c = \pm\ell$ and

$$
\pm\ell(1, 0, 0, -1, 0, 0)
$$

when $c = 0$. When $c = \pm\ell$ it follows from the definition of $M_{\ell,c}$ that $M_{\ell,\pm\ell}$ is a point. Thus the fixed points $\pm\ell(1, 0, 0, 1, 0, 0)$ are not interesting, being all of $M_{\ell,\pm\ell}$. On the other hand when $c = 0$, $M_{\ell,0}$ is not just a point. The presence of fixed points on $M_{\ell,0}$ means that we can *not* apply the Marsden-Weinstein theorem to construct the reduced space. Instead, we must use the technique of singular reduction [2]. In the literature this point has either been ignored, leading to incorrect results, or avoided, by removing the fixed points from the phase space, leading to loss of significant geometric information.

   To construct the reduced phase space for *all* values of c, we again use invariant theory.

Lemma 5..2 *The algebra of polynomials on* $\mathbf{R}^3 \times \mathbf{R}^3$ *invariant under the linear* S^1 *action defined by (8) is generated by*

$$
\begin{array}{ll}
\pi_1 = x_1 \quad \pi_2 = x_2 y_2 + x_3 y_3 \quad \pi_3 = x_3 y_2 - x_2 y_3 \\
\pi_4 = y_1 \quad \pi_5 = x_2^2 + x_3^2 \qquad \pi_6 = y_2^2 + y_3^2
\end{array}
\tag{9}
$$

subject to the relation

$$
\pi_2^2 + \pi_3^2 = \pi_5 \pi_6, \quad \pi_5 \geq 0 \ \ \pi_6 \geq 0.
\tag{10}
$$

In addition, every polynomial relation among the generators $\pi_1, \ldots, \pi_6$ *is a consequence of (10)*

Proof. The lemma follows from results of [24] and [39]. Further details are omitted. □

On the algebraic variety $M_{\ell,c}$ the algebra of polynomials invariant under Φ is generated by $\pi_1, \ldots, \pi_6$. In addition to the relation (10) there are the relations

$$
\pi_5 + \pi_1^2 = \ell^2
$$
$$
\pi_6 + \pi_4^2 = \ell^2
$$
$$
\pi_1 + \pi_4 = 2c,
\tag{11}
$$

which just define $M_{\ell,c}$. Eliminating π_4, π_5 and π_6 from (10) and (11) gives the semialgebraic variety $V_{\ell,c}$ defined by

$$
\pi_2^2 + \pi_3^2 = \left(\ell^2 - \pi_1^2 \right) \left(\ell^2 - (2c - \pi_1)^2 \right)
\tag{12}
$$

where

$$
\pi_1 \in I_{\ell,c} = \begin{cases} [-\ell + 2c, \ell] \ \text{if } c > 0 \\ [-\ell, \ell] \qquad \text{if } c = 0 \\ [-\ell, \ell + 2c] \ \text{if } c < 0 . \end{cases}
\tag{13}
$$

The variety $V_{\ell,c}$ is nonempty if $|c| \leq \ell$, and is a point if $|c| = \ell$. From now on we will assume that $|c| < \ell$. For $0 < |c| < \ell$, $V_{\ell,c}$ is a smooth manifold, which is diffeomorphic to a two sphere S^2. For $c = 0$, $V_{\ell,0}$ is defined by

$$
\pi_2^2 + \pi_3^2 = (\ell^2 - \pi_1^2)^2, \quad |\pi_1| \leq \ell.
\tag{14}
$$

The variety $V_{\ell,0}$ has two singular points $\pm(1, 0, 0)$ at which the tangent cone is nondegenerate. Therefore $V_{\ell,0}$ is homeomorphic, but *not* diffeomorphic to a two sphere.

We now prove

Proposition 5..3 $V_{\ell,c}$ *is the reduced space* $P_{\ell,c} = M_{\ell,c}/S^1$ *and the reduction mapping is*

$$
r_2 : M_{\ell,c} \longrightarrow V_{\ell,c} : (x, y) \longrightarrow (\pi_1, \pi_2, \pi_3) = (x_1, x_2 y_2 + x_3 y_3, x_2 y_3 - x_3 y_2) \tag{15}
$$

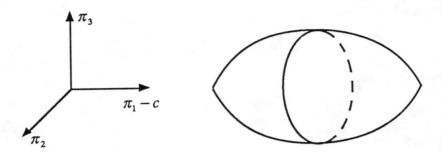

Figure 5. The variety $V_{\ell,0}$

Proof: We must show that every fiber of r_2 is precisely one orbit of $X_{S_{12}}$ on $M_{\ell,c}$. The following argument explicitly constructs the fibers of the mapping r_2. Provided that $y_2^2 + y_3^2 > 0$, we may solve the defining equations of π_2 and π_3 for x_2 and x_3. We obtain

$$x_2 = (y_2^2 + y_3^2)^{-1}(y_2\pi_2 - y_3\pi_3)$$
$$x_3 = (y_2^2 + y_3^2)^{-1}(y_2\pi_3 + y_3\pi_2). \tag{16}$$

Since $\pi = (\pi_1, \pi_2, \pi_3) \in V_{\ell,c}$ and $(x,y) = r_2^{-1}(\pi) \in M_{\ell,c}$, we find that

$$
\begin{aligned}
(\ell^2 - \pi_1^2)(y_1^2 + y_2^2) &= (x_1^2 + x_2^2 + x_3^2 - \pi_1^2)(y_2^2 + y_3^2) \\
&= (x_2^2 + x_3^2)(y_2^2 + y_3^2) \qquad \text{by definition of } \pi_1 \\
&= (x_2 y_2 + x_3 y_3)^2 + (x_3 y_2 - x_2 y_3)^2 \\
&= \pi_2^2 + \pi_3^2 \qquad \text{by definition of } \pi_2 \text{ and } \pi_3 \\
&= (\ell^2 - \pi_1^2)(\ell^2 - (2c - \pi_1)^2) \qquad \text{by definition of } V_{\ell,c}.
\end{aligned}
$$

Provided that $\pi_1 \neq \pm\ell$, we obtain

$$y_2^2 + y_3^2 = \ell^2 - (2c - \ell)^2. \tag{17}$$

From (17) we see that $\pi_1 = \pm\ell$ or $y_2^2 + y_3^2 = 0$ if

$$
\pi \in E = \begin{cases}
\{(\ell, 0, 0), (-\ell + 2c, 0, 0)\} & \text{if } 0 < c < \ell \\
\{(-\ell, 0, 0), (\ell, 0, 0)\} & \text{if } c = 0 \\
\{(-\ell, 0, 0), (\ell + 2c, 0, 0)\} & \text{if } -\ell < c < 0.
\end{cases}
$$

Therefore for $\pi \in V_{\ell,c} - E$, the fiber

$$r_2^{-1}(\pi) = \{(\pi_1, \frac{y_2\pi_2 - y_3\pi_3}{y_2^2 + y_3^2}, \frac{y_2\pi_3 + y_3\pi_2}{y_2^2 + y_3^2}, 2c - \pi_1, y_2, y_3) \in M_{\ell,c}|$$
$$y_2^2 + y_3^2 = \ell^2 - (2c - \pi_1)^2\}, \tag{18}$$

which is diffeomorphic to S^1. We now examine the exceptional fibers $r_2^{-1}(\pi)$ where $\pi \in E$. Suppose that $c > 0$, then

$$r_2^{-1}(\ell, 0, 0) = \{(\ell, 0, 0, 2c - \ell, y_2, y_3) \in M_{\ell,c}|y_2^2 + y_3^2 = \ell^2 - (2c - \ell)^2\}$$

and

$$r_2^{-1}(-\ell + 2c, 0, 0) = \{(-\ell + 2c, x_2, x_3, -\ell, 0, 0) \in M_{\ell,c}|x_2^2 + x_3^2 = \ell^2 - (2c - \ell)^2\}$$

both of which are diffeomorphic to S^1. When $c < 0$, a similar argument shows that the exceptional fibers of r_2 are diffeomorphic to S^1. When $c = 0$,

$$r_2^{-1}(\ell, 0, 0) = \ell(1, 0, 0, -1, 0, 0)$$

and

$$r_2^{-1}(-\ell, 0, 0) = -\ell(1, 0, 0, -1, 0, 0),$$

which are the fixed points of the S^1 action Φ on $M_{\ell,c}$. Therefore $V_{\ell,c}$ is the reduced space $P_{\ell,c} = M_{\ell,c}/S^1$. □

The next proposition gives the basic geometric property of the reduction mapping of the axial symmetry.

Proposition 5..4 *For $0 < c < |\ell|$ the bundle*

$$r_2 : M_{\ell,c} \longrightarrow P_{\ell,c} : (x, y) \longrightarrow (\pi_1, \pi_2, \pi_3)$$

is a Hopf fibration.

Proof. For simplicity we assume that $c > 0$. The case $c < 0$ is similar and the details are omitted.

First we must show that $M_{\ell,c}$ is a locally trivial S^1 bundle over $P_{\ell,c}$. This would follow if we could show that the mapping r_2 is a submersion. But this is a messy calculation, which we will not do. Instead we exhibit explicit bundle charts for $M_{\ell,c}$. We claim that they are given by

$$\varphi_1 : (V_{\ell,c} \cap \{-\ell + 2c < \pi_1 \leq \ell\}) \times S^1 \longrightarrow M_{\ell,c} - r_2^{-1}(-\ell + 2c, 0, 0) :$$
$$(\pi_1, \pi_2, \pi_3, \theta) \longrightarrow \left(\pi_1, \frac{\cos\theta\pi_2 - \sin\theta\pi_3}{\Delta_1}, \frac{\sin\theta\pi_2 + \cos\theta\pi_3}{\Delta_1},\right.$$
$$\left. 2c - \pi_1, \cos\theta\,\Delta_1, \sin\theta\,\Delta_1\right) \tag{19}$$

where $\Delta_1 = \sqrt{\ell^2 - (2c - \pi_1)^2}$ and

$$\varphi_2 : (V_{\ell,c} \cap \{-\ell + 2c \le \pi_1 < \ell\}) \times S^1 \longrightarrow M_{\ell,c} - r_2^{-1}(\ell, 0, 0) :$$
$$(\pi_1, \pi_2, \pi_3, \theta) \longrightarrow (\pi_1, \Delta_2 \cos\theta, \Delta_2 \sin\theta, 2c - \pi_1,$$
$$\frac{\cos\theta\,\pi_2 + \sin\theta\,\pi_3}{\Delta_2}, \frac{\sin\theta\,\pi_2 - \cos\theta\,\pi_3}{\Delta_2}) \qquad (20)$$

where $\Delta_2 = \sqrt{\ell^2 - \pi_1^2}$. The formula for φ_1 was obtained by parameterizing (18); while the formula for φ_2 follows by parameterizing an analogous expression for the fiber of r_2 which involves x_2 and x_3. For each fixed π, φ_i is a mapping of S^1 into the fiber $r_2^{-1}(\pi)$. Since $r_2 \circ \varphi_i(\pi, \theta) = \pi$, the mapping φ_i is bijective and hence is a homeomorphism.

We now determine the transition mapping

$$\varphi_{12} = \varphi_1^{-1} \circ \varphi_2 : (V_{\ell,c} - E) \times S^1 \longrightarrow (V_{\ell,c} - E) \times S^1$$

between the bundle charts. Let $\chi = \chi(\pi_2, \pi_3)$ be the angle determined by

$$\cos\chi = \frac{\pi_2}{\sqrt{\pi_2^2 + \pi_3^2}} \quad \text{and} \quad \sin\chi = \frac{\pi_3}{\sqrt{\pi_2^2 + \pi_3^2}}.$$

Using $\sqrt{\pi_2^2 + \pi_3^2} = \Delta_1 \Delta_2$, we may rewrite (19) as

$$\varphi_1(\pi, \theta) = (\pi_1, \Delta_1 \cos(\chi + \theta), \Delta_1 \sin(\chi + \theta), 2c - \pi_1, \Delta_2 \cos\theta, \Delta_2 \sin\theta)$$

and (20) as

$$\varphi_2(\pi, \theta) = (\pi_1, \Delta_1 \cos\theta, \Delta_1 \sin\theta, 2c - \pi_1, \Delta_2 \cos(\theta - \chi), \Delta_2 \sin(\theta - \chi)).$$

Therefore

$$\varphi_1(\pi, \theta - \chi) = \varphi_2(\pi, \theta)$$

which implies that

$$\varphi_{12}(\pi, \theta) = (\pi, \theta - \chi). \qquad (21)$$

Since $\pi_2^2 + \pi_3^2 > 0$ on $V_{\ell,c} - E$, the mapping φ_{12} is smooth with smooth inverse

$$\varphi_{21}(\pi, \theta) = \varphi_2^{-1} \circ \varphi_1(\pi, \theta) = (\pi, \theta + \chi).$$

Thus $M_{\ell,c}$ is a locally trivial S^1 bundle over $P_{\ell,c}$.

Next we classify the S^1 bundle defined by the mapping r_2, that is, we determine in which isomorphism class the bundle r_2 lies. From (21) we see that $M_{\ell,c}$ is the bundle formed by gluing the trivial bundles

$$(V_{\ell,c} \cap \{-\ell + 2c \le \pi_1 < \varepsilon\}) \times S^1 \quad \text{and} \quad (V_{\ell,c} \cap \{-\varepsilon < \pi_1 \le \ell\}) \times S^1$$

together by the mapping

$$\zeta : S^1 = (\{\pi_1 = 0\} \cap V_{\ell,c}) \times \{0\} \longrightarrow S^1 : (0, \pi_2, \pi_3, 0) \longrightarrow -\chi.$$

The mapping ζ has degree -1, because as (π_2, π_3) traverses S^1 counterclockwise, the angle $-\chi$ strictly decreases from 0 to -2π. Therefore by the classification of

S^1 bundles over S^2 (see [38]), the bundle r_2 is topologically isomorphic to the Hopf fibration.   □

An easy corollary of proposition 5.4 is that the total space of the bundle r_2 is homeomorphic to a three sphere S^3. Actually for $c \neq 0$ total space $M_{\ell,c}$ is diffeomorphic to S^3. This follows from

Lemma 5..3 *The variety* $M_{\ell,c} \subseteq \mathbf{R}^3 \times \mathbf{R}^3$ *defined by*

$$x_1^2 + x_2^2 + x_3^2 = \ell^2$$
$$y_1^2 + y_2^2 + y_3^2 = \ell^2$$
$$x_1 + y_1 = 2c$$

with $0 < |c| < \ell$ *is smooth. Moreover the function*

$$F : M_{\ell,c} \longrightarrow \mathbf{R} : (x,y) \longrightarrow x_3 + y_3$$

is a Morse function on $M_{\ell,c}$ *with two nondegenerate critical points.*

Proof. The proof is a straightforward exercise in vector calculus and no further details will be provided.   □

Using lemma 5.3 and a theorem of Reeb [40, p. 154] it follows that $M_{\ell,c}$ is the union of two closed three discs with smooth boundaries, which are diffeomorphic to S^2. The boundary two spheres are identified by a diffeomorphism. Since every diffeomorphism of S^2 is smoothly isotopic to the identity [41], $M_{\ell,c}$ is *diffeomorphic* to S^3.

6. Analysis of Normalized Hamiltonian

Let H be the twice normalized truncated perturbed Keplerian system. Let $H_{\ell,c}$ be the Hamiltonian on the reduced phase space $P_{\ell,c}$, which is obtained by reducing the Keplerian and axial symmetries. In this section we describe the geometry of the singular toral fibration defined by the Liouville integrable Hamiltonian system H on T^+S^3. To do this we we study the level sets of the associated one degree of freedom Hamiltonian $H_{\ell,c}$ on $P_{\ell,c}$. The critical level sets of $H_{\ell,c}$ are of special interest because they correspond to the singular fibers of the toral fibration. The inverse image of a critical level set of $H_{\ell,c}$ under the composition of the reduction mappings is an invariant manifold, which is called a *relative equilibrium* of X_H [42].

6.1 The Second Reduced Hamiltonian

Before we can determine the relative equilibria, we must have an explicit expression for the second reduced Hamiltonian $H_{\ell,c}$. To find this we need to express the variables $\pi_1, \ldots, \pi_6$ in terms of the Plücker coordinates S_{ij}, $1 \leq i < j \leq 4$. Using the definiton of π_i in terms of x, y (9) and the definition of x, y in terms of S_{ij} (4) we obtain

$$\pi_1 = x_1 = S_{12} + S_{34}$$
$$\pi_2 = x_2 y_2 + x_3 y_3 = S_{13}^2 - S_{24}^2 - S_{14}^2 + S_{23}^2$$
$$\pi_3 = x_3 y_2 - x_2 y_3 = 2(S_{13} S_{14} + S_{23} S_{24})$$
$$\pi_4 = y_1 = S_{12} - S_{34}$$
$$\pi_5 = x_2^2 + x_3^2 = S_{13}^2 + S_{14}^2 + S_{23}^2 + S_{24}^2 - 2(S_{13} S_{24} - S_{14} S_{23})$$
$$\pi_6 = y_2^2 + y_3^2 = S_{13}^2 + S_{14}^2 + S_{23}^2 + S_{24}^2 + 2(S_{13} S_{24} - S_{14} S_{23}).$$

Solving the above equations for the generators of $ker\, ad_{S_{12}}$ (see (4..14)) and using the definition of $P_{\ell,c}$ (5..11) and (5..12) gives

$$S_{12} = c$$
$$S_{34} = \frac{1}{2}(\pi_1 - \pi_4) = \pi_1 - c$$
$$S_{13}^2 + S_{23}^2 = \frac{1}{4}(\pi_5 + \pi_6 + 2\pi_2) = \frac{1}{2}\left(\ell^2 - c^2 - (c - \pi_1)^2 + \pi_2\right)$$
$$S_{14}^2 + S_{24}^2 = \frac{1}{4}(\pi_5 + \pi_6 - 2\pi_2) = \frac{1}{2}\left(\ell^2 - c^2 - (c - \pi_1)^2 - \pi_2\right)$$
$$S_{13} S_{24} - S_{14} S_{23} = \frac{1}{4}(\pi_6 - \pi_5) = c^2 - c\pi_1$$
$$S_{13} S_{14} + S_{23} S_{24} = \frac{1}{2}\pi_3. \tag{1}$$

Using (1) we can write the reduced truncated Hamiltonian H_ℓ (4..15) as a function on $P_{\ell,c}$.

For the quadratic Zeeman effect, substituting (1) into the truncated normalized Hamiltonian (4..5) gives the second reduced Hamiltonian

$$H_{\ell,c} = 3(\pi_1 - c)^2 + 2\pi_2 \tag{2}$$

on $P_{\ell,c}$. In (2) we have dropped the constants and rescaled the time.

In the orbiting dust problem, substituting (1) into the truncated normalized reduced Hamiltonian H_ℓ (4..20), (4..21) gives the second reduced Hamiltonian

$$H_{\ell,c}(\pi) = \beta_1(\pi_1 - c)^2 + \beta_2 \pi_2 \tag{3}$$

on $P_{\ell,c}$ where

$$\beta_1 = -\frac{1}{4}(\alpha_4 + \alpha_5) + \alpha_6$$
$$\beta_2 = \frac{1}{4}(\alpha_5 - \alpha_4.) \tag{4}$$

Here $\alpha_1, \ldots, \alpha_6$ are given by (4..22). Repeating this process for the lunar problem (4..16), (4..17), we obtain the second reduced Hamiltonian (3) where

$$
\begin{aligned}
\beta_1 &= -\frac{1}{2}(\alpha_2 + \alpha_3) + \alpha_4 + c^2(\alpha_6 - \frac{1}{2}\alpha_5) \\
\beta_2 &= \frac{1}{2}(\alpha_3 - \alpha_2) - \frac{1}{2}c^2\alpha_5
\end{aligned}
\tag{5}
$$

and $\alpha_1, \ldots, \alpha_6$ are given by (4..18).

In the artificial satellite problem, the second reduced Hamiltonian is

$$
K_{L,H} = \frac{\mu^4\alpha^2}{L^3G^3}\left(\frac{1}{2} - \frac{3}{4}s^2\right) + \varepsilon\frac{\mu^6\alpha^4}{L^3G^7}\left[P(s^2, G) - 2m^*_{2,0}(s^2)(es\sin g)^2\right]
\tag{6}
$$

where $P(s^2, G)$ and $m^*_{2,0}(s^2)$ are given by (4..10) and

$$
\begin{aligned}
\sqrt{2}G &= \sqrt{L^2 + \pi_3 - \pi_1^2 + 2H\pi_1} \\
2G^2s^2 &= L^2 - 2H^2 + \pi_3 + 2H\pi_1 \\
Les\sin g &= \pi_1 - H.
\end{aligned}
\tag{7}
$$

6.2 Level Sets of $H_{\ell,c}$: I

In this section we determine the level sets of

$$
H_{\ell,c}(\pi) = \beta_1(\pi_1 - c)^2 + \beta_2\pi_2
\tag{8}
$$

on $P_{\ell,c}$. In particular we obtain the critical points of $H_{\ell,c}$ for the quadratic Zeeman effect, the orbiting dust and lunar problems.

We begin by treating a degenerate case where

$$
h\beta_1 > 0 \text{ and } \beta_2 = 0.
$$

The level set $H_{\ell,c}^{-1}(h)$ is the intersection of two planes

$$
\pi_1 = c \pm \left(\frac{h}{\beta_1}\right) = d_\pm
$$

with the two sphere $P_{\ell,c}$. This intersection is

(i) one or two circles, depending on whether $[d_-, d_+] \cap int\, I_{\ell,c} \neq \emptyset$ and $[d_-, d_+] \not\subseteq I_{\ell,c}$, (see (5..13) for the definition of $I_{\ell,c}$) or $[d_-, d_+] \subseteq int\, I_{\ell,c}$;

(ii) one or two points, depending on whether $d_\pm$ is a boundary point of $I_{\ell,c}$.

In general, when $\beta_2 \neq 0$ a straightforward calculation shows that the critical points of $H_{\ell,c}$ lie on the topological circle $S^1_{\ell,c} = P_{\ell,c} \cap \{\pi_3 = 0\}$. In the π_1–π_2 plane, the restricted level set

$$
\left(H_{\ell,c}|S_{\ell,c}\right)^{-1}(h) = H_{\ell,c}^{-1}(h) \cap S^1_{\ell,c}
$$

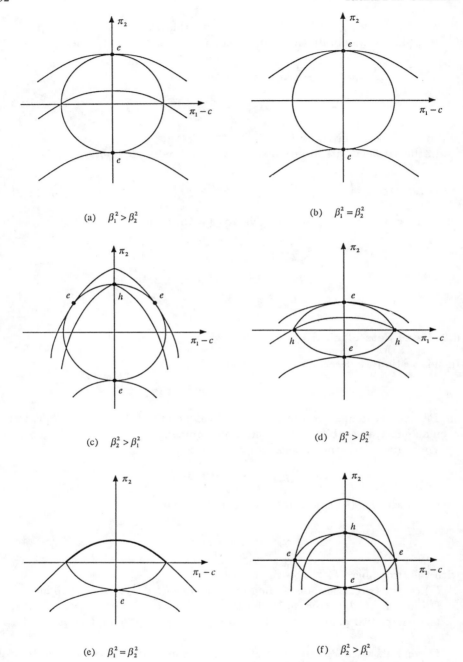

Figure 6. The restricted level sets of $H_{\ell,c}|S_{\ell,c}$ when $\beta_1\beta_2 < 0$. If $\beta_1\beta_2 > 0$ the figures are the same but the direction of the π_2–axis is reversed. Elliptic critical points of $H_{\ell,c}$ are marked with the letter "e" and hyperbolic critical points with the letter "h"

is the intersection of a parabola

$$\beta_1(\pi_1 - c)^2 + \beta_2\pi_2 = h$$

with symmetry axis $\{\pi_1 = c\}$ and the circle $S^1_{\ell,c}$ (see figure 6).
There are four possibilities for the restricted level set:
- (i) When the restricted level set is a point, the full level set $H^{-1}_{\ell,c}(h)$ is a nonsingular point of $P_{\ell,c}$.
- (ii) When the restricted level set is two points, there are two cases:
  - (a) If the two points are nonsingular, then the full level set is a circle.
  - (b) If the two points are singular points of $P_{\ell,c}$, then the full level set is either a topological circle or two points.
- (iii) When the restricted level set is three points, the full level set is an immersed circle with a normal crossing at a nonsingular point of $P_{\ell,c}$, which is a critical point of $H_{\ell,c}$.
- (iv) When the restricted level set is an arc joining two singular points of $P_{\ell,c}$, then the full level set is the same arc, which consists entirely of critical ponts of $H_{\ell,c}$.

From figure 6 we can read off the stability type of the critical points of $H_{\ell,c}$ which are nonsingular points of $P_{\ell,c}$. This we do as follows. When every full level set near the critical point is a circle, the the critical point is *elliptic*. When every full level set near the critical point is the disjoint union of two circles, then the critical point is *hyperbolic*. If the critical point is a singular point of $P_{\ell,c}$, then it is "elliptic" when nearby full level set are circles which shrink to the singular point as the value of $H_{\ell,c}$ approaches the critical value. A singular point is "hyperbolic" if it is isolated and the level set of $H_{\ell,c}$ containing the critical point is not contained in an arbitrarily small neighborhood of the critical point.

For example, in the quadratic Zeeman effect we have $\beta_1 = 3$ and $\beta_2 = 2$ for the second reduced Hamiltonian $H_{\ell,c}$ (5..1). Therefore figures 6(c) and 6(f) give the restricted level sets of $H_{\ell,c}$. In particular, it follows from figure 6(f) that the full level sets of $H_{\ell,0}$ on $P_{\ell,0}$ are as depicted in figure 7. This completely describes the dynamics on the ground state $P_{\ell,0}$.

Figure 6 has a major shortcoming: it gives no information about the organization of the critical values of $H_{\ell,c}$ into families and thus no information about the organization of the critical points of $H_{\ell,c}$ into families. To get this information we need to know the critical values of the energy momentum mapping

$$\mathcal{EM} : T^+S^3 \longrightarrow \mathbf{R}^3 : (q,p) \longrightarrow (H, |p|, S_{12})$$

of the Liouville integrable Hamiltonian H, whose twofold reduction is $H_{\ell,c}$. A point on $P_{\ell,c}$ is a critical point of the reduced Hamiltonian corresponding to the critical value h if and only if the polynomial Q obtained by eliminating π_2 from the defining equation of $H^{-1}_{\ell,c}(h)$:

$$h = \beta_1(\pi_1 - c)^2 + \beta_2\pi_2$$

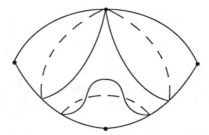

Figure 7. The level sets of $H_{\ell,0}$ on $P_{\ell,0}$. They describe the dynamics on the reduced ground state $P_{\ell,0}$ of the twice normalized reduced quadratic Zeeman effect

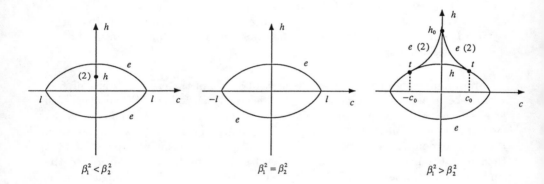

Figure 8. The ℓ =const. slice of the range of the energy momentum mapping $\mathcal{EM}$. The critical values of $\mathcal{EM}$ are the dark curves with the letters "e" (elliptic), "h" (hyperbolic), and "t" (transitional) indicating the stability type of the critical point of $H_{\ell c}$. Here $c_0 = \ell\left(\frac{\beta_1-\beta_2}{\beta_1+\beta_2}\right)^{\frac{1}{2}}$ and $h_0 = \beta_1^2\ell$

and the defining equation of $S^1_{\ell,c}$:

$$\pi_2^2 = \left(\ell^2 - \pi_1^2\right)\left(\ell^2 - (2c - \pi_1)^2\right)$$

(see (5.12)) has a double root $\pi_1 \in I_{\ell,c}$. Putting $\sigma_1 = \pi_1 - c$, a short calculation gives

$$Q(\sigma_1) = (\beta_1^2 - \beta_2^2)\sigma_1^4 + 2\left(-h\beta_1 + (\ell^2 + c^2)\right)\sigma_1^2 + \left(h^2 - \beta_1^2(\ell^2 - c^2)\right)$$

where

$$|\sigma_1| \leq \ell - |c| \quad \text{and} \quad |c| \leq \ell, \ \ell > 0. \tag{9}$$

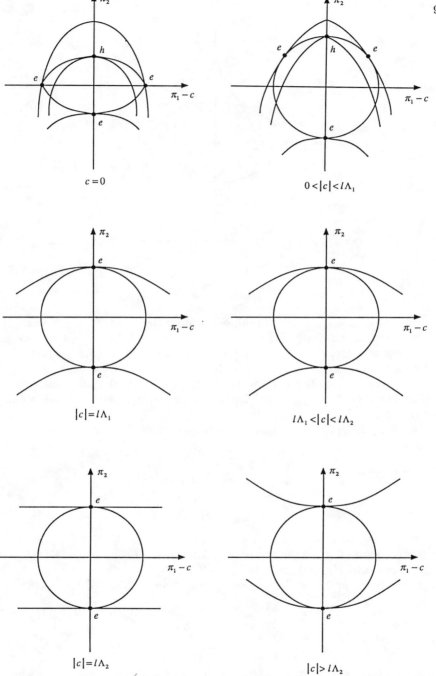

Figure 9. The restricted level sets of $H_{\ell,c}|S^1_{\ell,c}$. Critical values of $H_{\ell,c}$ corresponding to elliptic critical points are marked with the letter "e" and hyperbolic critical values are marked with the letter "h". Here $\Lambda_1 = \left(\frac{18(1-\nu)}{30(1-\nu)+k(\ell+c)} \right)^{\frac{1}{2}}$ and $\Lambda_2 = \left(\frac{18(1-\nu)}{k(\ell+c)} \right)^{\frac{1}{2}}$

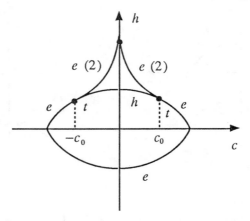

Figure 10. An ℓ =const. slice of the range of the energy momentum mapping $\mathcal{EM}$ of the lunar problem. Here $c_0 = \ell \Lambda_1$ and $h_0 = \frac{3}{2} \frac{(1-\nu)}{k^3} \ell^3$

In other words, the set of critical values of $\mathcal{EM}$ is the set of (h, ℓ, c) where Q has a multiple zero σ_1 which satisfies (9). As is shown in [16], this set is a semialgebraic subvariety of the discriminant locus of Q whose ℓ =const. cross section is given in figure 8.

In the quadratic Zeeman effect, the second reduced Hamiltonian (8) has coefficients $\beta_1 = 3$ and $\beta_2 = 2$. Therefore figure 8(c) determines the families of critical values of $H_{\ell,c}$.

In the orbiting dust problem, the second reduced Hamiltonian (8) has coefficients

$$\beta_1 = \frac{a^2 \ell (81a^2 + 9amk + 42m^2 k^2)}{32k^6 (9a^2 + 4k^2 m^2)} \tag{10}$$

$$\beta_2 = \frac{3a^2 m \ell (3a - 4mk)}{32k^6 (9a^2 + 4k^2 m^2)} \tag{11}$$

These expressions come from substituting (4..22) into (4). Here $\beta_1 > 0$. As long as $\beta_2 \neq 0$, figure 6 gives the restricted level sets of $H_{\ell,c}$ on $S_{\ell,c}^1$. The families of critical values of $H_{\ell,c}$ are given in figure 8.

In the lunar problem, the second reduced Hamiltonian (8) has coefficients

$$\beta_1 = \frac{3}{2} \frac{(1-\nu)}{k^3} \ell - \frac{1}{16k^2} (\frac{1}{2} + \frac{1}{\ell}) c^2 \tag{12}$$

$$\beta_2 = \frac{3}{8} \frac{(1-\nu)}{k^3} \ell + \frac{1}{16k^2} (\frac{1}{2} + \frac{1}{\ell}) c^2. \tag{13}$$

Note that these coefficients depend on the value c of the integral S_{12}, while the corresponding coefficients in the quadratic Zeeman effect and orbiting dust problem do not. The expressions (12) and (13) for β_1 and β_2 come from substituting (4.18) into (5). The restricted level sets of $H_{\ell,c}$ on $S_{\ell,c}$ are given in figure 9. The families of critical values of $H_{\ell,c}$ are given in figure 10 (see [43]).

6.3 Singular Toral Fibration: I

In this section we describe the topology of the fibers of the energy momentum mapping

$$\mathcal{EM} : T^\ell S^3 \longrightarrow \mathbf{R}^3 : (q, p) \longrightarrow (H, |p|, S_{12}).$$

We assume that after reducing the Keplerian and axial symmetries, the Hamiltonian H becomes the Hamiltonian

$$H_{\ell,c} = \beta_1(\pi_1 - c)^2 + \beta_2 \pi_2^2$$

on the second reduced phase space $P_{\ell,c}$. The main results of this section are summarized in table 2.

$H_{\ell,c}^{-1}(h)$	$\mathcal{EM}^{-1}(h, \ell, c)$
1. nonsingular point	T^2
2. smooth S^1	T^3
3. two singular points	disjoint union of two S^1
4. closed interval with singular boundary points	$S^1 \times S^2$
5. S^1 with two singular points	$S^1 \times$ (immersed S^2 with two normal crossings)
6. immersed S^1 with one nonsingular normal crossing	$T^2 \times$ (immersed S^1 with one nonsingular normal crossing).

Table 2. Topology of the level sets of the energy momentum mapping $\mathcal{EM}$ for the quadratic Zeeman effect, orbiting dust, and lunar problems

Let $r = r_2 \circ r_1 : T^\ell S^3 \longrightarrow P_{\ell,c}$ be the composition of the reduction mapping $r_1 : T^\ell S^3 \longrightarrow S_\ell^2 \times S_\ell^2$ which removes the Keplerian symmetry and the reduction mapping $r_2 : M_{\ell,c} \subseteq S_\ell^2 \times S_\ell^2 \longrightarrow P_{\ell,c}$ which removes the axial symmetry. From the construction of the reduction mappings, it follows that

$$\mathcal{EM}^{-1}(h, \ell, c) = r^{-1}\Big(H_{\ell,c}(h)\Big).$$

This is the basic fact which allows us to determine the topology of the fibers of the energy momentum mapping.

We now justify the entries in the second column of the table 2. For the justfication of the entries in the first column see §6.2. We treat the entries in the order in which they appear in the table.

1. If the full level set $H_{\ell,c}^{-1}(h)$ is a nonsingular point p of $P_{\ell,c}$, then the fiber $r^{-1}(p)$ is diffeomorphic to a two dimensional torus. This follows from the construction of the reduction mappings r_1 and r_2.

2. If $H_{\ell,c}^{-1}(h)$ is a smooth submanifold of $P_{\ell,c}$ which is diffeomorphic to S^1, then the level set $\mathcal{EM}^{-1}(h,\ell,c)$ is diffeomorphic to a smooth three dimensional torus. The connectedness and compactness of this level set follows from the construction of the reduction mappings. The fact that the level set is a three dimensional torus is a consequence of the theorem of Arnold–Liouville about completely integrable Hamiltonian systems.

3. If $H_{\ell,0}^{-1}(h)$ is the two singular points $P_{\ell,0}$, then $r^{-1}(H_{\ell,0}^{-1}(h))$ is the disjoint union of two S^1.

4. Suppose that $H_{\ell,0}^{-1}(h)$ is a closed arc $\Gamma \subseteq P_{\ell,0}$ with end points p_1 and p_2 which are singular points of $P_{\ell,0}$. By an isotopy which leaves the points p_i fixed we may suppose that

$$\Gamma = \{(\pi_1, -(\ell^2 - \pi_1^2), 0) \in P_{\ell,0}| \, |\pi_1| \le \ell\}.$$

The isotopy does not change the topology of $r^{-1}\left(H_{\ell,0}^{-1}(h)\right)$. The following argument shows that $r_2^{-1}(\Gamma)$ is the topological two sphere

$$\mathcal{S}^2 = \{(x, -x) \in S_\ell^2 \times S_\ell^2| \, |x|^2 = \ell^2\}.$$

Because $S_{12}|\mathcal{S}^2 = 0$, we have $\mathcal{S}^2 \subseteq M_{\ell,0}$. On $\mathcal{S}^2$ consider the arc

$$\gamma : [-\ell, \ell] \longrightarrow \mathcal{S}^2 : t \longrightarrow (t, 0, \sqrt{\ell^2 - t^2}, -t, 0, -\sqrt{\ell^2 - t^2})$$

Since

$$r_2 : S_\ell^2 \times S_\ell^2 \longrightarrow P_{\ell,0} : (x,y) \longrightarrow (\pi_1, \pi_2, \pi_3) = (x_1, x_2y_2 + x_3y_3, x_3y_2 - x_2y_3),$$

we have $r_2(\gamma(t)) = (t, -(\ell^2 - t^2), 0)$, which implies that

$$r_2\left(\gamma\left([-\ell, \ell]\right)\right) = \Gamma.$$

As is easily seen, $\gamma([-\ell, \ell])$ is a cross section for the S^1 action on $S_\ell^2 \times S_\ell^2$ given by

$$t, (x,y) \longrightarrow (\mathbf{R}_t x, \mathbf{R}_t y) \text{ where } \mathbf{R}_t = \begin{pmatrix} 1 & 0 & 0 \\ 0 & \cos t & -\sin t \\ 0 & \sin t & \cos t \end{pmatrix}.$$

Since this S^1 action is the flow of $X_{S_{12}}$, it follows from the definition of the reduction mapping r_2 that $r_2^{-1}(\Gamma) = \mathcal{S}^2$.

We now show that $W_{\ell,0} = r_1^{-1}(\mathcal{S}^2)$ is topologically $S^1 \times S^2$. From the definition of the variables (x,y) (5..4), it follows that $\mathcal{S}^2$ as a subset of $\mathbf{R}^6$ with coordinates (S_{ij}) is defined by

$$S_{12} = S_{13} = S_{23} = 0 \text{ and } S_{14}^2 + S_{24}^2 + S_{34}^2 = \ell^2.$$

A straightforward calculation shows that the mapping

$$s : \mathcal{S}^2 \longrightarrow T^\ell S^3 : (0,0,0,S_{14}.S_{24},S_{34}) \longrightarrow \left((0,0,0,1), (-S_{14},-S_{24},-S_{34},0)\right)$$

is a section for the bundle

$$r_1 : r_1^{-1}(\mathcal{S}^2) \subseteq T^\ell S^3 \longrightarrow \mathcal{S}^2 \subseteq S_\ell^2 \times S_\ell^2 : (q, p) \longrightarrow q \wedge p.$$

In other words, $r_1 \circ s = id_{\mathcal{S}^2}$. Because

$$W_{\ell,0} = \{(q, p) \in T\mathbf{R}^4 |\, |q|^2 = 1,\ \langle q, p \rangle = 0,\ |p|^2 = \ell^2,\ q_1 p_2 - q_2 p_1 = 0\}$$

is invariant under the geodesic flow on $T^+ S^3$ and the geodesic flow acts without fixed points on $W_{\ell,0}$, the bundle $r_1 : W_{\ell,0} \longrightarrow \mathcal{S}^2$ is a principal S^1 bundle. Since it has a section, the bundle r_1 is trivial. Consequently, $W_{\ell,0}$ is topologically $S^1 \times S^2$.

5. Suppose that $H_{\ell,0}^{-1}(h)$ is a topological S^1 with two singular points which are the singular points of $P_{\ell,c}$. Then this S^1 is the union of two closed arcs Γ_1 and Γ_2 which intersect at their end points which are the two singular points of $P_{\ell,0}$. Using a result from the proof of entry 4, we see that $r_2^{-1}(S^1) = r_2^{-1}(\Gamma_1) \cup r_2^{-1}(\Gamma_2)$. Thus $r_2^{-1}(S^1)$ is the union of two topological two spheres which are identified at two points that are mapped by r_2 onto the ends of Γ_1 and Γ_2. One may also describe $r_2^{-1}(S^1)$ by saying that topologically it is an immersed two sphere with two normal crossings. From the results of the proof of entry 4, it follows that $r^{-1}(S^1)$ is the union of two copies of $S^1 \times S^2$ which are identified along two S^1. These S^1 are hyperbolic periodic orbits of X_H of index 2 which are heteroclinic. Thus the level set of the energy momentum mapping is $S^1 \times r_2^{-1}(S^1)$.

6. The proof of this entry is analgous to the proof of entry 5. Further details are omitted.

6.4 Level Sets of $K_{L,H}$: II.

In this section we discuss the level sets of the second reduced Hamiltonian

$$K_{L,H} = \mathcal{H}_1 + \varepsilon \mathcal{H}_2 \tag{14}$$

(see (6..6)) of the artificial satellite problem. Our discussion follows [24,26] (see also [25]).

If we forget about the second term in $K_{L,H}$, then $\mathcal{H}_1$ is a Bott-Morse function when

$$0 < H < L^* = \frac{1}{\sqrt{5}} L.$$

Moreover $\mathcal{H}_1$ has two nondegenerate critical points of index two at the north and south poles of the second reduced phase space $P_{H,L}$ and a nondegenerate critical circle C of index zero at the critical inclination

$$\sin^2 i = \frac{4}{5}.$$

As H increases toward L^*, the critical circle C collapses to the north pole of P_{L,L^*}.

We now treat the full second reduced Hamiltonian $K_{L,H}$, when H is not close to L^*. If $0 < H < L^*$, then $K_{L,H}$ is a Morse function with six nondegenerate

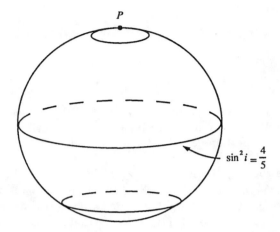

Figure 11. Level sets of $\mathcal{H}_1$ of the artificial satellite problem. The north and the south poles are nondegenerate critical points. The darkened circle is a nondegenerate critcal manifold

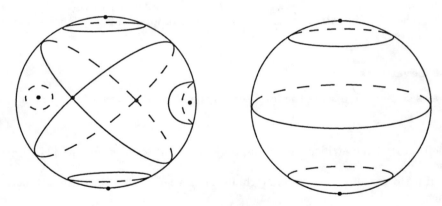

Figure 12. Critical points of $K_{L,H}$

critical points: two of index zero, one, and two, respectively. If $H > L^*$, then $K_{L,H}$ is a Morse function with two nondegenerate critical points: one of index zero and the other of index two (see figure 12).

In other words, the critical circle C of $\mathcal{H}_1$ has broken up into four nondegenerate critical points of $K_{L,H}$ provided that the critical circle C is not too close to the north pole of P_{L,L^*}.

To understand what happens when H is approximately L^* and the critical circle is near the north pole of P_{L,L^*} is a delicate matter. Calculating the Hessian

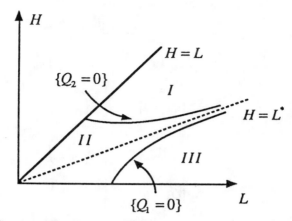

Figure 13. Curves where Hessian of $K_{L,H}$ at the north pole degenerates

of $K_{L,H}$ at the north pole of $P_{L,H}$ gives

$$\mathcal{Q} = \begin{pmatrix} Q_1 & 0 \\ 0 & Q_2 \end{pmatrix}$$

where Q_i are rational functions in H and L. The graphs of $Q_i = 0$ and the signs of Q_i are displayed in table 3.

In the interior of the regions I, II, or III, the north pole of $P_{L,H}$ is a non-degenerate critical point of $K_{H,L}$ of index two, one or zero respectively. For values of (L, H) where $Q_1 = 0$ or $Q_2 = 0$, the Hessian of $K_{L,H}$ degenerates. To see what happens there we introduce coordinates at the north pole p. Let $\phi : U \subseteq \mathbf{R}^2 \longrightarrow P_{L,H}$ be the chart defined by

$$\phi(\sigma_1, \sigma_2) = \left(\sigma_1, \sigma_2, \sqrt{L^4 - 2L^2(\sigma_1^2 + H^2) + (\sigma_1^2 - H^2)^2} \right)$$

where

$$\sigma_1 = \pi_1 - H$$
$$\sigma_2 = \pi_2$$
$$\sigma_3 = \pi_3. \tag{15}$$

The third component of the chart mapping ϕ is obtained by solving the defining equation (5.12) of $P_{L,H}$ for π_3 and then substituting the defining equations (15) of the variables σ_i. Note that $\phi(0,0) = p$. From (6) and (7), it is easy to see that $\mathcal{K}_{L,H} = \phi^* K_{L,H}$ is a function of σ_1^2 and σ_2^2. Hence $\mathcal{K}_{L,H}$ is invariant under the $\mathbf{Z}_2 \times \mathbf{Z}_2$ symmetry generated by the reflections

$$(\sigma_1, \sigma_2) \longrightarrow (-\sigma_1, \sigma_2) \text{ and } (\sigma_1, \sigma_2) \longrightarrow (\sigma_1, -\sigma_2).$$

Condition on (L, H)	Signs of $Q_{1,2}$
I	$\begin{pmatrix} - \\ & - \end{pmatrix}$
$\{Q_1 = 0\}$	$\begin{pmatrix} 0 \\ & - \end{pmatrix}$
II	$\begin{pmatrix} - \\ & + \end{pmatrix}$
$\{Q_2 = 0\}$	$\begin{pmatrix} + \\ & 0 \end{pmatrix}$
III	$\begin{pmatrix} + \\ & + \end{pmatrix}$

Table 3. Hessian of $K_{L,H}$ at the north pole

A computation shows that the fourth order Taylor polynomial $\mathcal{K}^{(4)}_{L,H}$ of $\mathcal{K}_{L,H}$ at $(0,0)$ is

$$\begin{cases} A_2\sigma_2^2 + B_1\sigma_1^4, & \text{where } Q_1(L,H) = 0 \\ A_1\sigma_1^2 + B_2\sigma_2^4, & \text{where } Q_2(L,H) = 0. \end{cases}$$

Using equivariant singularity theory, it can be shown that $\mathcal{K}^{(4)}_{L,H}$ is $\mathbf{Z}_2 \times \mathbf{Z}_2$ four determined and has codimension one. Consequently the universal unfolding of $\mathcal{K}^{(4)}_{L,H}$ near $(0,0)$ is

$$\begin{cases} \mu_1\sigma_1^2 + A_2\sigma_2^2 + B_1\sigma_1^4, & \text{where } Q_1(L,H) = 0 \\ A_1\sigma_1^2 + \mu_2\sigma_2^2 + B_2\sigma_2^4, & \text{where } Q_2(L,H) = 0. \end{cases} \tag{16}$$

In other words, the topology of the level sets of $\mathcal{K}_{L,H}$ near $(0,0)$ when (L,H) is in an open neighborhood of of a point on $\{Q_1 = 0\}$ or $\{Q_2 = 0\}$ is determined by the fourth order Taylor polynomial $\mathcal{K}^{(4)}_{L,H}$ at $(0,0)$. In addition, the level sets of $K_{L,H}$ near p and the level sets of the normal form (16) of $\mathcal{K}_{L,H}$ near $(0,0)$ are topologically the same. The level sets of $K_{L,H}$ near p are given in figure 14.

6.5 Singular Toral Fibration: II

In this section we describe the topology of the fibers of the energy momentum mapping

$$\mathcal{EM} : T^\ell S^3 \longrightarrow \mathbf{R}^3 : (q, p) \longrightarrow (K, |p|, S_{12})$$

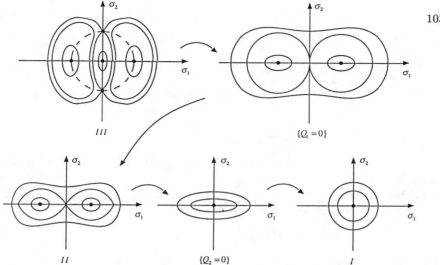

Figure 14. Level sets of $K_{L,H}$ near p when (L, H) lies in the region given in figure 12

where K is Brouwer's Hamiltonian (4..9). After reducing the Keplerian and axial symmetries, we obtain the second reduced Hamiltonian $K_{L,H}$ (6). The topology of the level sets of $\mathcal{EM}$ is given in table 4.

$K_{L,H}^{-1}(h)$	$\mathcal{EM}^{-1}(h, L, H)$
1. point	T^2
2. smooth S^1	T^3
3. two S^1 with two distinct transversal crossings	two T^3 intersecting cleanly along two T^2
4. an immersed S^1 with one normal crossing	two T^3 intersecting cleanly along a T^2

Table 4. Topology of the level set of the energy momentum mapping for the artificial satellite problem

The entries 1 and 2 in the second column of table 4 follow from the definition of the reduction mappings. Entry 3 follows from the observation that each S^1 on the second reduced space $P_{L,H}$ bounds a contractible disc. Hence $r^{-1}(S^1)$ is a three torus. If p_1 and p_2 are the points of normal crossing of the circles, then $r^{-1}(p_i)$ is a critical two torus of H of index one. For entry 4, we note that an immersed S^1 with one normal crossing is the union of two topological circles which are identified at the point q of normal crossing. Again these topological circles are contractible on $P_{L,H}$. Since $r^{-1}(q)$ is a nondegenerate critical two torus of H, entry 4 follows.

7. Appendix 1

In this appendix we provide a detailed proof of lemma 5.1.

Let V be the algebraic variety defined by the equations

$$f_1(x, y) = x_1^2 + x_2^2 + x_3^2 - \ell^2$$
$$f_2(x, y) = y_1^2 + y_2^2 + y_3^2 - \ell^2$$

which are the relations in the algebra of polynomials on $G_0^{-1}(\ell) \cap T^+ S^3$ invariant under the geodesic flow. Let $\mathbf{R}[\mathbf{R}^3 \times \mathbf{R}^3]$ be the ring of polynomials on $\mathbf{R}^3 \times \mathbf{R}^3$. Recall that a polynomial on V is the restriction of a polynomial on $\mathbf{R}^3 \times \mathbf{R}^3$ to V. In other words, the mapping

$$\theta : \mathbf{R}[\mathbf{R}^3 \times \mathbf{R}^3] \longrightarrow \mathbf{R}[V] : f \longrightarrow f|V$$

is a homomorphism onto the ring $\mathbf{R}[V]$ of polynomials on V.

To start with we want to show that $\mathbf{R}[V]$ is isomorphic to $\mathbf{R}[\mathbf{R}^3 \times \mathbf{R}^3]/I$ where I is the ideal of polynomials on $\mathbf{R}^3 \times \mathbf{R}^3$ generated by f_1 and f_2. To do this we must show that $ker\, \theta = I$. Suppose that $f|V = 0$. Now complexify everything in sight. Let $f^{\mathbf{C}}$ be the complexification of f and let $V^{\mathbf{C}}$ be the complex variety defined by $f_1^{\mathbf{C}} = f_2^{\mathbf{C}} = 0$. Then $f^{\mathbf{C}}|V^{\mathbf{C}} = 0$. Therefore, by the Hilbert nullstellensatz [44], there is a positive integer r such that $(f^{\mathbf{C}})^r \in I^{\mathbf{C}}$, where $I^{\mathbf{C}}$ is the ideal of complex polynomials on $\mathbf{C}^3 \times \mathbf{C}^3$ generated by $f_1^{\mathbf{C}}$ and $f_2^{\mathbf{C}}$. As is shown in lemma 1 below, $I^{\mathbf{C}}$ is a radical ideal. Consequently $f^{\mathbf{C}} \in I^{\mathbf{C}}$. Thus for some complex polynomials a, b on $\mathbf{C}^3 \times \mathbf{C}^3$,

$$f^{\mathbf{C}} = a f_1^{\mathbf{C}} + b f_2^{\mathbf{C}}.$$

Let
$$\overline{f}^{\mathbf{C}} = \overline{a} \overline{f_1}^{\mathbf{C}} + \overline{b}\, \overline{f_2}^{\mathbf{C}}.$$

Here $\overline{a}$ is the polynomial formed by taking the complex conjugate of the coefficients of the polynomial a. Therefore

$$f = \frac{1}{2}(f^{\mathbf{C}} + \overline{f}^{\mathbf{C}})|(\mathbf{R}^3 \times \mathbf{R}^3)$$
$$= \left(\frac{1}{2}(a + \overline{a})|\mathbf{R}^3 \times \mathbf{R}^3 \right) f_1 + \left(\frac{1}{2}(b + \overline{b})|\mathbf{R}^3 \times \mathbf{R}^3 \right) f_2$$
$$= A f_1 + B f_2$$

where $A, B \in \mathbf{R}[\mathbf{R}^3 \times \mathbf{R}^3]$. This shows that $f \in I$. Consequently $ker\, \theta = I$ as desired.

Next we show that $\mathbf{R}[V]$ is isomorphic to the ring $\mathbf{R}[G_0^{-1}(\ell)]^{S^1}$ of polynomials on $G_0^1(\ell) \subseteq T\mathbf{R}^4$ which are invariant under the geodesic flow. Recall that in §5.1 we have shown that the reduction mapping $r_1 : T^\ell S^3 \longrightarrow V$ is surjective with fiber S^1 which is a geodesic of length ℓ. Then r_1 induces a ring homomorphism r_1^*.

$$r_1{}^* : \mathbf{R}[V] \longrightarrow \mathbf{R}[G_0^{-1}(\ell)] : f \longrightarrow f \circ r_1 = F$$

Because r_1 is surjective, r_1^* is injective. We claim that the image of r_1^* is contained in $\mathbf{R}[G_0^{-1}(\ell)]^{S^1}$. To see this, suppose that $\gamma \subseteq G_0^{-1}(\ell)$ is a geodesic of energy ℓ. Then for some $(x, y) \in V$, we have $\gamma = r_1^{-1}(x, y)$. Therefore

$$F(\gamma) = F(r_1^{-1}(x, y)) = \{f(x, y)\},$$

that is, F is constant on each geodesic of energy ℓ. This says that $F \in \mathbf{R}[G_0^{-1}(\ell)]^{S^1}$. Actually, the image of r_1^* is $\mathbf{R}[G_0^{-1}(\ell)]^{S^1}$. To prove this, we note that the algebra $\mathbf{R}[G_0^{-1}(\ell)]^{S^1}$ is generated by

$$S_{ij} = (q_i p_j - q_j p_i)|G_0^{-1}(\ell) \ 1 \leq i < j \leq 4.$$

This is equivalent to saying that

$$
\begin{array}{ll}
X_1 = S_{12} + S_{34} & Y_1 = S_{12} - S_{34} \\
X_2 = S_{13} - S_{24} & Y_2 = S_{13} + S_{24} \\
X_3 = S_{23} + S_{14} & Y_3 = S_{23} - S_{14}
\end{array}
$$

generate $\mathbf{R}[G_0^{-1}(\ell)]^{S^1}$. But $r_1^* x_i = X_i$ and $r_1^* y_i = Y_i$ for $1 \leq i \leq 4$. Therefore r_1^* is surjective, which proves that r_1^* is an isomorphism.

We are now in a position to show that

$$X_1^2 + X_2^2 + X_3^2 = \ell^2 \text{ and } Y_1^2 + Y_2^2 + Y_3^2 = \ell^2 \tag{1}$$

are the only polynomial relations among the generators of $\mathbf{R}[G_0^{-1}(\ell)]^{S^1}$. Suppose that $F = 0$ is a polynomial relation among the variables X_i, Y_i. Then for some polynomial f on V, we have $F = r_1^*(f)$. Since the mapping r_1^* is a ring isomorphism, the condition $F = 0$ implies that $f = 0$. In other words, $f \in I$. Therefore for some polynomials $a, b \in \mathbf{R}[V]$ we have

$$
\begin{aligned}
f &= af_1 + bf_2 \\
&= a(x_1^2 + x_2^2 + x_3^2 - \ell^2) + b(y_1^2 + y_2^2 + y_3^2 - \ell^2).
\end{aligned}
$$

Consequently,

$$
\begin{aligned}
F &= r_1^*(f) = r_1^*(a)r_1^*(f_1) + r_1^*(b)r_1^*(f_2) \\
&= A(X_1^2 + X_2^2 + X_3^2 - \ell^2) + B(Y_1^2 + Y_2^2 + Y_3^2 - \ell^2)
\end{aligned}
$$

where $A = r_1^*(a), B = r_1^*(b) \in \mathbf{R}[G_0^{-1}(\ell)]^{S^1}$. Thus the relation $F = 0$ follows from the relations (1).

We now prove

Lemma 1. *The ideal I is a radical ideal.*

Proof: The proof given below is analgous to the one given in [45]. Let the tableau

$$T = \begin{pmatrix} i_1 \ j_1 \\ i_2 \ j_2 \\ i_3 \ j_3 \end{pmatrix}$$

represent the monomial

$$x_1^{i_1} x_2^{i_2} x_3^{i_3} y_1^{j_1} y_2^{j_2} y_3^{j_3}.$$

The tableau T is *straight* if $i_1 = 0$ or 1 and if $j_1 = 0$ or 1. From the defining relations of I:

$$x_1^2 = 1 - x_2^2 - x_3^2$$
$$y_1^2 = 1 - y_2^2 - y_3^2,$$

we have the tableaux relations

$$-\begin{pmatrix} i_1 \ j_1 \\ i_2 \ j_2 \\ i_3 \ j_3 \end{pmatrix} = \begin{pmatrix} i_1 - 2 \ j_1 \\ i_2 + 2 \ j_2 \\ i_3 \quad j_3 \end{pmatrix} + \begin{pmatrix} i_1 - 2 \ j_1 \\ i_2 \quad j_2 \\ i_3 + 2 \ j_3 \end{pmatrix} - \begin{pmatrix} i_1 - 2 \ j_1 \\ i_2 \quad j_2 \\ i_3 \quad j_3 \end{pmatrix}$$

$$-\begin{pmatrix} i_1 \ j_1 \\ i_2 \ j_2 \\ i_3 \ j_3 \end{pmatrix} = \begin{pmatrix} i_1 \ j_1 - 2 \\ i_2 \ j_2 + 2 \\ i_3 \quad j_3 \end{pmatrix} + \begin{pmatrix} i_1 \ j_1 - 2 \\ i_2 \quad j_2 \\ i_3 \ j_3 + 2 \end{pmatrix} - \begin{pmatrix} i_1 \ j_1 - 2 \\ i_2 \quad j_2 \\ i_3 \quad j_3 \end{pmatrix}$$

From the above two equations, which are called the *straightening rules*, it is easy to see that every tableau is a linear combination of straight tableaux. Define an order relation between the tableaux

$$T = \begin{pmatrix} i_1 \ j_1 \\ i_2 \ j_2 \\ i_3 \ j_3 \end{pmatrix} \quad \text{and} \quad T' = \begin{pmatrix} i_1' \ j_1' \\ i_2' \ j_2' \\ i_3' \ j_3' \end{pmatrix}$$

as follows:

case 1. Suppose that $i_1, j_1 \notin \{0,1\}$ or $i_1', j_1' \notin \{0,1\}$. Then $T < T'$ provided that either

$$\sum_{\ell=1}^{3} (i_\ell + j_\ell) < \sum_{\ell=1}^{3} (i_\ell' + j_\ell')$$

or

$$\sum_{\ell=1}^{3} (i_\ell + j_\ell) = \sum_{\ell=1}^{3} (i_\ell' + j_\ell')$$

and

$$(i_1, i_2, i_3, j_1, j_2, j_3) < (i_1', i_2', i_3', j_1', j_2', j_3')$$

where $<$ is the lexicographic order on $\mathbf{N}^6$.

case 2. Suppose that $i_1, j_1, i_1', j_1' \in \{0, 1\}$. Then $T < T'$ provided that either

$$i_1 < i_1'$$

or

$$i_1 = i_1' \text{ and } j_1 < j_1'$$

or

$$i_1 = i_1' \text{ and } j_1 = j_1' \text{ and } i_2 + i_3 + j_2 + j_3 < i_2' + i_3' + j_2' + j_3'$$

or

$$i_1 = i_1' \text{ and } j_1 = j_1'$$

and

$$i_2 + i_3 + j_2 + j_3 = i_2' + i_3' + j_2' + j_3'$$

and

$$i_2 + i_3 + j_2 + j_3 < i_2' + i_3' + j_2' + j_3'$$

where $<$ is the lexicographic order on $\mathbf{N}^6$.

From the definition of the tableaux ordering and the straightening rules, it follows that the straight tableaux are linearly independent. Thus the algebras $\mathbf{C}[x, y]/I$ and

$$R \oplus x_1 R \oplus y_1 R \oplus x_1 y_1 R \text{ where } R = \mathbf{C}[x_2, x_3, y_2, y_3]$$

are isomorphic.

Using the straightening rules we see that

(a) Every tableau T can be written uniquely as $\sum_i c_i T_i$ where T_i are straight tableaux which are smaller than T.

(b) If $T = \begin{pmatrix} i_1 \ j_1 \\ i_2 \ j_2 \\ i_3 \ j_3 \end{pmatrix}$, then the largest straight tableaux in $\sum_i c_i T_i$ is

$$T^* = \begin{pmatrix} i_1 - 2[i_1/2] \ j_1 - 2[j_1/2] \\ i_2 + 2[i_1/2] \ j_2 + 2[j_1/2] \\ i_3 \qquad\qquad j_3 \end{pmatrix}$$

where $[x]$ is the greatest integer less than or equal to x.

(c) If $T < S$, then $T^* < S^*$.

(d) If $T < S$, then $UT < US$ for every tableau U.

After all this preparation we are ready to prove that the ideal I is a radical ideal. Suppose that $T^m = 0$ for some nonnegative integer m. Write $T = \sum_{i=1}^{N} c_i T_i$ where T_i are straight and $T_1 < T_2 \cdots < T_N$. Then

$$T^m = \left(\sum_{i=1}^{N} c_i T_i \right)^N$$

$$= \sum_{i_1, i_2, \ldots i_m = 1}^{N} \frac{c_{i_1 \cdots i_m}}{i_1! i_2! \cdots i_m!} T_1^{i_1} \cdots T_m^{i_m}.$$

Since $T_1 < T_2 \cdots < T_N$, we have

$$T_N^m > T_1^{i_1} \cdots T_N^{i_N}$$

for all $1 \le i_1, i_2, \ldots, i_m \le N$ with $(i_1, \ldots, i_m) \ne (N, \ldots, N)$. In other words,

$$T^m = c_N^m (T_N^*)^m + \text{lower straight monomials.} \tag{2}$$

Since $T^m = 0$ by hypothesis and straight monomials are linearly indedpendent, it follows from (2) that $c_N = 0$. Thus $T = \sum_{i=1}^{N-1} c_i T_i$. Repeating this argument $N - 1$ more times gives $T = 0$, that is, $T \in I$. Hence I is a radical ideal.

8. Appendix 2

In this appendix we prove part (i) of proposition 5.2.

We begin our argument by noting that the reduction mapping

$$\varrho : TS^3 \longrightarrow \bigwedge\nolimits^2 (\mathbf{R}^4) : (q, p) \longrightarrow q \wedge p$$

is equivariant in the sense that if $A \in SO(4, \mathbf{R})$ then

$$\varrho(Aq, Ap) = Aq \wedge Ap = \bigwedge\nolimits^2 A \,(q \wedge p). \tag{1}$$

If the matrix of A with respect to the standard basis $\{e_1, \ldots, e_4\}$ of $\mathbf{R}^4$ is (a_{ij}), then then matrix of the linear mapping $\bigwedge^2 A : \bigwedge^2 \mathbf{R}^4 \longrightarrow \bigwedge^2 \mathbf{R}^4$ with respect to the standard basis $\{e_i \wedge e_j \,|\, 1 \le i < j \le 4\}$ is $(A_{ij;k\ell}) = (a_{ij}a_{k\ell} - a_{i\ell}a_{kj})$. In other words, the matrix of $\bigwedge^2 A$ is made up of the 2×2 minors of the matrix of A. For example, if

$$A = \begin{pmatrix} R_t & 0 \\ 0 & R_s \end{pmatrix} \quad \text{where } R_t = \begin{pmatrix} \cos t & \sin t \\ -\sin t & \cos t \end{pmatrix} \tag{2}$$

then

$$\bigwedge\nolimits^2 A = \begin{pmatrix} 1 & 0 & 0 & 0 \\ 0 & R_{s+t} & 0 & 0 \\ 0 & 0 & 1 & 0 \\ 0 & 0 & 0 & R_{s+t} \end{pmatrix}. \tag{3}$$

The mapping

$$\tau : SO(4, \mathbf{R}) \longrightarrow Gl(\bigwedge\nolimits^2 \mathbf{R}^4, \mathbf{R}) : A \longrightarrow \bigwedge\nolimits^2 A$$

is a group homorphism. Actually the image of τ is contained in $SO(\bigwedge^2 \mathbf{R}^4, \mathbf{R})$. In other words, $\bigwedge^2 A$ is a proper rotation on $\bigwedge^2 \mathbf{R}^4$ with respect to the Euclidean innerproduct

$$\langle u \wedge v, r \wedge s \rangle = 2 \det \begin{pmatrix} \langle u, r \rangle & \langle u, s \rangle \\ \langle v, r \rangle & \langle v, s \rangle \end{pmatrix}. \tag{4}$$

It is mechanical to check that $\bigwedge^2 A$ is an orthogonal linear mapping. The fact that $\det \bigwedge^2 A = 1$ follows because the equivariance property (1) of the mapping ϱ given by (1) implies that for every $P \in SO(4, \mathbf{R})$

$$\varrho(PBP^{-1}q, PBP^{-1}p) = (\bigwedge^2 P)(\bigwedge^2 B)(\bigwedge^2 P)(q \wedge p).$$

But every $B \in SO(4, \mathbf{R})$ is conjugate by a $P \in SO(4, \mathbf{R})$ to a matrix A of the form (2) for some $s, t \in \mathbf{R}$. Therefore $\bigwedge^2 B$ is conjugate to a matrix $\bigwedge^2 A$ of the form (3), which has determinant 1. Thus

$$\tau : SO(4, \mathbf{R}) \longrightarrow SO(\bigwedge^2 \mathbf{R}^4, \langle \, , \, \rangle) : A \longrightarrow \bigwedge^2 A$$

is an orthogonal representation.

The next argument shows that the representation τ decomposes into the sum of two three dimensional orthogonal representations. To proceed we recall some fact about the Hodge star operator $*$. The star operator is a linear mapping of $\bigwedge^2 \mathbf{R}^2$ into itself which is defined by the condition: given $\lambda \in \bigwedge^2 \mathbf{R}^4$

$$\mu \wedge *\lambda = \langle \mu, \lambda \rangle \, vol_{\mathbf{R}^4}$$

for all $\mu \in \bigwedge^2 \mathbf{R}^4$. Here $vol_{\mathbf{R}^4} = e_1 \wedge e_2 \wedge e_3 \wedge e_4$ is the standard volume element of $\mathbf{R}^4$. This definition is all right because if $0 = \mu \wedge *\lambda$ for all $\mu \in \bigwedge^2 \mathbf{R}^4$, then $0 = \langle \mu, \lambda \rangle$ for all $\mu \in \bigwedge^2 \mathbf{R}^4$. Therefore $\lambda = 0$ and consequently $*\lambda = 0$. A straightforward calculation shows that if $\{i, j, k, \ell\} = \{1, 2, 3, 4\}$ then

$$*(e_i \wedge e_j) = (sgn \, \sigma)e_k \wedge e_\ell, \tag{5}$$

where $sgn \, \sigma$ is the sign of the permutation

$$\sigma = \begin{pmatrix} 1 \; 2 \; 3 \; 4 \\ i \; j \; k \; \ell \end{pmatrix}.$$

From (5) we see that $*^2 = id$. Therefore the star operator has eigenvalues ± 1. Let $E_\pm$ be the ± 1 eigenspace of the star operator. The eigenspaces E_+ and E_- are orthogonal, for if $\lambda_\pm \in E_\pm$ then

$$\langle \lambda_+, \lambda_- \rangle = \langle *\lambda_+, \lambda_- \rangle = \langle \lambda_+, *\lambda_- \rangle = -\langle \lambda_+, \lambda_- \rangle$$

where the second equality follows from

$$\begin{aligned} \langle \lambda_-, *\lambda_+ \rangle \, vol_{\mathbf{R}^4} &= \lambda_- \wedge *(*\lambda_+) \\ &= \lambda_- \wedge \lambda_+ \\ &= \lambda_+ \wedge \lambda_- \\ &= \langle \lambda_+, *\lambda_- \rangle \, vol_{\mathbf{R}^4}. \end{aligned}$$

Therefore $\bigwedge^2 \mathbf{R}^4$ is an orthogonal direct sum of E_+ and E_-. As is easily checked

$$\tfrac{1}{2}(e_1 \wedge e_2 + e_3 \wedge e_4) \; \tfrac{1}{2}(e_2 \wedge e_3 - e_2 \wedge e_4) \; \tfrac{1}{2}(e_1 \wedge e_4 + e_2 \wedge e_3)$$

$$\tfrac{1}{2}(e_1 \wedge e_2 - e_3 \wedge e_4) \; \tfrac{1}{2}(e_1 \wedge e_3 + e_2 \wedge e_4) \; \tfrac{1}{2}(e_1 \wedge e_4 - e_2 \wedge e_3)$$

is an orthonormal basis of $E_+ \oplus E_-$. Now we come to the crucial property of the star operator, namely, for $A \in SO(4, \mathbf{R})$

$$*\bigwedge^2 A = \bigwedge^2 A *.$$ (6)

This implies that $\bigwedge^2 A$ maps $E_\pm$ into itself. To prove (6) we calculate as follows: for $\mu, \lambda \in \bigwedge^2 \mathbf{R}^4$ we have

$$\begin{aligned}
\bigwedge^2 A\mu \wedge \bigwedge^2 A\lambda &= \langle \bigwedge^2 A\mu, \bigwedge^2 A\lambda \rangle \, vol_{\mathbf{R}^4} \\
&= \langle \mu, \lambda \rangle vol_{\mathbf{R}^4} = (det\, A)\, \mu \wedge *\lambda \\
&= \bigwedge^4 A(\mu \wedge *\lambda) = \bigwedge^2 A\mu \wedge \bigwedge^2 A*\lambda.
\end{aligned}$$

In addition $\bigwedge A_\pm = \bigwedge^2 A | E_\pm$ is an orthogonal linear mapping of $(E_\pm, \langle\,,\,\rangle_\pm)$ where $\langle\,,\,\rangle_\pm = \langle\,,\,\rangle | E_\pm$. Therefore the representation τ decomposes into the representation

$$\tilde{\tau} : SO(4, \mathbf{R}) \longrightarrow SO(E_+, \langle\,,\,\rangle_+) \times SO(E_-, \langle\,,\,\rangle_-) : A \longrightarrow (\bigwedge^2 A_+, \bigwedge^2 A_-).$$

Using the definition of the mapping $\tilde{\tau}$ we may write the equivariance property (1) of ϱ as

$$\varrho(Aq, Ap) = (\bigwedge^2 A_+ x, \bigwedge^2 A_- y)$$ (7)

where x is the projection of $q \wedge p$ along E_- onto E_+ and y is the projection of $q \wedge p$ along E_+ onto E_-. Restricting the mapping ϱ to $T^\ell S^3$ gives the desired equivariance property of the reduction mapping r_1. This completes the proof of proposition 5.2.

References

1. Marsden, J. and Weinstein, A., Reduction of manifolds with symmetry, Rep. Math. Phys., **5** (1974), 121–130
2. Arms, J., Cushman, R.H., and Gotay, M.J., A universal reduction procedure for Hamiltonian group actions, (to appear in Proc. Integrable Hamiltonian Systems, eds. T. Ratiu and H. Flaschka, MSRI series, Springer Verlag, 1990)
3. Abraham, R. and Marsden, J., "Foundations of Mechanics", Benjamin/Cummings, Reading, Mass., 1978
4. Duistermaat, J.J., Bifurcations of periodic solutions near equilibrium points of Hamiltonian systems, in: "Bifurcation Theory and Applications", Montecatini, 1983, 55–105, ed. L. Salvadori, Lect. Notes in Math., **1057**, Springer Verlag, New York, 1984
5. van der Meer, J.-C., The Hamiltonian Hopf bifurcation, Lect. Notes in Math., **1160**, Springer Verlag, New York, 1985
6. Cotter, C., The semisimple 1:1 resonance, Thesis, University of California at Santa Cruz, 1986
7. Arnold, V.I., "Mathematical Methods in Classical Mechanics", Graduate Texts in Math., **60**, Springer Verlag, New York, 1978
8. Coffey, S., Deprit, A., and Williams, C.A., The quadratic Zeeman effect, Ann. N.Y. Acad. Sci., **497** (1986), 22–36

9. Zimmerman, M.L., Kash, M.M., and Kleppner, D., Evidence of an approximate symmetry for hydrogen in a uniform magnetic field, Phys. Rev. Lett., **45** (1980), 1092–94

10. Solovév, E.A., The hydrogen atom in a weak magnetic field, Sov. Phys. JETP, **55** (1982), 1017–1021

11. Reinhardt, W. and Farelley, D., The quadratic Zeeman effect in hydrogen, J. de Physique, coll. 2, suppl. vol 43. no. 11 (1982), 29–43

12. Deprit, A. and Ferrar, S., On polar orbits for the Zeeman effect in a moderately strong magnetic field, preprint, NIST, Gaithersburg, MD, l989

13. Cushman, R., Normal form for Hamiltonian vectorfields with periodic flow, in: "Differential Geometric Methods in Mathematical Physics", 125–144, ed. S. Sternberg, Reidel, Dordrecht, 1984

14. Cushman, R. and Sanders, J.A., The constrained normal form algorithm, Celest. Mech., **45** (1989), 181–187

15. Bertaux, J.L. and Blamont, J.E., Interpretation of Ogo 5 Lyman alpha measurements in the upper geocorona, J. Geophys. Res., **78** (1973), 80–91

16. van der Meer, J-C. and Cushman, R., Orbiting dust under radiation pressure, in: "Differential Geometric Methods in Theoretical Physics", 403–414, ed. H. Doebner, World Scientific, Singapore, 1987

17. Conley, C., On some new long periodic solutions of the plane restricted three body problem, Comm. Pure Appl. Math., **41** (1963), 449–467

18. Kummer, M., On the stability of Hill's solutions of the planar restricted three body problem, Amer. J. Math., **101** (1979), 1333–1345

19. Kummer, M., On the 3-dimensional lunar problem and other perturbations of the Kepler problem, J. Math. Anal. Appl., **93** (1983), 142–194

20. van der Meer, J-C. and Cushman, R., Constrained normalization of Hamiltonian systems and perturbed Keplerian motion, J. Appl. Math. and Phys. (ZAMP), **37** (1986), 402–424

21. Brouwer, D., Solution of the problem of artificial satellite theory without drag, Astron. J., **64** (1959), 378–397

22. Orlov, V.V., Almost circular periodic motions of a particle of matter under the gravitational attraction of a spheroid, Reports of the state astronomical institute in Shternberg, no. 88–89, Moscow University, 1953

23. Eckstein, M., Shi, Y., and Kevorkian, J., Satellite motion for all inclinations around an oblate planet, in: IAU Symposium 25, 291–322, ed. G. Contopoulos, Academic Press, London, 1966

24. Cushman, R., Reduction, Brouwer's Hamiltonian and the critical inclination, Celest. Mech., **31** (1983), 409–429; errata Celest. Mech., **33** (1984), 297

25. Coffey, S., Deprit, A., and Miller, B., The critical inclination in artificial satellite theory, Celest. Mech., **39** (1986), 365–405

26. Cushman, R., An analysis of the critical inclination problem using singularity theory, Celest. Mech., **42** (1988), 39–51

27. Moser, J., Regularization of Kepler's problem and the averaging method on a manifold, Comm. Pure Appl. Math., **23** (1970), 604–636

28. Milnor, J., On the geometry of the Kepler problem, Amer. Math. Monthly, **90** (1983), 353–365

29. Weinstein, A., Poisson structures and Lie algebras, in: "The Mathematical Heritage of Élie Cartan", Asterique (1985), Numéro Hors Sèrie, 421–434

30. Deprit, A., Canonical transformations depending on a parameter, Celest. Mech., **1** (1969), 12–30

31. Baider, A., and Churchill, R., The Campbell Baker Hausdorff group, Pac. J. Math., **131** (1988), 219–235

32. Arnold, V., "Geometrical Methods in the Theory of Ordinary Differential Equations", Grundl. Math. Wiss., vol. 260, Springer Verlag, New York, 1983
33. Birkhoff, G.D., "Dynamical Systems", AMS colloquium publications, vol. 9, AMS, Providence, 1927; revised ed. 1966
34. Deift, P., Lund, F. and Trubowitz, E., Nonlinear wave equations and constrained harmonic motion, Comm. Math. Phys., 74 (1980), 144–188
35. Moser, J., Geometry of quadrics and spectral theory, in: "The Chern Symposium 1979", 147–188, ed. W.Y. Hsiang, et. al., Springer Verlag, New York, 1980
36. Cushman, R. and Rod, D.L., Reduction of the 1:1 semisimple resonance, Physica D, 6 (1982), 105–112
37. Cushman, R. and Knörrer, H., The energy momentum mapping of the Lagrange top, in: "Differential Geometric Methods in Physics", 12-24, ed. H. Doebner et al., Lecture notes in math., 1139, Springer Verlag, New York, 1985
38. Steenrod, N., "The Topology of Fiber Bundles", Princeton Univ. Press, Princeton, 1951
39. Billera, L., Cushman, R. and Sanders, J., The Stanley decomposition of the harmonic oscillator, Proc. Ned. Akad. Wet., Series A 91 (1988), 375–393
40. Hirsch, M., "Differential Topology", Graduate texts in math., vol. 33, Springer Verlag, New York, 1976
41. Smale, S., Diffeomorphisms of the 2-sphere, Proc. AMS, 10 (1959), 621–629
42. Smale, S., Topology and mechanics, Inventiones Math., 10 (1970), 305–331
43. van der Meer, J-C., On integrability and reduction of normalized perturbed Keplerian systems, preprint, Technical University of Eindhoven, 1988
44. Mumford, D. "Algebraic Geometry I: Complex Projective Varieties", Grundl. Math. Wiss. 221, Springer Verlag, New York, 1976
45. Arbarello, E., Cornalba, M., Griffiths, P.A., and Harris, J., "Geometry of Algebraic Curves I", Springer Verlag, New York, 1985

On Littlewood's Counterexample of Unbounded Motions in Superquadratic Potentials

Mark Levi

1. Introduction

Littlewood [11] constructed an example of an equation of the form $\ddot{x} + V'(x) = p(t)$ with $\frac{V'(x)}{x} \to \infty$ and yet possessing unbounded solutions. This note contains a considerable simplification of Littlewood's construction together with rather precise information on the behavior of $\frac{V'(x)}{x} \to \infty$ under which the resonances of the type constructed by Littlewood are possible. The original construction [11] contained an error, as was pointed out by Yiming Long, who also corrected the original proof [12].

The above equation is a model Hamiltonian system for which the problem of stability (i.e. of the boundedness of solutions for all time) arises in its full difficulty. The Poincaré period map (also called the stroboscopic map) which maps the plane of initial conditions $(x, \dot{x})$ into itself[1] is area-preserving due to the conservative character of the equation. If the potential $V(x)$ happens to be superquadratic, i.e. if it grows faster than x^2 as $|x| \to \infty$, then one might expect that the map possesses a twist at infinity, i.e. that the points that are further from the origin undergo more revolutions during one period of the forcing. In physical rather than the geometrical terms, the twist corresponds to the dependence of the frequency on the amplitude. Intuitively speaking, the twist may be expected to destroy the resonances that could cause the accumulation of energy and thus the unboundedness. By contrast, in the case of a *quadratic* potential, the equation is linear: $\ddot{x} + \omega^2 x = p(t)$, and it is well known that resonances can occur, with the solutions growing without bound. In some examples of superquadratic potentials it has in fact been shown that all solutions stay bounded for all time [3], [4], [14] (see also [10], [18] for the case of potentials periodic in x). The proofs of boundedness all use Moser's twist theorem [7], [15], [19]. The Poincaré-Birkhoff fixed point theorem [2], [5], [9] has also been used to show the existence of periodic solutions [6], [8]. The Aubry-Mather theory and other recent results on

---

[1] This map is well-defined unless the solutions blow up in finite time, as happens, for instance, to all solutions of $\ddot{x} - x^2 = 1$ at both ends of the time interval.

monotone twist maps [1], [9], [13], [16], [17] shed new light on the qualitative behavior of the problem; we do not discuss here the implications of these results for our problem.

2. Results

Returning to the discussion of the construction of an unbounded solution, we will start with the equation

$$\ddot{x} + 4x^3 = p(t) \tag{1}$$

where $p(t) = (-1)^{[t]+1}$, with $[t]$ denoting the integer part of t.

Theorem. *There exists a C^∞-modification $V(x)$ of the potential $V_0(x) = x^4$ satisfying for some $C > c > 0$ the estimates*

$$cx^4 \leq V(x) \leq Cx^4, \quad cx^2 \leq |V'(x)| \leq C|x|^3,$$

such that the equation

$$\ddot{x} + V'(x) = p(t) \tag{2}$$

has an unbounded solution, whose rate of growth, moreover, is given by

$$ct^{\frac{1}{3}} < (\dot{x}^2 + x^4)^{\frac{1}{4}} < Ct^{\frac{1}{3}},$$

where c, C are some constants which can be estimated more explicitly.

Remark 1. A Twist Criterion
We will derive here a simple sufficient condition on the potential for the Poincaré map of an *autonomous* system to possess a twist, and show that this condition is violated by the potential constructed here. Let $z(t) = (x(t), \dot{x}(t))$ be a solution of $\ddot{x} + V'(x) = 0$ in the phase plane, and let $\zeta = (\xi(t), \eta(t))$ be a solution of the system linearized around $z(t)$. Assume that each solution vector $z(t)$ rotates clockwise in the phase plane. The criterion is based on the following geometrical observation, Fig. 2.

Take any solution $z(t)$ and let $\zeta(0)$ be parallel to $z(0)$. If ζ turns clockwise faster than $z(t)$, then the period $T(E)$ of the oscillations is a decreasing function of the energy (or the amplitude, or the area enclosed by the curve). In other words, then the Poincaré map possesses a monotone twist (with radial lines as the reference foliation). Expressing the above idea analytically, we rewrite the condition on the angular velocity in the form

$$\frac{d}{dt}\left(\frac{y}{x}\right) > \frac{d}{dt}\left(\frac{\eta}{\xi}\right), \quad \text{whenever} \quad \frac{y}{x} = \frac{\eta}{\xi}.$$

Using the governing equations $\dot{x} = y, \dot{y} = -V'(x), \quad \dot{\xi} = \eta, \dot{\eta} = -V''(x)\xi$, the above criterion reduces to

$$\frac{V'}{x} < V''.$$

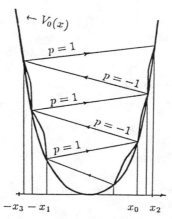

Fig. 1. Resonance conditions and the modification of the potential. Each arrow represents an odd number of swings which takes exacly one half-period. If the graph of $V_0 \equiv x^4$ is replaced by $U_0 = V_0(x) \pm x$, then the arrows marked $p = \mp 1$ become horizontal.

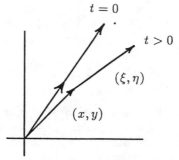

Fig. 2. A sufficient condition for monotone twist: any solution vector turns slower than the collinear to it linearized solution vector.

This twist condition is violated by the modifications of the potential below, as one can see easily from the fact that V'' changes sign as $x \to \infty$ while V' does not.

Physical interpretation of the above twist criterion. We will give the physical meaning to both sides of the last inequality. To that end, we think of the equation $\ddot{x} = -V'(x)$ as governing the oscillations of a particle moving along the x-axis subject to the restoring force $-V'$ of a nonlilnear spring. The geometrical property of a twist translates into the physical property of the frequency of oscillations growing monotonically with the amplitude. Since there is zero twist for linear springs ($V' = const \cdot x$), we expect there to be a twist for springs for which V' is superlinear; the last word is, in fact, made precise by the last inequality, which we finally proceed to interpret physically. Fixing x_0, we interpret $\frac{V'(x_0)}{x_0} \equiv k(x_0)$ as the "cumulative" Hooke's constant of the spring at x_0, i.e. as the Hooke's constant of an imagined linear spring whose force is $k(x_0)x$ when the elongation is x. (In particular, the imagined spring has the same tension

$V'(x_0)$ as the given one at $x = x_0$.) On the other hand, $V''(x_0)$ is the "local" Hooke's constant which measures the increment of the tension force $V'(x)$ per unit change of x at $x = x_0$. We can now restate the above twist condition as saying:

If the global Hooke's constant $\frac{V'(x_0)}{x_0}$ is greater than the local Hooke's constant $V''(x_0)$ for all x_0, then the period of oscillations is a monotonically decreasing function of the energy.

3. Proof of the Theorem

In the first subsection we outline the idea of the construction; the details are carried out in later subsections.

3.1 An Outline of the Construction

Referring to Fig. 1, we start with $x_0 > 0$ chosen so that the solution $x(t)$ with an initial condition $x(0) = x_0$, $\dot{x}(0) = 0$ swings left and stops at $x < 0$ at $t = 1$, i.e. with $x(1) \equiv -x_1 < 0$, $\dot{x}(1) = 0$. We will modify $V_0(x) \equiv x^4$ in such a way that the solution $x(t)$ of the equation (2) is in resonance with $p(t)$:

$$x(2n) \equiv x_{2n} > 0, \quad \dot{x}(2n) = 0, \tag{3a}$$

$$x(2n+1) \equiv -x_{2n+1} < 0, \quad \dot{x}(2n+1) = 0, \tag{3b}$$

for all integers $n \geq 0$. The modification of x^4 will preserve the values of V_0 at the points $(-1)^k x_k$ where the solution turns around, i.e. $V((-1)^k x_k) = x_k^4$ for all integers $k \geq 0$. Once the potential $V_0(x) = x^4$ has been modified to achieve the resonance conditions (3), the unboundedness of the solution $x(t)$ follows at once. Indeed, during the first half-periods, when $2n \leq t \leq 2n + 1$, we have $p = -1$ and thus $\frac{\dot{x}^2}{2} + V(x) + x = \text{const.}$, while for the second half-periods $2n + 1 \leq t \leq 2n + 2$ we have $\frac{\dot{x}^2}{2} + V(x) - x = \text{const.}$ Using these conservation relations for the endpoints $t = 2n$ and $t = 2n + 1$, we obtain:

$$V(x_{2n}) + x_{2n} = V(-x_{2n+1}) + (-x_{2n+1}),$$

$$V(-x_{2n+1}) - (-x_{2n+1}) = V(x_{2n+2}) - (x_{2n+2}),$$

both of which yield the same relation

$$x_{k+1}^4 - x_k^4 = x_k + x_{k+1}, \tag{4}$$

where $V((-1)^k x_k) = x_k^4$ was used. This difference equation says simply that the net gain in potential energy V during each half-period equals the product of the external force $p(t) = (-1)^{k+1}$ acting during k-th half-period and the net distance $x(k+1) - x(k) = (-1)^{k+1} x_{k+1} - (-1)^k x_k = (-1)^{k+1}(x_{k+1} + x_k)$ traveled during that half-period, i.e. $x_{k+1} + x_k$. This energy gain is the key idea of Littlewood's example. It should be pointed out that the difference equation (4) defines the sequence $x_k > 0$ uniquely for any $x_0 > 0$, so that from now on the x_k's are the fixed quantities. The following lemma implies in particular that Eq. (4) and thus the resonance conditions (3) imply the unboundedness of $x(t)$.

Lemma 1. *Any positive sequence $\{x_k\}$ with $x_0 > 0$ defined by the recurrence relation (4) satisfies the following estimates, for some $C > c > 0$, with $c = c(x_0)$, $C = C(x_0)$:*

$$ck^{\frac{1}{3}} < x_k < Ck^{\frac{1}{3}}, \tag{5a}$$

$$x_{k+1} - x_k < Ck^{-\frac{2}{3}}, \tag{5b}$$

$$cn^{\frac{4}{3}} < \sum_0^n x_k < Cn^{\frac{4}{3}}, \tag{5c}$$

$$cx_k < x_{k+2}^4 - x_k^4 < Cx_k, \tag{5d}$$

$$1 < \frac{x_{k+1}}{x_k} < C, \tag{5e}$$

for all $k \geq 1$.

The proof of the lemma is given in Sect. 3.5 below. At this stage we use only the implication that $x_k \to \infty$.

Remark 2. Avoiding virtually all computation, one can easily produce a modification of the potential x^4 satisfying the resonance conditions (4); this argument, however, does not resolve the main difficulty, which is to estimate the minimal necesary size of the modification, and in particular to see if one can keep the property $\frac{V'}{x} \to \infty$. To describe the argument, we start with Eq. (1) and choose the initial position x_0 so that the solution makes exactly one swing during the first half of the period, arriving at $-x_1$. If the potential is left unmodified, the solution will make more than one full swing during the second half period: it will reach the point x_2 defined above at least once. The potential can be modified in the interval $[x_0, x_2]$ in such a way that the solution is slowed down so that the point x_2 is reached exactly at the end of the period. A simple argument based on the superquadratic character of x^4 shows that during the next half-period the solution will again make at least one trip from x_2 to $-x_3$. By modifying V in the interval $[-x_1, -x_3]$ (by making $V'(x_3)$ small enough) we slow the solution down so that $x(3) = -x_3$, etc., thus achieving the resonance conditions. This argument is, however, too crude as it gives no estimate on the how small a change of V would suffice to slow the solution. It should be pointed out also that speeding the solution up rather than slowing it down cannot produce the resonance condition.

3.2 Modification of the Potential

The potential $V_0 = x^4$ will be modified inductively on the intervals I_n given by $I_{2k} = [x_{2k}, x_{2k+2}]$ and $I_{2k+1} = [-x_{2k+3}, -x_{2k+1}]$, $k \geq 0$, by replacing x^4 on I_n by a piecewise linear function as shown in Fig. 1 and as described below. We concentrate on the case of an even interval, I_{2n}; odd intervals are treated in the same way. Assume that the modification of the potential has been carried out in all previous intervals I_k, $k \leq 2n$ in such a way as to achieve the resonance conditions (3) and satisfying the growth estimates stated in the theorem on the interval $[-x_{2n-1}, x_{2n}]$. We will change the potential x^4 into a piecewise linear continuous function on the interval I_{2n}, with the slopes σ_1 and σ on the left and the right halves of I_{2n} respectively. The slope σ will serve as the parameter with which we will achieve the resonance condition. To make the modification of the potential more explicit, we denote $\xi = x - x_{2n+2}$, $a = x_{2n+2} - x_{2n}$, $b = x_{2n+2}^4 - x_{2n}^4$, (subscripts for a and b are omitted), and define $V_\sigma(x) = x_{2n+2}^4 + W(\xi)$, where

$$W(\xi) = \begin{cases} \sigma\xi & \text{for } -\frac{a}{2} \leq \xi \leq 0 \\ -b + \sigma_1(\xi + a) & \text{for } -a \leq \xi \leq -\frac{a}{2} \end{cases} ;$$

the slope σ is the parameter with which we will control the arrival time at the end of the period, and $\sigma_1 = \frac{2b}{a} - \sigma$. This modification $V_\sigma(x)$ of the potential on I_{2n} is continuous; it can be smoothed to a C^∞-function in small neighborhoods of the corners while preserving the statement of Lemma 2 below. This smoothing is described in the proof of that lemma.

3.3 Proof of the Resonance Condition

According to our inductive assumption, the resonance equations (3) hold for all x_k with $k \leq 2n + 1$ and $V'(x)/x > cx$ in the interval $-x_{2n-1} < x < x_{2n}$, with some $c > 0$ independent of n. Our aim is to show that for some $\sigma = \sigma^*$ the next resonance condition at $t = 2n + 2$ is satisfied. To that end, consider the vector $z_\sigma = (x_\sigma(2n + 2), \dot{x}_\sigma(2n + 2))$ at which the solution $(x_\sigma(t), \dot{x}_\sigma(t))$ in question finds itself at $t = 2n + 2$ (after making many oscillations, i.e. when n is large, during the preceding time interval of length one). We have to chose $\sigma = \sigma^*$ so that z_{σ^*} lies on the positive x-axis. To prove that such a choice exists, we will show that z_σ makes one full revolution as σ decreases from $\sigma = \sigma_0 \equiv \frac{b}{a}$; denoting by $\tau(\sigma)$ the time of a one-way swing (which is one half of the period of oscillation of the solution of $\ddot{x} + V_\sigma(x) = 1$ starting at $(x, \dot{x}) = (-x_{2n+1}, 0)$), we observe that if for some $\sigma < \sigma_0$ the numbers of one-way swings differ by at least two, or more precisely, if

$$\frac{1}{\tau(\sigma_0)} - \frac{1}{\tau(\sigma)} \geq 2, \tag{6}$$

that is

$$\tau(\sigma) - \tau(\sigma_0) \geq 2\tau(\sigma)\tau(\sigma_0), \tag{7}$$

then for some σ^* in $\sigma < \sigma^* < \sigma_0$ we have the desired resonance condition. To show that the modified potential satisfies the estimate $V'(X) > cx^2$, in addition to the resonance conditions (3), it suffices to show that Eq. (7) holds with $\sigma \approx x^2$ – more precisely, with some σ in $cx_{2n}^2 < \sigma < Cx_{2n}^2$, with c, C independent of n. Indeed, then for any , say, positive, x we have $x_{2n} \leq x \leq x_{2n+2}$. Then $\sigma > cx_{2n}^2 = c(\frac{x_{2n}}{x})^2 x^2 \geq c(\frac{x_{2n}}{x_{2n+2}})^2 x^2 \geq c_1 x^2$, using (5e) in the last inequality. It remains, thus, to prove that (7) holds with such σ. We do so by estimating both sides of (7) in (8) and (9) below.

Lemma 2. *With the modification of the potential on the interval I_{2n} described above there exist constants $C > c > 0$ independent of n and x_0 such that for all $0 < \sigma \leq \sigma_0$ the times $\tau(\sigma)$ of one-way trips (for $p = 1$) of the solution starting at $(-x_{2n+1}, 0)$ satisfy the estimates*

$$\sqrt{a}(2(\sigma-1)^{-\frac{1}{2}} - \sqrt{2}(\sigma_0-1)^{-\frac{1}{2}}) > \tau(\sigma) - \tau(\sigma_0) > \sqrt{a}((\sigma-1)^{-\frac{1}{2}} - \sqrt{2}(\sigma_0-1)^{-\frac{1}{2}}),$$
(8)

where $a = x_{2n+2} - x_{2n}$ and

$$\tau(\sigma_0) < Kx_{2n}^{-1},$$
(9)

for some K independent of n. Furthermore, there exists a C^∞-smoothing of the potential which still satisfies the above estimates.

The lemma is proven in Sect. 3.6 below.

3.4 End of Proof of the Theorem

To verify the inequality (7) it suffices to make sure that the lower bound on $\tau(\sigma) - \tau(\sigma_0)$ is strictly greater than the upper bound on $2\tau(\sigma)\tau(\sigma_0)$. Substituting the bounds from (8) and (9), this amounts to

$$\sqrt{a}((\sigma-1)^{-\frac{1}{2}} - \sqrt{2}\sigma_0 - 1^{-\frac{1}{2}}) > 2Kx_{2n}^{-1}(Kx_{2n}^{-1} + \sqrt{a}(2(\sigma-1)^{-\frac{1}{2}} - \sqrt{2}(\sigma_0-1)^{-\frac{1}{2}})).$$

This inequality reduces to an equivalent one

$$(\sigma-1)^{-\frac{1}{2}}(1 - 4Kx_{2n}^{-1}) > 2K^2 a^{-\frac{1}{2}} x_{2n}^{-2} + \sqrt{2}(\sigma_0-1)^{-\frac{1}{2}} - 2\sqrt{2}Kx_{2n}^{-1}(\sigma_0-1)^{-\frac{1}{2}}.$$
(10)

The first term in the right-hand side in (10) is the leading one, and is on the order of x_{2n}^{-1}, so that the last inequality should be satisfied with a choice of $\sigma \approx x^2$. To make this precise, we use the estimates $a \equiv x_{2n+2} - x_{2n} > cx_{2n}^{-2}$ and $\sigma_0 = \frac{b}{a} > cx_{2n}^3$ from Lemma 1 (Eqs. (4), (5d), (5e)) to conclude that the right-hand side of (10) is exceeded by Cx_{2n}^{-1}. Taking x_0 so large that the coefficient $1 - 4Kx_{2n}^{-1} > \frac{1}{2}$, we conclude that for some constant C independent of n, (10) and thus (6) hold if $0 < \sigma - 1 \leq Cx_{2n}^2$. This proves that Littlewood's counterexample can be implemented with the quadratic lower bound: $cx^2 < V'$, as explained in the paragraph preceding the statement of Lemma 2. The upper estimate $V' < Cx^3$ is obvious from the fact that the slope of x^4 is not more than doubled in our construction. We emphasize that the choice of x_0 was made independently of n. To complete the proof of the theorem, it remains to observe that the estimates $cx^4 < V(x) < Cx^4$ and $ct^{\frac{1}{3}} < (\dot{x}^2 + x^4)^{\frac{1}{4}} < ct^{\frac{1}{3}}$ follow directly from the above estimates.

3.5 Proof of Lemma 1

We prove (5a); the other inequalities follow trivially from this one and from (4). Given any $x_k > 0$, the recurrence relation defines the next positive value x_{k+1} uniquely; furthermore, $x_k < x_{k+1}$. The recurrence relation (4) gives $x_{k+1}^4(1 - x_{k+1}^{-3}) = x_k^4(1 + x_k^{-3})$, and thus

$$1 < \left(\frac{x_{k+1}}{x_k}\right)^4 = \frac{1 + x_k^{-3}}{1 - x_{k+1}^{-3}} < \frac{1 + x_0^{-3}}{1 - x_0^{-3}} \equiv r^4 \,;$$

using (4) again, we obtain a homogeneous expression in x_k, x_{k+1} for the difference

$$
\begin{aligned}
x_{k+1}^3 - x_k^3 &= \frac{(x_k + x_{k+1})(x_k^2 + x_k x_{k+1} + x_{k+1}^2)}{(x_k^3 + x_k^2 x_{k+1} + x_k x_{k+1}^2 + x_{k+1}^3)} \\
&= \frac{(1 + \rho_k)(1 + \rho_k + \rho_k^2)}{(1 + \rho_k + \rho_k^2 + \rho_k^3)} \equiv Q(\rho_k)\,.
\end{aligned}
$$

Since $Q(\rho)$ is a decreasing function for $\rho > 1$, and since $1 < \rho_k < r$ by the first estimate, we conclude that $\frac{3}{2} = Q(1) > x_{k+1}^3 - x_k^3 > Q(r) > 1$. Adding these inequalities for $k = 0, 1, ..., n - 1$, we obtain

$$\frac{3}{2}n > x_n^3 - x_0^3 > Q(r)n\,,$$

which proves (5a). All other estimates (5b–e) follow easily; actually, (5e) has been proven already.

3.6 Proof of Lemma 2

To prove the estimate (8) we note that the potentials V_σ and V_{σ_0} differ only on the interval I_{2n} and thus $\tau(\sigma) - \tau(\sigma_0)$ equals the difference $T(\sigma) - T(\sigma_0)$ of the times it takes the solution to cross the interval I_{2n} once. It is easy (but a little messy) to compute $T(\sigma)$ explicitly; instead of doing that we write $T(\sigma) = T_1(\sigma) + T_2(\sigma)$ as the sum of the times it takes for the solution to cross the first and the second halves of I_{2n}, and observe that $T_1(\sigma) < T_2(\sigma)$ (if $0 < \sigma < \sigma_0$, which we assume throughout), so that $T_2(\sigma) < T(\sigma) < 2T_2(\sigma)$, and only T_2 has to be estimated. One computes easily that

$$T_2(\sigma) = \sqrt{a}(\sigma - 1)^{-\frac{1}{2}}\,, \tag{11}$$

and $T(\sigma_0) = \sqrt{2a}(\sigma_0 - 1)^{-\frac{1}{2}}$. The last three estimates yield (8) at once.

The validity of the estimate (9) is suggested by the fact that it holds for the unmodified potential $U_0(x) = x^4 - x$, as one can check by estimating the period of one oscillation given by the derivative $\frac{\partial A(E)}{\partial E}$ of the area of the level curve with respect to the energy. However, we have to make sure that the cumulative effect of the changes to the potential on successive intervals I_k does not violate this asymptotic behavior. This can be done following Littlewood, by adding-up the times the solution spends in each of the intervals I_k; this is done in the appendix.

An alternative, slightly shorter method is to show that the ratios of these times to the times in the unmodified potential are all bounded uniformly in n. We give yet another much shorter method; it is based on a comparison idea, sketched in Fig. 3. By its definition, $\tau(\sigma_0)$ is the time of one one-way trip (when $p = 1$) in the potential $V(x) = V_{\sigma_0}(x)$ that has been modified on the intervals I_k, $k < 2n$, and is linear: $V' = \sigma_0$ on I_{2n}. For $p(t) = 1$ we have $\frac{1}{2}\dot{x}^2 + U(x) = $ const., where $U(x) = V(x) - x$, and

$$\tau(\sigma_0) = \int_{-x_{2n+1}}^{x_{2n+2}} \frac{dx}{\sqrt{U(x_{2n+2}) - U(x)}} \, .$$

To estimate this integral, we break it up into the sum

$$\tau(\sigma_0) = \left(\int_{-x_{2n+1}}^{-x_{2n-1}} + \int_{x_{2n}}^{x_{2n+2}} + \int_{-x_{2n-1}}^{x_{2n}} \right) \frac{dx}{\sqrt{U(x_{2n+2}) - U(x)}}$$

of the times of crossing the two extreme intervals I_{2n-1} and I_{2n} and the rest, Fig. 3.

We observe that the second integral is just $T(\sigma_0)$, which was essentially estimated in (11). Specifically,

$$T(\sigma_0) < 2T_2(\sigma_0) = \sqrt{x_{2n+2} - x_{2n}}(\sigma_0 - 1)^{-\frac{1}{2}} \leq cx_{2n}^{-\frac{5}{2}} \, ,$$

where we used (5d,e) to estimate $x_{2n+2} - x_{2n} \leq cx_{2n}^{-2}$ and (5e) to estimate $\sigma_0 > x_{2n}^3$. The first integral is estimated in the same way with the same result; the estimate depends only on the inductive assumption $\frac{V'}{x} > cx$ which is valid on I_{2n-1} and on the length of that interval estimated by Lemma 1 with the constants independent of n. With our goal (9) in mind, the end intervals make a negligible contribution to the time of one trip. The main difficulty is to estimate the integral over the middle interval and it is here that the main simplification is achieved. We introduce the auxiliary potential $P(x) = U_0(x) + U(x_{2n+2}) - U(x_{2n})$ where $U_0 = V_0(x) - x \equiv x^4 - x$, and note that $P(x) > U(x)$ on $-x_{2n-1} < x < x_{2n}$, as follows from the fact that the jumps $U(x_{k+2}) - U(x_k)$ are increasing with k (see Fig. 3). Comparison with the new potential P gives

$$\int_{-x_{2n-1}}^{x_{2n}} \frac{dx}{\sqrt{U(x_{2n+2}) - U(x)}} < \int_{-x_{2n-1}}^{x_{2n}} \frac{dx}{\sqrt{U_0(x_{2n+2}) - P(x)}}$$
$$= \int_{-x_{2n-1}}^{x_{2n}} \frac{dx}{\sqrt{U_0(x_{2n}) - U_0(x)}} \, .$$

The last integral represents the time of one swing in the potential $U_0(x) = x^4 - x$ (Fig. 3), and thus is bounded by $\frac{c}{x_{2n}}$, as a simple comparison with the motion in a quartic potential shows. It remains to observe that the potential can be smoothed to a C^∞-function in arbitrarily small neighborhoods of the points where the slope of V jumps in such a way that the effect on the times τ is arbitrarily small.

This completes the proof of Lemma 2.

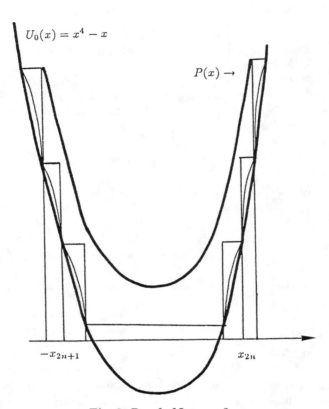

$$U_0(x) = x^4 - x$$

$$P(x) \rightarrow$$

$$-x_{2n+1} \qquad x_{2n}$$

Fig. 3. Proof of Lemma 2

3.7 Appendix: An Alternative Proof of the Estimate on $\tau(\sigma)$

This is essentially the original proof of Littlewood. To estimate $\tau(\sigma)$, we add up the contributions of each subinterval between $\pm x_k$ and $\pm x_{k+2}$; the integrals over the two extreme intervals I_{2n} and I_{2n-1} are bounded by $C x_{2n}^{-2}$, as shown above, and thus are insignificant, with the same result for the middle interval $[-x_1, x_0]$. The main contribution therefore comes from the remaining sum. Breaking up the integral in the way just indicated, we obtain

$$\tau(\sigma_0) = \left(\int_{-x_{2n+1}}^{-x_{2n-1}} + \int_{x_{2n}}^{x_{2n+2}} + \int_{-x_1}^{x_0} + \sum_{k=1}^{n-1} \int_{-x_{2k+1}}^{-x_{2k-1}} + \sum_{k=0}^{n-1} \int_{x_{2k}}^{x_{2k+2}} \right)$$
$$\times \frac{dx}{\sqrt{U(x_{2n+2}) - U(x)}} ,$$

and it remains to prove the bound (9) on the remaining two sums; we do it for the first one. We replace each integrand by its maximum over the interval of integration, and estimate the resulting greater sum

$$\sum_{k=1}^{n-1} \frac{x_{2k+1} - x_{2k-1}}{\sqrt{U(x_{2n+2}) - U(x_{2k-1})}} + \sum_{k=0}^{n-1} \frac{x_{2k+2} - x_{2k}}{\sqrt{U(x_{2n+2}) - U(x_{2k})}} . \qquad (12)$$

We replaced $U(x)$ by its maximum on each interval I_k, using the fact that U is increasing for $x > 0$ and decreasing for $x < 0$. The numerators of each summand in (12) are bounded by $Ck^{-\frac{2}{3}}$, according to Lemma 1. To estimate the denominators we first note that $U(x_{2k}) = x_{2k}^4 - x_{2k}$, while $U(x_{2k+1}) = x_{2k+1}^4 + x_{2k+1}$. Adding up the recurrence relations for the sequence $\{x_k\}$, we obtain the expressions for the denominators in (12) as the sums (we abbreviate $2n + 2 = m$):

$$U(x_m) - U(x_{2k-1}) = (x_{2n+1}^4 + x_{2n+1}) - (x_{2k+1}^4 + x_{2k+1}) = 2 \sum_{j=2k+2}^{2n+1} x_j, \quad (13a)$$

$$U(x_m) - U(x_{2k}) = (x_m^4 - x_m) - (x_{2k}^4 - x_{2k}) = 2 \sum_{j=2k}^{2n+1} x_j. \quad (13b)$$

We bound these sums from below using the estimates $x_k \geq ck^{\frac{1}{3}}$ from Lemma 1, together with the inequality $\sum_{j=l}^{m} j^{\frac{1}{3}} > \frac{3}{4} m^{\frac{4}{3}} \left(1 - \left(\frac{l}{m}\right)^{\frac{4}{3}}\right)$ which one obtains by observing that it is an upper Riemann sum for the integral $m^{\frac{4}{3}} \int_{\frac{l}{m}}^{1} x^{\frac{1}{3}} dx$. Substitution of these estimates in (13a) gives

$$\sum_{j=2k+2}^{2n+1} x_j > C(2n+1)^{\frac{4}{3}} \left(1 - \left(\frac{2k+2}{2n+1}\right)^{\frac{4}{3}}\right).$$

Using this in the denominator of the first sum in (12) results in the upper bound for that sum:

$$C \sum_{k=1}^{n-1} (k+1)^{-\frac{2}{3}} (2n+1)^{-\frac{2}{3}} \left(1 - \left(\frac{2k+2}{2n+1}\right)^{\frac{4}{3}}\right)^{-\frac{1}{2}}.$$

Letting $\frac{k+1}{2n+1} = t_k$ and $\Delta t_k \equiv \frac{1}{2n+1}$, we note that the above sum is less than

$$(2n+1)^{-\frac{2}{3}} \sum_{t_k=\frac{2}{2n+1}}^{\frac{n}{2n+1}} t_k^{-\frac{2}{3}} (1-(2t_k)^{\frac{4}{3}})^{-\frac{1}{2}} \Delta t_k < 2(2n+1)^{-\frac{1}{3}} \int_0^{\frac{1}{2}} t^{-\frac{2}{3}} (1-(2t)^{\frac{4}{3}})^{-\frac{1}{2}} dt.$$

Since $(2n+1)^{-\frac{1}{3}} < Cx_k^{-1}$, this estimate gives the desired bound on the first sum in (12). The second sum is estimated in the same way. This proves Lemma 2 (again).

Acknowledgement. I am grateful to the Forschungsinstitut für Mathematik, where this work has been carried out, for its hospitality. I would like to thank Jürgen Moser for encouraging me to write down these remarks and for pointing out some errors in the manuscript, and the referee for very useful remarks to help improve the exposition.

References

1. S. Aubry, P. Y. LeDaeron, The discrete Frenkel-Kontorova model and its extensions I: Exact results for the ground states. Physica **8D** (1983), 381–422
2. G.D. Birkhoff, Dynamical Systems. AMS Colloq. Publ., vol. IX, 1966, 165–169
3. R. Dieckerhoff and E. Zehnder, An "a priori" estimate for oscillatory equation. Dyn. Systems and Bifurcations, Groningen, 1984. LNM 1125. Springer, Berlin New York 1985, pp. 9–14
4. R. Dieckerhoff and E. Zehnder, Boundedness of solution via the twist-theorem. Ann. Scuola Norm. Sup. Pisa **14**(1) 1987, 79–75
5. J. Franks, Generalization of the Poincaré-Birkhoff Theorem, to appear in Annals of Math.
6. P. Hartman, On boundary value problems for superlinear second order differential equations. JDE **26** (1977), 37–53
7. M. R. Herman, Sur les courbes invariantes par des difféomorphismes de l'anneau, vol. 1, Astérisque 103–104, 1983 and vol. 2, Astérisque 144, 1986
8. H. Jacobowitz, R.A. Struble, Periodic solutions of $x'' + f(x,t) = 0$ via the Poincaré-Birkhoff Theorem. J. Diff. Eq. **20** (1976), no. 1, 37–52. Corrigendum: The existence of the second fixed point: a correction to "Periodic solutions..." above, J.D.E. **25** (1977), no. 1, 148–149
9. A. Katok, Some remarks on the Birkhoff and Mather twist theorems. Erg. Th. Dyn. Sys. **2** (1982), 183–194
10. M. Levi, KAM theory for particles in periodic potentials, Erg. Th. Dyn. Sys. **10** (1990), 777–785
11. J.E. Littlewood, Unbounded solutions of an equation $\ddot{y} + g(y) = p(t)$, with $p(t)$ periodic and bounded, and $\frac{g(y)}{y} \to \infty$ as $y \to \pm\infty$. J. Lond. Math. Soc. **41** (1966), 497–507
12. Y. Long, an unbounded solution of a superlinear Duffing's equation. Research report, Nankai Institute of Mathematics, Nankai University, Tianjin, China, June 1989
13. J.N. Mather, Existence of quasi-periodic orbits for twist homeomorphisms of the annulus. Topology **21** (1982), 457–476
14. G.R. Morris, A case of boundedness in Littlewood's problem on oscillatory differential equation. Bull. Austr. Math. Soc. **14** (1976), 71–93
15. J.K. Moser, On invariant curves of area-preserving mappings of an annulus. Nachr. Akad. Wiss. Göttingen, Math.-Phys. Kl. II (1962), 1–20
16. J.K. Moser, Break-down of stability. Lect. Notes in Phys. 247, J.M. Jowett, M. Month and S. Turner (eds.), Springer, Berlin New York, 1986 pp. 492–518
17. J.K. Moser, Monotone twist mappings and the calculus of variations. To appear in Erg. Th. Dyn. Sys.
18. J.K. Moser, A stability theorem for minimal foliations on a torus. Erg. Th. Dyn. Sys. (1988)8*, 251–281
19. H. Rüssmann, Über invariante Kurven differenzierbarer Abbildungen eines Kreisringes. Nachr. Akad. Wiss. Göttingen, Math.-Phys. Kl. II (1970), 67–105

Center Manifold Theory in Infinite Dimensions

A. Vanderbauwhede
G. Iooss

1. Introduction

Center manifold theory forms one of the cornerstones of the theory of dynamical systems. This is already true for finite-dimensional systems, but it holds a fortiori in the infinite-dimensional case. In its simplest form center manifold theory reduces the study of a system near a (non-hyperbolic) equilibrium point to that of an ordinary differential equation on a low-dimensional invariant center manifold. For finite-dimensional systems this means a (sometimes considerable) reduction of the dimension, leading to simpler calculations and a better geometric insight. When the starting point is an infinite-dimensional problem, such as a partial, a functional or an integro differential equation, then the reduction forms also a qualitative simplification. Indeed, most infinite-dimensional systems lack some of the nice properties which we use almost automatically in the case of finite-dimensional flows. For example, the initial value problem may not be well posed, or backward solutions may not exist; and one has to worry about the domains of operators or the regularity of solutions. Therefore the reduction to a finite-dimensional center manifold, when it is possible, forms a most welcome tool, since it allows us to recover the familiar and easy setting of an ordinary differential equation.

Center manifolds for infinite-dimensional systems have been studied in many different settings and by many different authors; let us just mention here the work of Henry [14], Chow and Lu [6,7], Iooss [16], Bates and Jones [2], Kirchgässner [20], Fischer [10], Mielke [22,23,24] and Scarpellini [29]. In a recent paper [31] one of us gave a comprehensive treatment of finite-dimensional center manifold theory, using the exponential asymptotic growth rate of the solutions explicitly in the definitions and in the formulations of the results. The aim of this paper is to describe some minimal conditions which allow to generalize the approach of [31] to infinite-dimensional systems. By isolating the difficulties and reducing as much as possible the unavoidable technicalities we have tried to present the theory in a form which more or less parallels the one given in [31]. This allows us to refer to [31] for part of the proofs.

As for the technicalities our main treatment uses only some elementary spectral theory and avoids the use of semigroups (either analytical or strongly continuous); the only place where semigroups and fractional powers come into play is at the end of Sect. 3, when we compare our hypotheses with some of the classical settings for this kind of problems. Besides our didactical purpose there is a second reason for avoiding semigroups: our treatment also covers cases where the spectrum is unbounded both to the left and to the right of the imaginary axis, and which therefore do not allow a semigroup approach. Center manifold theory for this type of problems was first introduced by Kirchgässner [20] and has recently been fully developed by Mielke [22,23,24]. Our main results are merely reformulations of some of this work, which has motivated and inspired us to a large extend.

In Sect. 2 we describe the setting and give some general and abstract hypothesis which allows to develop a basic center manifold theory (existence and smoothness). The main differences with [31] in the formulation of the results arise from the fact that here we do not assume that the initial value problem is well posed. We also pay some attention to the cut-off problem and to problems with parameters. In Sect. 3 we study a number of spectral hypotheses on the linear part of the equation which imply the abstract hypothesis of Sect. 2 and therefore the applicability of the center manifold theory. In Sect. 4 we show how our hypotheses can be verified for some simple examples, including a parabolic, an elliptic and a hyperbolic equation. These examples are certainly not new, and specialists know quite well why center manifold theory works in situations much more general than the ones treated here. Our reason for including these examples is mainly didactical, and intended towards the non-specialists. We want to show how center manifolds appear in a number of different situations, and illustrate some elementary techniques which allow to verify the necessary hypotheses. For one of the examples we also show how the center manifold can be used to obtain bifurcation results. The applications treated in Sect. 5 are more substantial, and involve evolutionary and stationary Navier-Stokes equations. Because of the technicalities involved we just describe the set-up and survey the further reduction to a center manifold, referring the reader to the literature for details and applications.

Acknowledgement. We like to thank the referees for their careful reading of the manuscript and for their constructive remarks.

2. General Theory

2.1 Main Theorems

Let X, Y and Z be Banach spaces, with X continuously embedded in Y, and Y continuously embedded in Z. In most applications the embeddings will be dense, but (except when explicitly stated) we do not need this for our theory. Let $A \in \mathcal{L}(X, Z)$ and $g \in C^k(X, Y)$ for some $k \geq 1$. We will consider differential equations of the form

$$\dot{x} = Ax + g(x). \tag{1}$$

By a solution of (1) we mean a continuously differentiable mapping $x : I \to Z$, where I is an open interval, and such that the following properties hold:

(i) $x(t) \in X, \forall t \in I$, and $x : I \to X$ is continuous;

(ii) $\dot{x}(t) = Ax(t) + g(x(t)), \forall t \in I$.

Definitions and notations. Let E and F be Banach spaces, $V \subset E$ an open subset, $k \in \mathbf{N}$ and $\eta \geq 0$. Then we define

$$C_b^k(V; F) := \left\{ w \in C^k(V; F) \mid |w|_{j,V} := \sup_{x \in V} \|D^j w(x)\| < \infty, 0 \leq j \leq k \right\},$$

and

$$C_b^{0,1}(E; F) := \left\{ w \in C^{0,1}(E; F) \mid |w|_{\mathrm{Lip}} := \sup_{x,y \in E, x \neq y} \frac{\|w(x) - w(y)\|}{\|x - y\|} < \infty \right\}.$$

In case $V = E$ we write $|w|_j$ for $|w|_{j,E}$.

We also define

$$BC^\eta(\mathbf{R}; E) := \left\{ w \in C^0(\mathbf{R}, E) \mid \|w\|_\eta := \sup_{t \in \mathbf{R}} e^{-\eta|t|} \|w(t)\|_E < \infty \right\}.$$

Remark that $BC^\eta(\mathbf{R}; E) \subset BC^\zeta(\mathbf{R}; E)$ if $0 \leq \eta < \zeta$, and that

$$\|w\|_\zeta \leq \|w\|_\eta \quad , \quad \forall w \in BC^\eta(\mathbf{R}; E),$$

i.e. $(BC^\eta(\mathbf{R}, E))_{\eta \geq 0}$ forms a scale of Banach spaces.

In this section we will impose the following basic hypothesis on A.

(H) There exists a continuous projection $\pi_c \in \mathcal{L}(Z; X)$ onto a finite-dimensional subspace $Z_c = X_c \subset X$, such that

$$A\pi_c x = \pi_c Ax \quad , \quad \forall x \in X,$$

and such that if we set

$$Z_h := (I - \pi_c)(Z) \quad , \quad X_h := (I - \pi_c)(X) \quad , \quad Y_h := (I - \pi_c)(Y),$$
$$A_c := A|_{X_c} \in \mathcal{L}(X_c) \quad , \quad A_h := A|_{X_h} \in \mathcal{L}(X_h, Z_h),$$

then the following hold

(i) $\sigma(A_c) \subset i\mathbf{R}$ (where $\sigma(A)$ denotes the spectrum of A);

(ii) there exists some $\beta > 0$ such that for each $\eta \in [0, \beta)$ and for each $f \in BC^\eta(\mathbf{R}; Y_h)$ the linear problem

$$\dot{x}_h = A_h x_h + f(t) \quad , \quad x_h \in BC^\eta(\mathbf{R}; X_h)$$

has a unique solution $x_h = K_h f$, where $K_h \in \mathcal{L}(BC^\eta(\mathbf{R}; Y_h); BC^\eta(\mathbf{R}; X_h))$ for each $\eta \in [0, \beta)$, and

$$\|K_h\|_\eta \leq \gamma(\eta) \quad , \quad \forall \eta \in [0, \beta),$$

for some continuous function $\gamma : [0, \beta) \to \mathbf{R}_+$.

Under the hypothesis (H) we will be interested in solutions of (1) which belong to $BC^\eta(\mathbf{R}; X)$ for some $\eta \in (0, \beta)$. The results which follow characterize such solutions; in the statements we use the notation $\pi_h := I_Z - \pi_c$.

Lemma 1. *Assume* (H) *and* $g \in C_b^0(X, Y)$. *Let* $\widetilde{x} : \mathbf{R} \to X$ *be a solution of (1), and let* $\eta \in (0, \beta)$. *Then the following statements are equivalent:*

(i) $\widetilde{x} \in BC^\eta(\mathbf{R}; X)$;
(ii) $\widetilde{x} \in BC^\zeta(\mathbf{R}; X)$, $\quad \forall \zeta > 0$;
(iii) $\pi_h \widetilde{x} \in C_b^0(\mathbf{R}; X_h)$.

Proof. Let $\widetilde{x}_c := \pi_c \widetilde{x}$ and $\widetilde{x}_h := \pi_h \widetilde{x}$. Then $\widetilde{x}_c$ is a solution of the ordinary differential equation

$$\dot{x}_c = A_c x_c + \pi_c g\left(\widetilde{x}(t)\right), \tag{2}$$

and hence

$$\widetilde{x}_c(t) = e^{A_c t} \widetilde{x}_c(0) + \int_0^t e^{A_c(t-s)} \pi_c g\left(\widetilde{x}(s)\right) ds \quad , \quad \forall t \in \mathbf{R}. \tag{3}$$

Using the fact that $\sigma(A_c) \subset i\,\mathbf{R}$ and that g is globally bounded this easily implies that $\widetilde{x}_c \in BC^\zeta(\mathbf{R}, X_c)$ for all $\zeta > 0$. Similarly, $\widetilde{x}_h$ is a solution of the equation

$$\dot{x}_h = A_h x_h + \pi_h g\left(\widetilde{x}(t)\right). \tag{4}$$

Now $\pi_h g(\widetilde{x}(.)) \in C_b^0(\mathbf{R}; Y_h)$, and hence, by (H)(ii), (4) has a unique solution in $C_b^0(\mathbf{R}; X_h)$, given by $K_h(\pi_h g(\widetilde{x}(.)))$; moreover, this solution $K_h(\pi_h g(\widetilde{x}(.)))$ is also the unique solution of (4) in $BC^\eta(\mathbf{R}, X_h)$, for each $\eta \in (0, \beta)$.

Now suppose (i) holds. Since $\widetilde{x}_h \in BC^\eta(\mathbf{R}; X_h)$ and $\eta \in (0, \beta)$ the foregoing argument shows that

$$\widetilde{x}_h = K_h(\pi_h g(\widetilde{x}(.))). \tag{5}$$

But we have already remarked that $K_h(\pi_h g(\widetilde{x}(.)))$ belongs in fact to $BC^0(\mathbf{R}; X_h) = C_b^0(\mathbf{R}; X_h)$. This proves that (i) $\Longrightarrow$ (iii).

Next assume (iii); since $C_b^0(\mathbf{R}; X_h) \subset BC^\zeta(\mathbf{R}; X_h)$ for each $\zeta > 0$ it follows that $\widetilde{x}_h \in BC^\zeta(\mathbf{R}; X_h)$ for all $\zeta > 0$. Since also $\widetilde{x}_c \in BC^\zeta(\mathbf{R}; X_c)$ for each $\zeta > 0$ we conclude that $\widetilde{x} = \widetilde{x}_c + \widetilde{x}_h \in BC^\zeta(\mathbf{R}; X)$ for all $\zeta > 0$; so (iii) $\Longrightarrow$ (ii). Since the implication (ii) $\Longrightarrow$ (i) is obvious, the proof is complete.

Lemma 2. *Assume* (H) *and* $g \in C_b^0(X; Y)$. *Let* $\widetilde{x} \in BC^\eta(\mathbf{R}; X)$ *for some* $\eta \in (0, \beta)$. *Then* $\widetilde{x}$ *is a solution of (1) if and only if*

$$\widetilde{x}(t) = e^{A_c t} \pi_c \widetilde{x}(0) + \int_0^t e^{A_c(t-s)} \pi_c g(\widetilde{x}(s)) ds + K_h(\pi_h g(\widetilde{x}(.)))(t) \quad , \quad \forall t \in \mathbf{R}. \tag{6}$$

Proof. If $\widetilde{x}$ is a solution of (1) then adding (3) and (5) shows that $\widetilde{x}$ satisfies (6). Conversely, if $\widetilde{x}$ satisfies (6) then projecting with π_c shows that $\widetilde{x}_c := \pi_c \widetilde{x}$ is a solution of (2), while projecting with π_h gives (5), and hence, by (H)(ii),

$\widetilde{x}_h := \pi_h \widetilde{x}$ is a solution of (4). Adding (2) and (4) shows that $\widetilde{x}$ is a solution of (1).

Theorem 1. *Assume* (H). *Then there exists a $\delta_0 > 0$ such that for all $g \in C_b^{0,1}(X, Y)$ satisfying*

$$|g|_{\mathrm{Lip}} < \delta_0 \tag{7}$$

there exists a unique $\psi \in C_b^{0,1}(X_c; X_h)$ with the property that for all $\widetilde{x} : \mathbf{R} \to X$ the following statements are equivalent:
(i) $\widetilde{x}$ is a solution of (1) and $\widetilde{x}$ belongs to $BC^\eta(\mathbf{R}; X)$ for some $\eta \in (0, \beta)$;
(ii) $\pi_h \widetilde{x}(t) = \psi(\pi_c \widetilde{x}(t))$ for all $t \in \mathbf{R}$, and $\pi_c \widetilde{x} : \mathbf{R} \to X_c$ is a solution of the ordinary differential equation

$$\dot{x}_c = A_c x_c + \pi_c g(x_c + \psi(x_c)). \tag{8}$$

Proof. We start by rewriting (6) in the abstract form

$$\widetilde{x} = S\pi_c \widetilde{x}(0) + KG(\widetilde{x}), \tag{9}$$

where $S : X_c \to \bigcap_{\eta \in (0,\beta)} BC^\eta(\mathbf{R}; X)$, $G : C^0(\mathbf{R}; X) \to C_b^0(\mathbf{R}; Y)$ and $K : \bigcup_{\eta \in (0,\beta)} BC^\eta(\mathbf{R}; Y) \to \bigcup_{\eta \in (0,\beta)} BC^\eta(\mathbf{R}; X)$ are given by

$$(Sx_c)(t) := e^{A_c t} x_c \quad , \quad \forall t \in \mathbf{R},$$
$$G(\widetilde{x})(t) := g(\widetilde{x}(t)) \quad , \quad \forall t \in \mathbf{R},$$

and

$$(K\widetilde{x})(t) := \int_0^t e^{A_c(t-s)} \pi_c \widetilde{x}(s) ds + K_h(\pi_h \widetilde{x})(t) \quad , \quad \forall t \in \mathbf{R}.$$

These operators have the same properties as in the finite-dimensional case (see Sect. 1.2 of [31]). In particular $K \in \mathcal{L}(BC^\eta(\mathbf{R}, Y), BC^\eta(\mathbf{R}; X))$ for each $\eta \in (0, \beta)$, and there exists some continuous function $\gamma_c : (0, \beta) \to \mathbf{R}_+$ such that

$$\|K\|_\eta \leq \gamma_c(\eta) \quad , \quad \forall \eta \in (0, \beta)$$

(here we use (H)(ii)). The mapping $G : BC^\eta(\mathbf{R}, X) \to BC^\eta(\mathbf{R}, Y)$ is globally Lipschitzian, with Lipschitz constant $|g|_{\mathrm{Lip}}$. Now let

$$\delta_0 := \sup_{\eta \in (0,\beta)} \gamma_c(\eta)^{-1};$$

then, assuming (7), the mapping KG is a contraction on $BC^\eta(\mathbf{R}; X)$ for an appropriate $\eta \in (0, \beta)$, and therefore the equation

$$\widetilde{x} = \widetilde{u} + KG(\widetilde{x}) \tag{10}$$

has for each $\widetilde{u} \in BC^\eta(\mathbf{R}; X)$ a unique solution $\widetilde{x} = \Psi(\widetilde{u}) \in BC^\eta(\mathbf{R}, X)$. The mapping $\Psi : BC^\eta(\mathbf{R}; X) \to BC^\eta(\mathbf{R}; X)$ is of class $C^{0,1}$ (more precisely : $\Psi - I \in C_b^{0,1}(BC^\eta(\mathbf{R}; X))$), and satisfies

$$\Psi(\widetilde{u}) = \widetilde{u} + KG(\Psi(\widetilde{u})) \quad , \quad \forall \widetilde{u} \in BC^\eta(\mathbf{R}; X). \tag{11}$$

Assuming that (7) holds, let $x_c \in X_c$ and take $\widetilde{u} = Sx_c$ in (10):

$$\widetilde{x} = Sx_c + KG(\widetilde{x}). \tag{12}$$

This equation has a unique solution $\widetilde{x} = \Psi(Sx_c) \in BC^\eta(\mathbf{R}; X)$ (observe that $S \in \mathcal{L}(X_c; BC^\eta(\mathbf{R}, X)))$; moreover, (12) implies that $\pi_c\widetilde{x}(0) = x_c$, and hence $\widetilde{x}$ satisfies (9). Using lemma 2 we conclude that for each $x_c \in X_c$ the equation (1) has a unique solution $\widetilde{x} = \Psi(Sx_c)$ belonging to $BC^\eta(\mathbf{R}; X)$ and satisfying $\pi_c\widetilde{x}(0) = x_c$.

Next we set

$$\psi(x_c) := \pi_h\Psi(Sx_c)(0) = K_h(\pi_h G(\Psi(Sx_c)))(0) \quad , \quad \forall x_c \in X_c. \tag{13}$$

It follows that $\psi \in C^{0,1}(X_c; X_h)$, with

$$\|\psi(x_c)\| \leq \|K_h(\pi_h G(\Psi(Sx_c)))\|_\eta \leq \|K_h\|_\eta \|\pi_h\|_{\mathcal{L}(Y)} |g|_0 \quad , \quad \forall x_c \in X_c.$$

Also, ψ is globally Lipschitzian, since Ψ is. We conclude that $\psi \in C_b^{0,1}(X_c; X_h)$.

Now let $\widetilde{x}$ be a solution of (1), with $\widetilde{x} \in BC^\eta(\mathbf{R}; X)$ for some $\eta \in (0, \beta)$; using lemma 1 we may without loss of generality assume that η is such that the foregoing results (in particular the existence of Ψ) apply. For each $s \in \mathbf{R}$ we define $\Gamma_s\widetilde{x} : \mathbf{R} \to X$ by $(\Gamma_s\widetilde{x})(t) := \widetilde{x}(t + s)$. Then $\Gamma_s\widetilde{x} \in BC^\eta(\mathbf{R}; X)$, $\Gamma_s\widetilde{x}$ is a solution of (1), and $\pi_c(\Gamma_s\widetilde{x})(0) = \pi_c\widetilde{x}(s)$. We conclude that

$$\Gamma_s\widetilde{x} = \Psi(S\pi_c\widetilde{x}(s)) \quad , \quad \forall s \in \mathbf{R},$$

and hence

$$\pi_h\widetilde{x}(s) = \pi_h(\Gamma_s\widetilde{x})(0) = \pi_h\Psi(S\pi_c\widetilde{x}(s))(0) = \psi(\pi_c\widetilde{x}(s)) \quad , \quad \forall s \in \mathbf{R}.$$

Using this identity and projecting the equation (1) onto X_c proves that $\pi_c\widetilde{x}$ is a solution of (8). This argument also proves the uniqueness of ψ.

Conversely, let $\widetilde{x} : \mathbf{R} \to X_c$ be a solution of (8); we want to show that $\widetilde{x}(t) := \widetilde{x}_c(t) + \psi(\widetilde{x}_c(t))$ is a solution of (1) belonging to $BC^\eta(\mathbf{R}; X)$. We know from the foregoing that $\widehat{x} := \Psi(S\widetilde{x}_c(0))$ is the unique solution of (1) belonging to $BC^\eta(\mathbf{R}; X)$ and satisfying $\pi_c\widehat{x}(0) = \widetilde{x}_c(0)$. But our foregoing arguments then imply that $\pi_h\widehat{x}(t) = \psi(\pi_c\widehat{x}(t))$, while $\pi_c\widehat{x}$ is a solution of (8). Since the initial value problem for (8) has a unique solution we conclude that $\pi_c\widehat{x} = \widetilde{x}_c$, and hence $\widehat{x} = \widetilde{x}$. This proves that $\widetilde{x}$ is indeed a solution of (1) belonging to $BC^\eta(\mathbf{R}; X)$.

As an immediate consequence we have

Corollary 1. Assume (H), and let $g \in C_b^{0,1}(X; Y)$ be such that (7) holds. Then the problem

$$\begin{cases} \dot{x} = Ax + g(x) \\ \pi_c x(0) = x_c \quad , \quad x \in BC^\eta(\mathbf{R}; X) \end{cases} \tag{14}$$

has for each $x_c \in X_c$ and each $\eta \in (0, \beta)$ a unique solution given by

$$\widetilde{x}(t; x_c) = \widetilde{x}_c(t; x_c) + \psi(\widetilde{x}_c(t, x_c)), \tag{15}$$

where $\widetilde{x}_c(t; x_c)$ is the unique solution of (8) satisfying $x_c(0) = x_c$.

Definition. *Under the foregoing hypotheses we call*

$$M_c := \{x_c + \psi(x_c) \mid x_c \in X_c\} \subset X \qquad (16)$$

the unique global center manifold of (1).

We now consider the problem of the smoothness of this center manifold.

Theorem 2. *Assume* (H). *Then there exists for each $k \geq 1$ a number $\delta_k > 0$ such that if $g \in C_b^{0,1}(X,Y) \cap C_b^k(V_\varrho, Y)$, with $V_\varrho := \{x \in X \mid \|\pi_h x\| < \varrho\}$ and $\varrho > \|K_h\|_0 |\pi_h g|_0$, and if moreover*

$$|g|_{\mathrm{Lip}} < \delta_k, \qquad (17)$$

then the mapping ψ given by theorem 1 belongs to the space $C_b^k(X_c; X_h)$.
  Moreover, if $g(0) = 0$ and $Dg(0) = 0$, then also $\psi(0) = 0$ and $D\psi(0) = 0$.

Proof. Fix $k \geq 1$, and suppose first that $g \in C_b^k(X; Y)$. It follows from (13) that the conclusion $\psi \in C_b^k(X_c; X_h)$ would follow immediately if we could show that $\Psi : BC^\eta(\mathbf{R}; X) \to BC^\eta(\mathbf{R}, X)$ is of class C_b^k; this in turn would be a consequence of (11) and the implicit function theorem if $G : BC^\eta(\mathbf{R}; X) \to BC^\eta(\mathbf{R}, Y)$ would be of class C_b^k. Unfortunately this is not the case, and we have to refine the argument. As in [31] one proves that

$$G : BC^\eta(\mathbf{R}, X) \to BC^\zeta(\mathbf{R}; Y)$$

is of class C_b^k if $\eta \geq 0$ and $\zeta > k\eta$. Suppose now that we can find $\eta, \zeta \in (0, \beta)$ such that

$$\sup_{\xi \in [\eta, \zeta]} \|K\|_\xi |g|_{\mathrm{Lip}} < 1. \qquad (18)$$

Then Ψ is a well-defined mapping on $BC^\eta(\mathbf{R}; X)$, and one can use a fiber contraction theorem in combination with the differentiability properties of G to show that Ψ is of class C^k when considered as a mapping from $BC^\eta(\mathbf{R}; X)$ into $BC^\zeta(\mathbf{X}; X)$. More precisely, we have that $\Psi(\widetilde{u}) = \widetilde{u} + \widetilde{\Psi}(\widetilde{u})$, with $\widetilde{\Psi} \in C_b^k(BC^\eta(\mathbf{R}; X); BC^\zeta(\mathbf{R}; X))$. This part of the proof is somewhat lengthy and technical, but completely parallels the treatment given in Sect. 1.3 of [31] for the finite-dimensional case; the only difference is that one has to make some obvious changes in the choice of spaces used in [31], since here G maps $BC^\eta(\mathbf{R}; X)$ into $BC^\eta(\mathbf{R}; Y)$ while K maps $BC^\eta(\mathbf{R}; Y)$ back into $BC^\eta(\mathbf{R}; X)$. The smoothness properties of Ψ combined with (13) then show that $\psi \in C_b^k(X_c; X_h)$. Moreover, the arguments in [31] show that the derivatives of Ψ can be calculated by formal differentiation of the identity (11); this implies easily that $\psi(0) = 0$ and $D\psi(0) = 0$ if $g(0) = 0$ and $Dg(0) = 0$.

In order to realize the condition (18) needed for the foregoing arguments we define

$$\delta_k := \sup_{\eta \in (0, \beta/k)} \inf_{\xi \in [\eta, k\eta]} \gamma_c(\xi)^{-1},$$

where, as before, $\gamma_c : (0, \beta) \to \mathbf{R}_+$ is a continuous function such that $\|K\|_\eta \leq \gamma_c(\eta)$. If (17) holds then the definition of δ_k and the continuity of γ_c imply that there exist some $\eta, \zeta \in (0, \beta)$ such that $\zeta > k\eta$ and such that (18) holds. This completes the proof in the case that $g \in C_b^k(X; Y)$.

Suppose next that g has only the smoothness indicated in the statement of the theorem, that is, we have $g \in C_b^{0,1}(X; Y) \cap C_b^k(V_\varrho; Y)$; we will need this weaker smoothness assumption when we consider local center manifolds (see theorem 3): it will help us to avoid the use of a smooth cut-off function on the Banach space X. To see why the conclusion of theorem 2 still holds under thus weaker assumption on g we observe that in (13) we have $Sx_c \in BC^\eta(\mathbf{R}; X_c)$. Therefore, in order to study the smoothness properties of ψ it is sufficient to consider the smoothness properties of the restriction of Ψ to $BC^\eta(\mathbf{R}, X_c)$. But if $\widetilde{u} \in BC^\eta(\mathbf{R}; X_c)$ then it follows from (11) and (H) that $\pi_h \Psi(\widetilde{u}) \in BC^0(\mathbf{R}; X_h)$, with

$$\|\pi_h \Psi(\widetilde{u})\|_0 = \|K_h \pi_h G(\widetilde{u})\|_0 \leq \|K_h\|_0 |\pi_h g|_0.$$

This shows that we can consider Ψ as on element of the set X_0 consisting of all $\Phi \in C^0(BC^\eta(\mathbf{R}; X_c); BC^\eta(\mathbf{R}, X))$ such that

$$\sup_{\widetilde{u} \in BC^\eta(\mathbf{R}, X_c)} \|\Phi(\widetilde{u}) - \widetilde{u}\|_0 < \infty$$

and

$$\sup_{\widetilde{u} \in BC^\eta(\mathbf{R}; X_c)} \|\pi_h \Phi(\widetilde{u})\|_0 \leq \|K_h\|_0 |\pi_h g|_0.$$

Now X_0 is a complete metric space when we use the metric

$$d_0(\Phi, \widetilde{\Phi}) := \sup_{\widetilde{u} \in BC^\eta(\mathbf{R}; X_c)} \|\Phi(\widetilde{u}) - \widetilde{\Phi}(\widetilde{u})\|_\eta,$$

and Ψ is the fixed point of the contraction $F_0 : X_0 \to X_0$ defined by

$$F_0(\Phi)(\widetilde{u}) := \widetilde{u} + KG(\Phi(\widetilde{u})) \quad , \quad \forall \Phi \in X_0 \, , \, \forall \widetilde{u} \in BC^\eta(\mathbf{R}; X_c).$$

It is now a straightforward (but somewhat lengthy) exercise to adapt the treatment given in Sect. 1.3 of [31] to the new situation considered here. We will just indicate a few crucial points, leaving the details to the reader. The spaces X_j $(0 \leq j \leq k)$ used in [31] should be replaced as follows: for X_0 we take the metric space defined above, while for X_j $(1 \leq j \leq k)$ we take the Banach space of all continuous and globally bounded mappings

$$\Phi^{(j)} : BC^\eta(\mathbf{R}; X_c) \to \mathcal{L}^{(j)}(BC^\eta(\mathbf{R}; X_c); BC^{j\eta + (2j-1)\mu}(\mathbf{R}; X)),$$

with $\mu > 0$ chosen as in [31]. The mappings F_j $(0 \leq j \leq k)$ are defined in a similar way as in [31]. Finally, instead of lemma 3.7 of [31] one should use the following result.

Lemma 3. *Let E be a Banach space, $\varrho > 0$ and $w \in C_b^1(V_\varrho; E)$, where $V_\varrho := \{x \in X \mid \|\pi_h x\| < \varrho\}$. Let $\eta \geq 0$ and $V_\varrho^\eta := \{\widetilde{u} \in BC^\eta(\mathbf{R}; X) \mid \widetilde{u}(t) \in V_\varrho, \forall t \in \mathbf{R}\}$. Define $W : V_\varrho^\eta \to BC^\eta(\mathbf{R}; E)$ and $W^{(1)} : V_\varrho^\eta \to \mathcal{L}(BC^\eta(\mathbf{R}; X); BC^\eta(\mathbf{R}; E))$ by*

$$W(\widetilde{u})(t) := w(\widetilde{u}(t)) \quad \text{and} \quad \left(W^{(1)}(\widetilde{(u)} \cdot \widetilde{v}\right)(t) := Dw(\widetilde{u}(t)) \cdot \widetilde{v}(t),$$

$$\forall t \in \mathbf{R} \,, \; \forall \widetilde{u} \in V_\varrho^\eta \,, \; \forall \widetilde{v} \in BC^\eta(\mathbf{R}; X).$$

Let $\Phi \in C^0(BC^\eta(\mathbf{R}; X_c); V_\varrho^\eta)$ be such that

(a) *Φ is of class C^1 from $BC^\eta(\mathbf{R}, X_c)$ into $BC^{\eta+\mu}(\mathbf{R}; X)$, for each $\mu > 0$;*
(b) *its derivative takes the form*

$$D\Phi(\widetilde{u}) \cdot \widetilde{v} = \Phi^{(1)}(\widetilde{u}) \cdot \widetilde{v} \quad, \quad \forall \widetilde{u}, \widetilde{v} \in BC^\eta(\mathbf{R}; X_c),$$

for some globally bounded $\Phi^{(1)} : BC^\eta(\mathbf{R}; X_c) \to \mathcal{L}(BC^\eta(\mathbf{R}; X_c); BC^\eta(\mathbf{R}; X))$.

Then $W \circ \Phi \in C_b^0(BC^\eta(\mathbf{R}; X_c); BC^\eta(\mathbf{R}; E))$. Moreover, $W \circ \Phi$ is of class C^1 from $BC^\eta(\mathbf{R}; X_c)$ into $BC^{\eta+\mu}(\mathbf{R}; E)$, for each $\mu > 0$, with

$$D(W \circ \Phi)(\widetilde{u}) \cdot \widetilde{v} = W^{(1)}(\Phi(\widetilde{u})) \cdot \Phi^{(1)}(\widetilde{u}) \cdot \widetilde{v} \,, \; \forall \widetilde{u}, \widetilde{v} \in BC^\eta(\mathbf{R}; X_c).$$

The proof of this lemma uses the same arguments as used in the proof of lemma 3.7 of [31].

Using the theorems 1–2 on global center manifolds we can now prove the following theorem on the existence of a local center manifold for (1).

Theorem 3. *Assume* (H), *and let $g \in C^k(X; Y)$ for some $k \geq 1$, with $g(0) = 0$ and $Dg(0) = 0$. Then there exist a neighborhood Ω of the origin in X and a mapping $\psi \in C_b^k(X_c; X_h)$, with $\psi(0) = 0$ and $D\psi(0) = 0$, and such that the following properties hold:*

(i) *if $\widetilde{x}_c : I \to X_c$ is a solution of (8) such that $\widetilde{x}(t) := \widetilde{x}_c(t) + \psi(\widetilde{x}_c(t)) \in \Omega$ for all $t \in I$, then $\widetilde{x} : I \to X$ is a solution of (1);*
(ii) *if $\widetilde{x} : \mathbf{R} \to X$ is a solution of (1) such that $\widetilde{x}(t) \in \Omega$ for all $t \in \mathbf{R}$, then*

$$\pi_h \widetilde{x}(t) = \psi(\pi_c \widetilde{x}(t)) \quad, \quad \forall t \in \mathbf{R},$$

and $\pi_c \widetilde{x} : \mathbf{R} \to X_c$ is a solution of (8).

Proof. In order to use the global results of theorems 1–2 we will modify $g(x)$ outside a neighborhood of the origin. The easiest way to do this is to replace g in (1) by

$$g_\varrho(x) := g(x)\chi(\varrho^{-1}x), \tag{19}$$

with $\varrho > 0$ sufficiently small, and with $\chi \in C_b^k(X; \mathbf{R})$ a cut-off function, i.e. such that $\chi(x) = 1$ for $\|x\| \leq 1$ and $\chi(x) = 0$ for $\|x\| \geq 2$. Such cut-off functions exist for example in Hilbert spaces, but for a general Banach space X such χ does not necessarily exist. Therefore we use a slightly different approach which avoids the use of such smooth cut-off function on the whole of X.

For each $\varrho > 0$ we set $\omega_\varrho := \{x \in X \mid \|\pi_c x\| \leq \varrho, \|\pi_h x\| \leq \varrho\}$. Since $g \in C^k(X; Y)$ we can find some $\varrho_0 > 0$ such that g and its derivatives up to order k are bounded in $\omega_{2\varrho_0}$. Let

$$\alpha(\varrho) := \sup_{x \in \omega_\varrho} \|Dg(x)\| \quad , \quad 0 < \varrho < 2\varrho_0.$$

Then we have $\alpha(\varrho) \to 0$ as $\varrho \to 0$ and $\|g(x)\| \leq 2\varrho\alpha(\varrho)$ for $x \in \omega_\varrho$. Let $\chi_c \in C_b^\infty(X_c; \mathbf{R})$ and $\widetilde{\chi} \in C_b^\infty(\mathbf{R})$ be smooth cut-off functions on respectively X_c and $\mathbf{R}$ (i.e. we have $\chi_c(x_c) = 1$ for $\|x_c\| \leq 1$, $\chi_c(x_c) = 0$ for $\|x_c\| \geq 2$, $\widetilde{\chi}(s) = 1$ for $|s| \leq 1$ and $\widetilde{\chi}(s) = 0$ for $|s| \geq 2$). Remark that such χ_c exists since X_c is finite-dimensional. Setting

$$\chi(x) := \chi_c(\pi_c x)\widetilde{\chi}(\|\pi_h x\|) \quad , \quad \forall x \in X$$

we see that $\chi \in C_b^{0,1}(X; \mathbf{R})$.

For each $\varrho \in (0, \varrho_0]$ we now define $g_\varrho : X \to Y$ by (19); then $g_\varrho \in C_b^{0,1}(X, Y)$, and since $g_\varrho(x) = g(x)\chi_c(\varrho^{-1}\pi_c x)$ for $x \in V_\varrho = \{x \in X \mid \|\pi_h x\| \leq \varrho\}$ we conclude that $g_\varrho \in C_b^{0,1}(X, Y) \cap C_b^k(V_\varrho; Y)$ for each $\varrho \in (0, \varrho_0]$. One can also easily verify that

$$|g_\varrho|_0 \leq 4\varrho\alpha(2\varrho)|\chi|_0 \quad \text{and} \quad |g_\varrho|_{\text{Lip}} \leq \alpha(2\varrho)(|\chi|_0 + 4|\chi|_{\text{Lip}}).$$

Now fix $\varrho \in (0, \varrho_0]$ such that

$$\alpha(2\varrho)(|\chi|_0 + 4|\chi|_{\text{Lip}}) < \delta_k \quad \text{and} \quad 4\alpha(2\varrho)|\chi|_0\|K_h\|_0\|\pi_h\|_{\mathcal{L}(Y)} < 1.$$

Then $|g_\varrho|_{\text{Lip}} < \delta_k$ and $\|K_h\|_0\|\pi_h g_\varrho\|_0 \leq \|K_h\|_0\|\pi_h\|_{\mathcal{L}(Y)}|g_\varrho|_0 < \varrho$, and hence we can apply theorems 1–2 to the equation

$$\dot{x} = Ax + g_\varrho(x). \tag{20}$$

This equation has a unique global center manifold $M_c = \{x_c + \psi(x_c) \mid x_c \in X_c\}$ with the properties described in theorem 1 and with $\psi \in C_b^k(X_c; X_h)$.

Let $\Omega := \{x \in X \mid \|\pi_c x\| < \varrho, \|\pi_h x\| < \varrho\}$, and let $\widetilde{x}_c : I \to X_c$ be a solution of (8) such that $\widetilde{x}(t) := \widetilde{x}_c(t) + \psi(\widetilde{x}(t)) \in \Omega$ for all $t \in I$. Since $g_\varrho(x) = g(x)$ for $x \in \Omega$ it follows that $\widetilde{x}_c$ is also a solution of the equation

$$\dot{x}_c = A_c x_c + \pi_c g_\varrho(x_c + \psi(x_c)). \tag{21}$$

But (21) has a unique solution $\widehat{x}_c : \mathbf{R} \to X_c$ such that $\widehat{x}_c(t) = \widetilde{x}_c(t)$ for $t \in I$. Then theorem 1 implies that $\widehat{x}(t) := \widehat{x}_c(t) + \psi(\widehat{x}_c(t))$ is a solution of (20). Since $\widehat{x}(t) = \widetilde{x}(t) \in \Omega$ for $t \in I$, it follows that $\widetilde{x} : I \to X$ is a solution of (1).

To prove (ii) let $\widetilde{x} : \mathbf{R} \to X$ be a solution of (1) such that $\widetilde{x}(t) \in \Omega$ for all $t \in \mathbf{R}$. Then $\widetilde{x}$ is a solution of (20), and since Ω is bounded in X we also have that $\widetilde{x} \in BC^0(\mathbf{R}; X) \subset BC^\eta(\mathbf{R}; X)$ for all $\eta \in (0, \beta)$. We conclude then from theorem 1 that $\pi_h \widetilde{x}(t) = \psi(\pi_c(t))$, while $\pi_c \widetilde{x}$ is a solution of (21); since $\widetilde{x}(t) \in \Omega$ this implies that $\pi_c \widetilde{x}$ is also a solution of (8), and the proof is complete.

Corollary 2. Under the conditions of theorem 4 there exists a neighborhood Ω of the origin in X such that all solutions $\widetilde{x} : \mathbf{R} \to X$ of (1) which satisfy $\widetilde{x}(t) \in \Omega$ for all $t \in \mathbf{R}$ are of class C^k as a mapping from $\mathbf{R}$ into X.

This result should be compared with the definition of a solution of (1). See also Hale and Scheurle [13] for a more systematic study of the smoothness of bounded solutions of equations such as (1).

Remark. The foregoing theory can be modified in several ways. For example, most of our results still hold if in the hypothesis (H)(ii) we replace the interval $[0, \beta)$ by the open interval $(0, \beta)$ (i.e. $\eta = 0$ not included). Then one has to delete (iii) in lemma 1, assume $g \in C_b^k(X, Y)$ in theorem 2, and assume the existence of a smooth cut-off function on X in theorem 3.

It is also possible to abandon the condition $\dim X_c < \infty$; in this case one has to assume that the problem

$$\dot{x}_c = A_c x_c + f(t) \qquad , \qquad x_c(0) = x_c \tag{22}$$

has for each $x_c \in X_c$, each $\eta \in (0, \beta)$ and each $f \in BC^\eta(\mathbf{R}; X_c)$ a unique solution $\widetilde{x}_c = S x_c + K_c f \in BC^\eta(\mathbf{R}; X_c)$, where S and K_c have the properties needed to prove theorems 1 and 2; one also needs a smooth cut-off function on X_c. We refer to recent work of Mielke [25,26] and Scarpellini [29] for more details on this case.

2.2 Special Cases

An important modification of the foregoing theory consists in the inclusion of parameters in the equation (1). First consider the case of an equation of the form

$$\dot{x} = A_0 x + h(x, \lambda), \tag{23}$$

where $A_0 \in \mathcal{L}(X, Z)$ satisfies the hypothesis (H), while $h \in C^k(X \times \mathbf{R}^m, Y)$ ($k \geq 1$, $m \geq 1$) is such that $h(0, 0) = 0$ and $D_x h(0, 0) = 0$. A particular case, which arises frequently in applications, is given by equations of the form

$$\dot{x} = A_0 x + \lambda B x + \widetilde{h}(x), \tag{24}$$

where $B \in \mathcal{L}(X, Y)$, $\lambda \in \mathbf{R}$ (i.e. $m = 1$), $\widetilde{h} \in C^k(X, Y)$, $\widetilde{h}(0) = 0$ and $D\widetilde{h}(0) = 0$.
In order to apply the foregoing theory we write

$$h(x, \lambda) = \widetilde{A} \cdot \lambda + h_1(x, \lambda),$$

where $\widetilde{A} := D_\lambda h(0, 0) \in \mathcal{L}(\mathbf{R}^m; Y) \subset \mathcal{L}(\mathbf{R}^m; Z)$. (Remark that $\widetilde{A} = 0$ for the equation (24)). Then (23) is equivalent to

$$\begin{cases} \dot{x} = A_0 x + \widetilde{A} \cdot \lambda + h_1(x, \lambda), \\ \dot{\lambda} = 0. \end{cases} \tag{25}$$

This has the form (1) when we replace X, Y and Z by respectively $X \times \mathbf{R}^m$, $Y \times \mathbf{R}^m$ and $Z \times \mathbf{R}^m$, and define A and g by $A(x, \lambda) := (A_0 x + \tilde{A} \cdot \lambda, 0)$ and $g(x, \lambda) := (h_1(x, \lambda), 0)$. The center subspace corresponding to A is given by $X_c \times \mathbf{R}^m$, where X_c is the center subspace corresponding to A_0. An application of theorem 3 to (25) gives us then a local center manifold of the form

$$M_c = \{(x_c + \psi(x_c, \lambda), \lambda) \mid x_c \in X_c, \lambda \in \mathbf{R}^m\},$$

with $\psi \in C_b^k(X_c \times \mathbf{R}^m, X_h)$, and with the properties described in the statement of theorem 3. A reinterpretation of these properties shows that for each sufficiently small $\lambda \in \mathbf{R}^m$ the equation (23) has a local center manifold, given by

$$M_c(\lambda) = \{x_c + \psi(x_c, \lambda) \mid x_c \in X_c\}. \tag{26}$$

Remark that we can have $\psi(0, \lambda) \neq 0$ and $D_{x_c}\psi(0, \lambda) \neq 0$ for $\lambda \neq 0$, since theorem 3 only implies that $\psi(x_c, \lambda) = O((|x_c| + |\lambda|)^2)$. Of course if $h(0, \lambda) = 0$ for all λ then also $\psi(0, \lambda) = 0$ for all λ.

A different and more complicated situation arises when the parameters appear in an essential way in the linear part of the equation, i.e. when we have an equation of the form

$$\dot{x} = A_\lambda x + h(x, \lambda), \tag{27}$$

with h as above and $\lambda \mapsto A_\lambda$ a sufficiently smooth mapping from $\mathbf{R}^m$ into $\mathcal{L}(X, Z)$. For example A_λ could be a holomorphic family of type (A), as studied by Kato in [19]. In this case one is forced to work out a parameter-dependent version of our center manifold theory. Without going into details, let us briefly describe the general idea of such a theory. Assume that A_0 satisfies the hypothesis (H). Intuitively, when we change λ, then the center spectrum will slightly move off the imaginary axis. Therefore we should assume that the projection π_c in the hypothesis (H) depends smoothly on λ, and restrict ourselves to sufficiently small parameter values such that

$$\mu \in \sigma(A_c(\lambda)) \implies |\text{Re}\,\mu| < \varepsilon, \tag{28}$$

where $\varepsilon > 0$ is fixed and sufficiently small. In (H)(ii) we should only consider $\eta \in (\varepsilon, \beta)$, and assume a uniform estimate for $\|K_h(\lambda)\|$, i.e.

$$\|K_h(\lambda)\|_\eta \leq \gamma(\eta) \quad , \quad \forall \eta \in (\varepsilon, \beta),$$

valid for all sufficiently small λ. Then, instead of considering solutions belonging to $BC^\eta(\mathbf{R}; X)$ for some $\eta \in (0, \beta)$ (as we did in the foregoing theorem), we should here consider solutions belonging to $BC^\eta(\mathbf{R}; X)$ for some $\eta \in (\varepsilon, \beta)$. The theory should then become very similar to the one we have worked out above and in [31]. However, there is a drawback: the smaller ε is chosen, the smaller the parameter range for which the theory will hold (see (28)); but larger values of ε impose stronger restrictions on the differentiability of the center manifold, which will maximally be of the order $[\beta \varepsilon^{-1}]$ (see (18), Sect. 1.3 of [31], [32] and [16]).

Another important special case arises when the equation (1) commutes with a group representation. This means that there exists a group $\Gamma \subset \mathcal{L}(Z) \cap \mathcal{L}(Y) \cap \mathcal{L}(X)$ of linear operators, representing the symmetries of (1), such that

$$SAx = ASx \quad \text{and} \quad Sg(x) = g(Sx), \qquad \text{for all } x \in X \text{ and } S \in \Gamma.$$

The group Γ leaves then the subspace X_c invariant. A basic assumption one has to make is that the action of Γ leaves the cut-off function χ used in the proof of theorem 3 invariant:

$$\chi(Sx) = \chi(x) \qquad , \qquad \forall x \in X \ , \ \forall S \in \Gamma. \tag{29}$$

Usually this can be realized by choosing norms such that the symmetry operators $S \in \Gamma$ are unitary.

Assuming (29) the modified nonlinearity g_ϱ appearing in (20) will commute with the symmetry operators S; it follows then from the uniqueness of the global center manifold that we have

$$S\psi(x_c) = \psi(Sx_c) \qquad , \qquad \forall x_c \in X_c \ , \ \forall S \in \Gamma. \tag{30}$$

This means that the center manifold is invariant under the action of Γ, and that the reduced ordinary differential equation (21) on this center manifold is equivariant under the action of Γ in X_c. The first reference for this type of results seems to be the paper [28] of Ruelle. Such results are extremely fruitful in a lot of physical problems which have symmetries, since they considerably simplify the study of the flow on the center manifold. For an example, see [5].

Another result of the same type is when the system anticommutes with a symmetry R (case of reversible systems):

$$RAx = -ARx \quad , \quad Rg(x) = -g(Rx) \qquad , \qquad \forall x \in X.$$

Modulo an assumption similar to (29) one shows then that $R\psi(x_c) = \psi(Rx_c)$, and that the reduced vectorfield on the center manifold anticommutes with R_c, the restriction of R to X_c.

3. Spectral Theory

The aim of this section is to state some quite general spectral hypotheses on the linear operator A appearing in (1.1) and to show that these spectral hypotheses imply the hypothesis (H) of Sect. 1, and hence the applicability of the center manifold theory of that section. For the standard results from spectral theory used in this section we refer to Kato [19].

Let Z be a Banach space, and $A : D(A) \subset Z \to Z$ a closed linear operator. We set $X := D(A)$ with the graph norm. We denote by $\sigma(A)$ and $\varrho(A)$ the spectrum, respectively the resolvent set of A. Let Y be a Banach space such that X is continuously embedded in Y and Y continuously embedded in Z. We make the following assumptions:

(Σ)(i) $\sigma(A) \cap i\mathbf{R}$ consists of a finite number of isolated eigenvalues, each with a finite-dimensional generalized eigenspace;

(ii) there exist constants $\omega_0 > 0$, $C > 0$ and $\alpha \in [0,1)$ such that for all $\omega \in \mathbf{R}$ with $|\omega| \geq \omega_0$ we have $i\omega \in \varrho(A)$,

$$\|(i\omega - A)^{-1}\|_{\mathcal{L}(Z)} \leq \frac{C}{|\omega|} \tag{1}$$

and

$$\|(i\omega - A)^{-1}\|_{\mathcal{L}(Y;X)} \leq \frac{C}{|\omega|^{1-\alpha}}. \tag{2}$$

Several examples of operators satisfying these hypotheses will be discussed in later sections. It should be noted that in applications the choice of the intermediate space Y is imposed by the nonlinearity $g(x)$ (see (1.1)). In some applications, such as for example water waves and certain problems from elasticity theory, one is forced to take $Y = Z$ and hence $\alpha = 1$ in (2). For a discussion of this so-called quasi-linear case we refer to the work of Mielke ([23,24,25]).

Assuming (Σ) there exists a closed path Γ_c in $\mathbf{C}$ surrounding the eigenvalues of A on the imaginary axis and not including any other elements of $\sigma(A)$. We define

$$\pi_c := \frac{1}{2\pi i} \int_{\Gamma_c} (\lambda - A)^{-1} d\lambda. \tag{3}$$

Then $\pi_c \in \mathcal{L}(Z;X)$ is a projection onto the finite-dimensional subspace $X_c := \pi_c(Z)$ of X spanned by the generalized eigenvectors corresponding to the purely imaginary eigenvalues of A; we also have $A\pi_c x = \pi_c A x$ for $x \in X$. As in Sect. 1 we let $\pi_h : I_Z - \pi_c$, $Z_h := \pi_h(Z)$, $X_h := \pi_h(X)$, $Y_h := \pi_h(Y)$, $A_c := A|_{X_c} \in \mathcal{L}(X_c)$ and $A_h := A|_{X_h} \in \mathcal{L}(X_h; Z_h)$. Then $\sigma(A_c) = \sigma(A) \cap i\mathbf{R}$ and $\sigma(A_h) \cap i\mathbf{R} = \emptyset$. Together with (1) and (2) this implies the existence of some $C_1 > 0$ such that

$$\|(i\omega - A_h)^{-1}\|_{\mathcal{L}(Z_h)} \leq \frac{C_1}{1 + |\omega|} \quad , \quad \forall \omega \in \mathbf{R} \tag{4}$$

and

$$\|(i\omega - A_h)^{-1}\|_{\mathcal{L}(Y_h; X_h)} \leq \frac{C_1}{(1 + |\omega|)^{1-\alpha}} \quad , \quad \forall \omega \in \mathbf{R}. \tag{5}$$

Using the graph norm in X_h and the identity $A_h(i\omega - A_h)^{-1}x = (i\omega - A_h)^{-1}A_h x$, which holds for all $x \in X_h$, it follows easily from (4) that

$$\|(i\omega - A_h)^{-1}\|_{\mathcal{L}(X_h)} \leq \frac{C_1}{1 + |\omega|} \quad , \quad \forall \omega \in \mathbf{R}. \tag{6}$$

Lemma 1. *There exist constants $\delta > 0$ and $M > 0$ such that for all $\lambda \in \mathbf{C}$ satisfying*

$$|\mathrm{Re}\,\lambda| \leq \delta(1 + |\mathrm{Im}\,\lambda|) \tag{7}$$

we have $\lambda \in \varrho(A_h)$,

$$\|(\lambda - A_h)^{-1}\|_{\mathcal{L}(Z_h)} \le \frac{M}{1 + |\lambda|}, \tag{8}$$

$$\|(\lambda - A_h)^{-1}\|_{\mathcal{L}(Z_h; X_h)} \le M, \tag{9}$$

and

$$\|(\lambda - A_h)^{-1}\|_{\mathcal{L}(Y_h; X_h)} \le \frac{M}{(1 + |\lambda|)^{1-\alpha}}. \tag{10}$$

It follows in particular that

$$\beta := \min\left\{|\text{Re}\,\lambda| \mid \lambda \in \sigma(A_h)\right\} \ge \delta > 0. \tag{11}$$

Proof. We set $\delta := (2C_1)^{-1}$, where $C_1 > 0$ is as in (4)–(6). Let $\lambda = \mu + i\omega$, with $\mu, \omega \in \mathbf{R}$ and $|\mu| \le \delta(1 + |\omega|)$. We have then

$$\lambda - A_h = \left[I_{Z_h} + \mu(i\omega - A_h)^{-1}\right](i\omega - A_h),$$

with

$$\|\mu(i\omega - A_h)^{-1}\|_{\mathcal{L}(Z_h)} \le \delta C_1 = \frac{1}{2}.$$

It follows that $I_{Z_h} + \mu(i\omega - A_h)^{-1} \in \mathcal{L}(Z_h)$ has a bounded inverse, with norm less that or equal to 2. This implies that $\lambda \in \varrho(A_h)$, with

$$\|(\lambda - A_h)^{-1}\|_{\mathcal{L}(Z_h)} \le 2\|(i\omega - A_h)^{-1}\|_{\mathcal{L}(Z_h)} \le \frac{2C_1}{1 + |\omega|} \le \frac{2C_1(1 + \delta)}{1 + |\lambda|}.$$

Setting $M := 2C_1(1 + \delta) + 1$ we see that (8) holds, while using the identity

$$A_h(\lambda - A_h)^{-1} = -I_{Z_h} + \lambda(\lambda - A_h)^{-1} \quad , \quad \forall \lambda \in \varrho(A_h), \tag{12}$$

we find also that

$$\|(\lambda - A_h)^{-1}\|_{\mathcal{L}(Z_h; X_h)} \le \|(\lambda - A_h)^{-1}\|_{\mathcal{L}(Z_h)} + \|A_h(\lambda - A_h)^{-1}\|_{\mathcal{L}(Z_H)}$$
$$\le 1 + (1 + |\lambda|)\|(\lambda - A_h)^{-1}\|_{\mathcal{L}(Z_h)} \le 1 + 2C_1(1 + \delta) = M.$$

To obtain (10) we write

$$\lambda - A_h = (i\omega - A_h)\left[I_{X_h} + \mu(i\omega - A_h)^{-1}\right]$$

and use the fact that $\|\mu(i\omega - A_h)^{-1}\|_{\mathcal{L}(X_h)} \le \frac{1}{2}$ to show that $I_{X_h} + \mu(i\omega - A_h)^{-1} \in \mathcal{L}(X_h)$ has a bounded inverse with norm less than or equal to 2. It follows that

$$\|(\lambda - A_h)^{-1}\|_{\mathcal{L}(Y_h; X_h)} \le \left\|[I_{X_h} + \mu(i\omega - A_h)^{-1}]^{-1}\right\|_{\mathcal{L}(X_h)} \left\|(i\omega - A_h)^{-1}\right\|_{\mathcal{L}(Y_h; X_h)}$$
$$\le \frac{2C_1}{(1 + |\omega|)^{1-\alpha}} \le \frac{2C_1(1 + \delta)^{1-\alpha}}{(1 + |\lambda|)^{1-\alpha}} \le \frac{M}{(1 + |\lambda|)^{1-\alpha}}.$$

This completes the proof.

Next we construct two paths Γ_+ and Γ_- in $\mathbf{C}$, given by

$$\Gamma_+ := \{-\delta|\omega| + i\omega \mid \omega \in \mathbf{R}\} \quad \text{and} \quad \Gamma_- := \{\delta|\omega| + i\omega \mid \omega \in \mathbf{R}\}; \tag{13}$$

we orient Γ_+ in the sense of increasing ω and Γ_- in the sense of decreasing ω. Remark that lemma 1 implies that $\Gamma_+ \cup \Gamma_- \subset \varrho(A_h)$.

Lemma 2. *For each $t > 0$ we have that*

$$S_+(t) := \frac{1}{2\pi i} \int_{\Gamma_+} e^{\lambda t}(\lambda - A_h)^{-1} d\lambda \tag{14}$$

defines an element of $\mathcal{L}(Z_h; X_h)$; moreover, the mapping $S_+ : (0, \infty) \to \mathcal{L}(Z_h; X_h)$ is C^∞, with

$$\frac{d^n S_+}{dt^n}(t) = A_h^n S_+(t) \quad , \quad \forall t > 0 , \ \forall n \geq 1. \tag{15}$$

Similarly, we have that

$$S_-(t) := \frac{1}{2\pi i} \int_{\Gamma_-} e^{\lambda t}(\lambda - A_h)^{-1} d\lambda, \qquad (t < 0), \tag{16}$$

defines a C^∞ mapping $S_- : (-\infty, 0) \to \mathcal{L}(Z_h; X_h)$ with

$$\frac{d^n S_-}{dt^n}(t) = A_h^n S_-(t) \quad , \quad \forall t < 0 , \ \forall n \geq 1. \tag{17}$$

Proof. The proof of this lemma is essentially the same as for the construction of a holomorphic semigroup (see e.g. chapter IX, §1.6 of Kato [19]). For completeness we give here briefly the main argument.

From the definitions (13) and (14) and from the estimate (9) one easily finds that

$$\|S_+(t)\|_{\mathcal{L}(Z_h; X_h)} \leq \frac{C_2}{t} \quad , \quad \forall t > 0,$$

for some constant $C_2 > 0$. By dominated convergence this proves that $S_+ : (0, \infty) \to \mathcal{L}(Z_h; X_h)$ is well-defined and continuous. Differentiating in (14) any number of times under the integral sign gives always convergent integrals. Again by dominated convergence this proves that $S_+ : (0, \infty) \to \mathcal{L}(Z_h; X_h)$ is C^∞. To prove (15) we consider $dS_+(t)/dt$ as an element of $\mathcal{L}(Z_h)$; using (12) and the closedness of A_h one obtains easily (15) for $n = 1$. Repeating the argument proves (15) for general $n \geq 1$. As is shown in [19] S^+ can be extended to a holomorphic mapping on a small sector containing the positive real axis.

Remark. Since on X_h we have $A_h(\lambda - A_h)^{-1} = (\lambda - A_h)^{-1}A_h$, it follows from the definitions (14) and (16) that

$$A_h S_+(t)|_{X_h} = S_+(t)A_h \ (t > 0) \quad \text{and} \quad A_h S_-(t)|_{X_h} = S_-(t)A_h \ (t < 0). \tag{18}$$

Lemma 3. *The limits*

$$\pi_s := \lim_{t \to 0^+} S_+(t)|_{Y_h} \quad \text{and} \quad \pi_u := \lim_{t \to 0^-} S_-(t)|_{Y_h} \qquad (19)$$

exist in $\mathcal{L}(Y_h; Z_h)$ (i.e. in the uniform operator norm of $\mathcal{L}(Y_h; Z_h)$), and

$$(\pi_s + \pi_u)y = y \quad , \qquad \forall y \in Y_h. \qquad (20)$$

Proof. For each $\eta > 0$ we define paths Γ_+^η and Γ_-^η in $\mathbf{C}$ by

$$\Gamma_+^\eta := \left\{ -\delta|\omega| + i\omega \mid \omega \in \mathbf{R}, |\omega| \geq \delta^{-1}\eta \right\} \cup \left\{ -\eta + i\omega \mid \omega \in \mathbf{R}, |\omega| \leq \delta^{-1}\eta \right\}$$

and

$$\Gamma_-^\eta := \left\{ \delta|\omega| + i\omega \mid \omega \in \mathbf{R}, |\omega| \geq \delta^{-1}\eta \right\} \cup \left\{ \eta + i\omega \mid \omega \in \mathbf{R}, |\omega| \leq \delta^{-1}\eta \right\};$$

we orient Γ_+^η and Γ_-^η in the sense of increasing, respectively decreasing ω (see Fig. 1.a).

Using lemma 1, and in particular (11), we have then for each $\eta \in (0, \beta)$ that

$$S_+(t) = \frac{1}{2\pi i} \int_{\Gamma_+^\eta} e^{\lambda t} (\lambda - A_h)^{-1} d\lambda \quad , \quad \forall t > 0. \qquad (21)$$

Using (12) to replace the integrandum in (21) gives us

$$S_+(t) = \left(\frac{1}{2\pi i} \int_{\Gamma_+^\eta} \frac{e^{\lambda t}}{\lambda} d\lambda \right) I_{Z_h} + \frac{1}{2\pi i} \int_{\Gamma_+^\eta} \frac{e^{\lambda t}}{\lambda} A_h(\lambda - A_h)^{-1} d\lambda. \qquad (22)$$

The first integral at the right hand side of (22) is independent of $\eta > 0$ and therefore can be calculated by taking the limit for $\eta \to \infty$; some easy estimates show that it vanishes. Hence we have

$$S_+(t) = \frac{1}{2\pi i} \int_{\Gamma_+^\eta} \frac{e^{\lambda t}}{\lambda} A_h(\lambda - A_h)^{-1} d\lambda \quad , \quad \forall t > 0, \forall \eta \in (0, \beta). \qquad (23)$$

Using (10) and the fact that $\alpha \in [0, 1)$ it follows that

$$\|S_+(t)\|_{\mathcal{L}(Y_h; Z_h)} \leq \frac{Me^{-\eta t}}{2\pi} \|A_h\|_{\mathcal{L}(X_h; Z_h)} \int_{\Gamma_+^\eta} \frac{d|\lambda|}{|\lambda|^{2-\alpha}} \leq C_\eta e^{-\eta t} \ , \ \forall t > 0. \qquad (24)$$

We conclude (by dominated convergence) that

$$\pi_s := \lim_{t \to 0^+} S_+(t)|_{Y_h} = \frac{1}{2\pi i} \int_{\Gamma_+^\eta} \frac{A_h}{\lambda} (\lambda - A_h)^{-1} d\lambda \in \mathcal{L}(Y_h; Z_h) \qquad (25)$$

is well defined. In a similar way we have

$$\pi_u := \lim_{t \to 0^-} S_-(t)|_{Y_h} = \frac{1}{2\pi i} \int_{\Gamma_-^\eta} \frac{A_h}{\lambda} (\lambda - A_h)^{-1} d\lambda \in \mathcal{L}(Y_h; Z_h); \qquad (26)$$

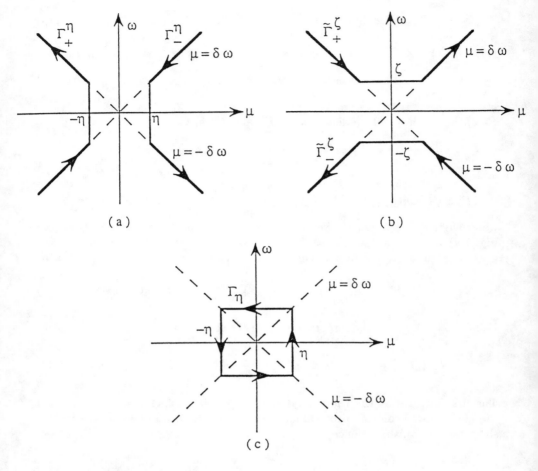

Fig. 1. The paths Γ^η_+, Γ^η_-, $\widetilde{\Gamma}^\zeta_+$ $\widetilde{\Gamma}^\zeta_-$ and Γ_η

in (25) and (26) we have to take $\eta \in (0, \beta)$.

In order to prove (20) we define for each $\zeta > 0$ paths $\widetilde{\Gamma}^\zeta_+$ and $\widetilde{\Gamma}^\zeta_-$ in $\mathbf{C}$ by

$$\widetilde{\Gamma}^\zeta_+ = \{\mu + i\delta^{-1}|\mu| \mid \mu \in \mathbf{R}, |\mu| \geq \delta\zeta\} \cup \{\mu + i\zeta \mid \mu \in \mathbf{R}, |\mu| \leq \delta\zeta\}$$

and

$$\widetilde{\Gamma}^\zeta_- = \{\mu - i\delta^{-1}|\mu| \mid \mu \in \mathbf{R}, |\mu| \geq \delta\zeta\} \cup \{\mu - i\zeta \mid \mu \in \mathbf{R}, |\mu| \leq \delta\zeta\};$$

we orient $\widetilde{\Gamma}_+^\zeta$ and $\widetilde{\Gamma}_-^\zeta$ in the sense of increasing, respectively decreasing μ (see Fig. 1.b). Next we let

$$B_+ := \frac{1}{2\pi i} \int_{\widetilde{\Gamma}_+^\zeta} \frac{A_h}{\lambda} (\lambda - A_h)^{-1} d\lambda \ \text{ and } \ B_- := \frac{1}{2\pi i} \int_{\widetilde{\Gamma}_-^\zeta} \frac{A_h}{\lambda} (\lambda - A_h)^{-1} d\lambda;$$

these expressions are independent of $\zeta > 0$. Using (10) we find

$$\|B_+\|_{\mathcal{L}(Y_h; Z_h)} \le \frac{M}{2\pi} \|A_h\|_{\mathcal{L}(X_h; Z_h)} \int_{\widetilde{\Gamma}_+^\zeta} \frac{d|\lambda|}{|\lambda|^{2-\alpha}} \longrightarrow 0 \text{ as } \zeta \to \infty.$$

We conclude that $B_+ = B_- = 0$.

Now fix some $\eta \in (0, \beta)$; using (25)–(26), and taking $\zeta = \delta^{-1}\eta$ in the definition of B_+ and B_- we find

$$\pi_s + \pi_u = \pi_s + \pi_u + B_+ + B_- = \frac{-1}{2\pi i} \oint_{\Gamma_\eta} \frac{A_h}{\lambda} (\lambda - A_h)^{-1} d\lambda,$$

where $\Gamma_\eta = -(\Gamma_+^\eta + \widetilde{\Gamma}_+^\zeta + \Gamma_-^\eta + \widetilde{\Gamma}_-^\zeta)$ is a clockwise oriented closed path around the origin and contained in the resolvent set of A_h (see Fig. 1.c). Using once more (12), and denoting by $J_{Y_h; Z_h}$ the canonical injection of Y_h into Z_h, we obtain

$$\pi_s + \pi_u = \left(\frac{1}{2\pi i} \oint_{\Gamma_\eta} \frac{d\lambda}{\lambda} \right) J_{Y_h; Z_h} - \frac{1}{2\pi i} \oint_{\Gamma_\eta} (\lambda - A_h)^{-1} d\lambda = J_{Y_h; Z_h}.$$

This proves (20) and concludes the proof of the lemma.

Remark 1. Since X_h is continuously embedded in Y_h it follows from (24) that for each $\eta \in (0, \beta)$ there exists a constant $C_\eta > 0$ such that

$$\|S_+(t)\|_{\mathcal{L}(X_h; Z_h)} \le C_\eta e^{-\eta t} \ (t > 0) \ \text{ and } \ \|S_-(t)\|_{\mathcal{L}(X_h; Z_h)} \le C_\eta e^{-\eta|t|} \ (t < 0). \tag{27}$$

Remark 2. There exist quite general additional hypotheses which imply that the operators π_s and π_u extend to bounded linear projections on Z; the proof however requires much more sophisticated techniques (see e.g. Burak [4] or Grisvard and da Prato [11]).

Lemma 4. *Assume* (Σ), *with* $\alpha \in (0, 1)$. *Then there exists a constant* $\widetilde{M} = \widetilde{M}(\alpha) > 0$ *such that*

$$\|S_+(t)\|_{\mathcal{L}(Y_h; X_h)} \le \widetilde{M}(\alpha)(1 + t^{-\alpha}) e^{-\beta t} \ , \quad \forall t > 0, \tag{28}$$

and

$$\|S_-(t)\|_{\mathcal{L}(Y_h; X_h)} \le \widetilde{M}(\alpha)(1 + |t|^{-\alpha}) e^{-\beta|t|} \ , \quad \forall t < 0. \tag{29}$$

If (Σ) *holds with* $\alpha = 0$, *then (28) and (29) hold for each* $\alpha \in (0, 1)$.

Proof. If (Σ) holds with $\alpha = 0$, then (10) holds for $\alpha = 0$, and hence also for each $\alpha \in (0, 1)$. So we can suppose, without loss of generality, that (10) holds for some $\alpha \in (0, 1)$. Fixing some $\eta \in (0, \beta)$ we find from (10) and (21) that for each $t > 0$:

$$\|S_+(t)\|_{\mathcal{L}(Y_h; X_h)} \leq \frac{M}{2\pi} \int_{\Gamma_+^\eta} |e^{\lambda t}| \frac{d|\lambda|}{(1 + |\lambda|)^{1-\alpha}}$$

$$\leq \frac{M}{\pi} \left(\delta^{-1} \eta e^{\eta t} + (1 + \delta)^\alpha \int_{\delta^{-1}\eta}^\infty e^{-\delta\omega t} \frac{d\omega}{\omega^{1-\alpha}} \right)$$

$$\leq \frac{M}{\pi\delta} \left(\beta + \frac{1+\delta}{t^\alpha} \int_0^\infty e^{-s} \frac{ds}{s^{1-\alpha}} \right) e^{-\eta t}.$$

Taking the limit for $\eta \to \beta$ one obtains (28) for an appropriate $\widetilde{M} = \widetilde{M}(\alpha)$; (29) is obtained in a similar way.

Using the foregoing estimates we can now prove the main result of this section.

Theorem 1. *Assume* (Σ) *and let* $\eta \in [0, \beta)$. *Then the equation*

$$\dot{x}_h = A_h x_h + f(t) \tag{30}$$

has for each $f \in BC^\eta(\mathbf{R}; Y_h)$ *a unique solution* $\widetilde{x}_h \in BC^\eta(\mathbf{R}; X_h)$, *given by*

$$\widetilde{x}_h(t) = (K_h f)(t) := \int_{-\infty}^t S_+(t-s)f(s)ds - \int_t^\infty S_-(t-s)f(s)ds. \tag{31}$$

Moreover, there exists a continuous function $\gamma : [0, \beta) \to \mathbf{R}_+$ *such that*

$$\|K_h\|_{\mathcal{L}(BC^\eta(\mathbf{R}, Y_h); BC^\eta(\mathbf{R}; X_h))} \leq \gamma(\eta) \quad , \quad \forall \eta \in [0, \beta). \tag{32}$$

Proof. Fix some $\eta \in [0, \beta)$ and some $f \in BC^\eta(\mathbf{R}; Y_h)$, and let $\widetilde{x}_h(t)$ be given by (31). Let $\widetilde{S}(t) := S_+(t)$ for $t > 0$ and $\widetilde{S}(t) := -S_-(t)$ for $t < 0$. Then we have

$$\widetilde{x}_h(t) = \int_{-\infty}^\infty \widetilde{S}(t-s)f(s)ds = \int_{-\infty}^\infty \widetilde{S}(s)f(t-s)ds. \tag{33}$$

Now $\|f(t-s)\| \leq \|f\|_\eta e^{\eta(t-s)} \leq \|f\|_\eta e^{\eta(|t|+|s|)}$, and hence, using lemma 4:

$$\|\widetilde{x}_h(t)\|_{X_h} \leq \|f\|_\eta e^{\eta|t|} \int_{-\infty}^\infty \|\widetilde{S}(s)\|_{\mathcal{L}(Y_h; X_h)} e^{\eta|s|} ds$$

$$\leq \widetilde{M} \|f\|_\eta e^{\eta|t|} \int_{-\infty}^\infty e^{-(\beta-\eta)|s|}(1 + |s|^{-\alpha})ds = \gamma(\eta)\|f\|_\eta e^{\eta|t|}.$$

Since $f : \mathbf{R} \to Y_h$ is continuous it follows from these estimates and from dominated convergence that $\widetilde{x}_h : \mathbf{R} \to X_h$ is continuous, that $\widetilde{x}_h \in BC^\eta(\mathbf{R}; X_h)$, and that (32) holds.

Next we calculate, in Z_h, the derivative $\dot{\widetilde{x}}_h(t)$; using lemma's 2 and 3 and the fact that f takes its values in the intermediate space Y_h we find

$$
\begin{aligned}
\dot{\widetilde{x}}_h(t) &= \lim_{s \to t^-} S_+(t-s)f(s) + \lim_{s \to t^+} S_-(t-s)f(s) \\
&\quad + \int_{-\infty}^{t} A_h S_+(t-s)f(s)ds - \int_{t}^{\infty} A_h S_-(t-s)f(s)ds \\
&= A_h \widetilde{x}_h(t) + (\pi_s + \pi_u)f(t) \\
&= A_h \widetilde{x}_h(t) + f(t).
\end{aligned}
$$

We conclude that $\widetilde{x}_h$ is indeed a solution of (30).

To prove the uniqueness of this solution we show that if $\widetilde{x}_h \in BC^\eta(\mathbf{R}; X_h)$ is any solution of

$$\dot{x}_h = A_h x_h, \tag{34}$$

then $\widetilde{x}_h = 0$. To prove this, fix some $t_0 \in \mathbf{R}$ and define $\widetilde{x}_+ : (-\infty, t_0) \to X_h$ and $\widetilde{x}_- : (t_0, \infty) \to X_h$ by

$$\widetilde{X}_+(t) := S_+(t_0 - t)\widetilde{x}_h(t) \ (t < t_0) \quad \text{and} \quad \widetilde{x}_-(t) := S_-(t_0 - t)\widetilde{x}_h(t) \ (t > t_0).$$

Using (18) and considering $\widetilde{x}_+$ as a mapping in Z_h we find

$$\dot{\widetilde{x}}_+(t) = -S_+(t_0 - t)A\widetilde{x}_h(t) + S_+(t_0 - t)\dot{\widetilde{x}}_h(t) = 0 \quad , \quad \forall t < t_0,$$

and hence

$$\widetilde{x}_+(t) = \lim_{s \to -\infty} \widetilde{x}_+(s) \quad , \quad \forall t < t_0. \tag{35}$$

Taking $s < \min(0, t_0)$ and $\varepsilon \in (0, \beta - \eta)$ we obtain from (27) that

$$\|\widetilde{x}_+(s)\|_{Z_h} \leq \|S_+(t_0 - s)\|_{\mathcal{L}(X_h; Z_h)} \|\widetilde{x}_h(s)\|_{X_h} \leq C_{\eta+\varepsilon} e^{-(\eta+\varepsilon)t_0} e^{\varepsilon s} \|\widetilde{x}_h\|_\eta. \tag{36}$$

It follows from (35) and (36) that $\widetilde{x}_+(t) = 0$ for all $t < t_0$; in the same way one proves that $\widetilde{x}_-(t) = 0$ for all $t > t_0$. But then

$$\widetilde{x}_h(t_0) = \pi_s \widetilde{x}_h(t_0) + \pi_u \widetilde{x}_h(t_0) = \lim_{t \to t_0^-} \widetilde{x}_+(t) + \lim_{t \to t_0^+} \widetilde{x}_-(t) = 0.$$

Since this holds for all $t_0 \in \mathbf{R}$ we conclude that $\widetilde{x}_h = 0$, and the proof is complete.

A particular case: analytic semigroups

In many examples where the equation (1.1) represents a parabolic equation the operator A is the generator of an analytic semigroup. We want to show now that our hypothesis (Σ) is satisfied for this important class of applications. To prove this we need some results from the theory of analytic semigroups and fractional powers of operators. For the details of this theory we refer to Henry [14] or Pazy [27].

Consider the following hypothesis:

(S) $A : D(A) \subset Z \to Z$ is a densely defined closed linear operator, with the following properties:

(i) $\sigma(A) \cap i\mathbf{R}$ consists of a finite number of isolated eigenvalues, each with a finite-dimensional generalized eigenspace;

(ii) there exist constants $a \in \mathbf{R}$, $\delta^* > 0$ and $C > 0$ such that if $\lambda \in \mathbf{C}$ and

$$\operatorname{Re}\lambda \geq a - \delta^*|\operatorname{Im}\lambda|, \tag{37}$$

then $\lambda \in \varrho(A)$ and

$$\|(\lambda - A)^{-1}\|_{\mathcal{L}(Z)} \leq \frac{C}{1 + |\lambda|}. \tag{38}$$

It follows from (S)(ii) that A generates an analytic semigroup $\{e^{At} \mid t \geq 0\}$ of bounded linear operators on Z. We want to show that the hypothesis (S) implies (Σ) for an appropriate choice of the space Y. As before we set $X := D(A)$ with the graph norm. It follows directly from (S)(ii) that for $\omega \in \mathbf{R}$ and $|\omega|$ sufficiently large we have $i\omega \in \varrho(A)$, $\|(i\omega - A)^{-1}\|_{\mathcal{L}(Z)} \leq C|\omega|^{-1}$, and $\|(i\omega - A)^{-1}\|_{\mathcal{L}(X)} \leq C|\omega|^{-1}$.

In order to define the space Y we set

$$B := aI - A; \tag{39}$$

then $-B$ generates an analytic semigroup $e^{-Bt} = e^{-at}e^{At}$ ($t \geq 0$) and moreover B satisfies the conditions needed to construct the fractional powers B^α ($\alpha \in \mathbf{R}$); in particular there exists a number $\gamma > 0$ such that $\operatorname{Re}\lambda > \gamma$ for all $\lambda \in \sigma(B)$. The fractional powers B^α ($\alpha \in \mathbf{R}$) have the following properties (see [14] or [27] for the details and proofs):

(a) $B^\alpha \in \mathcal{L}(Z)$ is injective for each $\alpha \leq 0$;

(b) $B^\alpha : D(B^\alpha) = R(B^{-\alpha}) \subset Z \to Z$ is a densely defined closed linear operator, for each $\alpha > 0$;

(c) $B^0 = I_Z$ and $B^1 = B$ (and hence $D(B^1) = D(B) = D(A)$);

(d) if $\alpha_1 \geq \alpha_2 > 0$ then $D(B^{\alpha_1}) \subset D(B^{\alpha_2})$;

(e) $B^{\alpha_1}B^{\alpha_2} = B^{\alpha_2}B^{\alpha_1} = B^{\alpha_1+\alpha_2}$ on $D(B^\alpha)$, where $\alpha = \max(\alpha_1, \alpha_2, \alpha_1 + \alpha_2)$;

(f) for each $\alpha \geq 0$ and $t > 0$ we have $e^{-Bt} \in \mathcal{L}(Z, D(B^\alpha))$, $B^\alpha e^{-Bt} \in \mathcal{L}(Z)$, and

$$\|B^\alpha e^{-Bt}\|_{\mathcal{L}(Z)} \leq M_\alpha t^{-\alpha}e^{-\gamma t} \quad, \quad \forall t > 0, \tag{40}$$

for some constant $M_\alpha > 0$ depending only on $\alpha \geq 0$;

(g) $B^\alpha e^{-Bt} = e^{-Bt}B^\alpha$ on $D(B^\alpha)$, for each $t > 0$ and each $\alpha \geq 0$.

Now fix some $\alpha \in [0, 1)$, and let $Y := D(B^{1-\alpha})$, with the graph norm

$$\|y\|_Y := \|y\|_Z + \|B^{1-\alpha}y\|_Z;$$

it follows easily that X is continuously embedded in Y and Y continuously embedded in Z; remark that in $X = D(B)$ we can use the graph norm of B, which is equivalent to the graph norm of A. Since $e^{-Bt} \in \mathcal{L}(Z; X)$ for $t > 0$ we have also $e^{-Bt} \in \mathcal{L}(Y; X)$; using the properties (a)–(g) we find then for each $y \in Y$ and each $t > 0$ that

$$
\begin{aligned}
\|e^{-Bt}y\|_X &= \|e^{-Bt}y\|_Z + \|Be^{-Bt}y\|_Z \\
&= \|e^{-Bt}y\|_Z + \|B^\alpha e^{-Bt}B^{1-\alpha}y\|_Z \\
&\leq M_0 e^{-\gamma t}\|y\|_Z + M_\alpha t^{-\alpha}e^{-\gamma t}\|B^{1-\alpha}y\|_Z \\
&\leq C_1(1 + t^{-\alpha})e^{-\gamma t}\|y\|_Y,
\end{aligned}
$$

where $C_1 > 0$ is an appropriate constant; we conclude that

$$
\|e^{-Bt}\|_{\mathcal{L}(Y;X)} \leq C_1(1 + t^{-\alpha})e^{-\gamma t} \quad, \quad \forall t > 0. \tag{41}
$$

Now we have for real $\mu \geq 0$ that

$$
(\mu + B)^{-1} = \int_0^\infty e^{-\mu t}e^{-Bt}dt; \tag{42}
$$

using (41) it follows then for $\mu \geq 1$ that

$$
\|(\mu + B)^{-1}\|_{\mathcal{L}(Y;X)} \leq C_1 \int_0^\infty e^{-\mu t}(1 + t^{-\alpha})dt \leq \frac{C_2}{\mu^{1-\alpha}}. \tag{43}
$$

Finally, let $\omega_0 \geq 1$ be such that $i\omega \in \varrho(A)$ for $\omega \in \mathbf{R}$, $|\omega| \geq \omega_0$, while $\|(i\omega - A)^{-1}\|_{\mathcal{L}(X)} \leq C|\omega|^{-1}$. Combining this with (43) and with the identity

$$
(i\omega - A)^{-1} - (\mu + B)^{-1} = (\mu + a - i\omega)(i\omega - A)^{-1}(\mu + B)^{-1}, \tag{44}
$$
$$
\forall \omega \in \mathbf{R}, \; |\omega| \geq \omega_0, \; \forall \mu > 0,
$$

we find, for $|\omega| \geq \omega_0$ and $\mu \geq 1$:

$$
\begin{aligned}
\|(i\omega - A)^{-1}\|_{\mathcal{L}(Y)} &\leq \left(1 + |\mu + a - i\omega|\|(i\omega - A)^{-1}\|_{\mathcal{L}(X)}\right)\|(\mu + b)^{-1}\|_{\mathcal{L}(Y;X)} \\
&\leq \frac{C_1}{\mu^{1-\alpha}}\left(1 + C\frac{|\mu + a - i\omega|}{|\omega|}\right);
\end{aligned}
$$

taking $\mu = |\omega|$ proves that

$$
\|(i\omega - A)^{-1}\|_{\mathcal{L}(Y;X)} \leq \frac{C_2}{|\omega|^{1-\alpha}} \quad, \quad \forall \omega \in \mathbf{R}, \; |\omega| \geq \omega_0. \tag{45}
$$

We conclude that the hypothesis (Σ) is satisfied.

In certain cases, such as e.g. the first example given in Sect. 3, it is easier to verify directly (Σ) than to verify (S); our approach then allows to apply center manifold theory without using fractional powers. In other cases the hypothesis (Σ) holds, although (S) does not.

Remark. Under the hypothesis (S) one can show that the operators π_u and π_s given by lemma 3 can be extended to bounded linear operators on Z. In fact, $\pi_u \in \mathcal{L}(Z)$ is a projection, with $X_u := \pi_u(Z) \subset X$ such that $A_u := A|_{X_u}$ is a bounded linear operator on X_u, with $\sigma(A_u) = \{\lambda \in \sigma(A) \mid \text{Re } \lambda > 0\}$. Also π_s is a projection in Z, given by $\pi_s = I_Z - \pi_u - \pi_c$, and hence $\pi_h = \pi_s + \pi_u$. Moreover, we also have

$$S_-(t) = e^{A_u t} \pi_u|_{Z_h} \qquad , \qquad \forall t < 0$$

and

$$S_+(t) = e^{At} \pi_s|_{Z_h} \qquad , \qquad \forall t > 0.$$

We conclude this section with some brief remarks on a class of equations for which the center manifold theory of Sect. 1 applies but which do not necessarily satisfy the hypothesis (Σ) of this section. It follows from the proof of theorem 1 that in order to reach the conclusions of that theorem it is sufficient to have operators $S_+(t)$ $(t > 0)$, $S_-(t)$ $(t < 0)$, π_s and π_u satisfying the conclusions of lemma's 2-4, together with (18) and (27). A particular case for which such operators can be constructed is when the operator A generates a strongly continuous semigroup. To be more precise, consider the following hypothesis:

(C) $Z = X_{cu} \times Z_s$ and $A(x_{cu}, x_s) = (A_{cu} x_{cu}, A_s x_s)$, where X_{cu} and Z_s are Banach spaces, $A_{cu} \in \mathcal{L}(X_{cu})$, $A_s : D(A_s) \subset Z_s \to Z_s$ is a densely defined closed linear operator, and $(x_{cu}, x_s) \in X_{cu} \times D(A_s)$; it is assumed that these operators satisfy the following conditions:

(i) $\operatorname{Re} \lambda \geq 0$ for all $\lambda \in \sigma(A_{cu})$, and $\sigma(A_{cu}) \cap i\mathbf{R}$ consists of a finite number of isolated eigenvalues, each with a finite-dimensional generalized eigenspace;

(ii) A_s is the infinitesimal generator of a strongly continuous semigroup $\{e^{A_s t} \mid t \geq 0\}$ of bounded linear operators on Z_s, satisfying

$$\|e^{A_s t}\|_{\mathcal{L}(Z_s)} \leq M e^{-\beta t} \quad , \quad \forall t \geq 0 \tag{46}$$

for some $M \geq 1$ and $\beta > 0$.

As shown in [19] or [27] the condition (C)(ii) is equivalent to the condition that $\{\mu \in \mathbf{R} \mid \mu > -\beta\} \subset \varrho(A_s)$ and

$$\|(\mu - A_s)^{-n}\|_{\mathcal{L}(Z_s)} \leq \frac{M}{(\mu + \beta)^n} \quad , \quad n = 1, 2, \ldots . \tag{47}$$

When $M = 1$ it is sufficient that (47) holds for $n = 1$.

Assuming (C) we set $X = X_{cu} \times X_s$, where $X_s := D(A_s)$ is equiped with the graph norm of A_s. Defining $\pi_c \in \mathcal{L}(X_{cu})$ by (3) (in which we replace A by A_{cu}), and setting $X_u := (I - \pi_c)(X_{cu})$ we take then $Z_h = X_u \times Z_s$, $X_h = X_u \times X_s$, $\pi_u(x_u, z_s) = (x_u, 0)$, $\pi_s(x_u, z_s) = (0, z_s)$, $S_+(t)(x_u, z_s) = (0, e^{A_s t} z_s)$ for $t > 0$, and $S_-(t)(x_u, z_s) = (e^{A_{cu} t} x_u, 0)$ for $t < 0$. Taking $Y = X$ and hence $\alpha = 0$ we can then repeat the proof of theorem 1 to show that although the mapping $S_+ : (0, \infty) \to \mathcal{L}(Z_h)$ is in general not C^1, we have that for each $x \in X_h$ the mapping $t \mapsto S_+(t)x$ is continuously differentiable, which is sufficient to carry out the proof.

We conclude that either of the hypotheses (Σ), (S) or (C) imply (H) for appropriate choices of Y; these hypotheses are therefore sufficient for the existence of a local center manifold for (1.1), with the properties described in Sect. 1.

4. Examples

In this section we consider in detail some simple examples on which we show how our hypotheses can be verified. These examples are: a parabolic equation, which is usually treated using the theory of analytic semigroups; an elliptic equation in a strip, on which we illustrate the approach of Kirchgässner; and a nonlinear wave equation which fits into the framework of C_0 semigroups. For this last example we also use the existence of a center manifold to make a brief bifurcation analysis. To the specialists these examples will probably appear trivial, but, as we already pointed out in the introduction, we have written them out with the non-specialist in mind.

As a first example we consider the parabolic equation

$$\begin{cases} \dfrac{\partial u}{\partial t} = \dfrac{\partial^2 u}{\partial x^2} + u + g\left(u, \dfrac{\partial u}{\partial x}\right), \\ u(0,t) = u(\pi,t) = 0 \quad, \quad (x,t) \in (0,\pi) \times \mathbf{R}. \end{cases} \tag{1}$$

We suppose that $g \in C^{k+1}(\mathbf{R}^2; \mathbf{R})$ for some $k \geq 1$, and that $g(u,v) = O(|u|^2 + |v|^2)$ as $(u,v) \to (0,0)$. We can rewrite (1) in the form (1.1) by introducing the following spaces and operators. We set $Z := L_2(0,\pi)$, $X := H_2(0,\pi) \cap \overset{\circ}{H}_1(0,\pi)$, and define $A \in \mathcal{L}(X;Z)$ by

$$Au := \frac{d^2 u}{dx^2} + u = (D^2 + 1)u, \tag{2}$$

where $D := d/dx$. Since $H_1(0,\pi) \subset C^0([0,\pi])$ we have for each $u \in X$ that $g(u, Du)$, $(\partial g/\partial u)(u, Du)$ and $(\partial g/\partial v)(u, Du)$ are in $C^0([0,\pi])$; from this it follows that the mapping $u \mapsto g(u, Du)$ is of class C^k from X into $Y := H_1(0,\pi)$. We want to show now that the operator A defined by (2) satisfies the hypothesis (Σ) of Sect. 3.

The spectrum of A is well known; it consists of the simple eigenvalues $\lambda_n := 1 - n^2$, with $n = 1, 2, \ldots$, corresponding to the eigenfunctions $u_n(x) := \sin nx$. Hence we have just one simple eigenvalue on the imaginary axis, namely $\lambda_1 = 0$. Next let $\lambda \in \varrho(A)$, $v \in Z = L_2(0,\pi)$ and $u := (\lambda - A)^{-1}v \in X$. Then we have

$$- D^2 u + (\lambda - 1)u = v. \tag{3}$$

Multiplying (3) by $\bar{u}$ and integrating over $(0,\pi)$ shows that

$$\|Du\|_{L_2}^2 + (\lambda - 1)\|u\|_{L_2}^2 = \int_0^\pi v\bar{u}\, dx. \tag{4}$$

Taking $\lambda = i\omega$ with $\omega \in \mathbf{R} \backslash \{0\}$, and considering the imaginary part of (4) gives $|\omega|\|u\|_{L_2}^2 \leq \|v\|_{L_2}\|u\|_{L_2}$, and hence

$$\|(i\omega - A)^{-1}\|_{\mathcal{L}(Z)} \leq |\omega|^{-1} \quad, \quad \forall \omega \in \mathbf{R} \backslash \{0\}. \tag{5}$$

As an intermediate step to proving the estimate (3.2) we consider the equation

$$- D^2 u + s^2 u = v, \tag{6}$$

with $s \in \mathbf{R}$; throughout the following discussion we restrict attention to the case $|s| \geq 1$. Using Fourier series it is easy to show that the equation (6) has for each $v \in H_m(0, \pi)$ $(m \geq -1)$ a unique solution $u \in H_{m+2}(0, \pi) \cap \overset{\circ}{H}_1(0, \pi)$. Let us use the notation $\|u\|_m := \|u\|_{H_m(0,\pi)}$ and $|u|_m := \|D^m u\|_{L_2(0,\pi)}$.

First we take $v \in H_{-1}(0, \pi)$ and $u \in \overset{\circ}{H}_1(0, \pi)$; then (6) is an equality in $H_{-1}(0, \pi) = (\overset{\circ}{H}_1(0, \pi))^*$ which we can apply to u to find

$$|u|_1^2 + s^2 \|u\|_0^2 \leq \|v\|_{-1} \|u\|_1;$$

this implies

$$\|u\|_1 \leq \|v\|_{-1} \quad \text{and} \quad |s| \|u\|_0 \leq \|v\|_{-1}. \tag{7}$$

Next we take $v \in L_2(0, \pi)$ and $u \in H_2(0, \pi) \cap \overset{\circ}{H}_1(0, \pi)$. Taking the inner product in $L_2(0, \pi)$ of (6) with u gives

$$|u|_1^2 + s^2 \|u\|_0^2 \leq \|v\|_0 \|u\|_0,$$

from which we find

$$|s|^2 \|u\|_0 \leq \|v\|_0 \quad \text{and} \quad |s| \|u\|_1 \leq \|v\|_0. \tag{8}$$

Taking the inner product in $L_2(0, \pi)$ of (6) with $D^2 u$ gives

$$|u|_2^2 + s^2 |u|_1^2 \leq \|v\|_0 |u|_2, \tag{9}$$

and hence $|u|_2 \leq \|v\|_0$, which in combination with (8) gives

$$\|u\|_2 \leq C \|v\|_0 \tag{10}$$

for some appropriate $C > 0$.

If $v \in H_1(0, \pi)$ then we can rewrite (9) as

$$|u|_2^2 + s^2 |u|_1^2 \leq |v|_1 |u|_1 + |v(0)| |Du(0)| + |v(\pi)| |Du(\pi)|. \tag{11}$$

Let $\theta \in C^\infty([0, \pi], \mathbf{R})$ be such that $\theta(0) = 1$ and $\theta(\pi) = 0$; then

$$v(0) = -\int_0^\pi (D\theta \cdot v + \theta \cdot Dv) dx,$$

and hence $|v(0)| \leq C_1 \|v\|_1$; in a similar way we have $|v(\pi)| \leq C_1 \|v\|_1$, and then (8) and (11) imply

$$|u|_2^2 \leq C_1 (|Du(0)| + |Du(\pi)|) \|v\|_1 + s^{-1} \|v\|_1^2. \tag{12}$$

In order to estimate $Du(0)$ and $Du(\pi)$ we take the inner product of (6) with θu; considering the real part and after some integration by parts we find

$$|Du(0)|^2 = -\int_0^\pi D\theta |Du|^2 du + s^2 \int_0^\pi D\theta |u|^2 dx$$
$$- \int_0^\pi [D(\theta \bar{v})u + D(\theta v)\bar{u}] dx;$$

using (8) it follows that

$$|Du(0)|^2 \le C_2 s^{-2} \|v\|_1^2.$$

In a similar way one estimates $|Du(\pi)|$; bringing these estimates in (12) and combining with (8) then gives

$$\|u\|_2 \le C_3 s^{-1/2} \|v\|_1. \tag{13}$$

Now let us return to the equation (3), in which we take $\lambda = \mu \in \mathbf{R}$ with $\mu \ge 2$. Comparing with (6) and using (13) then proves that

$$\|(\mu - A)^{-1}\|_{\mathcal{L}(Y;X)} \le C_3 \mu^{-1/4} \quad , \quad \forall \mu \in \mathbf{R}, \, \mu \ge 2. \tag{14}$$

Finally, using the identity

$$(i\omega - A)^{-1} - (\mu - A)^{-1} = (\mu - i\omega)(i\omega - A)^{-1}(\mu - A)^{-1}$$

and the estimate $\|(i\omega - A)^{-1}\|_{\mathcal{L}(X)} \le |\omega|^{-1}$ which follows from (5), we find by taking $\mu = |\omega|$ that

$$\|(i\omega - A)^{-1}\|_{\mathcal{L}(Y;X)} \le C|\omega|^{-1/4} \quad , \quad \forall \omega \in \mathbf{R}, \, |\omega| \ge 2. \tag{15}$$

We conclude that the operator A defined by (2) satisfies the hypothesis (Σ), with $\alpha = 3/4$.

Remark. By considering complex λ with $\operatorname{Re} \lambda \ge 0$ and adapting the estimates one proves that A satisfies (S), and hence generates an analytic semigroup. Since $H_1(0, \pi) \subset D(B^{1-\alpha})$ for $\alpha > 3/4$ (we use the notation of Sect. 3) the usual approach (see e.g. [14]) consists in setting $Y = D(B^{1-\alpha})$ for some $\alpha \in (3/4, 1)$ and apply the interpolation theory summarized in Sect. 3. The elementary approach which we have used here gives the optimal result for $Y = H_1(0, \pi)$, namely $\alpha = 3/4$. (See [3] and [15] for more details).

Our second example is an elliptic problem on a strip:

$$\begin{cases} \dfrac{\partial^2 u}{\partial x^2} + \dfrac{\partial^2 u}{\partial y^2} + \mu u + g\left(u, \dfrac{\partial u}{\partial x}, \dfrac{\partial u}{\partial y}\right) = 0, \\ u(x, 0) = u(x, \pi) = 0, \forall x \in \mathbf{R}\, ; \, (x, y) \in \mathbf{R} \times (0, \pi). \end{cases} \tag{16}$$

We suppose that $g \in C^{k+1}(\mathbf{R}^3, \mathbf{R})$ $(k \ge 1)$, with $g(u, v, w) = O(|u|^2 + |v|^2 + |w|^2)$ as $(u, v, w) \to 0$. This example has been discussed before by Mielke in [23]; the basic idea, due to Kirchgässner [20], is to consider the x-coordinate in (16) as the time-variable, and to rewrite (16) as an evolution equation, as follows. Fix some $\mu_0 \in \mathbf{R}$ and let $\mu = \mu_0 + \nu$. We then rewrite (16) as

$$\frac{d}{dx}\begin{pmatrix} u_1 \\ u_2 \end{pmatrix} = A\begin{pmatrix} u_1 \\ u_2 \end{pmatrix} + \begin{pmatrix} 0 \\ -\nu u_1 - g(u_1, u_2, Du_1) \end{pmatrix}, \tag{17}$$

where

$$A = \begin{pmatrix} 0 & 1 \\ -D^2 - \mu_0 & 0 \end{pmatrix} \quad , \quad D = \frac{d}{dy}. \tag{18}$$

We have $A \in \mathcal{L}(X; Z)$, where $Z := \overset{\circ}{H}_1(0, \pi) \times L_2(0, \pi)$ and $X := (H_2(0, \pi) \cap \overset{\circ}{H}_1(0, \pi)) \times \overset{\circ}{H}_1(0, \pi)$. The same argument as for the example (1) proves that the mapping $(u_1, u_2) \mapsto (0, -\nu u_1 - g(u_1, u_2, Du_1))$ is of class C^k from X into the space $Y := (H_2(0, \pi) \cap \overset{\circ}{H}_1(0, \pi)) \times H_1(0, \pi)$. Remark that (17) depends on the scalar parameter ν, and has the form (2.24). Therefore we have for each sufficiently small ν a corresponding center manifold, on condition that the operator A satisfies the spectral hypotheses of Sect. 3.

To determine the spectrum of A fix some $\lambda \in \mathbf{C}$ and some $v = (v_1, v_2) \in Z$, and consider the equation

$$Au = \lambda u + v, \tag{19}$$

or more explicitly (with $u = (u_1, u_2)$):

$$\begin{aligned} u_2 &= \lambda u_1 + v_1, \\ -D^2 u_1 - \mu_0 u_1 &= \lambda u_2 + v_2. \end{aligned} \tag{20}$$

Eliminating u_2 we find

$$-D^2 u_1 - (\lambda^2 + \mu_0) u_1 = \lambda v_1 + v_2. \tag{21}$$

If this equation has for each $v \in Z$ a unique solution $u_1 \in H_2(0, \pi) \cap \overset{\circ}{H}_1(0, \pi)$, then also (19) has, via the first equation of (20), a unique solution $u \in X$, and λ is in the resolvent set of A. It follows that

$$\begin{aligned} \sigma(A) &= \{\lambda \in \mathbf{C} \mid \lambda^2 + \mu_0 = n^2, n = 1, 2, \dots\} \\ &= \{\lambda_{\pm n} := \pm\sqrt{n^2 - \mu_0} \mid n = 1, 2, \dots\}. \end{aligned} \tag{22}$$

The eigenfunctions corresponding to the eigenvalues $\lambda_{\pm n}$ are given by

$$\Phi_{\pm n}(y) = \begin{pmatrix} \sin ny \\ \lambda_{\pm n} \sin ny \end{pmatrix}, \quad n \geq 1.$$

If $n^2 \neq \mu_0$ then $\lambda_{\pm n}$ are simple eigenvalues; however, if $n^2 = \mu_0$, then $\lambda_{\pm n} = 0$ is non-semisimple, since the equation (20) with $(v_1, v_2) = (\sin ny, 0)$ has a solution $(u_1, u_2) = (0, \sin ny)$; in that case $\lambda_{\pm n} = 0$ has algebraic multiplicity two.

Now suppose that $\mu_0 \in [m^2, (m+1)^2)$ for some $m \geq 1$. Then $\operatorname{Re} \lambda_{\pm n} = 0$ for $1 \leq n \leq m$ and $\operatorname{Re} \lambda_{\pm n} \neq 0$ for $n > m$; more precisely:

$$|\operatorname{Re} \lambda_{\pm n}| \geq \beta := \sqrt{(m+1)^2 - \mu_0}, \quad \forall n \geq m + 1.$$

We conclude that the center subspace X_c is $2m$-dimensional.

To verify that A satisfies (Σ) we will use again the estimates (7)–(13) satisfied by the solutions of the equation (6). We consider (19), or equivalently (20), for $\lambda = i\omega$, with $\omega \in \mathbf{R}$ and $\omega^2 \geq \mu_0 + 1$. We first take $v_1 = 0$ and $v_2 \in L_2(0, \pi)$, then (21) in combination with (8) gives

$$(\omega^2 - \mu_0)\|u_1\|_0 \leq \|v_2\|_0 \quad \text{and} \quad (\omega^2 - \mu_0)^{1/2}\|u_1\|_1 \leq \|v_2\|_0.$$

Since $u_2 = i\omega u_1$ it follows that

$$\|u_2\|_0 \leq \frac{|\omega|}{\omega^2 - \mu_0}\|v_2\|_0 \leq \frac{C_1}{|\omega|}\|v_2\|_0$$

and

$$\|u_1\|_1 \leq \frac{1}{(\omega^2 - \mu_0)^{1/2}}\|v_2\|_0 \leq \frac{C_2}{|\omega|}\|v_2\|_0,$$

where C_1 and C_2 are constants independent of ω. Next we take $v_2 = 0$ and $v_1 \in \overset{\circ}{H}_1(0, \pi)$; eliminating u_1 from (20) we find the following equation in $H_{-1}(0, \pi)$:

$$- D^2u_2 + (\omega^2 - \mu_0)u_2 = -D^2v_1 - \mu_0 v_1. \tag{23}$$

Using (7) we conclude that

$$\|u_2\|_1 \leq \|D^2v_1 + \mu_0 v_1\|_{-1} \leq C_3\|v_1\|_1$$

and

$$(\omega^2 - \mu_0)^{1/2}\|u_2\|_0 \leq C_3\|v_1\|_1;$$

since $u_1 = (i\omega)^{-1}(u_2 - v_1)$ it follows that

$$\|u_1\|_1 \leq \frac{C_4}{|\omega|}\|v_1\|_1 \quad \text{and} \quad \|u_1\|_0 \leq \frac{C_4}{|\omega|}\|v_1\|_1.$$

These estimates in combination with the linearity of $(i\omega - A)^{-1}$ then imply that

$$\|(i\omega - A)^{-1}\|_{\mathcal{L}(Z)} \leq \frac{C}{|\omega|} \quad , \quad \forall \omega \in \mathbf{R} , \ \omega^2 \geq \mu_0 + 1. \tag{24}$$

Next suppose that $(v_1, v_2) \in Y = (H_2(0, \pi) \cap \overset{\circ}{H}_1(0, \pi)) \times H_1(0, \pi)$. If $v_1 = 0$ then it follows from (21), (8) and (13) that

$$\|u_1\|_1 \leq C_5(\omega^2 - \mu_0)^{-3/4}\|v_2\|_1 \quad \text{and} \quad \|u_1\|_2 \leq C_5(\omega^2 - \mu_0)^{-1/4}\|v_2\|_1;$$

since $u_2 = i\omega u_1$ it follows that

$$\|u_1\|_2 \leq C_6|\omega|^{-1/2}\|v_2\|_1 \quad \text{and} \quad \|u_2\|_1 \leq C_6|\omega|^{-1/2}\|v_2\|_1. \tag{25}$$

From the other side, if $v_2 = 0$ then $(v_1, 0) \in X$, and we can use the estimate $\|(i\omega - A)^{-1}\|_{\mathcal{L}(X)} \leq C|\omega|^{-1}$ which follows from (24). In combination with (25) and the linearity of $(i\omega - A)^{-1}$ this proves that

$$\|(i\omega - A)^{-1}\|_{\mathcal{L}(Y;X)} \leq \frac{C'}{|\omega|^{1/2}} \quad , \quad \forall \omega \in \mathbf{R} , \ \omega^2 \geq \mu_0 + 1. \tag{26}$$

We conclude that the operator A defined by (18) satisfies (Σ), and hence we can apply our center manifold theory to the equation (16); in particular, all sufficiently small, globally bounded solutions of (16) will be in the local center manifold of (16). We also remark that for this example the hypothesis (S) is not satisfied, and hence the semigroup approach does not apply.

As a third example we consider the following damped nonlinear wave equation, discussed (among others) by Hale and Scheurle in [13]:

$$\begin{cases} \dfrac{\partial^2 u}{\partial t^2} = \dfrac{\partial^2 u}{\partial x^2} - 2\delta \dfrac{\partial u}{\partial t} + \nu u + f(u), \\ x \in (0, \pi), u(0, t) = u(\pi, t) = 0. \end{cases} \tag{27}$$

In this equation δ is a positive constant satisfying $0 < \delta^2 < 3$, ν is a real parameter varying near 1, and $f : \mathbf{R} \to \mathbf{R}$ is supposed to be of class C^{k+1} for some $k \geq 1$, with $f(u) = O(|u|^2)$ as $u \to 0$. We rewrite (27) in the form

$$\frac{d}{dt} \begin{pmatrix} u_1 \\ u_2 \end{pmatrix} = A \begin{pmatrix} u_1 \\ u_2 \end{pmatrix} + \begin{pmatrix} 0 \\ (\nu - 1)u_1 + f(u_1) \end{pmatrix}, \tag{28}$$

with

$$A = \begin{pmatrix} 0 & 1 \\ D^2 + 1 & -2\delta \end{pmatrix} \quad , \quad D = \frac{d}{dx}. \tag{29}$$

The operator $A : D(A) = X := (H_2(0, \pi) \cap \overset{\circ}{H}_1(0, \pi)) \times \overset{\circ}{H}_1(0, \pi) \to Z = H_1(0, \pi) \times L_2(0, \pi)$ is densely defined and closed, while the map $(u_1, u_2) \mapsto (0, (\nu - 1)u_1 + f(u_1))$ is of class C^k from X into itself.

Let $(v_1, v_2) \in Z$ and $\lambda \in \mathbf{C}$; then the equation

$$A(u_1, u_2) = \lambda(u_1, u_2) + (v_1, v_2)$$

for $(u_1, u_2) \in X$ takes the more explicit form

$$D^2 u_1 + (1 - 2\delta\lambda - \lambda^2)u_1 = (2\delta + \lambda)v_1 + v_2 \quad , \quad u_2 = \lambda u_1 + v_1.$$

It follows that

$$\sigma(A) = \{\lambda_0 = 0, \lambda_1 = -2\delta\} \cup \{\lambda_n, \bar{\lambda}_n \mid n \geq 2\} \ , \ \lambda_n := -\delta + i(n^2 - 1 - \delta^2)^{1/2}. \tag{30}$$

All the elements in the spectrum of A are simple eigenvalues; except for the zero eigenvalue they all satisfy $\operatorname{Re} \lambda \leq -\delta$. The eigenvectors corresponding to λ_0, λ_1 and λ_n $(n \geq 2)$ are respectively $\phi_0 := (\sin x, 0)$, $\phi_1 := (1, -2\delta) \sin x$ and $\phi_n := (1, \lambda_n) \sin nx$ $(n \geq 2)$. We have $Z = X_0 \oplus Z_s$, with $X_0 := \operatorname{span} \phi_0$ and

$$Z_s := \left\{ (u_1, u_2) \in Z \mid \int_0^\pi u_2(x) \sin x \, dx = -2\delta \int_0^\pi u_1(x) \sin x \, dx \right\}.$$

We want to show now that the restriction A_s of A to $Z_s \cap X$ generates a strongly continuous semigroup $\{e^{A_s t} \mid t \geq 0\}$ on Z_s satisfying the estimate

$$\|e^{A_s t}\|_{\mathcal{L}(Z_s)} \leq M e^{-\delta t} \quad , \quad \forall t \geq 0. \tag{31}$$

In order to prove (31) we introduce an equivalent norm on Z_s. Let $(u_1, u_2) \in Z_s$; we can write

$$(u_1, u_2) = \alpha_1 \phi_1 + \sum_{n \geq 2} (a_n, b_n) \sin nx \tag{32}$$

and
$$\|(u_1, u_2)\|_{Z_s}^2 = \alpha_1^2 + \sum_{n \geq 2} \left((1 + n^2)|a_n|^2 + |b_n|^2\right). \tag{33}$$

For each $n \geq 2$ we set
$$(a_n, b_n) \sin nx = \alpha_n \phi_n + \beta_n \bar{\phi}_n; \tag{34}$$

this is equivalent to
$$a_n = \alpha_n + \beta_n \quad , \qquad b_n = \alpha_n \lambda_n + \beta_n \bar{\lambda}_n \tag{35}$$

and to
$$\alpha_n = (\bar{\lambda}_n - \lambda_n)^{-1}(a_n \bar{\lambda}_n - b_n), \beta_n = (\lambda_n - \bar{\lambda}_n)^{-1}(a_n \lambda_n - b_n). \tag{36}$$

We have then
$$(1 + n^2)|a_n|^2 + |b_n|^2 \leq 2(1 + n^2 + |\lambda_n|^2)(|\alpha_n|^2 + |\beta_n|^2)$$
$$= 4n^2(|\alpha_n|^2 + |\beta_n|^2) \quad , \quad \forall n \geq 2 \tag{37}$$

and
$$n^2(|\alpha_n|^2 + |\beta_n|^2) \leq 4n^2|\lambda_n - \bar{\lambda}_n|^{-2} \left(|a_n|^2|\lambda_n|^2 + |b_n|^2\right)$$
$$= n^2(n^2 - 1 - \delta^2)^{-1} \left((n^2 - 1)|a_n|^2 + |b_n|^2\right)$$
$$\leq 4(3 - \delta^2)^{-1} \left((1 + n^2)|a_n|^2 + |b_n|^2\right). \tag{38}$$

It follows from (33), (37) and (38) that
$$\|(u_1, u_2)\|^2 := \alpha_1^2 + \sum_{n \geq 2} n^2 \left(|\alpha_n|^2 + |\beta_n|^2\right),$$
$$(u_1, u_2) = \alpha_1 \phi_1 + \sum_{n \geq 2}(\alpha_n \phi_n + \beta_n \bar{\phi}_n) \in Z_s, \tag{39}$$

defines an equivalent norm on Z_s.

Let now $\mu \in \mathbf{R}$, $\mu > -\delta$, $(v_1, v_2) \in Z_s$, and $(u_1, u_2) \in Z_s \cap X$ such that $A_s(u_1, u_2) = \mu(u_1, u_2) - (v_1, v_2)$. Writing
$$(u_1, u_2) = \alpha_1 \phi_1 + \sum_{n \geq 1}(\alpha_n \phi_n + \beta_n \bar{\phi}_n) \, , \, (v_1, v_2) = \gamma_1 \phi_1 + \sum_{n \geq 2}(\gamma_n \phi_n + \delta_n \bar{\phi}_n)$$

it follows immediately that
$$\alpha_1 = (\mu + 2\delta)^{-1}\gamma_1 \, , \, \alpha_n = (\mu - \lambda_n)^{-1}\gamma_n \, , \, \beta_n = (\mu - \bar{\lambda}_n)^{-1}\delta_n \ (n \geq 2),$$

and hence, since $|\mu - \lambda_n| \geq \mu + \delta \ (n \geq 2)$:
$$\|(u_1, u_2)\|^2 \leq (\mu + \delta)^{-2}\|(v_1, v_2)\|^2.$$

So we have
$$\|(A_s - \mu)^{-1}\|_{\mathcal{L}(Z_s)} \leq (\mu + \delta)^{-1} \quad , \quad \forall \mu > -\delta, \tag{40}$$

and it follows from the Hille-Yosida theorem (see e.g. [18] or [26]) that A_s generates a strongly continuous semigroup $\{e^{A_s t} \mid t \geq 0\}$ satisfying

$$\|e^{A_s t}\|_{\mathcal{L}(Z_s)} \leq e^{-\delta t} \quad , \quad \forall t \geq 0. \tag{41}$$

Returning to the original norm on Z_s then proves (31).

We conclude that the equation (28) satisfies the hypothesis (C) of Sect. 2, and hence the center manifold theory of Sect. 1 is applicable. The equation (28) has for each ν sufficiently close to 1 a one-dimensional local center manifold of class C^k.

In order to illustrate briefly how such local center manifold can be used to prove bifurcation results let us assume that $k \geq 3$ and that $f(-u) = -f(u)$; this implies that (27) (or equivalently (28)) has the symmetry $u \mapsto -u$. As a consequence the reduced equation on the center manifold will have the form

$$\dot{\varrho} = g(\varrho, \nu - 1), \tag{42}$$

with $\varrho \in \mathbf{R}$ and $g : \mathbf{R}^2 \to \mathbf{R}$ a C^k-function such that

$$g(-\varrho, \nu - 1) = -g(\varrho, \nu - 1) \tag{43}$$

and $D_\varrho g(0,0) = 0$. An easy calculation shows that g takes the form

$$g(\varrho, \nu - 1) = \frac{1}{2\delta}(\nu - 1)\varrho + \frac{3C}{4} \cdot \frac{1}{2\delta}\varrho^3 + O(\varrho((\nu - 1)^2 + \varrho^2)), \tag{44}$$

where $C := \frac{1}{3!}D^3 f(0)$. Assuming that $C \neq 0$ it follows that (42), and hence also (27), undergo at $\nu = 1$ a classical pitchfork bifurcation of equilibria: for all ν near 1 such that $(\nu - 1)C < 0$ the equation (42) has besides the trivial equilibrium $\varrho = 0$ two other equilibria, of the form

$$\varrho = \pm\varrho^*(\nu - 1) = \pm\left(\frac{4}{3C}(\nu - 1) + o(|\nu - 1|)\right)^{1/2}. \tag{45}$$

Moreover, (42) has then also two small bounded solutions, connecting $\varrho = 0$ to the two nontrivial equilibria. Lifting these solutions of (42) to solutions of (27) we find for $(\nu - 1)C < 0$ three steady-state solutions (the trivial one and two non-trivial ones, one symmetric to the other) connected by two heteroclinic solutions (i.e. transient waves). Our general results show that these transient waves will be of class C^k in the time variable t. The results of Hale and Scheurle in [13] show that in fact these transient waves will be analytic in time if f is analytic. This should be contrasted with the fact that even if f is analytic our theory gives us only a C^k local center manifold, for each $k \geq 1$. In general there will be no C^∞ or analytic local center manifold, since the domain of invariance may shrink down to $\{0\}$ as $k \to \infty$. See Sect. 1.4 of [31] for some examples and a further discussion of this point. We refer to the vast bifurcation literature for other illustrations on how center manifolds can be used to obtain bifurcation results; some elementary cases are treated in Sect. 3 of [31].

There are many other classes of equations to which one can associate strongly continuous semigroups, and hence center manifolds. For example, center manifold theory has been extensively used to study functional differential equations (see Hale and de Oliveira [12]) or Volterra integral equations of convolution type (see Diekmann and van Gils [8]). In [9] Diekmann and van Gils have shown how the center manifold theory given here can be extended to the framework of dual semigroups which is suitable for the treatment of retarded functional differential equations.

5. Application to Hydrodynamic Stability Problems

In this section we briefly describe how hydrodynamic stability problems may enter into the framework of the previous sections for applying the center manifold theorem. We will consider two types of applications. The first one is given by the classical Navier-Stokes equations which we write as a differential equation in a suitable function space; the part to the right of the imaginary axis of the spectrum of the associated linear operator is bounded, and this operator generates an analytic semigroup; in this case the Cauchy problem is well posed for $t > 0$. Our second application deals with steady solutions of the Navier-Stokes equations in a cylinder. As in the example (16) of the previous section the role of the time variable is played by the space variable x parallel to the generators of the cylinder. In this case the Cauchy problem has no meaning and the spectrum of the linear operator is unbounded as well to the left as to the right of the imaginary axis. For details and proofs on the functional analytic setting for the Navier-Stokes equations as used in what follows we refer to Ladyzhenskaya [21] and Témam [30].

5.1 The Classical Navier-Stokes Equations

Consider the following partial differential equation system, describing the time evolution of an incompressible fluid, and known as the Navier Stokes equations:

$$\begin{cases} \dfrac{\partial V}{\partial t} + (V \cdot \nabla)V + \nabla p = \nu \Delta V + f(x) \\[2mm] \nabla \cdot V = 0 \qquad\qquad\qquad\qquad\quad \text{for } x \in \Omega, \\[2mm] V|_{\partial\Omega} = a \ , \ \displaystyle\int_{\partial\Omega} a \cdot n d\sigma = 0. \end{cases} \qquad (1)$$

Here Ω is a bounded domain in $\mathbf{R}^3$ (or $\mathbf{R}^2$), with smooth boundary $\partial\Omega$ and exterior normal unit vector $n : \partial\Omega \to \mathbf{R}^3$, $V = V(t, x) \in \mathbf{R}^3$, $p = p(t, x) \in \mathbf{R}$, ν is a dimensionless positive number related to the Reynolds number, while $f : \Omega \to \mathbf{R}^3$ and $a : \partial\Omega \to \mathbf{R}^3$ are given vector fields. As we will see the problem (1) splits into two equations, one for V and one which gives ∇p in function of V, and hence determines p up to a constant once V is known. So the Cauchy problem associated to (1) consists in finding solutions $(V, p) : \mathbf{R}_+ \times \Omega \to \mathbf{R}^3 \times \mathbf{R}$ of (1) such that $V(0, x) = \overline{V}(x)$ for some given $\overline{V} : \Omega \to \mathbf{R}^3$ satisfying $\nabla \cdot \overline{V} = 0$.

In many cases one will want to consider the explicit dependence of (1) on some parameters. The parameter ν already appears explicitly in the equation, while the data f and a may depend on some further parameters $\widetilde{\mu} \in \mathbf{R}^m$. One can also consider domains Ω depending on a parameter; it is shown in [5] that in this case the problem can be rewritten as a parameter-dependent system similar to (1) and on a fixed domain Ω_0.

We set $\mu = (\nu, \widetilde{\mu})$ and suppose that for each μ we have a stationary solution $(V_\mu^{(0)}, p_\mu^{(0)}) = (V_\mu^{(0)}(x), p_\mu^{(0)}(x))$ of (1); in many practical cases such basic solution is easily available. Setting $V = V_\mu^{(0)} + U$, $p = p_\mu^{(0)} + \nu\widetilde{p}$, and performing a time rescale with scaling factor ν reduces (1) to the system

$$\begin{cases} \dfrac{\partial U}{\partial t} = \Delta U + \nu^{-1}\left[\widetilde{B}_\mu U + \widetilde{N}(U)\right] - \nabla\widetilde{p} \\[2mm] \nabla \cdot U = 0 \quad , \quad U|_{\partial\Omega} = 0, \end{cases} \tag{2}$$

with

$$\widetilde{B}_\mu U := -\left((U \cdot \nabla)V_\mu^{(0)} + (V_\mu^{(0)} \cdot \nabla)U\right) \quad , \quad \widetilde{N}(U) := -(U \cdot \nabla)U. \tag{3}$$

Now let $W \in (L_2(\Omega))^3$ be such that $\nabla \cdot W \in L_2(\Omega)$ (here $\nabla \cdot W$ is the divergence of W in the sense of distributions). It follows then from the identity

$$\int_\Omega \nabla\psi \cdot W \, dx + \int_\Omega \psi(\nabla \cdot W) \, dx = \int_{\partial\Omega} \psi W \cdot n \, dx, \tag{4}$$

which holds for regular functions, that we can define $W \cdot n|_{\partial\Omega}$ as an element of the dual space of the space $H_{1/2}(\partial\Omega)$ of the traces $\psi|_{\partial\Omega}$ of functions $\psi \in H_1(\Omega)$. We conclude that $W \cdot n|_{\partial\Omega} \in H_{-1/2}(\Omega)$ if $W \in (L_2(\Omega))^3$ and $\nabla \cdot W \in L_2(\Omega)$; this holds in particular if $\nabla \cdot W = 0$. This allows us to define the basic space

$$Z := \left\{ U \in (L_2(\Omega))^3 \mid \nabla \cdot U = 0, U \cdot n|_{\partial\Omega} = 0 \right\}, \tag{5}$$

equipped with the standard scalar product of $(L_2(\Omega))^3$. An equivalent way to define Z is to consider it as the closure in $(L_2(\Omega))^3$ of the space of C^∞ solenoidal vector fields with compact support in Ω. Let π_0 be the orthogonal projection on Z in $(L_2(\Omega))^3$; then one can show that $(I - \pi_0)((L_2(\Omega)^3)) = \{\nabla\psi \mid \psi \in H_1(\Omega)\}$ (compare with (4)), and projecting with π_0 makes the term $\nabla\widetilde{p}$ disappear in (2). This projection gives us the equation

$$\frac{dU}{dt} = A_\mu U + \nu^{-1}N(U), \tag{6}$$

where $A_\mu : D(A_\mu) = X := \{U \in Z \mid U \in (H_2(\Omega))^3, U|_{\partial\Omega} = 0\} \to Z$ is a densely defined closed linear operator given by

$$A_\mu U := TU + \nu^{-1}B_\mu U \quad , \quad TU = \pi_0 \Delta U \quad , \quad BU := \pi_0 \widetilde{B}_\mu U, \tag{7}$$

while

$$N(U) := \pi_o \widetilde{N}(U). \tag{8}$$

We have $A_\mu \in \mathcal{L}(X, Z)$ when we put on X the standard scalar product of $(H_2(\Omega))^3$.

Before we consider the operator A_μ in more detail let us show first that $N \in C^\infty(X; Y)$, where $Y := \{W \in Z \mid W \in (H_1(\Omega))^3\}$, equipped with the $(H_1(\Omega))^3$ scalar product. The Sobolev imbedding theorem gives us the continuous imbeddings $H_2(\Omega) \hookrightarrow C^0(\overline{\Omega})$ and $H_1(\Omega) \hookrightarrow L_4(\Omega)$. From this it follows easily that the mapping $(U_1, U_2) \in X^2 \mapsto V := (U_1 \cdot \nabla)U_2$ defines a bounded bilinear operator from X into $(H_1(\Omega))^3$; hence we have $\tilde{N} \in C^\infty(X; (H_1(\Omega))^3)$. Next take any $V \in (H_1(\Omega))^3$ and consider the Neumann problem

$$\begin{cases} \Delta\phi = \nabla \cdot V \in L_2(\Omega), \\ \dfrac{\partial\phi}{\partial n} = V \cdot n \in H_{1/2}(\Omega). \end{cases} \tag{9}$$

Let $\phi \in H_2(\Omega)$ be any solution of (9), and set $W := V - \nabla\phi$; then one easily verifies that $W = \pi_0 V \in Y$, and that $\|W\|_{H_1} \leq C\|V\|_{H_1}$. This proves that $Y = \pi_0((H_1(\Omega))^3)$, and hence we have $N = \pi_0 \tilde{N} \in C^\infty(X, Y)$, with

$$\|N(U)\|_Y \leq C\|U\|_X^2. \tag{10}$$

The same argument also shows that $B_\mu \in \mathcal{L}(X, Y)$, on condition that the basic solution $V_\mu^{(0)}$ is sufficiently regular.

Now we turn to the principal part of the operator A_μ, which is the so-called Stokes operator $T \in \mathcal{L}(X; Z)$. Solving the equation $TU = g$ for $U \in X$ and for given $g \in Z$ is equivalent to finding solutions $(U, \psi) \in (H_2(\Omega))^3 \times H_1(\Omega)$ of the system

$$\begin{cases} \Delta U + \nabla\psi = g \quad, \quad \nabla \cdot U = 0 \text{ on } \Omega, \\ U|_{\partial\Omega} = 0. \end{cases} \tag{11}$$

It was shown in [20] and in [29] that (11) has a unique solution, and hence T has a bounded inverse $T^{-1} \in \mathcal{L}(Z; X)$. Moreover, we have

$$(TU, V) = (U, TV) \quad, \quad \forall U, V \in X \tag{12}$$

and

$$(TU, U) = -\int_\Omega \sum_{i,j} \left|\frac{\partial U_i}{\partial x_j}\right|^2 dx \leq 0 \quad, \quad \forall U \in X. \tag{13}$$

It follows that T is selfadjoint and negative; moreover T has a compact resolvent, since the imbedding $X \hookrightarrow Z$ is compact. It results (see [18]) that

$$\|(\lambda - T)^{-1}\|_{\mathcal{L}(Z)} \leq \begin{cases} \dfrac{1}{|\lambda|} & \text{if Re } \lambda > 0, \\ \dfrac{1}{|\text{Im } \lambda|} & \text{if Im } \lambda \neq 0. \end{cases} \tag{14}$$

Using techniques similar to those explained in Sect. 3 one also proves that

$$\|(\lambda - T)^{-1}\|_{\mathcal{L}(Y;X)} \leq \begin{cases} \dfrac{M}{|\lambda|^{1/4}} & \text{if Re } \lambda > 0 \text{ and } |\lambda| \text{ sufficiently large}, \\ \dfrac{M}{|\text{Im } \lambda|^{1/4}} & \text{if Re } \lambda \leq 0 \text{ and } |\text{Im } \lambda| \text{ sufficiently large}. \end{cases} \tag{15}$$

(see [14] or [3] for details). Writing

$$\lambda - A_\mu = \lambda - (T + \nu^{-1} B_\mu) = \left[I_Z - \nu^{-1} B_\mu (\lambda - T)^{-1} \right] (\lambda - T)$$
$$= (\lambda - T) \left[I_X - \nu^{-1} (\lambda - T)^{-1} B_\mu \right] \qquad (16)$$

one then easily deduces from (14) and (15) that A_μ satisfies the hypotheses (Σ) and (S) of Sect. 3.

For a specific problem (that is, for specific f, a and Ω) one has to locate the spectrum of A_μ which consists of discrete eigenvalues with finite multiplicities. For critical values of the parameters there may be some eigenvalues on the imaginary axis; the center manifold theorem then applies for parameter values near such critical values. Indeed, for a fixed μ_0 we can rewrite (6) as

$$\frac{dU}{dt} = A_{\mu_0} U + g(U, \mu),$$

with $g(U, \mu) := \nu^{-1} \left[B_\mu U + N(U) \right] - \nu_0^{-1} B_{\mu_0} U$. The foregoing results show that $g(\cdot, \mu) \in C^\infty(X, Y)$, and hence the parameter-dependent center manifold theory explained in Sect. 2.2 applies.

Remark. The foregoing theory and estimates can be extended to the case where the domain Ω of the flow is unbounded but translationally invariant in one or more directions, and one looks for solutions which are spatially periodic in the unbounded directions. This is precisely the situation which one encounters in such classical problems as the Rayleigh-Bénard convection and the Taylor-Couette problem (flow between two concentric rotating cylinders).

5.2 Stationary Navier-Stokes Equations in a Cylinder

In this section we consider stationary solutions of the Navier-Stokes equations in an infinite cylinder $Q = \mathbf{R} \times \Omega$, where $\Omega \subset \mathbf{R}^2$ is a bounded, regular domain. We write the coordinates in Q as (x, y), with $x \in \mathbf{R}$ and $y \in \Omega$. We will use a similar approach as for the second example of Sect. 3.

The stationary solutions of the Navier-Stokes equations satisfy the system

$$\begin{cases} (V \cdot \nabla) V + \nabla p = \nu \Delta V + f_{\widetilde{\mu}}, \\ \nabla \cdot V = 0, \qquad\qquad\qquad \text{in } Q \\ V|_{\partial Q} = a_{\widetilde{\mu}}, \quad \text{where } \partial Q = \mathbf{R} \times \partial \Omega. \end{cases} \qquad (17)$$

(As before we suppose that f and a depend on parameters $\mu \in \mathbf{R}^m$, and set $\mu = (\nu, \widetilde{\mu})$). We also suppose that f and a are functions of the cross-sectional variable $y \in \Omega$ (respectively $\partial \Omega$) only. Finally we assume the existence of a family of sufficiently smooth x-independent solutions $(V_\mu^{(0)}, p_\mu^{(0)}) = (V_\mu^{(0)}(y), p_\mu^{(0)}(y))$.

We set

$$V = V^{(0)} + U \qquad \text{and} \qquad p = p_\mu^{(0)} + \nu \widetilde{p},$$

and write U as $U = (U_x, U_y)$, with $U_x \in \mathbf{R}$ and $U_y \in \mathbf{R}^2$. Then we define $W = (W_x, W_y) \in \mathbf{R} \times \mathbf{R}^2$ by

$$W_x := -\widetilde{p} \quad , \quad W_y := \frac{\partial U_y}{\partial x}, \tag{18}$$

and set $\mathcal{V} := (U, W)$. Then the system (17) can be rewritten in the form

$$\frac{d\mathcal{V}}{dx} = A_\mu \mathcal{V} + \nu^{-1} N(\mathcal{V}), \tag{19}$$

where $A_\mu = T + \nu^{-1} B_\mu$,

$$T\mathcal{V} = \begin{pmatrix} -\nabla_y \cdot U_y \\ W_y \\ -\Delta_y U_x + \nabla_y \cdot W_y \\ -\Delta_y U_y - \nabla_y W_x \end{pmatrix}, \tag{20}$$

$$B_\mu \mathcal{V} = \begin{pmatrix} 0 \\ 0 \\ (V_{\mu,y}^{(0)} \cdot \nabla_y) U_x + (U_y \cdot \nabla_y) V_{\mu,x}^{(0)} - V_{\mu,x}^{(0)} \nabla_y \cdot U_y \\ (V_{\mu,y}^{(0)} - \nabla_y) U_y + (U_y \cdot \nabla_y) V_{\mu,y}^{(0)} + V_{\mu,x}^{(0)} W_y \end{pmatrix}, \tag{21}$$

and

$$N(\mathcal{V}) = \begin{pmatrix} 0 \\ 0 \\ (U_y \cdot \nabla_y) U_x - U_x (\nabla_y \cdot U_y) \\ (U_y \cdot \nabla_y) U_y + U_x W_y \end{pmatrix}. \tag{22}$$

Remark that there are no differentiations in the variable x on the right hand side of (19). The boundary conditions take the form

$$U_x|_{\partial Q} = 0 \quad , \quad U_y|_{\partial Q} = 0 \quad , \quad W_y|_{\partial Q} = 0;$$

together with (19) this also implies

$$\nabla_y \cdot U_y|_{\partial Q} = 0.$$

The idea is now to consider the x-variable in (19) as a time variable, in order to obtain a local center manifold which contains all sufficiently small solutions which are globally bounded in the x-variable.

We have that $A_\mu \in \mathcal{L}(X, Z)$, with

$$Z := \left\{ (U, W) \in [H_1(\Omega)]^3 \times [L_2(\Omega)]^3 \mid U = 0 \text{ on } \partial\Omega \right\} \tag{23}$$

and

$$X := \left\{ (U, W) \in [H_2(\Omega)]^3 \times [H_1(\Omega)]^3 \mid U = 0, \nabla_y \cdot U_y = 0 \text{ and } W_y = 0 \text{ on } \partial\Omega \right\}. \tag{24}$$

Using the continuous imbeddings $H_2(\Omega) \hookrightarrow C^0(\overline{\Omega})$ and $H_1(\Omega) \hookrightarrow L_4(\Omega)$ one easily shows that N is a smooth mapping from X into itself; this allows us to take $Y = X$ and $\alpha = 0$ when we apply the general theory of Sects. 2 and 3 to the equation (19). One directly verifies that $B_\mu \in \mathcal{L}(Z)$ and $B_\mu \in \mathcal{L}(X)$.

In order to show that the operator A_μ satisfies the hypothesis (Σ) it is then sufficient to prove that

$$\|(i\omega - T)^{-1}\|_{\mathcal{L}(Z)} \leq \frac{C}{|\omega|} \quad , \quad \forall \omega \in \mathbf{R} \,, \, |\omega| \geq \omega_0. \tag{25}$$

Indeed, (27) and $B_\mu \in \mathcal{L}(Z)$ imply, via (16), that

$$\|(i\omega - A_\mu)^{-1}\|_{\mathcal{L}(Z)} \leq \frac{2C}{|\omega|} \quad , \quad \forall \omega \in \mathbf{R} \,, \, |\omega| \geq \omega_0'. \tag{26}$$

This in turn implies that $(i\omega - A_\mu)^{-1} \in \mathcal{L}(Z; X)$ for ω sufficiently large, and in combination with the compact imbedding $X \hookrightarrow Z$ we conclude that A_μ has compact resolvent. It results that the spectrum of A_μ consists of isolated eigenvalues with finite multiplicities, and hence that A_μ satisfies (Σ).

In order to prove (25) one can use a method due to Agmon [1] and further developed for the particular type of problems considered here by Mielke [23,24]. The idea is to deduce (25) from some estimates for solutions of the steady Stokes equation in Q which are periodic in the x-variable. We refer to [18] for the details.

Again one has to study how the spectrum of A_μ changes with the parameter μ. If for some value of μ there are some eigenvalues on the imaginary axis then there is a corresponding center manifold for all nearby values of μ. See [18] for a typical application of this center manifold.

Remark. The particular problem (17) is reversible, since with $V = (V_x(x,y), V_y(x,y))$ also $\widetilde{V} := (-V_x(-x,y), V_y(-x,y))$ is a solution of (17). If also $V_x^{(0)} = 0$ then, as is shown in Sect. 2.2, one can construct the center manifold in such a way that the reduced equation on the center manifold is also reversible.

References

1. S. Agmon. On the eigenfunctions and on the eigenvalues of general elliptic boundary value problems. Comm. Pure Appl. Math. **15** (1962), 119–147
2. P. Bates and C.K. Jones. Invariant manifolds for semilinear partial differential equations. Dynamics Reported, Vol. 2 (1989), 1–38
3. D. Brézis. Perturbations singulières et problèmes de défaut d'ajustement. C.R. Acad. Sci. Paris, **276A** (1973), 1597–1600
4. T. Burak. On semigroups generated by restrictions of elliptic operators to invariant subspaces. Israel J. Math. **12** (1972), 79–93
5. P. Chossat and G. Iooss. The Couette-Taylor problem, chapter V. In preparation
6. S.-N. Chow and K. Lu. Invariant manifolds for flows in Banach spaces. J. Diff. Eqns. **74** (1988), 285–317
7. S.-N. Chow and K. Lu. C^k centre unstable manifolds. Proc. Roy. Soc. Edinburgh, **108A** (1988), 303–320
8. O. Diekmann and S. van Gils. Invariant manifolds for Volterra integral equations of convolution type. J. Diff. Eqns. **54** (1984), 139–180

9. O. Diekmann and S. van Gils. The center manifold for delay equations in the light of suns and stars. In: M. Roberts and I. Stewart (eds.), Singularity Theory and Its Applications. Proc. Warwick 1989, Part II, Lect. Notes in Math. **1463** (1991), pp. 122–141, Springer-Verlag

10. G. Fischer. Zentrumsmannigfaltigkeiten bei elliptischen Differentialgleichungen. Math. Nachr. **115** (1984), 137–157

11. P. Grisvard and G. da Prato. Sommes d'opérateurs linéaires et équations differentielles opérationelles. J. Math. Pures et Appl. **54** (1975), 305–387

12. J.K. Hale and J. de Oliveira. Hopf bifurcation for functional equations. J. Math. Anal. Appl. **74** (1980), 41–59

13. J.K. Hale and J. Scheurle. Smoothness of bounded solutions of nonlinear evolution equations. J. Diff. Eqns. **56** (1985), 142–163

14. D. Henry. Geometric theory of semilinear parabolic equations. Lect. Notes in Math. **840** (1981), Springer-Verlag, NY

15. G. Iooss. Estimation au voisinage de $t = 0$, pour un exemple de problème d'évolution où il y a incompatibilité entre les conditions initiales et aux limites. C.R. Acad. Sci. Paris **271A** (1970), 187–190

16. G. Iooss. Bifurcations of maps and applications. Math. Studies **36** (1979), Elsevier-North-Holland, Amsterdam

17. G. Iooss. Bifurcation and transition to turbulence in hydrodynamics. In: L. Salvadori (ed.), Bifurcation Theory and Applications. Lect. Notes in Math. **1057**, Springer-Verlag, (1984) 152–201

18. G. Iooss, A. Mielke and Y. Demay. Theory of steady Ginzburg-Landau equation in hydrodynamic stability problems. Europ. J. Mech. B/Fluids **3** (1989), 229–268

19. T. Kato. Perturbation theory for linear operatos. Springer-Verlag, Berlin, 1966

20. K. Kirchgässner. Wave solutions of reversible systems and applications. J. Diff. Eqns. **45** (1982), 113–127

21. O.A. Ladyzhenskaya. The mathematical theory of viscous incompressible flow. Gordon and Breach, New York, 1963

22. A. Mielke. A reduction principle for nonautonomous systems in infinite-dimensional spaces. J. Diff. Eqns. **65** (1986), 68–88

23. A. Mielke. Reduction of quasilinear elliptic equations in cylindrical domains with applications. Math. Meth. Appl. Sci. **10** (1988), 51–66

24. A. Mielke. Saint-Venant's problem and semi inverse solutions in nonlinear elasticity. Arch. Rat. Mech. Anal. **102** (1988), 205–229

25. A. Mielke. Normal hyperbolicity of center manifolds and Saint-Venant's principle. Arch. Rat. Mech. Anal. **110** (1990), 353–372

26. A. Mielke. On nonlinear problems of mixed type: a qualitative theory using infinite-dimensional center manifolds. J. Dynamics Diff. Eqns. To appear

27. A. Pazy. Semigroups of linear operators and applications to partial differential equations. Applied Math. Sci. **44**, Springer-Verlag, New York, 1983

28. D. Ruelle. Bifurcations in the presence of a symmetry group. Arch. Rat. Mech. Anal. **51** (1973), 136–152

29. B. Scarpellini. Center manifolds of infinite dimensions. I. Main results and applications. Z. Angew. Math. Phys. **42** (1991), 1–32

30. R. Témam. Navier-Stokes equations, theory and numerical analysis. North-Holland, Amsterdam, 1979

31. A. Vanderbauwhede. Centre manifolds, normal forms and elementary bifurcations. Dynamics Reported, Vol. 2 (1989), 89–169

32. A. Vanderbauwhede. Invariant manifolds in infinite dimensions. In: S.-N. Chow and J.K. Hale (eds.), Dynamics of Infinite Dimensional Systems. Springer-Verlag (1987), 409–420

Oscillations in Singularly Perturbed Delay Equations

A.F. Ivanov, A.N. Sharkovsky

Introduction

This paper presents some recent results on the scalar singularly perturbed differentila delay equation

$$\nu \dot{x}(t) + x(t) = f(x(t-1)) . \tag{1}$$

The equation is of significant interest for both mathematicians dealing with qualitative theory of differential equations and for scientists applying the theory to real world problems in different areas.

Equations of form (1) have recently found a variety of applications in several fields of natural science. For instance, they model processes in radiophysics and optics (oscillations in linear arrays of tunnel diodes, high frequency generators, electro-optical bistable devices). In mathematical biology and physiology they describe systems with delayed response, particularly, the regulation of red blood cell populations, respiratory control circuits, neural interactions, etc. They were suggested to model commodity cycles in economics. Interested readers may find descriptions of applications or further references, for example in [6, 10–11, 14, 16–17, 19–25, 36, 40–42, 45, 48, 59]. Certain non-linear boundary value problems for hyperbolic equations are reducible to functional-differential equations which include equation (1). Such a procedure of reduction was proposed in 1936 by A.A. Vitt. Studies of nonlinear boundary value problems based on the mentioned reduction can be found in the monograph [55].

In spite of the simple form of equation (1) its dynamics is very rich and varifold. Apparently, the equation is one the most studied in the theory of differential functional equations, as recent results of many authors show (see list of references). These results show as well that we are rather far from a complete understanding of the dynamics given by equation (1). There is a series of natural and simple stated problems, which are still unsolved.

One efficient approach to equation (1) is to begin with step functions $f(x)$. Indeed, with $f(x)$ being finite valued any initial condition generates a piecewise exponential solution. For certain families of initial conditions the problem of the asymptotic behavior of solutions is reducible to the study of maps on finite dimensional sets, in particular, to one-dimensional maps in the simplest cases. This approach was used in a series of papers, including [1–3, 18–23, 36, 40, 48, 61] with step functions or smoothed step functions $f(x)$. Some of these papers deal with equations of the form $\dot{x}(t) = f(x(t-1))$. The idea is to determine a set Φ of initial conditions consisting of functions of special type characterized by a real parameter $z \in \Lambda$. For any $z \in \Lambda$ and $\varphi \in \Phi$ given by z there exists $t_0 = t_0(\varphi)$ such that the segment of the corresponding solution $x(t_0+t)$, $t \in [-1, 0]$, is again an element of Φ which belongs to some $\tilde{z} \in \Lambda$. Thus, one has an induced one-dimensional map $F : z \to \tilde{z}$ on the parameter set Λ. It turns out that the map F is a continuous and piecewise Moebius transformation. Therefore the dynamics given by equation (1) (on a subset of solutions) is as complicated as the dynamics of the corresponding piecewise Moebius map. In general, interval maps given by piecewise Moebius transformations may define complicated dynamical systems (see, e.g. [34]). In particular, for the solutions of the differential-difference equations of the form (1) and its modifications the authors of the papers [22, 23, 61] obtained an induced map $F_0(z)$ of the interval $[a, b]$ as shown in Fig. 1.

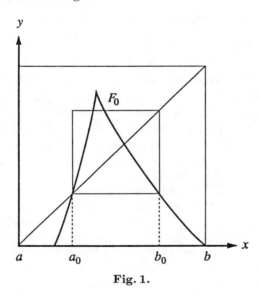

Fig. 1.

The map F_0 has a closed invariant repelling set $K_0 \subset [a_0, b_0]$ which is homeomorphic to a Cantor set. The dynamics of F_0 on the set K_0 is rather complicated (the description of the standard example is found in [55]). If $f(x)$ is smoothed in a small neighborhood of the discontinuity points the new induced map F_0' is proved to coincide with F_0 on the set K_0. Hence the dynamics of equation (1) is still complicated. As shown in [18] the described dynamics persists under small perturbations of step functions or smoothed step functions $f(x)$. In some cases the map F has an invariant measure which is absolutely continuous with respect to Lebesgue measure [3, 19].

The existence of such a measure implies in particular a probability distribution for successive maxima (or zeros) of the solutions generated by initial functions from the parameterized set Φ.

A natural approach to study equation (1) is to consider it as a singular perturbation of the difference equation with continuous argument

$$x(t) = f(x(t-1)), \quad t \in \mathbb{R}_+ . \tag{2}$$

To have a continuous solution of equation (2) for $t \geq -1$ one requires, together with continuity of f and φ, a so-called consistency condition $\lim_{t \to -0} \varphi(t) = f(\varphi(-1))$.

The asymptotic behavior of the solutions to equation (2) is determined by the dynamics of the one-dimensional map

$$f : x \to f(x) . \tag{3}$$

There exists a formal correspondence between trajectories $\{x_k = f^k(x_0), k = 1, 2, \cdots\}$ of the dynamical system given by equation (3) and step function solutions $x(t) = f^k(x_0), t \in [k-1, k)]$, of equation (2), generated by initial functions $\varphi(t) = x_0, t \in [-1, 0)$. The asymptotic behavior of the solutions of equation (2) depends entirely on the properties of the iteration sequence $\{x_k\}$, $x_{k+1} = f(x_k)$, $x_0 \in \mathbb{R}$ where $\varphi(t_0) \overset{\text{def}}{=} x_0$ and therefore $x(k+t_0) = f^k(x_0)$, $k \in \mathbb{Z}_+$. Consequently, to see the dynamics of solutions of equation (2) one should follow the continuum of trajectories of the map (3) $\{x_k : x_k = f(x_{k-1})\}$ with $x_0 \in \{x = \varphi(t) : t \in [-1, 0)\}$.

At present there is a sufficiently complete theory of the continuous argument difference equation (2) based on the properties of the one-dimensional dynamical system (3) [55]. Generically, equation (2) has continuous solutions of three types: asymptotically constant solutions, relaxation type solutions and turbulent type solutions. Asymptotically constant solutions have a finite limit as $t \to +\infty$. They are determined by the attracting fixed points of the map (3). Relaxation type solutions are undamped solutions with constant oscillation frequency on each unit time interval $[k-1, k)$. The Lipschitz constants of such a solution on the intervals $[k-1, k)$ are unbounded as $k \to \infty$. Their existence is tied to a repelling fixed point of the map (3), separating domains of attraction of attracting fixed points or splitting the domain of attraction of an attracting 2-cycle. Turbulent type solutions are undamped solutions with unlimitedly increasing oscillation frequency and unbounded Lipschitz constants on $[k-1, k)$ as $k \to \infty$. Equation (2) has turbulent type solutions if the map (3) has periodic points with periods greater than 2. The existence of relaxation and turbulent type solutions indicates the complexity of the dynamics given by equation (2).

The natural question is to what extent the dynamics of the map (3) determines properties of the solutions for equation (1)?

Solutions of equation (1) appear to have some simple properties which are intrinsic to the dynamical system defined by the map (3). An example is the following property of invariance. If the map f has an invariant interval $I(f(I) \subseteq I)$ then any initial function $\varphi(t)$ with $\varphi([-1,0]) \subset I$ gives rise to a solution with values in I for all $t \geq 0$. This allows us to define a semiflow $\mathcal{F}^t, t \geq 0$ on $X = C^0([-1,0], I)$, as usual, by setting $(\mathcal{F}^t \varphi)(s) = x\varphi^\nu(t+s)$, $s \in [-1,0]$. Moreover, if all points $x \in I$ are attracted under f by a fixed point $x_* \in I$ then any initial function φ satisfying $\varphi([-1,0]) \subseteq I$ generates a solution x for which $\lim_{t\to\infty} x(t) = x_*$. In other words, there is a correspondence between attracting fixed points of the map (3) and constant solutions of equation (1) which are asymptotically stable. This shows that asymptotically constant solutions persist under singular perturbations of equation (2).

What happens to relaxation and turbulent solutions when equation (2) is singularly perturbed? Clearly, the Lipschitz constant for the solutions of equation (1) can not grow infinitely. Indeed, if I is an f-invariant interval then for any $\nu > 0$ and $\varphi(t) \in I$, $t \in [-1,0]$ the derivative of the corresponding solution is bounded: $|\dot{x}(t)| \leq (1/\nu)|-x(t) + f(x(t-1))| \leq (1/\nu) \operatorname{diam} I$. Therefore, the oscillation frequency of solutions with amplitudes bounded away from zero can not increase infinitely.

With ν small one naturally expects a closeness (in a sense to be made precise) between solutions of equations (1) and (2). This happens to be true within finite time intervals provided the nonlinearity $f(x)$ and the initial conditions considered are continuous. In particular, if $f(x)$ is continuously differentiable and the (same) initial condition for equations (1) and (2) is also continuously differentiable then the corresponding solutions remain close within a time interval of length $O(1/\nu), \nu \to +0$. This means that the solutions of equations (1) are as complicated as the solutions of equation (2) in this time interval.

The question how the asymptotic properties for equations (1) and (2) are related when ν is small is much more difficult.

Suppose the interval map f has an attracting cycle $x_1 \to x_2 \to \cdots \to x_n \to x_1$ with components U_i, $i = 1, 2, \cdots, n$ of its domain of immediate attraction. Clearly, an initial condition with values in say U_1, for $t \in [-1, 0)$ defines a solution of equation (2) which is necessarily discontinuous at $t = i$, $i \in \mathbb{Z}_+$. This solution converges as $t \to +\infty$ to a step function solution of equation (2) defined by the initial condition $\varphi(t) = x_1$, $t \in [-1, 0)$, and the convergence is uniform on time intervals $[k, \infty)$ as $k \to \infty$.

Because of the closeness results mentioned above an important problem is to find conditions for the map f which guarantee that there is a correspondence between the attracting cycle of the map f and an asymptotically stable periodic solution of equation (1), with period close to n, for small $\nu > 0$.

It appears that, in general, there is no such correspondence. This is shown by the following simple example. Let $f_0(x)$ be a smooth function mapping the interval $[-1, 1]$ into itself such that $f_0(x) = 0$ for $|x| \le h, \frac{1}{2} < h < 1$, and f_0 has no fixed points outside the set $\{x \in \mathbb{R} : |x| \le h\}$. In addition $f_0(x)$ may be chosen in such a way that it has an attracting 2-cycle generating relaxation type solutions, and a cycle of period > 2 generating turbulent type solutions for equation (2). With $f_0(x)$ chosen in such a fashion, the difference equation (2) has continuous solutions of three possible types: asymptotically constant, relaxation, and turbulent ones. However, the asymptotic behavior of the solutions for equation (1) (with $f = f_0$) is very simple for any $\nu > 0$: all solutions satisfy $\lim_{t \to \infty} x(t) = 0$. This phenomenon of simplification for the asymptotic behavior of the solutions of equation (1) is caused by the existence of an attracting fixed point $x = 0$ of the map with "large" domain of immediate attraction.

Similar phenomena arise in more general cases. If an invariant interval I_0 attracts an interval $J_0 : I_0 \bigcap_{n \ge 0} f^n(J_0)$, and the part $I \backslash J_0$ which is not attracted is small enough compared to $J_0 \backslash I_0$ and does not contain fixed points then every solution x of equation (1) satisfies $x(t) \in J_0, t > t_0$, for some t_0 depending on the particular solution. Thus, an attractor with sufficiently large domain of immediate attraction "attracts" all solutions of equation (1).

Another aspect of the problem is an increase in complexity for the asymptotic behavior of solutions of equation (1) compared to the dynamics given by the map (3) (or equation (2)). Consider equation (1) with $f(x) = -\text{sign}(x)$ for $|x| > h, 0 < h < 1$, $f(x) = -a \, \text{sign}(x)$ for $|x| \le h, a > 1$. Then there exists an open set of parameters (a, h) so that the corresponding equation (1) has a set of solutions which are governed by a quasi-random variable as $t \to \infty$. This means for instance that successive maxima of the solutions (or distances between zeros) have a probability distribution with a density which is absolutely continuous with respect to the Lebesgue measure. Note that in this case the map (3) has a cycle of period two given by -1 and 1 and this cycle is globally attracting. This implies that the increase in complexity occures in a small Hausdorff neighbourhood of the generalized 2-periodic solution of equation (2) defined by $p_0(t) = 1, t \in (0, 1), p_0(t) = -1, t \in (1, 2) \, p_0(0) = p_0(1) = [-a, a]$. Moreover, the size of this neighbourhood goes to zero as $\nu \to +0$.

Very important are bifurcation problems for equation (1) when the non-linearity $f(x)$ is parameter dependent. Bifurcation problems for interval maps are rather well understood (see, e.g. [54]). For some families of interval maps (including the well-known family $f_\lambda(x) = \lambda x(1 - x), 0 \le \lambda \le 4$) the most important changes arise through period doubling bifurcations. The first bifurcation gives rise to a globally stable 2-cycle with a repelling fixed point in between. The previous example suggests that solutions of equation (1) which remain close to this 2-cycle may be very complex.

For equation (1) the problem of how the dynamics of its solutions mimics the dynamics of the interval map (3), when a parameter λ changes, was not in fact under systematic investigation. Computer simulations with equation (1) for different choices of f_λ indicate a correspondence between bifurcations for one-parameter families of equations (1) (with small ν) and one-parameter families of maps (3) [6]. In particular, for the family $f_\lambda = \lambda x(1 - x)$ there is evidence that, for ν sufficiently small, one has a correspondence between attracting cycles of period 2^n, $n \leq n_0(\nu)$ and attracting periodic solutions of equation (1) with period approximately 2^n. Unfortunately, there is no rigorous result available so far.

The most natural approach to prove existence of periodic solutions for equation (1) is by the use of interval cycles for the map (3). In the simplest case, when the map f has two intervals interchanged by f and a repelling fixed point in between, the existence of a periodic solution was shown in [16].

The existence of an attracting cycle of intervals does not necessarily produce the existence of periodic solutions for equation (1) as the previous example with $f = f_0$ shows. This implies that a cycle of intervals should be subjected to additional assumptions. Some sufficient conditions are given below which guarantee the existence of a periodic solution for equation (1) when the map f has an attracting cycle of intervals.

The paper is organized in the following way.

In Chapter 1 difference equations with continuous argument are considered. Simple properties of the solutions needed later are discussed. Preliminary basic notions on interval maps are given.

Chapter 2 deals with the simplest properties of equation (1) defined by the interval map (3).

Continuous dependence results showing closeness within finite time intervals between solutions of equations (1) and (2) for small positive ν are proved in Chap. 3.

In Chapter 4 a series of examples is considered showing specific features of solutions of equation (1) which are caused by the singular perturbation term.

The role of attracting periodic intervals with relatively large immediate attraction domains is studied in Chap. 5.

Chapter 6 deals with the existence of periodic solutions for equation (1).

Concluding discussions including some naturally posed unsolved problems are presented in Chap. 7.

We do not survey all the results available for differential-delay equations of the form (1) but rather make an attempt to present studies done at the Institute of Mathematics of the Ukrainian Academy of Sciences. Therefore some intersections may be found with other results, in particular, with those obtained in [40–42].

1. Difference Equations

Basic Notions for Interval Maps

We recall briefly some basic notions from the theory of one-dimensional maps which we use throughout the paper.

Every continuous map: $f : x \rightarrow f(x)$ of an interval $I \subset \mathbb{R}$ into itself generates a dynamical system on I. Every $x_0 \in I$ defines a trajectory $\{x_k, k \in \mathbb{Z}_+\}$ by $x_{k+1} = f(x_k)$. A point x_0 is called *periodic* with period n if the points $x_0, x_1, \cdots, x_{n-1}$ are pairwise distinct and $f(x_{n-1}) = x_0$. The points $x_0, x_1, \cdots, x_{n-1}$ are said to form a *cycle* of period n. Clearly, any point from the cycle is periodic with period n. Fixed points are periodic with period 1. Points from a cycle of period n are fixed points for the map $f^n = \underbrace{f \circ f \circ \cdots \circ f}_{n}$.

A fixed point $x_0 \in I$ is called *attracting* if $\lim_{k \rightarrow \infty} f^k(x) = x_0$ for all x in some neighbourhood of x_0. If the function $f(x)$ is differentiable at $x = x_0$ and $|f'(x_0)| < 1$ then the fixed point x_0 is attracting. A maximal connected open (with respect to I) set which is attracted by the fixed point is called a *domain of immediate attraction* of the fixed point. The domain of immediate attraction sometimes is called an *immediate basin*.

A fixed point $x_0 \in I$ is called *repelling* if it has a neighbourhood $U(x_0)$ such that for every $x' \in U(x_0) \backslash \{x_0\}$ there exists a positive integer $k = k(x')$ with $f^k(x') \notin U(x_0)$. This means that all points from some neighbourhood leave the neighbourhood (though, they may get back afterwards). If $f(x)$ is differentiable at $x = x_0$ and $|f'(x_0)| > 1$ then the fixed point x_0 is repelling.

A periodic point $x_0 \in I$ of period n is called *attracting* if it is an attracting fixed point of the map f^n. Then the corresponding cycle $\{x_0, x_1, \cdots, x_{n-1}\}$ is also called attracting. If $f^n(x)$ is differentiable at $x = x_0$ and $|(f^n)'(x_0)| < 1$ then the periodic point x_0 is attracting. Since $(f^n)'(x_0) = f'(x_0)f'(x_1) \cdots f'(x_{n-1})$ for smooth maps the inequality mentioned holds at any point of the cycle. Repelling periodic points and cycles are defined similarly. Sometimes attracting periodic points and cycles are called *sinks*, and repelling ones are called *sources*.

A set M is called *invariant* if $f(M) \subseteq M$. Sometimes the stronger condition $f(M) = M$ is meant by invariance. If it is not specified we use the broader first notion.

A closed set $A \subset I$ will be called an *attractor* if it is invariant and there exists a neighbourhood $U(A)$ with $\bigcap_{k>0} f^k(U(A)) = A$. Attracting fixed points and cycles are attractors. A maximal open set U which has a non-empty intersection with A for each connected component and such that $f^k(x) \rightarrow A$, $x \in U$ as $k \rightarrow \infty$ will be called the domain of immediate attraction for the attractor A.

The domain of immediate attraction for an attracting cycle $\{x_0, x_1, \cdots, x_{n-1}\}$ consists of n open intervals. Each of them contains a point x_i from the cycle for some i and is the domain of immediate attraction of the fixed point x_i of the map f^n, $i = 1, 2, \cdots, n$.

An interval $I_0 \subset I$ is called *periodic* with period n if $f^n(I_0) \subset I_0$ and the intervals $I_k = f^k(I_0)$, $k = 0, 1, \cdots, n - 1$ satisfy int $I_i \cap$ int $I_j = \emptyset$, $i \neq j$. Here we will deal only with closed periodic intervals. The set of intervals $\{I_0, I_1, \cdots, I_{n-1}\}$ is said to form an interval cycle of period n. If the map has an interval cycle of period n then it has a periodic point with period n or $n/2$ at least (the latter may happen if $n = 2q$ and if the intervals I_i and I_{i+q}, $i = 0, 1, \cdots, q - 1$, have common points on the boundary, which constitute the cycle of period $q = n/2$). A cycle of intervals $\{I_0, I_1, \cdots, I_{n-1}\}$ is called attracting if the set $\cup_i I_i$ is an attractor.

The domain of immediate attraction of an attracting cycle of intervals consists of n open (with respect to I) intervals each of them containing an element of the cycle.

Difference Equations with Continuous Argument

In this part we briefly describe properties of solutions of difference equations with continuous argument

$$x(t) = f(x(t - 1)), \quad t \in \mathbb{R}_+ \tag{2}$$

which are needed later.

Throughout we assume that the one-dimensional map

$$f : x \to f(x) \tag{3}$$

has an invariant interval I and is continuous on I.

To have solutions of equation (2) for $t \geq 0$ it is necessary to define some functions $\varphi(t)$ on the initial set $[-1, 0)$. Let $\varphi \in X = C([-1, 0), I)$. Then for $t \in [0, 1)$, $x(t) = f(\varphi(t - 1)) \in I$ because of the invariance property $f(I) \subseteq I$. By repeating the procedure we construct the solution for $t \in [1, 2)$ and so on. Thus, to any $\varphi \in X$ there corresponds an unique solution $x_\varphi(t)$ of the equation (2) for all $t \geq 0$.

Requiring $\lim_{t \to -0} \varphi(t) = f(\varphi(-1))$ for a given $\varphi \in X$ the solution $x_\varphi(t)$ is continuous for all $t \geq 0$ since $f(x)$ is continuous. We restrict ourselves here to continuous solutions by supposing $\varphi \in X^0 = \{\varphi \in X \,|\, \lim_{t \to -0} \varphi(t) = f(\varphi(-1))\}$.

Remark. Unlike differential equations, difference equations in form (2) do not require any assumptions of continuity or smoothness of $f(x)$ or $\varphi(t)$. In particular we shall consider difference equations with discontinuous (e.g. steplike) functions. Clearly, the restriction $\varphi \in X = C([-1, 0), I)$ is also not necessary.

Since the solution $x_\varphi(t)$ is defined by means of iterates of f the asymptotic behaviour of the solutions depends on properties of sequences $\{f^k(x_0), k \geq 0\}$ (i.e. on trajectories of the dynamical system $\{f^k, k \geq 0\}$ for distinct $x_0 \in \{\varphi(t), t \in [-1, 0)\}$). Generically, equation (2) has solutions which are asymptotic to upper semicontinuous functions (generally speaking, to discontinuous ones), see details in [55]. The complexity of the limit functions, determining the asymptotic behaviour of the solutions of equation (2), is characterized by the discontinuity set and by the jump spectrum which consists of the accumulation points of the function on the discontinuity set. Generically, the jump spectrum is finite though it may consist of countably many points. The discontinuity set usually has a complicated structure; in particular it may be homeomorphic to a Cantor set.

We shall not get into the detailed theory of equation (2) which is presented completely in the monograph [55]. Here we only consider the simplest properties of solutions which are needed in the sequel.

We distinguish three basic types of continuous solutions of equation (2): asymptotically constant solutions, relaxation type solutions and turbulent type solutions. We present simple examples which show the mechanisms of how the different types of solutions do appear.

a) Asymptotically Constant Solutions

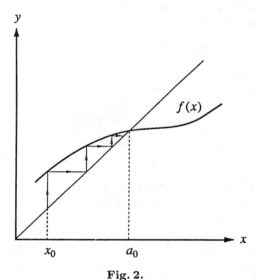

Fig. 2.

Suppose the interval map (3) has an attracting fixed point a_0 (Fig. 2) with domain of immediate attraction J_0, implying $\lim_{k \to \infty} f^k(x_0) = a_0$ for every $x_0 \in J_0$. Then, for every φ with $\varphi(t) \in J_0$ for all $t \in [-1, 0)$, the corresponding solution $x_\varphi(t)$ satisfies $\lim_{t \to +\infty} x_\varphi(t) = a_0$. We call such solutions asymptotically constant. Clearly their existence and stability is determined by the existence of the attracting fixed points of the map f. If a fixed point x_0 is repelling for the map then the solution $x(t) = a_0$ of equation (2) is Liapunov unstable.

b) Relaxation Type solutions

Relaxation type solutions appear in the following typical cases. (i) The map f has several (> 1) attracting fixed points and their attraction domains are separated by repelling fixed points. (ii) The map f has an attracting cycle of period two with a two component domain of attraction, separated by a repelling fixed point. The two cases can be realized by monotone maps. We show them in Fig. 3 a) and b), respectively.

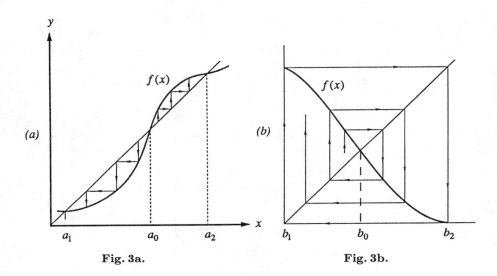

Fig. 3a.   Fig. 3b.

Consider case (i). If the initial function $\varphi \in X$ satisfies $a_0 < \varphi(t) \leq a_2$ for all $t \in [-1, 0)$ then $\lim x_\varphi(t) = a_2$ since $f^k(x_0) \to a_2$ for all $x_0 \in (a_0, a_2]$, $k \to \infty$. The corresponding solution $x_\varphi(t)$ is asymptotically constant. Similarly, $\lim_{t\to\infty} x_\varphi(t) = a_1$ provided $a_1 \leq \varphi(t) < a_0$ for all $t \in [-1, 0)$. The situation changes when $\varphi(t)$ has intersections with the graph $x(t) = a_0$. Consider the simplest case of two intersections: $\varphi(t) > a_0$ for $t \in [-1, t_1) \cup (t_2, 0)$ and $\varphi(t) < a_0$ for $t \in (t_1, t_2)$ (Fig. 4a). Since $f^k(x_0) \to a_2$ for every $x_0 \in (a_0, a_2]$ and $f^k(y_0) \to a_1$ for every $y_0 \in [a_1, a_0)$, the solution $x_\varphi(t)$ approaches a generalized 1-periodic function on $[k-1, k)$ as $k \to \infty$ (see Fig. 4b). Clearly, the convergence is uniform on each compact set not containing t_1 and t_2. This means that the family $\{f^k(\varphi(t)), k \in \mathbb{Z}_+\}$ converges uniformly on $[-1, 0\backslash U_\delta(t_1, t_2)$ where $U_\delta(t_1, t_2)$ is a δ neighbourhood of the points t_1 and t_2.

Case (ii) differs from (i) in that we have convergence to a 2-periodic limit function. For the initial function shown in Fig. 5a one obtains the limit function shown in Fig. 5b.

In both cases (i) and (ii), the oscillation frequency (number of zeros of $x_\varphi(t) - a_0$) of the solution $x_\varphi(t)$ on each unit segment $[k-1, k)$ is constant for all $k \in \mathbb{N}$ and is defined by the number of crossings of the initial function with

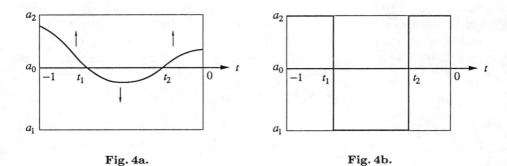

Fig. 4a.   Fig. 4b.

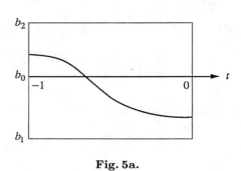

Fig. 5a.

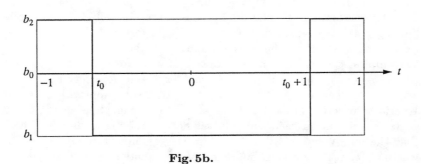

Fig. 5b.

the level of the repelling fixed point. The Lipschitz constant of the solution $x_\varphi(t)$ at the crossing points with $x = a_0$ (or $x = b_0$) increases infinitely as $t \to \infty$ and does not depend on the smoothness of $f(x)$ or $\varphi(t)$.

c) Turbulent Type Solutions

Turbulent type solutions are characterized by exponential (or polynomial) growth of oscillation frequency while their amplitudes do not damp out as $t \to \infty$. Smoothness of the solutions is predetermined by the smoothness of the map (3) and of the initial function φ, and does not change with t. Nevertheless, the Lipschitz constant for any solution on the unit interval $[t-1, t)$ grows infinitely as $t \to \infty$ (with exponential rate generically).

The generation of oscillations for turbulent type solutions can be illustrated as follows. Suppose the map f of the interval $I = [a, b]$ onto itself has the form as in Fig. 6.

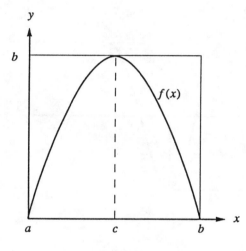

Fig. 6.

In this case there exist two intervals I_1 and I_2 such that each of them is mapped onto their union $I_1 \cup I_2$ ($I_1 = [a, c]$, $I_2 = [c, b]$ for the map in Fig. 6). Therefore, if the initial condition $\varphi(t)$ attains all the values from $I_1 = [a, c]$ on some time subinterval $[t_1, t_2]$ of $[-1, 0)$, then the solution $x_\varphi(t)$ will attain all the values from $I = I_1 \cup I_2$ for the time interval $[1 + t_1, 1 + t_2]$. Similar, initial conditions ranging within $I_2 = [c, b]$ give rise to a solution ranging through all the interval I after one time unit. One oscillation of the initial function I covering the interval I generates two similar oscillations within the same time interval but one time unit later. An initial condition φ with two oscillations (Fig. 7a) generates a solution $x_\varphi(t)$ with four oscillations on $[0, 1)$ (Fig. 7b). Clearly, the number of oscillations on the initial interval $[-1, 0)$ is increased by the factor 2^n for the time interval $[n-1, n)$.

The existence of turbulent type solutions with exponential growth of the frequency may be concluded in the case when the interval map f has periodic

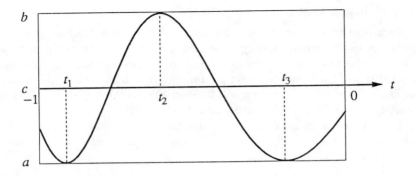

Fig. 7a.

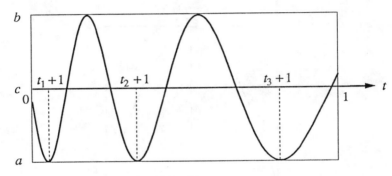

Fig. 7b.

points with periods which are not a power of two. Indeed, as it was shown in [49] in this case there exist two intervals I_1 and I_2 and a positive integer N such that $g(I_1) \supset I_1 \cup I_2$ and $g(I_2) \supset I_1 \cup I_2$ where $g = f^N$. Therefore, an oscillation of the initial function covering the union $I_1 \cup I_2$ gives rise to at least two oscillations covering $I_1 \cup I_2$ after a time interval of length N.

Turbulent type solutions with polynomial growth of the frequency (sometimes called preturbulent ones) always exist when the map f has periodic points of periods 2^i with $i > 1$ and no other periodic points. But they may exist also for some maps f which have only fixed points.

Summarizing, the existence of certain types of continuous solutions for equation (2) is defined by the dynamics of the map f. In particular, if the map f has attracting fixed points, equation (2) has asymptotically constant solutions: if there are no attracting fixed points, there are no asymptotically constant solutions (except trivial ones $x(t) = $ const); if the map has several attracting fixed points on some subinterval of I such that their immediate attraction domains are separated by repelling fixed points or if it has an attracting 2-cycle with two component domain of immediate attraction separated by a fixed point of by a cycle of period two, then equation (2) has relaxation type solutions; if the map f has a periodic point with period $\neq 2^i$, $i = 0, 1, 2, \cdots$ then equation (2) has turbulent type solutions. Cleary, equation (2) may have solutions of several types simultaneously. Examples of asymptotically constant, relaxation type, and turbulent type solutions are shown on the a), b), c) parts of Fig. 8 respectively.

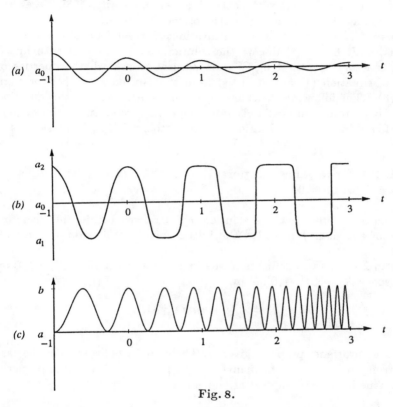

Fig. 8.

2. Singular Perturbations of Difference Equations with Continuous Argument: Simplest Properties

It is natural to consider the differential difference equation

$$\nu \dot{x}(t) + x(t) = f(x(t-1)) \tag{1}$$

as a singular perturbation ($\nu \ll 1$) of the difference equation with continuous argument

$$x(t) = f(x(t-1)) . \tag{2}$$

Properties of solutions for equation (2) can be understood rather well. The analysis is based on properties of the one-dimensional dynamical system generated by the corresponding map

$$f : x \rightarrow f(x) \, . \tag{3}$$

For a theory of equation (2) with scalar $f(x)$ see monograph [55]. Necessary preliminaries have been introduced in the previous chapter.

The map f is assumed to have an invariant interval $I = [a, b]$ and to be continuous on I. Let $x_\varphi^\nu(t)$ denote the solution of equation (1) with initial condition $\varphi \in X_I = C([-1, 0], I)$. It is natural to ask what properties of solutions of equation (1) are inherited from those of equation (2) (or from the map (3))? The following statements contain some answers to this question which can be obtained immediately from the dynamics given by the map f. They are found in earlier publications by the authors [2, 55], and also in [40–42].

Theorem 2.1 (Invariance property). *If $\varphi \in X_I$ then $x_\varphi^\nu(t) \in I$ for all $t \geq 0$ and any fixed $\nu > 0$.*

Theorem 2.1 states that the solution $x_\varphi^\nu(t)$ ranges within the invariant interval I of the map f provided the initial condition $\varphi(t)$ does so for all $t \in [-1, 0]$.

Theorem 2.1 allows to define in a well-known way a semiflow $\mathcal{F}^t$, $t \geq 0$ on the state space $X_I = C([-1, 0], I)$ by

$$(\mathcal{F}^t \varphi)(s) = x_\varphi^\nu(t + s), \ s \in [-1, 0] \, . \tag{4}$$

Remark. The invariance property given by Theorem 2.1 holds true for the case of a nonstrong invariance of the map f i.e., $f(I) \subseteq I$. The invariance property also holds true in the case of discontinuous maps f .

Proof. Suppose $\varphi \in X_I = C([-1, 0], I)$ and t_0 is the first time where the corresponding solution $x(t)$ leaves the interval I. To be definite we may assume that $t_0 = 0$ (due to the autonomy), $x(0) = b$, and that every right-sided neighborhood of $t_0 = 0$ contains a point t' with $x(t') > b$. Then this neighbourhood also contains a point t'' with $x(t'') > b$ and $\dot{x}(t'') > 0$. Admitting $t'' < 1$ we have $\nu \dot{x}(t'') = -x(t'') + f(x(t'' - 1)) < 0$ a contradiction. The other case, $x(0) = a$, is treated similarly. □

Suppose next that x_* is an attracting fixed point of the map f with immediate basin J_0 : $\lim_{n \rightarrow \infty} f^n(x_0) = x_*$ for any $x_0 \in J_0$. Define $X_{J_0} = C([-1, 0], J_0)$. In this situation the following holds.

Theorem 2.2. *For any $\nu > 0$ and $\varphi \in X_{J_0}, \lim_{t \rightarrow \infty} x_\varphi^\nu(t) = x_*$.*

The result shows that asymptotically constant solutions persist under singular perturbations of equation (2).

The proof of Theorem 2.2 is based on the following Lemma, which is also of independent interest.

Lemma 2.1. *Suppose an interval J is mapped by f into itself. If none of the endpoints of the interval $f(J)$ is a fixed point then for every $\varphi \in X_J = C([-1,0], J)$ there exists a finite time $t_0 = t_0(\varphi, \nu)$ such that $x_\varphi^\nu(t) \in f(J)$ for all $t \geq t_0$.*

Proof. Suppose first that $\varphi(0) \in \overline{f(J)}$. Then we claim that $x_\varphi^\nu(t) \in f(J)$ for all $t \leq 0$. Suppose not, and let t_0 be the first point at which the solution $x_\varphi^\nu(t)$ leaves the interval $\overline{f(J)}$. Then every right-sided neighbourhood of $t = t_0$ contains a point t' for which $x_\varphi^\nu(t') \notin \overline{f(J)}$. To be definite suppose $x_\varphi^\nu(t') > \sup\{\overline{f(J)}\}$. Then the same neighbourhood contains also a point t'' for which both $x_\varphi^\nu(t'') > \sup\{\overline{f(J)}\}$ and $d/dt[x_\varphi^\nu(t'')] > 0$ holds. Since $x_\varphi^\nu(t) \in J$ for all $t \in [t_0 - 1, t_0]$ and $t'' < t_0 + 1$ may be assumed, we then have $\nu \dot{x}_\varphi^\nu(t'') = -x_\varphi^\nu(t'') + f(x_\varphi^\nu(t'' - 1))$, a contradiction.

Suppose next that $\varphi(0) \notin \overline{f(J)}$. To be definite, let $\varphi(0) > \sup\{f(J)\}$ the case $\varphi(0) < \inf\{f(J)\}$ is treated similar). We claim that $x_\varphi^\nu(t)$ is decreasing for all $t \in [0, t_0]$ where $t_0 \leq \infty$ is the first point with $x_\varphi^\nu(t_0) = \sup\{f(J)\}$. Suppose $t_0 = \infty$. Then $x_\varphi^\nu(t) > \sup\{f(J)\}$ for all $t \geq 0$. According to equation (1) $\nu \dot{x}_\varphi^\nu(t) = -x_\varphi^\nu(t) + f(x_\varphi^\nu(t-1)) \leq 0$. Therefore there exists $x' = \lim_{t \to \infty} x_\varphi^\nu(t) \geq \sup\{f(J)\}$. Since x' is not a fixed point of the map f we have $-f(x') + x' := \delta > 0$. Equation (1) then replies $\nu \dot{x}_\varphi^\nu(t) = -x_\varphi^\nu(t) + f(x_\varphi^\nu(t-1) \leq -\delta/2$ for large t. This implies $x_\varphi^\nu(t) \to -\infty$ as $t \to \infty$, a contradiction. Therefore $t_0 < \infty$. Since $x_\varphi^\nu(t)$ is decreasing on $[0, t_0]$, by the above, and $x_\varphi^\nu(t) \in \overline{f(J)}$ we have $x_\varphi^\nu(t) \in f(J)$ for all $t \in [t_0 - 1, t_0]$. To complete the proof we repeat its first part.   □

Proof of Theorem 2.2. Let J_0 denote the immediate basin of the attracting fixed point $x = x_*$. Take an arbitrary $\varphi \in X_{J_0} = C([-1,0], J_0)$ and set $m = \inf\{\varphi(s), s \in [-1,0]\}$, $M = \sup\{\varphi(s), s \in [-1,0]\}$. Then $[m, M] \subset J_0$. Consider the smallest closed invariant interval J' containing the interval $[m, M]$, which is contained in J_0. Then one has $J' \supset f(J') \supset f^2(J') \supset \cdots$ and $\bigcap_{n \geq 0} f^n(J') = x_*$. The proof follows by repeated application of Lemma 2.1 and by using the invariance property.   □

Theorem 2.2 can be extended to the case of a general attractor of the map f. Suppose an interval I_0 is invariant and an attractor for the map f with immediate basin J_0:

$$\text{dist}(f^n(x), I_0) \to 0 \text{ for all } x \in J_0, \; n \to \infty.$$

Theorem 2.3. *For any $\nu > 0$ and $\varphi \in C([-1,0], J_0)$*
$\inf\{I_0\} \leq \lim_{t\to\infty} \inf x_\varphi^\nu(t) \leq \lim_{t\to\infty} \sup x_\varphi^\nu(t) \leq \sup\{I_0\}$.

The proof is the same as in the case of Theorem 2.2. with J being any invariant subinterval of J_0 containing I_0.

Let x_* be a repelling fixed point of the map f, satisfying $|f'(x_*)| > 1$. The following shows that the repelling property (in a sense) persists for the constant solution $x(t) = x_*$ of equation (1) if ν is small enough.

Theorem 2.4. *Suppose x_* is a repelling fixed point for the map f, $f'(x)$ is continuous in a neighbourhood of x_* and $|f'(x_*)| > 1$. Then there exists a positive ν_0 such that for all $0 < \nu \leq \nu_0$ the constant solution $x(t) = x_*$ of equation (1) is unstable.*

A constant solution $x(t) = x_*$ is called unstable if the stationary state $\varphi(t) = x_*$ of the semiflow $\mathcal{F}^t$ is unstable.

The proof of the theorem splits into two cases.
1. $f(x)$ is increasing in a neighbourhood of $x = x_*$. In this case the proof follows directly from the following Lemma.

Lemma 2.2. *Suppose the map f increases in some (half) neighbourhood of a repelling fixed point $x = x_*$. Then there exists a (half) neighbourhood $U(x_*)$ such that for every initial function $\varphi \in X_{U(x_*)} = C([-1,0], U(x_*))$ the corresponding solution $x_\varphi^\nu(t)$ has the property $x_\varphi^\nu(t_0 + s) \notin X_{U(x_*)}, s \in [-1,0]$, for some $t_0 = t_0(\varphi, \nu) \geq 0$.*

Proof. For definiteness we suppose $f(x_*) = x_*$ and $f(x) > x$ for all $x \in I' = (x_*, x_* + \delta]$. Take an arbitrary $\varphi \in X_{I'} = C([-1,0], I')$ and consider the corresponding solution $x_\varphi^\nu(t)$. Set $\inf\{\varphi(s), s \in [-1,0]\} = m > x_*$. We claim that there exists $t_0 \geq 0$ such that $x_\varphi^\nu(t) > f(m)$ for all $t \in [t_0, t_0 + 1]$. Indeed, in the case $\varphi(0) \geq f(m)$ one has $x_\varphi^\nu(t) \geq f(m)$ for all $t \in [0,1]$. This can be shown similar to the proof of Theorem 2.1. In the other case $\varphi(0) < f(m)$ there always exists a first point $t_0 > 0$ such that $x_\varphi^\nu(t_0) = f(m)$ and $x_\varphi^\nu(t)$ is strictly increasing for $t \in [0, t_0]$ (see the second part of the proof of Lemma 2.1). According to the first case and autonomy of equation (1) $x_\varphi^\nu(t) \geq f(m)$ for all $t \in [t_0, t_0 + 1]$. Using induction arguments one has $x_\varphi^\nu(t) > f^n(m)$ for all $t \in [t_n, t_n + 1]$ and some t_n. Since $f^n(m) \notin U(x_*) = (x_*, x_* + \delta]$ for every $m \in U(x_*)$ and some $n \in \mathbb{N}$, the proof follows. $\qquad\square$

2. $f(x)$ is decreasing in a neighbourhood of $x = x_*$ with $f'(x_*) < -1$.

The proof in this case follows from two facts: (i) Instability of the stationary state for the semiflow generated by the linear differential – delay equation $\nu\dot{y}(t) + y(t) = f'(x_*)y(t-1)$. The characteristic quasipolynomial $\lambda(z) = \nu z + 1 - f'(x_*)\exp(-z)$ has roots with positive real parts when $0 < \nu$ is small enough, and linear instability follows [13, 17, 43, 45]. (ii) The stationary state

$x = x_*$ of the semiflow $\mathcal{F}^t$ given by $\nu\dot{x}(t) + x(t) = f(x(t-1))$ is unstable provided $\lambda(z) = \nu z + 1 - f'(x_*)\exp(-z)$ has roots with positive real parts and $f(x)$ satisfies $[f(x) - f(x_*) - f'(x_*)(x - x_*)] = O(|x - x_*|)$ as $x \to x_*$ [12].

Another but similar proof is contained in [16] (Lemma 10).

In the case when the endpoints of the invariant interval I are not attracting fixed points the invariance property (Theorem 2.1) can be strengthened in the following way.

Theorem 2.5. *Suppose the interval $I = [a, b]$ is invariant under f and if $x = a$ (or $x = b$) is a fixed point then it is a repelling one. Then there exists a positive number δ, depending only on $f(x)$ and ν, such that if we denote $I' = [a + \delta, b - \delta]$ then the following holds: (1) for every $\varphi \in X_I$ there exists a time $t_0 = t_0(\varphi, \nu)$ such that $x_\varphi^\nu(t_0 + s) \in X_{I'}, s \in [-1, 0]$ (excepting $\varphi \equiv a$ or b when $x = a$ or $x = b$ is a fixed point); (2) for every $\psi \in X_{I'}$ $x_\psi^\nu(t) \in I'$ for all $t \geq 0$.*

Remark. It is clear that in the case that one of the endpoints of the interval is an attracting fixed point or a nonisolated fixed point Theorem 2.5 does not hold. This follows from Theorem 2.2 and from the fact that every fixed point of the map f gives rise to a corresponding stationary solution of equation (1).

Proof. We shall show the existence of a positive δ such that for every $\varphi \in X_I$ the corresponding solution $x_\varphi^\nu(t)$ satisfies $x_\psi^\nu(t) \geq a + \delta$ for sufficiently large t. In a similar way the existence of positive σ may be shown for which $x_\varphi^\nu(t) \leq b - \sigma$ for large t. This evidently implies the proof.

Since $I = [a, b]$ is invariant in every case (either $f(a) > a$ or $f(a) = a$ and $x = a$ is a repelling fixed point) there exists a positive γ such that $f(x) > x$ for all $x \in (a, a + \gamma]$. Set $(a, a + \gamma] = I_1$.

Claim 1. For every $\varphi \in X_{I_1}$ there exists a time moment $t_1 = t_1(\varphi, \nu)$ such that $x_\varphi^\nu(t_1) = a + \gamma$, $x_\varphi^\nu(t_1 + s) > a + \gamma$ for all $s \in (0, 1]$. Moreover, $x_\varphi^\nu(t)$ is increasing for $t \in [0, t_1]$.

The proof essentially repeats the proof of Lemma 2.2.

Claim 2. For every $\varphi \in X_I$, either $x_\varphi^\nu(t) - (a + \gamma) > 0$ for sufficiently large t, or $x_\varphi^\nu(t) - (a + \gamma)$ has arbitrarily large zeros.

Proof. The case $x_\varphi^\nu(t) - (a + \gamma) < 0$ for all large t is excluded by claim 1.

From claim 2 it follows that we only have to consider solutions which oscillate around $x = a + \gamma$). Consider a zero t_0 of $x_\varphi^\nu(t) - (a + \gamma)$ which contains in every right-side neighbourhood a point t' for which $x_\varphi^\nu(t') - (a + \gamma) < 0$. Then on the interval $[t_0, t_0 + 1]$ one has $x_\varphi^\nu(t) \geq a + \gamma \exp\{-(t - t_0)/\nu\}$, which implies $x_\varphi^\nu(t) \geq a + \gamma \exp(-1/\nu) \overset{\text{def}}{=} a + \delta$ for all $t \in [t_0, t_0 + 1]$. If $x_\varphi^\nu(t)$ has a zero t_1 on $(t_0, t_0 + 1]$ such that every right-sided neighbourhood contains a point t' satisfying $x_\varphi^\nu(t') - (a + \gamma) < 0$, we set $t_0 = t_1$ and repeat arguments. If $x_\varphi^\nu(t)$ does not have such a zero in $(t_0, t_0 + 1]$ then $x_\varphi^\nu(t) - (a + \gamma) < 0$ for all $t \in (t_0, t_0 + 1]$. This implies $x_\varphi^\nu(t_0 + 1 + s) \in X_{I_1}, s \in [-1, 0]$ and therefore $x_\varphi^\nu(t)$ increases for $t \geq t_0 + 1$ until the next zero t_1 of $x_\varphi^\nu(t) - a + \gamma)$. In every case one has $x_\varphi^\nu(t) \geq a + \delta$ for all $t \in [t_0, t_1]$. The Theorem is then proved by induction.   □

The following Theorem is a combination of Theorems 2.3 and 2.5.

Theorem 2.6. *Suppose the interval $I_0 \subset I$ is invariant under f and an attractor with domain of immediate attraction $J_0 \subset I : f(I_0) = I_0$, $f^n(x) \to I_0$ as $n \to \infty$ for every $x \in J_0$. If none of the endpoints of the interval I_0 is a fixed point then the following holds: there exists a positive δ depending on f and ν only such that solutions of equation (1) satisfy $x_\varphi^\nu(t) \in [\inf I_0 + \delta, \sup I_0 - \delta]$ for every $\varphi \in C([-1, 0], J_0)$ and large t.*

The proof is based essentially on the arguments given in the proofs of Theorems 2.3 and 2.5. We leave the details for the reader.

Remark. All results proved in this chapter extend for piecewise continuous nonlinearities $f(x)$ which we use in the sequel. In particular, Theorem 2.1 (invariance property) and Lemma 2.1 hold without any changes.

Example 2.1. Consider equation (1) with $f(x)$ being the logistic family $f_\lambda(x) = \lambda x(1 - x), 0 \leq \lambda \leq 4$, which map the interval $[0, 1]$ into itself.

We briefly recall some dynamical properties of the map f_λ, depending on particular values of the parameter λ.

If $0 \leq \lambda \leq 1$ the map f_λ has the only attracting fixed point $x = 0$ which attracts all others trajectories $(x_n)(x = 0$ is a global attractor, Fig. 9a).

For $\lambda > 1$ another fixed point $x = 1 - 1/\lambda$ bifurcates which attracts all other trajectories (x_n) for $1 < \lambda \leq 3$, (except $x = 0$). The fixed point $x = 0$ is repelling for every $\lambda > 1$ (Fig. 9b).

For $\lambda > 3$ the fixed point $x = 1 - 1/\lambda$ becomes repelling and an attracting cycle $\{a_1, a_2\}$ of period two bifurcates off. For $3 < \lambda \leq 1 + \sqrt{6}$ this cycle attracts almost all trajectories (x_n) (except the repelling fixed points $x = 0$ and $x = 1 - 1/\lambda$ and their preimages) (Fig. 9c).

The further development of dynamics for the map f_λ is well-known. There exists an increasing sequence $\lambda_0 < \lambda_1 < \lambda_2 < \cdots < \lambda_n < \cdots (\lambda_0 = 1, \lambda_1 = 3, \lambda_2 = 1 + \sqrt{6})$ such that for every $\lambda \in (\lambda_n, \lambda_{n+1}]$ the map f_λ has an attracting cycle of period 2^n which attracts almost all trajectories (x_n) (except repelling cycles of periods $1, 2, \cdots, 2^{n-1}$ and all their preimages). The sequence converges to $\lambda_* \approx 3,569$. For each $\lambda > \lambda_*$ the map f_λ has a cycle with a period which is not a power of two.

For every $\lambda > 3$, the interval $I_\lambda = [f_\lambda^2(1/2), f_\lambda(1/2)]$ is invariant for the map f_λ and is an attractor (Fig. 9d).

We shall see now what can be said about the asymptotic behavior as $t \to \infty$ of solutions to equation (1) when the initial conditions are taken from $X = C([-1, 0], [0, 1])$. To draw conclusions we use Theorems 2.1–2.6.

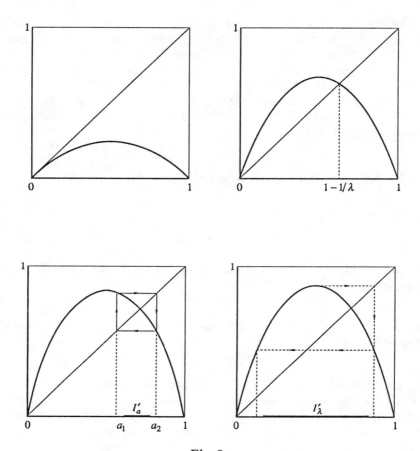

Fig. 9.

When $0 \leq \lambda \leq 1$ every solution of equation (1) satisfies $\lim_{t \to \infty} x(t) = 0$ (Fig. 9a).

When $1 < \lambda \leq 3$ every solution of equation (1) satisfies $\lim_{t \to \infty} x(t) = x_\lambda = 1 - 1/\lambda$ (except $x \equiv 0$) (Fig. 9b).

Now consider the case $\lambda > 3$ and let $\{a_1, a_2\}$ be the cycle of period two that appears for the map f_λ. There exists a parameter value $\lambda^0 \in (\lambda_1, \lambda_2) = (3, 1 + \sqrt{6})$ such that at $\lambda = \lambda^0$ the critical point $x = 1/2$ forms a cycle of period two which is evidently attracting.

For all $\lambda \in (3, \lambda^0]$ the points a_1 and a_2 lay on the right hand side of $x = 1/2$ and the interval $I_a = [a_1, a_2]$ is invariant and a global attractor for the map f_λ. In this case one has $x(t) \in I_a$ for all sufficiently large t and every solution $x(t)$ of equation (1) (except $x \equiv 0$). Moreover, there exists a positive $\delta = \delta(\lambda, \nu)$ such that $x(t) \in I_a'$ for all large t, where $I_a' = [a_1 + \delta, a_2 - \delta]$ (Fig. 9c)(Theorem 2.6).

When $\lambda \in (\lambda^0, 1 + \sqrt{6}]$ the interval $I_a = [a_1, a_2]$ is not invariant but the interval $I_\lambda = [f_\lambda^2(1/2), f_\lambda(1/2)]$ is. Similarly, every solution $x(t)(\not\equiv 0)$ of equation (1) satisfies $x(t) \in I_\lambda$ for large t. There exists $\delta = \delta(\lambda, \nu)$ such that $x(t) \in I_\lambda'$ for large t, where $I_\lambda' = [f_\lambda^2(1/2) + \delta, f_\lambda(1/2) - \delta]$ (Theorem 2.6).

The same situation holds true for every $4 \geq \lambda > \lambda^0$. The interval $I_\lambda = [f_\lambda^2(1/2), f_\lambda(1/2)]$ remains invariant. There exists a positive $\delta = \delta(\lambda, \nu)$ such that $x(t) \in I_\lambda' = [f_\lambda^2(1/2) + \delta, f_\lambda(1/2) - \delta]$ for every solution $x(t)$ of equation (1) and all large t (Fig. 9d).

3. Continuous Dependence on Parameter

Consider the differential-difference equation

$$\nu \dot{x}(t) + x(t) = f(x(t-1)) \tag{1}$$

with small positive ν and the corresponding difference equation with continuous argument

$$x(t) = f(x(t-1)) \tag{2}$$

which is obtained formally from equation (1) by letting $\nu = 0$. Assume that the one-dimensional map

$$f: \quad x \to f(x) \tag{3}$$

has a closed invariant interval $I \subseteq \mathbb{R}$ and is continuous on I.

Let $X_I = C([-1, 0], I)$ denote the continuous functions from $[-1, 0]$ into I. Clearly, if $\varphi \in X_I$ the corresponding solution $x_\varphi^\nu(t)$ of equation (1) is continuous (even smooth for $t > 0$), whereas the solution of equation (2) need not be continuous. It is continuous for all $t \geq -1$ if the consistency condition $\varphi(0) = f(\varphi(-1))$ holds. This motivates us to introduce the subset of initial functions $X_I^0 = \{\varphi \in X_I | \varphi(0) = f(\varphi(-1))\}$.

One naturally expects that close initial data $\varphi(t)$ and $\psi(t)$ generate solutions $x_\varphi(t)$ and $x_\psi^\nu(t)$ which are also close within (at least) a finite time interval, provided ν is small enough. In fact closeness between solutions of equations (1) and (2) holds uniformly on intervals $[0, T], T > 0$ for $\varphi \in X_I^0$, and uniformly on compact subsets of $\mathbb{R}_+ = \{t | t \geq 0\}$ which do not contain discontinuity points of $x_\varphi(t)$ for $\varphi \in X_I$. Precise statements are given in Theorems 3.1 and 3.4 below.

Let $\mathcal{M}$ be a subset of $\mathbb{R}$. By the norm of $\varphi : \mathcal{M} \to \mathbb{R}$ we mean the uniform norm, that is $\|\varphi\|_{\mathcal{M}} = \sup\{|\varphi(t)|, t \in \mathcal{M}\}$.

Theorem 3.1. *For any $\varphi \in X_I^0$ and positive T, ε there exist positive δ, ν_0 depending on φ, T, ε such that $\|x_\varphi - x_\psi^\nu\|_{[0,T]} \leq \varepsilon$ for all $0 < \nu \leq \nu_0$ provided $\|\varphi - \psi\|_{[-1,0]} \leq \delta$ and $\psi \in X_I$.*

Due to induction arguments it is sufficient to prove the theorem for $T = 1$. We first prove several lemmas.

Lemma 3.1. *For any $\varphi \in X_I$ and $\varepsilon > 0$ there exists $\delta = \delta(\varphi, \varepsilon) > 0$ such that $\|x_\varphi^\nu - x_\psi^\nu\|_{[0,1]} \leq \varepsilon$ for all $\nu > 0$ provided $\psi \in X_I$ and $\|\varphi - \Psi\|_{[-1,0]} \leq \delta$.*

Proof. Since the differential-difference equation (1) is equivalent to the integral equation $x(t) = x(0)\exp(-t/\nu) + (1/\nu)\int_0^t \exp\{(s-t)/\nu\}f(x(s-1))ds$, we have the following relation for $t \in [0,1]|x_\varphi^\nu(t) - x_\psi^\nu(t)| \leq |\varphi(0) - \psi(0)|\exp(-t/\nu) + (1/\nu) \times \int_0^t \exp\{(s-t)/\nu\}|f(\varphi(s-1)) - f(\psi(s-1))|ds$. The uniform continuity of f implies that for any $\varepsilon > 0$ there exists $\delta > 0$ with $|f(\varphi(t)) - f(\psi(t))| \leq \varepsilon$ provided $|\varphi(t) - \psi(t)| \leq \delta$. This yields $|x_\varphi^\nu(t) - x_\psi^\nu(t)| \leq \delta\exp(-t/\nu) - \varepsilon(1 - \exp(-t/\nu) \leq \max\{\delta, \varepsilon\}$ which completes the proof. $\square$

Lemma 3.2. *For any $\varphi \in X_I^0$ and $\varepsilon > 0$ there exists $\nu = \nu_0(\varphi, \varepsilon) > 0$ such that $\|x_\varphi^\nu - x_\varphi\|_{[0,1]} \leq \varepsilon$ for all $0 < \nu \leq \nu_0$.*

Proof. Taking into account that $1 - \exp(-t/\nu) = (1/\nu)\int_0^t \exp\{(s-t)/\nu\}ds$ we have for $t \in [0,1]$: $|x_\varphi^\nu(t) - x_\varphi(t)| \leq |\varphi(0) - f(\varphi(t-1))|\exp(-t/\nu) + (1/\nu)\int_0^t \exp\{(s-t)/\nu\}|f(\varphi(s-1)) - f(\varphi(t-1))|ds$. Since $f(\varphi(\cdot))$ is uniformly continuous for $t \in [-1,0]$ it follows that for any $\varepsilon' > 0$ there exists $\delta' > 0$ such that $|f(\varphi(t_1)) - f(\varphi(t_2))| \leq \varepsilon'$ provided $|t_1 - t_2| \leq \delta'$. Thus for $t \in [0, \delta']$. we have $|x_\varphi^\nu(t) - x_\varphi(t)| \leq \varepsilon'\exp(-t/\nu) + \varepsilon'(1 - \exp(-t/\nu)) \leq \varepsilon'$. Suppose next $t \in [\delta', 1]$. Then $|\varphi(0) - f(\varphi(t-1))|\exp(-t/\nu) = \operatorname{diam} I \exp(-\delta'/\nu) = \varepsilon'$ for all sufficiently small ν, say $0 < \nu \leq \nu'$. On the other hand $(1/\nu)\int_0^t \exp\{(s-t)/\nu\}|f(\varphi(s-1)) - f(\varphi(t-1))|ds = (1/\nu)(\int_0^{t-\delta'} + \int_{t-\delta'}^t) \leq \operatorname{diam} I \exp(-\delta'/\nu) + \varepsilon'(1 - \exp(-\delta'/\nu)) < 2\varepsilon'$ for all sufficiently small ν say $0 < \nu \leq \nu''$. Therefore, setting $\nu''' = \min(\nu', \nu'')$ we have $(1/\nu)\int_0^t \exp\{(s-t)/\nu\}|f(\varphi(s-1)) - f(\varphi(t-1))|ds = 2\varepsilon'$ for all $0 < \nu \leq \nu'''$. This implies $|x_\varphi^\nu(t) - x_\varphi(t)| \leq 3\varepsilon' = \varepsilon$ for all $0 < \nu \leq \nu'''$ and $t \in [\delta', 1]$ with $\varepsilon' = \varepsilon/3$. The proof is complete. $\square$

The proof of Theorem 3.1. follows easily from the inequality $\|x_\psi^\nu - x_\phi\|_{[0,1]} \leq \|x_\varphi - x_\varphi^\nu\|_{[0,1]} + \|x_\varphi^\nu - x_\psi^\nu\|_{[0,1]}$ and Lemmas 3.1 and 3.2.

It is not difficult to see that, similarly to the proof of Theorem 3.1, the closeness between solutions of equation (2) and solutions of equation (1) may be derived, when f in equation (1) is perturbed. For a precise statement we denote by $x_\varphi^\nu(t, f)$ and $x_\varphi(t, f)$ the solutions of equations (1) and (2), respectively, with particular $f(x)$.

Theorem 3.2. *For any $\varphi \in X_I^0$ and positive T, ε there exist positive δ, σ, ν_0 depending on φ, T, ε such that $\|x_\varphi(\cdot, f) - x_{\tilde\varphi}^0(\cdot, \tilde f))\|_{[0,T]} \leq \varepsilon$ for all $0 < \nu \leq \nu_0$ provided $\tilde\varphi \in X_I$, $\|\varphi - \tilde\varphi\|_{[-1,0]} \leq \delta$ and $\|f - \tilde f\|_I \leq \sigma$.*

With the closeness result proved the next natural question appears. How long do the solutions of equations (1) and (2) remain close, provided the initial data are close?

Suppose $\varphi \in X_I^0$ is fixed and consider arbitrary $\psi \in X_I$ with the initial deviation $\|\varphi - \psi\|_{[-1,0]} := \Delta_0$ being small. The solutions $x_\psi(t)$ and $x_\varphi^\nu(t)$ diverge, in general, as t increases. Since $\Delta_T := \|x_\psi - x_\varphi^\nu\|_{[0,T]} \le \|x_\varphi - x_\varphi^\nu\|_{[0,T]} + \|x_\varphi - x_\psi\|_{[0,T]}$ and $\|x_\varphi - x_\varphi^\nu\|_{[0,T]} \to 0$ as $\nu \to +0$, the value $\|x_\psi - x_\varphi^\nu\|_{[0,T]}$ may be estimated by $\|x_\varphi - x_\psi\|_{[0,T]}$. The latter is determined by the initial deviation Δ_0 and equation (2). Thus, the value of Δ_T depends on both the deviation induced by difference equation (2) with Δ_0 given and the deviation caused by solutions of equations (1) and (2) through the same initial condition. The latter depends essentially on the smoothness of $f(x)$.

Theorem 3.3. *Suppose f and $\varphi \in X_T^0$ are Lispschitz. Then $\|x_\varphi - x_\varphi^\nu\|_{[0,T]} = O(\nu)$ as $\nu \to +0$ for any fixed $T > 0$.*

Proof. Suppose the Lispschitz constants are L and L' for $f(x)$ and $\varphi(t)$, respectively. First consider the interval $[0,1]$. To estimate $\|x_\varphi^\nu - x_\varphi\|_{[0,1]}$ we use the inequality $|x_\varphi^\nu(t) - x_\varphi(t)| \le |\varphi(0) - f(\varphi(t-1))| \exp(-t/\nu) + (1/\nu) \times \int_0^t \exp\{(s-t)/\nu\}|f(\varphi(s-1)) - f(\varphi(t-1))|ds \overset{\text{def}}{=} d(t)$ (see the proof of lemma 3.2). Since $\varphi(t)$ is fixed and Lipschitz and $\varphi(0) = f(\varphi(-1))$ we have $|\varphi(0) - f(\varphi(t-1)|\exp(-t/\nu) \le LL'\nu \times (t/\nu)\exp(-t/\nu) \le LL'\nu/e \overset{\text{def}}{=} c_1\nu$. On the other hand $(1/\nu)\int_0^t \exp\{(s-t)/\nu\}|f(\varphi(s-1)) - f(\varphi(t-1))|ds \le LL' \int_0^t \exp\{(s-t)/\nu\}|s-t|ds = \nu \int_0^{t/\nu} \exp(-u)|u|du \le c_2\nu$. Therefore $d(t) \le c\nu$, where c is a constant depending on L and L' only. Thus $\|x_\varphi - x_\varphi^\nu\|_{[0,1]} \le c\nu$.

Now consider the solutions $x_\varphi(t)$ and $x_\varphi^\nu(t)$ for $t \in [0,1]$ as members of the space of initial functions. Denote them by $\varphi_1 \in X_I^0$ and $\psi_1 \in X_I$ respectively. Then $\|x_\varphi - x_\varphi^\nu\|_{[1,2]} \le \|x_{\varphi_1} - x_{\varphi_1}^\nu\|_{[0,1]} + \|x_{\varphi_1}^\nu - x_{\psi_1}^\nu\|_{[0,1]}$. But one has $\|x_{\varphi_1}^\nu - x_{\psi_1}^\nu\|_{[0,1]} \le \sup_{t\in[0,1]}\{\varphi_1(0) - \psi_1(0)|\exp(-t/\nu) + L(1 - \exp(-t/\nu))\sup_{(0,t)}|\varphi_1(s-1) - \psi_1(s-1)|$, which implies $\|x_{\varphi_1}^\nu - x_{\psi_1}^\nu\|_{[0,1]} \le \max\{L,1\}|\varphi_1 - \psi_1\|_{[-1,0]}$. Since $\varphi_1 = f(\varphi)$ and both φ and f are Lipschitz, φ_1 is Lipschitz too. Therefore $\|x_{\varphi_1} - x_{\varphi_1}^\nu\|_{[0,1]} \le c_1\nu$ again, and we have $\|x_\varphi - x_\varphi^\nu\|_{[1,2]} \le c_1\nu + c\max\{L,1\}c\nu = O(\nu)$. With T fixed the above arguments can be repeated, completing the proof. $\square$

It is worth to note that assuming $f(x)$ to be Lipschitz and $\varphi \in H^\alpha$, $0 < \alpha \le 1$, one would obtain $\|x_\varphi - x_\varphi^\nu\|_{[0,T]} = O(\nu^\alpha)$ as $\nu \to +0$ for any fixed T. We recall that $H^\alpha = \{\varphi \in X_I | |\varphi(t') - \varphi(t'')| \le K|t' - t''|^\alpha$ for all $t', t'' \in [-1,0], K - \text{const}\}$.

As we have noted earlier, the consistency condition $\varphi(0) = f(\varphi(-1))$ need not hold in the case $\varphi \in X_I$. Then the solution $x_\varphi(t)$ of equation (2) is in general discontinuous at each point $t = i$, $i \in \mathbb{N}$, although the solution $x_\varphi^\nu(t)$ of equation (1) is smooth for $t > 0$. Nevertheless the solutions $x_\varphi(t)$ and $x_\varphi^\nu(t)$ are close within finite time intervals for small ν, outside the discontinuity points of $x_\varphi(t)$. To be precise we define for positive T and κ the set $J_T^\kappa = [0, T] \setminus \bigcup_{i=0}^{[T+1]} [i, i + \kappa)$. where $[\cdot]$ stands for integer part of a number. Then the following holds.

Theorem 3.4. *For any $\varphi \in X_I$ and positive T, κ, ε there exist positive δ, ν_0 depending on $\varphi, T, \kappa, \varepsilon$ such that $\|x_\varphi - x_\psi^\nu\|_{J_T^\kappa} \leq \varepsilon$ for all $0 < \nu \leq \nu_0$ provided $\psi \in X_I$ and $\|\varphi - \psi\|_{[-1, 0]} \leq \delta$.*

The proof is similar to that of Theorem 3.1.

Finally we note that some continuous dependence results may be proved under weaker assumptions on f and φ than in Theorems 3.1. and 3.4. We consider here the particular case of nonlinearities $f(x)$ as needed in the next chapter. Assume: (i) $f(x)$ has a finite discontinuity set Λ, is continuous on $I \setminus \Lambda$ and $\lim_{x \to x^* \pm 0} f(x)$ exists for any $x^* \in \Lambda$; (ii) $f(I \setminus \Lambda) \bigcap \Lambda = \emptyset$.

Introduce an initial function space X_I^1 by setting $X_I^1 = \{\varphi \in X_I|$ all zeros of $\varphi(t) - x^*$, $x^* \in \Lambda$, are isolated$\}$.

With $\varphi \in X_I^1$, the solution $x_\varphi(t)$ of equation (2) is defined as usual by the above iteration procedure. By a solution $x_\varphi^\nu(t)$ of equation (1) we mean a continuous and piecewise continuously differentiable function satisfying the equation for all $t > 0$ except at isolated points. Clearly, with given φ the corresponding solution $x_\varphi^\nu(t)$ is constructed for $t > 0$ through step by step integration.

Suppose $\varphi \in X_I^1$ is fixed. We enumerate all zeros of $\varphi(t) - x^*$, $x^* \in \Lambda$, on the initial set $[-1, 0]$ by $t_1 < t_2 < \cdots < t_N$. The number of zeros is finite according to the definition. Take any positive κ and T and set $J_T^\kappa = J_T^\kappa(\varphi) = [0, T] \setminus \bigcup_{k=1}^{N} \bigcup_{i=0}^{[T+1]} U_\kappa(t_k + i)$ where $U_\kappa(z)$ is the κ-neighbourhood of z. The set J_T^κ is the interval $[0, T]$ excepting κ-neighbourhoods of points $t_k + i$, where $0 \leq i \leq [T + 1]$, t_k is a zero of $\varphi(t) - x^*$, $x^* \in \Lambda$, $1 \leq \kappa \leq N$. Clearly, for any $\kappa > 0$ the solution $x_\varphi(t)$ is continuous on J_T^κ.

Theorem 3.5. *Let f satisfies conditions (i) and (ii). For any $\varphi \in X_I^1$ and positive T, κ, ε there exist positive δ and ν_0 depending on $\varphi, T, \kappa, \varepsilon$ such that $\|x_\varphi - x_\psi^\nu\|_{J_T^\kappa} \leq \varepsilon$ for all $0 < \nu \leq \nu_0$ provided $\psi \in X_I^1$ and $\|\varphi - \psi\|_{[-1, 0]} \leq \delta$.*

Essentially the proof is similar to that of Theorem 3.1.

4. Impact of Singular Perturbations: Examples

In this chapter we consider several simple examples showing that the asymptotic behaviour as $t \to +\infty$ of solutions for equation (1) with positive ν may differ essentially from the asymptotic behaviour of solutions for equation (2) (though, as was shown in the previous chapter, the solutions of the equations are close within any sufficiently large but fixed time interval, for small $\nu > 0$).

In the examples considered the function $f(x)$ is piecewise constant (hence, the map $x \to f(x)$ is not continuous). This allows us to find an explicit form for the shift operator along solutions of equation (1) and to carry out a sufficiently complete analysis of the properties of the solutions. If it is not specified otherwise the parameter ν is assumed to be positive and small throughout the chapter.

The examples show in particular that the singular term $\nu \dot{x}(t)$ may lead to both a simplification of the limit behavior for the solutions (Examples 4.1–4.3) and a complication (Example 4.4). For the latter, the attractor of the difference equation (2) consists of generalized periodic functions, whereas the attractor of the corresponding singularly perturbed equation is described by oscillating solutions governed (in a sense) by a quasi-random quantity for which the density distribution is absolutely continuous with respect to Lebesgue measure.

In the examples which follow the map f has a maximal invariant interval I. Set $X = C([-1,0], I)$. According to Theorem 2.1 (the invariance property) and its generalization to the case of the discontinuous f, for an arbitrary $\varphi \in X$ the corresponding solution satisfies $x_\varphi^\nu(t+s) \in X$, $s \in [-1,0]$, for all $t \geq 0$ and each $\nu > 0$. This allows us to consider initial conditions from X only.

Example 4.1. Consider equation (1) with f satisfying: $f(x) = a > 0$ for $x > 0$; $f(x) = -b < 0$ for $x < 0$; $f(0) = 0$.

With $f(x)$ given, the corresponding interval map has two attracting fixed points $x_1 = a$ and $x_2 = -b$ with basins $x > 0$ and $x < 0$ respectively. Both equations (1) and (2) have three constant solutions $x_0(t) = 0$ and $x_1(t) = a$, $x_2(t) = -b$ with the latter two being attracting. Any initial function $\varphi(t) > 0$ gives rise to a solution $x(t)$ satisfying $\lim_{t \to \infty} x(t) = a$. Similarly, any initial function $\varphi(t) < 0$ generates a solution with $\lim_{t \to \infty} x(t) = -b$. This is the case for both equation (1) and equation (2) (see Chaps. 1 and 2).

Equation (2) also has relaxation type solutions, and they are the typical ones. They are generated by initial conditions having both positive and negative values. Small perturbations give rise to relaxation type solutions as well.

On the other hand for equation (1) oscillatory solutions are rare. According to the following proposition almost all solutions are asymptotically constant.

Proposition 4.1. *Almost all solutions of equation (1) satisfy one of the following* $\lim_{t \to \infty} x(t) = a$ *or* $\lim_{t \to \infty} x(t) = -b$.

"Almost all" is used in the following meaning. The set of initial conditions for which the solutions have limits a or b is an open and dense subset of $X = C([-1,0], \mathbb{R})$.

Proof. First consider a set of initial functions with at most two zeros: $\varphi_u = \{\varphi \in X | \varphi(0) = \varphi(-u) = 0, \varphi(t) < 0$ for $t \in (-u, 0), \varphi(t) > 0$ for $t \in [-1, -u)\}$, depending on the real parameter $u \in [0, 1]$.

Integrating (1) for $t > 0$ and u given, we have $x^u(t) = a - a \exp(-t/\nu)$ for $t \in [0, 1 - u]$, $x^u(1 - u) \overset{\text{def}}{=} x_1 = a[1 - \exp\{-(1 - u)/\nu\}]$; $x^u(t) = -b + (x_1 + b) \exp\{-(t - 1 + u)/\nu\}$ for $t \in [1 - u, 1]$, $x^u(1) \overset{\text{def}}{=} x_2 = -b + (x_1 + b) \exp(-u/\nu)$; $x^u(t) = a + (x_2 - a) \exp\{-(t - 1)/\nu\}$ for $t \in [1, 2 - u]$.

Claim 1. With u fixed there exists a unique solution $x^u(t)$ of equation (1) generated by φ_u. The solution does not depend on the particular $\varphi \in \Phi_u$.

Since $f(x)$ takes constant values for $x < 0$ and $x > 0$ the claim is obvious.

Claim 2. Given $u \in [0, 1]$ either (a) there exists $t_1 \in (0, 1]$ with $x^u(t_1) = 0$, $x^u(t) > 0$ for $t \in (0, t_1)$ and $x^u(t) < 0$ for $t \in (t_1, 1]$, or (b) $x^u(t) = a + (x^u(1) - a) \exp\{-(t - 1)/\nu\}$, $t \geq 1$.

Clearly, $x^u(t)$ is increasing for $t \in (0, 1 - u)$ and decreasing for $t \in (1 - u, 1)$. Thus, either $x^u(1) > 0$ meaning $x^u(t) > 0$ for all $t \in (0, 1]$, implying $x^u(t) = a + (x^u(1) - a) \exp\{-(t - 1)/\nu\}$ (Fig. 10).

Claim 3. With ν fixed there exists $u_1 > 0$ such that $x^{u_1}(t) > 0$ for $t \in (0, 1)$ and $x^{u_1}(1) = 0$. For any $u \in [0, u_1)$ $x^u(t) > 0$ for all $t > 0$ (therefore $x^u(t) = a + (x^u(1) - a) \exp\{-(t - 1)/\nu\}$, $t \geq 1$).

The claim is obvious and u_1 is calculated directly $u_1 = \nu \ln[(a + b)/a \exp(-1/\nu) + b)]$. The claim states the existence of a threshold value for the parameter u: for every $u < u_1$ the solution $x^u(t)$ has no zeros for $t > 0$, while for $u \geq u_1$ it has at least one zero $t_1 > 0$.

Claim 4. In case $x^u(1) < 0$ there either (a) exists $1 < t_2 < t_1 + 1$ with $x^u(t_2) = 0$, or (b) $x^u(t) < 0$ for all $t \in [1, 2]$.

The claim is obvious.

Similarly to claim 3 the following holds.

Claim 5. With ν fixed there exists $u_2 > 0$ such that $x^{u_2}(t) < 0$ for $t \in (t_1, t_2)$, $t_2 = t_1 + 1$, $x^{u_2}(t_2) = 0$. For any $u \in (u_2, 1]$ $x^u(t) < 0$ for all $t > t_1$ (therefore $x^u(t) = -b + (x^u(1 + t_1) + b) \exp\{-(t - t_1 - 1)/\nu\}$).

The claim follows as a symmetric counterpart of claim 3. Indeed, for any $u > u_1$ there always exists $t_1 > 0$ such that $x^u(t_1) = 0$, and $x^u(t) > 0$ for all $t \in (0, t_1)$ (see claim 3). Due to the symmetry arguments to those of claim 3, there is $t_1^* = \nu \ln[(a + b)/(b \exp(-1/\nu) + a)]$ and a corresponding value u_2 of the parameter u such that $x^{u_2}(t_1^* + 1) = 0$, $x^{u_2}(t) < 0$ for all $t \in (t_1^*, t_1^* + 1)$. The parameter value u_2 is a real root of the equation $1 - u_2 + \nu \ln[1 + (a/b)(1 - \exp\{(u_2 - 1)/\nu\})] = \nu \ln[(a + b)/(b \exp(-1/\nu) + a)]$.

Claims 2–5 allow to define a map $\mathcal{F}$ on the parameterized sets Φ_u in the following way. To any Φ_u, $u \in (u_1, u_2)$, there corresponds $\Phi_{u'}$ with $u' = t_2 - t_1$. In the case $u \in [0, u_1]$ we set $u' = 0$, and in the case $u \in [u_2, 1]$ we set $u' = 1$.

The map $\mathcal{F}$ induces an one-dimensional map by $u' = F(u)$. We shall find the explicit form of F next. If both t_2 and t_1 exist then it is easy to calculate:

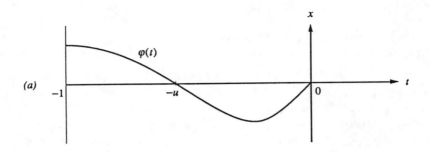

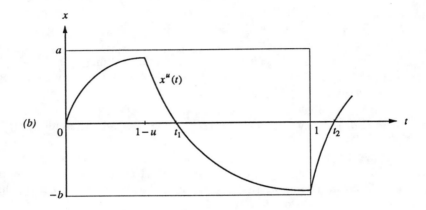

Fig. 10.

$$\Delta_1 \overset{\text{def}}{=} t_1 - (1-u) = \nu \ln[1 + a(1 - \exp\{(u-1)/\nu\})/b] \,,$$

$$\Delta_2 \overset{\text{def}}{=} t_2 - 1 = \nu \ln[1 + b/a + \exp(-1/\nu) - (b/a+1)\exp(-u/\nu)] \,.$$

In this case: $F(u) = u' = u + \Delta_2 - \Delta_1$, implying

$$F : u \to u + \nu \ln[1 + b/a + \exp(-1/\nu) - (b/a+1)\exp(-u/\nu)]$$
$$- \nu \ln[1 + \frac{a}{b}(1 - \exp\frac{u-1}{\nu})] \,.$$

Changing the variable u to $z = h(u) \overset{\text{def}}{=} \exp(-u/\nu)$ we get the toplogically equivalent map

$$G : z \to z \frac{1 + (a/b)(1 - \exp(-1/\nu)/z)}{1 + b/a + \exp(-1/\nu) - (b/a+1)z} \,, z \in [\exp(-1/\nu), 1] \,,$$

with F and G being conjugate by $G \circ h = h \circ F$ for $u \in [0,1]$. Denoting $a/b = k$ and $a \exp(-1/\nu)/(a+b) = \varepsilon$ we obtain

$$G : z \to k\frac{z - \varepsilon}{1 + \varepsilon - z}, \quad z \in [\exp(-1/\nu), 1] .$$

Note that F is defined for all $u \in [0, 1]$. This implies that $z = h(u)$ varies within $[\exp(-1/\nu), 1]$ and the latter interval is the domain of G. The function $k(z - \varepsilon)/(1 + \varepsilon - z)$ is defined for all real $z \neq 1 + \varepsilon$ and is strictly increasing (Fig. 11). If $\nu > 0$ is small enough then there exist $z_1 < z_2$ such that $G(z_1) = \exp(-1/\nu)$, $z_1 > \exp(-1/\nu)$ and $G(z_2) = 1$, $z_2 < 1$ (by direct calculation one obtains from the formula for G : $G(1) > 1$, $G(z_1) = \exp(-1/\nu)$, $z_1 = \varepsilon[1 - (k + 1)/\{k^2 + \varepsilon(k + 1)\}] > \exp(-1/\nu)$, $0 < \nu \ll 1$. It is clear that the values z_1 and z_2 are related to u_1 and u_2 in the following way: $z_1 = \exp(-u_1/\nu)$, $z_2 = \exp(-u_2/\nu)$. According to the definition of the map F and claims 3, 5 we have to set $G(z) = \exp(-1/\nu)$, $z \leq z_1$, and $G(z) = 1$, $z \geq z_2$. Then the map G has a form as shown in Fig. 11 by continuous curve.

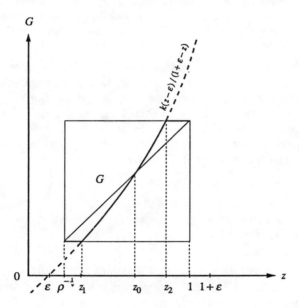

Fig. 11.

The map G is related to the dynamics given by (1) in the following way. For any particular $u \in [0, 1]$ equation (1) has a unique solution $x^u(t)$, $t \geq 0$ generated by Φ_u. The distance u' between its successive zeros t_1, and t_2 (Fig. 10) is given for u by $u' = F(u)$, where $F = h^{-1} \circ G \circ h$, $h = \exp(-u/\nu)$. Therefore, if the solution $x^u(t)$ oscillates with successive zeros $t_1 < t_2 < t_3 < t_4 < \cdots$ then the distance u_n between zeros t_{2n-1} and t_{2n} is governed by G as follows: $u_n = h^{-1} \circ G^n \circ h$, where G^n is n-th iterate of G.

The map G has one repelling fixed point z_0 (Fig. 11). (The value z_0 is found as a larger (real) root of the equation $z = k(z - \varepsilon)/(1 + \varepsilon - z)$). Clearly, the corresponding value $u_0 = \nu \ln(1/z_0)$ gives rise to an unstable periodic solution of the equation (1). For any $z \neq z_0$ the sequence $z_n = G^n(z)$ is monotone. There always exists a first $n_0 \in \mathbb{N}$ with either $z_{n_0} = \exp(-1/\nu)$ or $z_{n_0} = 1$. This implies monotonicity of the corresponding $u_n = \nu \ln(1/z_n)$ with $u_{n_0} = 1$ or $u_{n_0} = 0$, respectively. Recall that we set $u' = F(u) = 0$ for $u \in [0, u_1]$ and $u' = F(u) = 1$ for $u \in [u_2, 1]$. If the initial value satisfies $u \in [0, u_1] \cup [u_2, 1]$ then $x^u(t)$ has no zeros for $t > 0$, and either $x^u(t) \to a$ or $x^u(t) \to -b$ as $t \to \infty$ (see Claims 3, 5). Therefore, the solution $x^u(t)$ for which $u_{n_0} = 0$ (or $u_{n_0} = 1$) monotonically tends to a (or to $-b$) for large t.

Similar (but more complicated) calculations show that for any even $m \geq 4$ there exists precisely one unstable periodic solution with m zeros per period. Almost all other solutions are asymptotically constant. There exist infinitely many solutions which merge into the mentioned periodic solutions. Almost all small perturbations within the initial set give rise to asymptotically constant solutions. Details are found in [2].

Since the solutions depend continuously on initial conditions for the non-linearity f of Example 4.1, the set of asymptotically constant solutions (which have limits a or b as $t \to \infty$) is open. For every initial function $\varphi \in C([-1, 0], \mathbb{R})$ and arbitrary $\varepsilon > 0$ there exists an initial function $\varphi_m \in C([-1, 0], \mathbb{R})$ which has an even number m of zeros on the inital set $[-1, 0]$ and is in an ε-neighbourhood of φ. Together with the previous arguments this gives density and completes the proof of Proposition 4.1.

Next, we briefly describe the second

Example 4.2. Consider equation (1) with $f(x)$ satisfying: $f(x) = a > 0$ for $x > 0$ and $f(x) = -b < 0$ for $x \geq 0$.

The corresponding interval map has a globally attracting cycle of period 2: $a \to -b \to a$ (Fig. 12). All solutions of equation (2) oscillate. Initial functions having m zeros on $[-1, 0)$ produce solutions having m zeros on each interval $[k, k+1)$, $k \in \mathbb{N}$. This follows from the fact that each solution of equation (2) is obtained by successive iterations of the corresponding initial function (see Chap. 2).

For equation (1) the situation is different as the following proposition shows.

Proposition 4.2. *Equation (1) has an asymptotically stable periodic solution generated by any initial function $\varphi(t)$ satisfying $\varphi(t) > 0$ for all $t \in [-1, 0]$ (or $\varphi(t) < 0$). Almost all other inital functions generate solutions which merge into this periodic solution.*

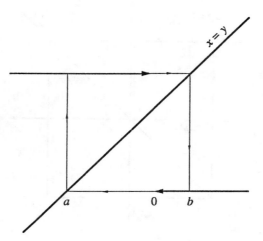

Fig. 12.

"Almost all" means that the corresponding set is open and dense in $X = C([-1, 0], \mathbb{R})$. The details of the proof can be found in [2].

Thus both Examples 4.1 and 4.2 show that the term $\nu\dot{x}(t)$ added to equation (2) leads to the disappearance of solutions having more than one zero on intervals of length 1.

A similar phenomenon also takes place for the equation $\dot{x}(t) = g(x(t-1))$ if the nonlinearity g satisfies the negative feedback condition $xg(x) < 0$, $x \neq 0$. Strong results for the case of a general nonlinearity $g(x)$ are found in [60].

Example 4.3. Fix a constant $h \in (0,1)$ and consider equation (1) with $f(x) = f_h(x)$ where nonlinearity $f_h(x)$ is defined by $f_h(x) \equiv 0$ for $|x| \leq h$ and $f_h(x) = -\text{sign}(x)$ for $|x| > h$ (Fig. 13).

Proposition 4.3 *Any solution of equation (1) satisfies* $\lim_{t \to \infty} x_\varphi^\nu(t) = 0$ *provided $h \geq 1/2$.*

Note that $x = 0$ is an attracting fixed point of the map f_h in the interval $[-1, 1]$ with basin $|x| < h$ and $1 \to -1 \to 1$ is an attracting cycle with basin $|x| > h$. This means that equation (2) has both asymptotically constant solutions and relaxation type solutions. At the same time, if $h \geq 1/2$ all solutions of equation (1) are asymptotically constant.

Proof of the proposition.. It is clear that any initial function $\varphi(t)$ satisfying $|\varphi(t)| \leq h$ for $t \in [-1, 0]$ generates the solution $x_\varphi^\nu(t) = \varphi(0)\exp(-t/\nu)$ of equation (1) for which $\lim_{t \to \infty} x_\varphi^\nu(t) = 0$. $\qquad\square$

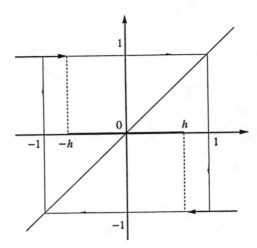

Fig. 13.

Introduce a family of sets of initial functions depending on the real parameter u, $0 \le u \le 1$, by $\varphi_u = \{\varphi \in X | \varphi(0) = \varphi(-u) = h, \varphi(t) > h$ for $t \in (-u, 0)$, $|\varphi(t)| \le h$ for $t \in [-1, -u]\}$.

Claim 1. With u fixed there exists a unique solution $x^u(t)$ of equation (1) generated by φ_u. The solution does not depend on the particular choice of $\varphi \in \varphi_u$.

Claim 1 is obvious.

Claim 2. Given $u \in [0, 1]$ there either (a) exists a $t_1 \in (0, 1)$ with $x^u(t_1) = -h$, or (b) $x^u(t) = c \exp\{-(t-1)/\nu\}$, $t \ge 1$.

Integrating (1) on $[0, 1]$ we have: $x^u(t) = h \exp(-t/\nu)$ for $t \in [0, 1-u]$, $x^u(t) = -1 + (x_1 + 1) \exp\{-(t-1+u)/\nu\}$ for $t \in [1-u, 1]$ with $x_1 = h \exp\{(u-1)/\nu\}$. Since $x^u(t)$ is monotone on $[0, 1]$ the claim follows.

Claim 3. In the case (a) of claim 2 there exists $t_2 > 1$ with $x^u(t_2) = -h$, $x^u(t) < -h$ for all $t \in (t_1, t_2)$.

Since $x^u(t) \in [-h, h]$ for $t \in [0, t_1]$ and $x^u(t) < -h$ for $t \in (t_1, 1]$, $x^u(t)$ is monotonically increasing for $t \ge 1$ with $x^u(t) \ge x^u(1) \exp\{-(t-1)/\nu\}$. This implies the existence of t_2 (Fig. 14).

It is natural to introduce a map $\mathcal{F}$ on the family φ_u in the following way. To given $u \in [0, 1]$ and φ_u there corresponds $v \in [0, 1]$ and φ_v such that $v = t_2 - t_1$. If the second zero t_2 of $x^u(t) + h$ does not exist we put $v = 0$ (the latter case means that the solution $x^u(t)$ has the form $x^u(t) = x^u(1) \exp\{-(t-1)/\nu\}, t \ge 1$ and goes to zero as $t \to \infty$. So do the solutions generated by φ_0).

The map $\mathcal{F}$ induces an one-dimensional map $F : u \to v$. We shall calculate the explicit form of F.

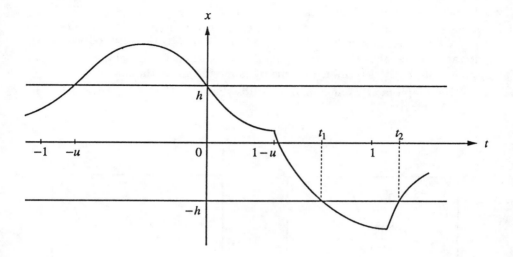

Fig. 14.

Denote $\Delta_1 = t_1 - (1 - u)$. Then $-h = -1 + (1 + x_1)\exp(-\Delta_1/\nu)$. This implies $\Delta_1 = \nu \ln[(1 + h\exp\{(u-1)/\nu\})/(1-h)]$. Denoting $\Delta_2 = t_2 - 1$ we have $x_2 \exp(-\Delta_2/\nu) = -h$ in the case $t_2 \le t_1 + 1$, with $x_2 = -1 + (x_1 + 1)\exp(-u/\nu)$ implying $\Delta_2 = \nu \ln[\{1 - h\exp(-1/\nu) - \exp(-u/\nu)\}/h]$. In the case $t_2 > t_1 + 1$ we set $v = F(u) = 1$. Let $F_1(u) = u + \nu \ln[1 - \beta - \exp(-u/\nu)]/[\alpha(1 + \beta\exp(u/\nu))]$ for all u where $F(u)$ exists. Here $\alpha = h/(1-h)$, $\beta = h\exp(-1/\nu)$. Then we have for $u \in [0, 1]$:

$$F : u \to \begin{cases} 0 & , \text{ if } \quad F_1(u) < 0 \\ u + \nu \ln \frac{1 - \beta - \exp(-u/\nu)}{\alpha(1 + \beta\exp(u/\nu))} & , \text{ if } \quad F_1(u) \in [0, 1] \\ 1 & , \text{ if } \quad F_1(u) > 1 \, . \end{cases}$$

Introducing a new variable by $z = h(z) \overset{\text{def}}{=} \exp(-u/\nu)$ and denoting $G_1(z) = \alpha(z + \beta)/[1 - (z + \beta)]$ we get the equivalent map

$$G : z \to \begin{cases} 1 & , \text{ if } \quad G_1(z) > 1 \\ \alpha \frac{z + \beta}{1 - (z + \beta)} & , \text{ if } \quad G_1(z) \in [\exp(-1/\nu), 1] \, , \\ \exp(-1/\nu) & , \text{ if } \quad G_1(z) < \exp(-1/\nu) \, , \end{cases}$$

where F and G are conjugate by $G \circ h = h \circ F$. The map G from the interval $[\exp(-1/\nu), 1]$ into itself and the dynamics of solutions of equation (1) for initial functions from φ_u, $0 \le u \le 1$, are related in the following way. Fix $u \in [0, 1]$, φ_u, and consider the corresponding solution $x^u(t)$ of equation (1). $x^u(t)$ either oscillates around $x = 0$ or tends to zero as $t \to +\infty$. Enumerate successive zeros of the function $z(t) = x^u(t) - h$ by $0 < t_1 < t_2 < t_3 < t_4 < \cdots$

(which are finite or infinite in number) and let $u_n = t_{2n} - t_{2n-1}$. Then u_n and u_{n-1} are related by $u_n = F^2(u_{n-1})$. Therefore $u_n = F^{2n}(u)$. Since $F = h^{-1} \circ G \circ h$ we have $u_n = h^{-1} \circ G^{2n} \circ h(u)$. Here f^{2n} and G^{2n} are the $2n$-th iterates of the maps. Thus, the dynamics of solutions for initial functions from φ_u is completely determined by the dynamics given by the map G.

The graph of $G(z)$ and small $\nu > 0$ is shown in Fig. 15a for $\alpha < 1$ and in Fig. 15b for $\alpha > 1$.

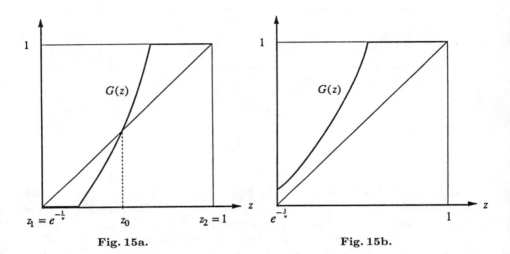

Fig. 15a.   **Fig. 15b.**

The case $\alpha < 1$ corresponds to $h < 1/2$. There exists a positive ν_0 such that for all $0 < \nu \leq \nu_0$ the map G has three fixed points $z_1 = \exp(-1/\nu)$, $z_2 = 1$, z_0 where z_0 is the root of the equation $G(z) = z$ which belongs to the interval (z_1, z_2). The fixed points z_1 and z_2 are attracting with domains of attraction $[z_1, z_0)$ and $(z_0, z_2]$ respectively, while the fixed point z_0 is repelling. Therefore, in this case equation (1) has two periodic solutions corresponding to $u = 1$ and $u = \nu \ln(1/z_0)$ (the value $u = 0$ corresponds to the solution $x(t) = h \exp(-t/\nu)$ which is attracted by the trivial periodic solution $x(t) \equiv 0$). The first one attracts all solutions from φ_u if $u > \nu \ln(1/z_0)$. If $u < \nu \ln(1/z_0)$ the corresponding solution $x^u(t)$ tends to zero exponentially as $t \to +\infty$.

The case $\alpha \geq 1$ corresponds to $h \geq 1/2$. For any $\nu > 0$, the map G has the only attracting fixed point $z = 1$ which corresponds to $u = 0$. Clearly, for a given $u \in (0, 1]$ we have $F(u) < u$ and there exists an integer $n_0 = n_0(u)$ with $F^n(u) = 0$ for all $n \geq n_0$ (Fig. 15b). Thus for any $\varphi \in \varphi_u$ there exists $t_0 = t_0(u)$ such that the solution $x_\varphi^\nu(t)$ is of the form $x_\varphi^\nu(t) = x_\varphi^\nu(t_0) \exp\{-(t - t_0)/\nu\}$ for $t \geq t_0$ and hence tends to zero.

To show that $\lim_{t \to \infty} x_\varphi^\nu(t) = 0$ for any $\varphi \in X$ in the case $h \geq 1/2$ we make use of the following observation. Take an arbitrary $\varphi \in X$ and consider the corresponding solution $x_\varphi^\nu(t)$. If $|x_\varphi^\nu(t)| \leq h$ then $x_\varphi^\nu(t) \to 0$ as $t \to \infty$. Therefore, we have to consider initial conditions for which the corresponding solutions oscillate with respect to both $x = h$ and $x = -h$. In this latter case there always exists a sequence (possibly finite) $0 < s_1 < s_2 < s_3 < \cdots$ such that $x_\varphi^\nu(s_{4k-3}) = x_\varphi^\nu(s_{4k}) = h$, $x_\varphi^\nu(s_{4k-2}) = x_\varphi^\nu(s_{4k-1}) = -h$, $x_\varphi^\nu(t) \in [-h, h]$ for all $s \in [s_{2k-1}, s_{2k}]$, and $x_\varphi^\nu(t) \leq h$ for all $t \in [s_{4k-3}, s_{4k}]$, $x_\varphi^\nu(t) \geq -h$ for all $t \in [s_{4k-2}, s_{4k-1}]$, $k \in \mathbb{N}$. Consider $\psi(s) = x_\varphi^\nu(t_1 + s)$, $s \in [-1, 0]$ as an element of X. Let $u = \sup\{v \in [0, 1] : |\psi(s)| \leq h$ for all $s \in [-1, -v]\}$. The value $-u$ is the largest point on the interval $[-1, 0]$ such that $|\psi(s)| \leq h$ for all $s \in [-1, -u]$. Compare now the solution $x_\psi^\nu(t)$, $t \geq 0$, and the solution $x^u(t)$ constructed by φ_u with given u. Define $w_k = s_{2k+1} - s_{2k}$ if s_{2k+1} exists and $w_k = 0$ otherwise, $k \in \mathbb{N}$ (in the latter case the sequence (s_k) is finite). Direct calculation shows that $s_3 - s_2 = w_1 \leq t_2 - t_1 = F(u)$, where t_1, t_2 are the first and second zeros of $x^u(t)$ constructed above. Induction arguments show that $w_k = s_{2k+1} - s_{2k} \leq F^k(u)$, $k \in \mathbb{N}$. Since $F^k(u) = 0 \,\forall k \geq k_0$ for some $k_0 \in \mathbb{N}$ we have $w_k = 0 \,\forall k \geq n_0$ for some positive integer $n_0 \leq k_0$. This implies that the sequence (s_k) is finite and therefore $x_\varphi^\nu(t) = c \exp\{-(t - t_0)/\nu\}$ for some $c, t_0 > 0$.

Example 4.4. Consider equation (1) with $f(x)$ given by $f(x) = 1$ for $x > h$, $0 < h < 1$, $f(x) = a > 1$ for $0 < x \leq h$, $f(0) = 0$, $f(x) = -f(-x)$ for $x < 0$ (Fig. 16).

Proposition 4.4. *For any positive integer n there exists an open subset of the parameter space $\{(a, h), a > 1, 0 < h < 1\}$ such that for any particular choice of a and h from this subset and any sufficiently small $0 < \nu < \nu_0 = \nu_0(h, a)$ the corresponding equation (1) has an asymptotically stable periodic solution with period $2n + O(\nu)$, $\nu \to +0$.*

Proposition 4.5. *There exists an open subset of the parameter space such that for any particular choice of (a, h) from this subset and any sufficiently small $\nu(0 < \nu \leq \nu_0(h, a))$ the corresponding equation (1) has a set of solutions such that subsequent maxima (or distances between zeros) behave quasi-randomly (the associated probability density is absolutely continuous with respect to Lebesgue measure).*

Given $f(x)$ for any $0 < h < 1$ and $a > 1$ the interval map f has a globally attracting cycle of period two formed by the points -1 and 1. The corresponding difference equation (2) has relaxation type solutions which are two-periodic for $t > 0$. Nevertheless, the asymptotic behavior of the solution for equation (1) is much more complicated as the propositions indicate.

We briefly sketch an approach to the proofs of the two propositions, as given in [1, 3] (see also [40]). Consider the set Φ of initial functions defined by

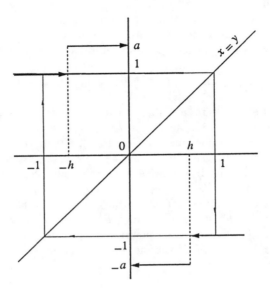

Fig. 16.

$\Phi = \{\varphi \in X | \varphi(-1) = h, \varphi(t)$ is unimodal on $[-1,0]$, that is, there exists a $t' \in (-1,0)$ such that $\varphi(t)$ is increasing on $(-1,t')$ and decrasing on $(t',0)\}$.

Straightforward calculations show that for ν sufficiently small and any $\varphi \in \Phi$, the corresponding solution $x_{\varphi}^{\nu}(t)$ has the property: there exists $t_1 > 0$ such that $x_{\varphi}^{\nu}(t_1 + t), t \in [-1,0]$ belongs to φ. This allows us to define a map $\mathcal{F}$ on Φ by $\mathcal{F}(\varphi) = \tilde{\varphi}, \tilde{\varphi}(t) = x_{\varphi}^{\nu}(t_1 + t), t \in [-1,0]$. Next consider the set $\Psi = \mathcal{F}(\Phi)$. Functions in Ψ depend on the real parameter $z = \varphi(0)$. Again, to any $\psi \in \Psi$ there corresponds an unique $\tilde{\psi} \in \Psi$ given by $\tilde{\varphi} = \mathcal{F}(\psi)$. Now $\mathcal{F}$ on Ψ induces an one-dimensional map of the parameter set $G :\mapsto z \to \tilde{z}$, which turns out to be piecewise Moebius and continuous. Simple, but technically rather complicated, calculations allow us to find the explicit form of G. All details can be found in the mentioned paper [3]. In particular, there exists a parameter subset such that G has a slope greater than 1 at each point of an invariant interval (Fig. 17). According to the theory of interval maps, this implies the existence of an invariant measure μ which is absolutely continuous with respect to Lebesque measure λ (that is $\mu(A) = \mu(G^{-1}(A))$ for every measurable $A \subset I$).

Similarly, for any n there exists an (a, h)-parameter subset for which equation (1) has an asymptotically stable periodic solution of period $2n + O(\nu)$ (ν is small) [1]. The results are based on the analysis of parametrized families of the obtained piecewise Moebius maps G [34].

We note that the asymptotic behaviors described by Propositions 4.4 and 4.5 occur in a δ-neigbourhood (in the Hausdorff metric) of the generalized peri-

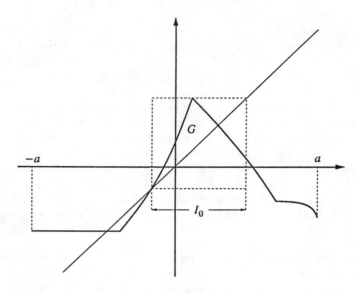

Fig. 17.

odic solution $p_0(t)$ of equation (2) defined by $p_0(t) = 1$ for $t \in (0,1)$, $p_0(t) = -1$ for $t \in (1,2)$, $p_0(0) = p_0(1) = [-a,a]$, $p_0(t)$ continued periodically outside $[0,2)$.

The following should be also noted. The induced interval map for the shift operator along solutions in the cases considered in Example 4.4 (and in many others examples in recent publications; see, e.g. [18–23, 40, 48, 61]) has Cantor sets or (as in the case of Proposition 4.4) closed intervals as invariant sets. The map on these sets is transitive (there exists a dense trajectory). Moreover it is mixing (a map G is said to be mixing on an invariant set F, if for any open (with respect to F) subset U there exist positive integers m and k such that $G^j(\cup_{i=1}^{m-1} G^i(U)) = F$ for $j \geq k$). The above sets contain trajectories (Liapunov unstable ones) with diverse asymptotic behavior: periodic trajectories with arbitrarily large periods; recurrent trajectories (for which the ω-limit sets are minimal sets different form cycles; there exists a continuum of such sets and they are pairwise disjoint Cantor-like sets); and simply Poisson stable trajectories (they are almost all trajectories), etc. Each such trajectory, as we know, gives rise to an unstable solution of equation (1) with a corresponding asymptotic behvior.

Since a set with the mixing property is invariant, every point of it has at least one preimage which belongs to the set. Therefore, any trajectory on the set may be prolonged for negative n (usually in several ways) to obtain a two-sided trajectory. Such two-sided trajectories may have the same asymptotic behaviors for both $n \to \infty$ and $n \to -\infty$, or different ones. In particular, in this way we obtain homoclinic trajectories, and each of them is attracted by a periodic trajectory or by a fixed point as $n \to \infty$ and $n \to -\infty$. To every two-sided trajectory there corresponds a solution of equation (1) defined for all $t \in \mathbb{R}$ (in fact a family of solutions differing by a shift in time). In particular, there exist solutions (homoclinic ones) modeling solitons (the corresponding trajectory for the interval map is homoclinic to a fixed point).

Every homoclinic trajectory on an invariant set with the mixing property is known to attract a continuum of trajectories as $n \to \infty$ [54, 55]. Hence, there exists a continuum of different solutions of equation (1), defined for $t \geq 0$ only (and differing not only by a shift along t). Every such solution will reproduce the original homoclinic solution, as $t \to \infty$, with increasing accuracy on time intervals of increasing length. In particular each such solution of equation (1), corresponding to a one-dimensional trajectory which is homoclinic to a fixed point, simulates a sequence of single waves (solitons) scattering away as $t \to +\infty$.

In the present paper we do not deal with bifurcation problems for equation (1) when the nonlinearity $f(x)$ is parameter dependent. Bifurcations for periodic solutions and possible paths of transition to chaos are studies extensively now in different classes of dynamical systems. The problem seems to be difficult for equation (1) and is not studied widely (some numerical results may be found in [6]).

In this situation the study of bifurcation problems for relatively simple examples seems to be worthwhile. (In particular, it is of interest what happens with the dynamics of solutions for example 4.4 as the parameters a, h vary, and how chaos may appear there). We shall not get into more detail but would like to conclude with a remark. If the shift operator $\mathcal{F}^t$ on a subset of solutions is reducible to an one-dimensional map G which is continuous and piecewise Moebius then its Schwartz derivative $S(G) = G'''/G' - 3/2(G''/G')^2$ equals zero (for all points where it exists). This implies [34] that period doubling bifurcations for the map G may occur only finitely many times. The scenary of the bifurcation itself is the following (see Fig. 18). An attracting cycle of period n (a fixed point on Fig. 18a) while losing stability is replaced by a parameterized family of cycles of period n (Fig. 18 (b)). After this an attracting cycle of period $2n$ (Fig. 18 (b)), or repelling cycle of period $2n$ (Fig. 18 (c) may appear. In the second case a local chaos in the vicinity of the $2n$ cycle appears. The cycle of period n itself becomes unstable in every case.

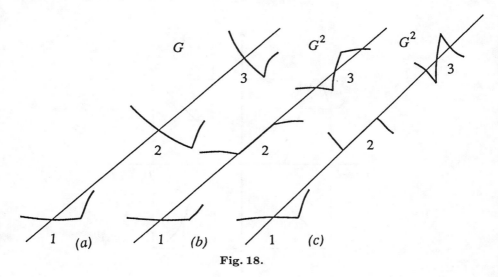

G G^2 G^2

Fig. 18.

5. Attractors of Interval Maps and Asymptotic Behavior of Solutions

In this chapter we try to show the role which is played by the attractors of interval maps with large domains of immediate attraction for the asymptotic behavior of the solutions of equation (1).

Consider first a simple but important generalization of the previous Example 4.3.

Example 5.1. Fix $h \in (0,1)$ and consider equation (1) with $f(x) = f_0(x)$, where $f_0(x)$ is smooth, $f_0(x) = 0$ for $|x| \leq h$, $|f_0(x)| < 1$ for $|x| > h$ and $x = 0$ is the only fixed point of the map f_0 (a particular $f_0(x)$ is shown in Fig. 19).

Proposition 5.1. *In the case $h \geq 1/2$ every solution of equation (1) satisfies* $\lim_{t \to \infty} x_\varphi^\nu(t) = 0 \, (\forall \nu > 0)$.

Proof. As in Example 4.2 we introduce a family of sets of initial functions by $\varphi_u = \{\varphi \in X | \varphi(0) = \varphi(-u) = h, \, \varphi(t) > h, \, t \in (-u, 0), \, |\varphi(t)| \leq h, \, t \in [-1, -u]\}$ depending on a real parameter $u \in [0, 1]$. Given u and a particular $\varphi \in \varphi_u$ there exists an unique solution $x^u(t)$ of equation (1) defined for all $t \geq 0$.

Claim. For any u there either, (a) exist $t_1 \in (0, 1)$ and $t_2 > 1$ with $x^u(t_1) = x^u(t_2) = -h$, $x^u(t) \in [-h, h]$ for $t \in [0, t_1]$ and $x^u(t) < -h$ for $t \in (t_1, t_2)$, or (b) $x^u(t) = c \exp\{-(t-1)/\nu\}$, $t \geq 1$.

The proof is quite similar as in the case of claims 2 and 3 of Example 4.2.

Denoting $w = t_2 - t_1$ we have an induced interval map F_1 on the parameter set $[0, 1]$ with $F_1(u) = w$. In the case that t_1 does not exist or $t_2 = t_1$ we set $w =$

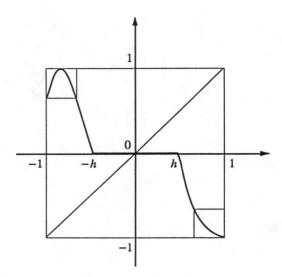

Fig. 19.

$F_1(u) = 0$. Compare now w and v obtained in Example 4.3. Since $|f_0(x)| \leq 1$ for $|x| > h$ and $f_0(x) \equiv f_h(x)$ for $|x| \leq h$ we have $w \leq v = F(u)$, where $F(u)$ is the same as in Example 4.3 (Fig. 20). Because of the monotonicity of F we conclude $F_1^n(u) \leq F^n(u)$. The exact form of $F(u)$ (see Fig. 15b) shows us that for any u there exists a positive integer $n_0 = n_0(h, u)$ with $F_1^n(u) = 0$ for all $n \geq n_0$. This implies the existence of t_0 such that $|x^u(t)| \leq h$ for all $t \geq t_0$. The proposition is proved.   □

Now we observe that generally $f_0(x)$ may be defined on $\{x | h < |x| < 1\}$, $h > \frac{1}{2}$ in an arbitrary way. In particular, f_0 can have an invariant subinterval with an attracting cycle of period two, a repelling cycle of period two and no other cycles on it (and the already existing fixed point $x = 0$). This guarantees that relaxation type solutions are typical for equation (1). In addition we can require f_0 to have periodic points with periods $(2k + 1)2^m$, k, m positive integers. The latter will ensure the existence of turbulent type solutions for equation (1) (see Chap. 1 for the details). An example of f_0 is shown in Fig. 19.

The proposition says, that for $h \geq 1/2$ all solutions of equation (1) are asymptotically constant, notwithstanding the particular form of $f_0(x)$ outside $[-h, h]$. For small positive ν the continuous dependence results of Chap. 3 imply that the solutions of equation (1) follow the solutions of equation (2) within finite time interval (which is the larger the smaller ν is). Then, after some transient time interval, they begin to decrease to zero exponentially. The duration of the transient state my be estimated generically as $O(1/\nu)$).

Thus the example suggests that the main factor to the determination of the asymptotic behaviour of solutions of equation (1) may be an attractor having

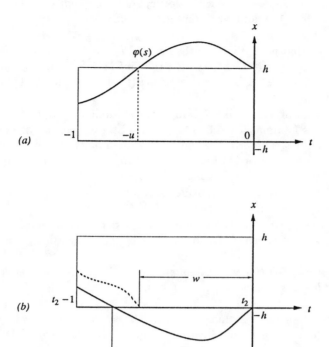

Fig. 20.

a large domain of immediate attraction compared with the remaining part of the invariant interval. The following theorem shows that this is the typical situation.

Theorem 5.1. *Suppose the map f of the compact interval I into itself has a compact invariant subinterval I_0 with immediate attraction domain $J_0 : I_0 \subset J_0 \subset I$, $f^k(x) \to I_0$ as $k \to \infty$ for any $x \in J_0$. If the set $I \backslash J_0$ does not contain fixed points and the value $meas(I \backslash J_0)/meas(J_0 \backslash I_0)$ is small enough then for every solution $x(t)$ of equation (1) there exists a time $t_0 = t_0(x, \nu)$ such that $x(t) \in J_0$ for all $t \geq t_0$. Moreover, $\inf I_0 \leq \lim_{t \to \infty} \inf x(t) \leq \lim_{t \to \infty} \sup x(t) \leq \sup I_0$.*

Remark. If $x(t) \in J_0$ for a unit time interval then one immediately obtains the required conclusion $\lim_{t \to \infty} \inf x(t) \geq \inf I_0$ and $\lim_{t \to \infty} \sup x(t) \leq \sup I_0$. This follows from Theorem 2.3.

Therefore, we only have to show that every solution of equation (1) satisfies $x(t) \in J_0$ for $t \in [s-1, s]$ and some (sufficiently large) s.

Remark. Suppose that no endpoint of the interval I_0 is a fixed point. Then there exists a positive number $\delta = \delta(f, \nu)$ such that $\inf I_0 + \delta \leq \lim_{t \to \infty} \inf x(t) \leq \lim_{t \to \infty} \sup x(t) \leq \sup I_0 - \delta$ for every solution $x(t)$ of equation (1). This follows from Theorem 2.5.

We give a proof of Theorem 5.2 using several auxilary propositions. They are listed below as Lemmas 5.1–5.3. The proofs of these Lemmas are technical and only outlined her. The proof of Lemma 5.2 is similar to the considerations of example 5.1, and the proof of Lemma 5.3 is similar to the arguments given in example 4.3 (case $h > 1/2$). For more details see [27, 28].

Let $x_0 \in I$ be arbitrary and consider a solution $x(t)$ of equation (1). We say that $x(t)$ oscillates with respect to x_0 if $x(t) - x_0$ has zeros for $t \geq 0$.

Under the assumptions of Theorem 5.1 there exist three intervals $I \supset J_0 \supset I_0$ which are invariant under f. Denote $I = [a, b]$, $\bar{J}_0 = [a_0, b_0]$, $I_0 = [a_1, b_1]$.

Lemma 5.1. *Every solution $x(t)$ of equation (1) either oscillates with respect to both a_0 and b_0 or satisfies $x(t) \in J_0$, $t \geq 0$.*

The statement of the Lemma is evident. If $x(t)$ does not oscillate then $x(t) \in \bar{J}_0$, $t \in [0, 1]$. Due to the invariance property (Theorem 2.1) we have $x(t) \in \bar{J}_0$ for all $t \geq 0$.

Lemma 5.1 allows us to consider only those solutions which oscillate with respect to both a_0 and b_0.

Now introduce a set Φ_u of initial functions depending on the real parameter $u \in [0, 1]$ by $\Phi_u = \{\varphi \in X_I | \varphi(0) = \varphi(-u) = a_0, \varphi(s) \in J_0, s \in [-1, -u)\}$. Let $x^u(t)$, $t \geq 0$ be a solution of equation (1) constructed by a particular $\varphi \in \Phi_u$ for a given u. Since we consider solutions which oscillate around a_0 and b_0, there always exist $t_1 < 1$ and $t_2 > 1$ such that $x^u(t_1) = x^u(t_2) = b_0$, $x^u(t) < b_0$ for $t \in [0, t_1)$ (a particular case is shown in Fig. 21). Consider now $x^u(t_2 + s) = \psi(s)$, $s \in [-1, 0]$ as an element of X_I. Then, similarly, we may assume that there exist $t_3 > t_2$ and $t_4 > t_2 + 1$ such that $x^u(t_3) = x^u(t_4) = a_0$, $x^u(t) > a_0$ for $t \in [t_2, t_3,)]$ (Fig. 21). Consider again $x^u(t_4 + u) = \tilde{\varphi}(s)$ as an element of X_I. It is clear that $\tilde{\varphi}(s)$ belongs to some $\Phi_{u'}$ with u' given by $u' = t_4 - t_3$. Define now a one-dimensional map $\mathcal{F}$ on the parameter set $\{u : 0 \leq u \leq 1\}$ by $\mathcal{F} : u \to u'$. In the case that zeros t_3, t_4 do not exist for some u and $\varphi \in \Phi_u$ we set $\mathcal{F}(u) = 0$. Due to the continuous dependence of solutions of equation (1) on initial conditions it is clear that for every fixed ν there exists $u_0 = u_0(f, \nu) \in (0, 1)$ such that $\mathcal{F}(u) = 0$ for every $0 \leq u \leq u_0$ and arbitrary $\varphi \in \Phi_u$.

Note that in general for every fixed u the value u' depends on the particular choice of $\varphi \in \Phi_u$. The following lemma shows that there exists an one-dimensional map to which the mapping $\mathcal{F}$ is subjected.

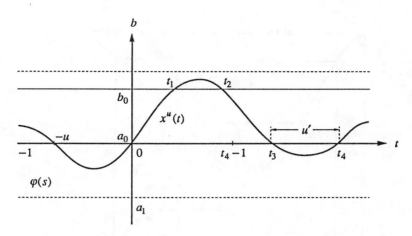

Fig. 21.

Lemma 5.2. *For $f(x)$ given and $\mathrm{meas}(I\setminus J_0)/\mathrm{meas}(J_0\setminus I_0)$ small, there exists an one-dimensional map F of the interval $[0,1]$ into itself which majorizes the map $\mathcal{F}$ in the following sense: $F(u) > u'$ for every particular $\varphi \in \Phi_u$ and arbitrary $u \in [0,1]$.*

The proof of the lemma is based on the properties of solutions of equation (1) with a step function $f^*(x)$ which is constructed on the basis of a given nonlinearity $f(x)$. It is similar to the considerations of Example 5.1. We suppose that $f(x)$ is fixed an continue with the construction of the function $f^*(x)$ which we will need.

We have the three invariant intervals $I = [a,b]$, $\bar{J}_0 = [a_0, b_0]$ and $I_0 = [a_1, b_1]$ which satisfy $I \supset J_0 \supset I_0$. Now $f^*(x)$ is defined as follows

$$
f^* = \begin{cases}
b, \ x \in [a, a_0] \\
a, \ x \in [b_0, b] \\
b_1, \ x \in [a_1, c) \\
a_1, \ x \in (c, b_1] \qquad \text{for some} \quad c \in (a_1, b_1) \ . \\
\text{an arbitrary step functions satisfying:} \\
x < f^*(x) \le b_0, \ f^*(x) \not\equiv b_0, \ x \in (a_0, a_1) \\
x > f^*(x) \ge a_0, \ f^*(x) \not\equiv a_0, \ x \in (b_1, b_0)
\end{cases}
$$

For a $f(x)$ and the three intervals $I \supset J_0 \supset I_0$ given, $f^*(x)$ is chosen to satisfy $f^*(x) \ge f(x)$ for $x \in (a_0, a_1)$ and $f^*(x) \le f(x)$ for $x \in (b_1, b_0)$. Then, due to the construction one has $f^*(x) \ge f(x)$ for $x \le c$ and $f^*(x) \le f(x)$ for $x > c$. A particular $f(x)$ and its $f^*(x)$ are shown in Fig. 22.

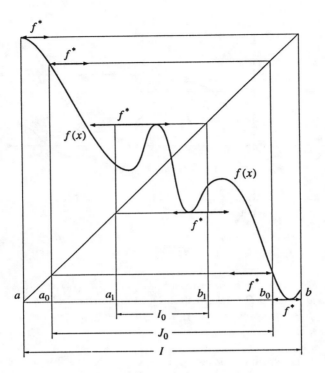

Fig. 22.

A technical calculation shows that, for every $u \in [0,1]$ and particular $\varphi \in \Phi_u$ the map $\mathcal{F}$ depending on f and f^* has the property $u'(f^*) > u'(f)$, where $u' = t_4 - t_3$ is defined above. This is proved by step by step comparison of the corresponding solutions depending on the particular f and f^* constructed above. Details are found in [27].

The map $\mathcal{F}$ associated to f^* induces an one-dimensional map F given by $u' = F(u)$. Indeed u', constructed by u and φ, does not depend on the particular choice of $\varphi \in \Phi_u$ when f is replaced by a step function f^* (cf. in Examples 4.1–4.4).

The following statement is verified by a direct calculation of the map F. They are similar to Example 4.3, case $h > 1/2$ (see Chap. 4).

Lemma 5.3. *The one-dimensional map $F : [0,1] \to [0,1]$ is conjugate by $z = \exp(-u/\nu)$ to a map $G : [\exp(-1/\nu), 1] \to [\exp(-1/\nu), 1]$. If $b - b_0$ and $a_0 - a$ are small enough then the map G has the only fixed point $z = 1$, which is globally attracting:* $\lim_{k \to \infty} G^k(z) = 1 \, \forall z \in [\exp(-1/\nu), 1]$. *The map G has the form shown in Fig. 15b.*

Remark. Since $G(z) \equiv 1$ for $z \in [z_0, 1]$ and $G(z) > z$ for all $z \in [\exp(-1/\nu), 1]$ it follows that for every fixed $z \in [\exp(-1/\nu), 1]$ there exists a positive integer n_0 such that $G^k(z) = 1 \, \forall k \geq n_0$.

With Lemmas 5.1–5.3 at hand, the proof of Theorem 5.1 is straightforward. Take an arbitrary $\varphi \in X$. If the function $x_\varphi^\nu(t) - a_0$ (or $x_\varphi^\nu(t) - b_0$) has no zeros for $t > 0$ then the theorem holds (Lemma 5.1). If it has a zero $t_0 > 0$ we consider $x_\varphi^\nu(t_0 + s)$, $s \in [1, 0]$ as an element of Φ_u for some $u \in [0, 1]$. Then the map $\mathcal{F}$ is defined, for this initial condition, as well as the induced one-dimensional map F majorizing $\mathcal{F}$ (Lemma 5.2). If meas $(I \backslash J_0)/\text{meas}(J_0 \backslash I_0)$ is small enough, then the map $G = h^{-1} \circ F \circ h$, $z = h(u) = \exp(-u/\nu)$ has the property: $\lim_{k \to \infty} G^k(z) = 1$ (Lemma 5.3). Moreover, with $z = \nu \ln(1/u)$ given there exists $k_0 \in \mathbb{N}$ such that $G^{k_0}(z) < 1$, $G^k(z) = 1$, $k > k_0$ (Remark 5.3). Therefore, the corresponding $u_k = F^k(u)$ satisfy $u_{k_0} > 0$, $u_k = 0 \, \forall k > k_0$. This implies that for every $u \in [0, 1]$ and every $\varphi \in \Phi_u$ there exists $k_1 \leq k_0$ such that $\mathcal{F}^{k_1}(u) = 0$. But for $u = 0$ one has $x_\varphi^\nu(t) \in J_0 \, \forall t > 0$. This completes the proof.

One naturally expects to extend (in a sense) Theorem 5.1. to cycles of intervals. What conditions should a cycle of intervals $\{I_k\}_{k=1}^n$ be subjected to, in order to guarantee existence of solutions for equation (1) which range cyclically in intervals $I_1, I_2, \cdots, I_n$? An answer is given by Theorem 5.2 below.

We suppose that a set of intervals $I_k = [a_k, b_k]$, $k = 1, 2, \cdots, n$, forms a cycle of period n for the map $f : I_1 \to I_2 \to \cdots \to I_n \to I_1$. For every k, $1 \leq k \leq n$, denote by J_k the interval which connects I_k and $I_{k+1(\text{mod } n)}$ and has joint endpoints with them: $J_k = [b_k, a_{k+1}]$ for $b_k \leq a_{k+1}$, and $J_k = [b_{k+1}, a_k]$ for $b_{k+1} \leq a_k$ (from now on we identify the indices $n+1$ and 1). J_k may consist of one point. For any k, $1 \leq k \leq n$, intervals I_k, I_{k+1}, J_k given we define the following numbers:

$$l_1(I_k) = [\sup f(J_k) - \sup I_{k+1}]/[\sup f(J_k) - \sup f(I_k)] ,$$
$$\text{if } \sup f(J_k) > \sup f(I_k) , \text{ and}$$
$$l_1(I_k) = 0 , \text{ if } \sup f(J_k) \leq \sup f(I_k) ,$$
$$l_2(I_k) = [\inf I_{k+1} - \inf f(J_k)]/[\inf f(I_k) - \inf f(J_k)] , \text{ if}$$
$$\inf f(I_k) > \inf f(J_k) , l_2(I_k) = 0 \text{ if } \inf f(I_k) \leq \inf f(J_k) ,$$
$$l(I_k) = \max\{l_1(I_k) , l_2(I_k)\} ,$$
$$m(I_k) = [\inf f(I_k) - \inf I_{k+1}]/[\inf f(I_k) - \sup I_k] ,$$
$$\text{if } \sup I_k < \inf f(I_k) ,$$
$$m(I_k) = [\sup I_{k+1} - \sup f(I_k)]/[\inf I_k - \sup f(I_k)] ,$$
$$\text{if } \sup f(I_k) < \inf I_k .$$

Introduce subsets X_k, $k = 1, 2, \cdots, n$, of X by setting $X_k = C([-1, 0], I_k)$.

Theorem 5.2. *Suppose the map f has an interval cycle $I_1 \to I_2 \to \cdots \to I_n \to I_1$, satisfying $m(I_k) > l(I_k)$ for $k = 1, 2, \cdots, n$. Then there exists a positive*

ν_0 such that for any $0 < \nu \leq \nu_0$ and arbitrary $\varphi \in X_1$, the corresponding solution $x_\varphi^\nu(t)$ has the following property: there exists a sequence $0 < t_1 < t_2 < t_3 < \cdots \to \infty$ with $t_{k+1} - t_k > 1$ for all $k \in \mathbb{N}$ and $x_\varphi^\nu(t_k + t) \in I_{k(\mathrm{mod}\,n)}$ for $t \in [0, 1]$.

Remark. Let $\mathcal{F}^t, t \geq 0$ be the semiflow on $X_I = C([-1, 0], I)$ given by $\mathcal{F}^t \varphi(s) = x_\varphi^\nu(t + s)$, $s \in [0, 1]$. The teorem says that if ν is sufficiently small for every $\varphi \in X_1$ there exists a sequence $(t_k) \to \infty$ such that $(\mathcal{F}^{t_k} \in X_{I_{k(\mathrm{mod}\,n)}}$. Every initial function $\varphi \in X_1$ generates a solution $x_\varphi^\nu(t)$ which ranges cyclically in the intervals $I_1, I_2, \cdots, I_n$ within time segments of length at least 1.

Remark. Since $l(I_k) \geq 0$ the conditions of Theorem 5.2 imply that $m(I_k) > 0$ for all $1 \leq k \leq n$. The inequality $m(I_k) > 0$ implies in turn (see the definition) of $m(I_k)$) that the set $\{f(I_k)\}$ is a proper subset of $\{I_{k+1}\}$. This means that each of the intervals I_k is mapped strictly inside the interval I_{k+1}, $k = 1, 2, \cdots, n$. Then it is not difficult to see that under the conditions of Theorem 5.2 there exists a cycle of intervals $\{I_1', I_2', \cdots, I_n'\}$ satisfying $I_k' \subset I_k$ $I_k' \neq I_k$, $f(I_k') = I_{k+1}'$. Indeed, it is enough to set $I_k' = \cap_{i \geq 0} f^{ni}(I_k)$. The interval cycle $\{I_1', I_2', \cdots, I_n'\}$ (which may coincide with the trajectory of a periodic point) is an attractor and the set $I_1 \cup I_2 \cup \cdots \cup I_n$ is a proper subset of its domain of immediate attraction. The conditions $m(I_k) > l(I_k)$, $k = 1, 2, \cdots, n$, can be considered (in a sense) as reflecting the fact that the set $I_1 \cup I_2 \cup \cdots \cup I_n$ is much larger than the remaining part $I \backslash (\cup_{k=1}^n I_k)$ of the invariant interval I.

A particular map of an interval into itself having a cycle of intervals of period two is depicted in Fig. 23. A cycle of intervals is formed by $I_1 = [a_1, b_1]$ and $I_2 = [a_2, b_2]$ with $f(I_1) = [a_2', b_2]$, $f(I_2) = [a_1, b_1']$ where $a_2' > a_2$, $b_1' < b_1$. The set J_1 coincides with the set J_2 and is the interval $[b_1, a_2]$. Define $\xi = \inf \{f(x), x \in J_1\}$, $\eta = \sup \{f(x), x \in J_1\}$. Directly from the definitions we have:

$$l_1(I_1) = 0, \; l_2(I_2) = (a_2) - \xi)/(a_2' - \xi) \Rightarrow l(I_1) = (a_2 - \xi)/(a_2' - \xi);$$
$$m(I_1) = (a_2' - a_2)/(a_2' - b_1) \,;$$
$$l_1(I_2) = (\eta - b_1)/(\eta - b_1'), \; l_2(I_2) = 0 \Rightarrow l(I_2) = (\eta - b_1)/(\eta - b_1');$$
$$m(I_2) = (b_1 - b_1')/(a_2 - b_1') \,.$$

The conditions of Theorem 5.2 in the case considered take the form $(a_2' - a_2)/(a_2' - b_1) > (a_2 - \xi)/(a_2' - \xi)$ and $(b_1 - b_1')/(a_2 - b_1') > (\eta - b_1)/(\eta - b_1')$. They hold always if the inequalities $(a_2' - a_2)/(a_2' - b_1) > (a_2 - a_1)/(a_2' - a_1)$ and $(b_1 - b_1')/(a_2 - b_1') > (b_2 - b_1)/(b_2 - b_1')$ are satisfied. This follows from the fact $a_1 \leq \xi \leq \eta \leq b_2$. In particular, the inequalities are justified when a_2' and b_1' are fixed and $a_2 - b_1$ is small enough.

The proof of Theorem 5.2 is based on the following lemma.

Lemma 5.4. *Suppose that the inequality $m(I_k) > l(I_k)$ holds. Then there exists a positive ν_0 such that for all $0 < \nu \leq \nu_0$ and any $\varphi \in X_k$ the corresponding*

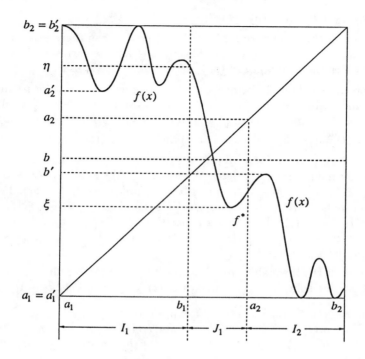

Fig. 23.

solution $x_\varphi^\nu(t)$ has the following property: there exists a time $t_* = t_*(\varphi, \nu) > 1$ with $x_\varphi^\nu(t_* + t) \in I_{k+1}$ for all $t \in [0, 1]$.

The proof is divided into several parts. To be definite we suppose $k = 1$, and set $I_1 = [a_1, b_1]$, $I_2 = [a_2, b_2]$, $a_1 < b_1 < a_2 < b_2$, $f(I_1) = [a_2', b_2'] \subset I_2$, $J_1 = [b_1, a_2]$, $\xi_1 = \inf f(J_1)$, $\eta_1 = \sup f(J_1)$; $X_1^0 = \{\varphi \in X_1 | \varphi(0) = b_1\}$.

Claim 1. For any $\varphi \in X_1$, there exists $t_1 = t_1(\varphi, \nu) > 0$ with $x_\varphi^\nu(t_1) = b_1$.

Since $f(I_1) \subset I_2$ and $b_1 < a_2'$, according to equation (1) the solution $x_\varphi^\nu(t)$ increases (for any $\nu > 0$ and $\varphi \in X_1$) in some righthand neighbourhood of $t = 0$. Clearly, $d/dt(x_\varphi^\nu(t)) > 0$ for all $t > 0$ where $x_\varphi^\nu(t) < a_2'$. Moreover $x_\varphi^\nu(t) \geq \alpha(t) \stackrel{\text{def}}{=} a_2' + [\varphi(0) - a_2']\exp(-t/\nu)$. The latter implies $t_1 \leq t_1^0 = \nu\ln[(a_2' - a_1)/(a_2' - b_1)]$.

Claim 1 allows to restrict the considerations to X_1^0 rather than X_1.

Claim 2. For any $\varphi \in X_1^0$ there exists $t_2 = t_2(\varphi, \nu)$ with $x_\varphi^\nu(t_2) = a_2$. Moreover, $x_\varphi^\nu(t)$ increases on $[0, t_2]$ and $t_2 \leq \nu\ln[(a_2' - b_1)/(a_2' - a_2)]$.

Let $\varphi \in X_1^0$. Then for $t \in [0, 1]$ we have $\varphi) \geq \alpha(t) \stackrel{\text{def}}{=} a_2' + (b_1 - a_2')\exp(-t/\nu)$. Clearly, $x_\varphi^\nu(t)$ is monotone for all those t from a righthand neighbourhood of $t = 0$ where $x_\varphi^\nu(t) < a_2'$.

Hence, $t_2 \leq t_2^0 = \nu\ln[(a_2' - b_1)/(a_2' - a_2)]$.

Claim 3. If the inequality $m(I_1) > l_2(I_1)$ holds, then there exists a positive ν_0^1 such that for all $0 < \nu \leq \nu_0^1$ and for any $\varphi \in X_1^0$ the corresponding solution $x_\varphi^\nu(t)$ satisfies the inequality $x_\varphi^\nu(t) \geq a_2$ for all $t \in [t_2, t_2 + 1]$.

According to claim 2, for any $\varphi \in X_1^0$ there exists $t_2 = t_2(\varphi, \nu)$ such that $x_\varphi^\nu(t)$ is increasing on $[0, t_2]$ and $x_\varphi^\nu(t_2) = a_2$. Moreover, $t_2 \leq t_2^0 = \upsilon\ln[(a_2' - b_1)/(a_2' - a_2)]$. We may choose ν_0^1 guaranteeing $t_2^0 < 1$ for all $0 < \nu \leq \nu_0^1$. Then $x_\varphi^\nu(t) \geq \alpha(t) \overset{\text{def}}{=} a_2' + (b_1 - a_2')\exp(-t)/\nu)$ and hence $x_\varphi^\nu(t) \geq b_1$ for all $t \in [t_2, 1]$. Put $\alpha_1 \overset{\text{def}}{=} \alpha(1) = a_2' + (b_1 - a_2')\exp(-1/\nu)$, and consider the solution $x_\varphi^\nu(t)$ within the time interval $[1, 1 + t_2]$. We have: $x_\varphi^\nu(t) \geq \xi_1 + (\alpha_1 - \xi_1)\exp\{-(t - 1)/\nu\} \geq \xi_1 + [a_2' + (b_1 - \alpha_1)\exp(-1/\nu) - \xi_1](a_2' - a_2)/(a_2' - b_1)$. From the definition we have $m(I_1) = (a_2' - a_2)/(a_2' - b_1)$ and $l_2(I_1) = (a_2 - \xi_1)/(a_2' - \xi_1)$. Since $m(I_1) > l_2(I_1)$, there exists a positive $\nu_0' < \nu_0^1$ with $\xi_1 + [a_2' + (b_1 - a_2')\exp(-1/\nu) - \xi_1](a_2' - a_2)/(a_2' - b_1) \geq a_2$ for all $0 < \nu < \nu_0'$. This implies $x_\varphi^\nu(t) \geq a_2$ for $t \in [1, 1 + t_2]$.

Claim 4. If the inequality $m(I_1) > l_1(I_1)$ holds, then for all $0 < \nu < \nu_0'$ and any $\varphi \in X_1^0$ the solution $x_\varphi^\nu(t)$ satisfies $x_\varphi^\nu(t) \leq b_2$ for $t \in [t_2, t_2 + 1]$.

Clearly $x_\varphi^\nu(t) \leq \beta(t) \overset{\text{def}}{=} b_2' + (b_1 - b_2')\exp(-t/\nu) \leq b_2'$ for all $t \in [0, 1]$. Suppose $\nu \leq \nu_0'$. Since $m(I_1) = (a_2' - a_2)/(a_2' - b_1)$ and $l_1(I_1) = (\eta_1 - b_2)/(\eta_1 - b_2')$ we have $x_\varphi^\nu(t) \leq \eta_1 + (b_2' - \eta_1) \times \exp\{-(t - 1)/\nu\} \leq \eta_1 + (b_2' - \eta_1)(a_2' - a_2)/(a_2' - b_1) = b_2$ for $t \in [1, 1 + t_2]$.

To complete the proof of the lemma we set $\nu_0 = \nu_0'$ and $t_* = t_2 + 1$. The case $b_2 < a_1$ is treated similarly.

With the proved Lemma, the proof of Theorem 5.2 is straight-forward.

The conditions involved in Theorem 5.2 are explained in the following example.

Example 5.2. Suppose δ is a small positive number. Define $f_\delta(x)$ by $f_\delta(x) = 0$ for $x < -1 - \delta$, $f_\delta(x) = 2$ for $x \in (-1 + \delta, 1 - \delta)$, $f_\delta(x) = a < -1 - \delta$ for $x > 1 + \delta$ and let $f_\delta(x)$ be an arbitrary monotone function for $x \in (1 - \delta, -1 + \delta) \cup (1 - \delta, 1 + \delta)$ such that $f_\delta(x) \in C^0(\mathbb{R})$ (Fig. 24). The map f_δ has an interval cycle of period three: $I_1 \to I_2 \to I_3 \to I_1$ with $I_1 = [a, -1 - \delta]$, $I_2 = [-1 + \delta, 1 - \delta]$, $I_3 = [1 + \delta, 2]$. Note that there exists an attracting cycle of period three $a \to 0 \to 2 \to a$ whose immediate attraction domain contains $I_1 \cup I_2 \cup I_3$ at least. For the interval cycle $\{I, I_2, I_3\}$ we have $J_1 = [-1 - \delta, -1 + \delta]$, $J_2 = [1 - \delta, 1 + \delta]$, $J_3 = [-1 - \delta, 1 + \delta]$. One easily obtains that $l_1(I_1) = 0$, $l_1(I_2) = 0$, $l_2(I_1) = 0$, $l_2(I_2) = (1 + \delta - a)/(2 - a)$, $l_1(I_3) = (3 + \delta)/(2 - a)$, $l_2(I_3) = 0$, , $m(I_1) = m(I_2) = (1 - \delta)/(1 + \delta)$, $m(I_3) = (-1 - \delta - a)/(1 + \delta - a)$. Then the conditions of Theorem 5.2 become $(1 - \delta)/(1 + \delta) > 0$, $(1 - \delta)/(1 + \delta) > (1 + \delta - a)/(2 - a)$, $(-1 - \delta - a)/(1 + \delta - a) > (3 + \delta)/(2 - a)$.

This means that for any $a < -1 - \sqrt{6}$ there exists a positive $\delta_0 = \delta_0(a)$ such that the assumptions of Theorem 5.2 hold for f_δ provided $0 < \delta \le \delta_0$. For the particular choice $a = -4$ a sufficient condition is $0 < \delta < \sqrt{52} - 7 \approx 0,21$.

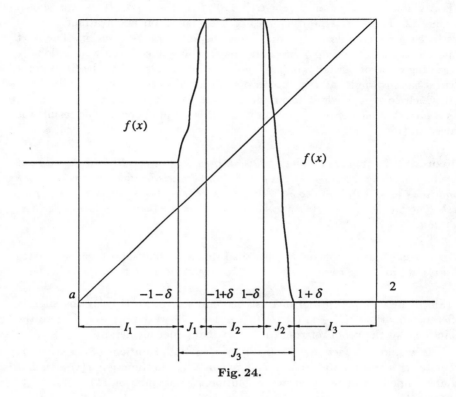

Fig. 24.

Note that if the conditions of Theorem 5.2 hold for a particular continuous function $f(x)$, then they are also satisfied for all sufficiently small C^0 perturbations of $f(x)$.

6. Existence of Periodic Solutions

The existence of nonconstant periodic solutions for funtional-differential equations has been studied in many papers. We refer, for example, to [5, 9, 15, 17, 30, 31, 33, 39, 42–45, 58, 59, 62] for autonomous differential-difference equations related to the equation considered here. Several methods were developed to prove the existence of periodic solutions including technique based on recent results of functional analysis. Some of them are applicable to the singularly perturbed differential-difference equation

$$\nu \dot{x}(t) + x(t) = f(x(t-1)) . \tag{1}$$

If the interval map f has only one attracting point and no other cycles, then all solutions of equation (1) are asymptotically constant. This means that the rest point of the semiflow $\mathcal{F}^t$ corresponding to the fixed point of the map f is a global attractor on $X_I = C([-1,0], I$ as $t \to +\infty$. This was shown in Chap. 2. Therefore, the dynamics of the map f on an invariant interval has to be more complex to produce nonconstant periodic solution. The next situation is when the map f has only one repelling fixed point and a globally attracting cycle of period two. This means, in particular, that the fixed point divides the invariant interval into two subintervals which are permuted by f and which cover the whole invariant interval. In this situation, equation (1) has a nonconstant periodic solution if $\nu > 0$ is small enough. This result was proved in [16].

Theorem 6.1. *Suppose the map f has an invariant interval I with exactly one repelling fixed point $x_* \in I$, $|f'(x_*)| > 1$, and f satisfies the negative feedback conditions $(x - x_*)[f(x) - x_*] < 0$, $x \neq x_*$. Then there exists a positive ν_0 such that for every $\nu \in (0, \nu_0]$ equation (1) has a slowly oscillating periodic solution.*

We recall that a solution $x(t)$ is called slowly oscillating if successive zeros of $x(t) - x_*$ for large t are spaced apart by distances more than the time delay 1.

Since the complete proof of this theorem is given in [16] for the slightly different equation $\dot{x}(t) + \nu x(t) + f(x(t-1)) = 0$ we briefly sketch here the main ideas of the proof refering to the original paper for details.

It is well known fact that for $0 < \nu < |f'(x_*)|$ all solutions of equation (1) oscillate with respect to $x = x_*$. This means that the function $x(t) - x_*$ has an unbounded set of zeros for every solution $x(t)$ of equation (1).

Consider a set of initial functions defined by $K = \{\varphi \in X_I | \varphi(-1) = x_*, \varphi(s) - x_* < 0$ for all $s \in (-1, 0]\}$.

For any $\varphi \in K$ there exists a sequence $\{t_k\}_{k=1}^{\infty}$ of zeros of $x_\varphi^\nu(t) - x_*$ with $t_{k+1} - t_k > 1$ for all $k \in \mathbb{N}$, $x_\varphi^\nu(t) - x_* < 0$ for $t \in (t_{2i-1}, t_{2i})$, $x_\varphi^\nu(t) - x_* > 0$ for $t \in (t_{2i}, t_{2i+1})$, $i \in \mathbb{N}$. In other words, any $\varphi \in K$ gives rise to a slowly oscillating solution. This makes it possible to define a map G on K in the following way. If $\varphi \in K$ and t_2 is the second zero of the function $x_\varphi^\nu(t) - x_*$ then $(G\varphi)(t) = x_\varphi^\nu(t_2 + 1 + t)$, $t \in [-1, 0]$. Clearly, G maps K into itself. It is convenient to consider the constant solution $x_\varphi^\nu(t) \equiv x_*$ as a fixed point of G. Other fixed points of G (if any) generate nontrivial periodic solutions of equation (1). The main result of [16] is to show the existence of a fixed point of G different from x_*.

It is possible to find a subset $K_0 = \{\varphi \in K | \varphi(t) \exp(t/\nu)$ does not decrease for $t \in [-1, 0]\}$ of K which is invariant under G.

Suppose next that $f'(x_*) < -1$. Then for all sufficiently small $\nu > 0$ the trivial solution $x(t) \equiv x_*$ is unstable. Using ideas of [33, 44, 64] this allows us to show that the fixed point $\varphi \equiv x_*$ is repelling under G on K_0. More precisely, it is possible to find a neighbourhood U_* in K_0 of the fixed point $\varphi = x_*$ such that for every $\varphi \in U_*$ there exist a positive integer $N = N(\varphi)$ such that $G^N(\varphi) \notin U_*$. Here G^N is the N-th iterate of the map G. This implies, according to [44], the existence of a fixed point of G different from the trivial one $\varphi = x_*$. As we have remarked before every nontrivial fixed point of G gives rise to a slowly oscillating periodic solution of equation (1).

Theorem 6.1 is existence theorem which does not say anything about the particular form of the periodic solutions when ν is small. In general, little can be said about it even when the structure of the map f is known in great detail. This is one of the unsolved problems (see Chap. 7).

However, when the map f has a globally attracting cycle of period two, the structure of periodic solutions and their asymptotics as $\nu \to +0$ can be studied. This is done in [42]. Here we cite only the following particular result.

Suppose the map f has a globally attracting cycle $\{a_1, a_2\}$ of period two on I and $f'(x_*) < -1$ for the repelling fixed point $x = x_*(H)$. Let $p_0(t) = a_1$, $t \in [0, 1)$, $p_0(t) = a_2$, $t \in [1, 2)$ and continuate $p_0(t)$ periodically for all $t \in \mathbb{R}$.

Theorem 6.2. *If the map f satisfies (H), then there exists a positive ν_0 such that for every $0 < \nu \leq \nu_0$ equation (1) has a periodic solution $p_\nu(t)$ with period $2 + O(\nu)$, $\nu \to +0$. The periodic solution $p_\nu(t)$ converges to $p_0(t)$ as $\nu \to +0$, uniformly on every compact interval not containing integer points $t = k$, $k \in \mathbb{Z}$.*

For a proof of this theorem see [42].

Remark. Note that neither stability nor uniqueness of the periodic solution $p_\nu(t)$ is asserted in Theorem 6.2. In fact, there may be several or even infinitely many periodic solutions (see Example 4.4 or [1, 3, 40]).

Example 6.1. Consider equation (1) with $f(x) = f_\lambda(x) = \lambda x(1 - x)$.

For every $0 \leq \lambda \leq 3$ all solutions have finite limits (see Example 2.1).

Suppose that $3 < \lambda \leq \lambda^*$. Here $\lambda^* \approx 3,57$ is the value of the parameter λ for which the map f_λ has cycles of every period 2^n, $n = 0, 1, 2, \cdots$ but no other cycles (Feigenbaum point). It is well-known (see, e.g. [54]) that for every $\lambda \in (3, \lambda^*)$ the fixed point $x_* = 1 - 1/\lambda$ is repelling and $(x - x_*)[f_\lambda(x) - x_*] < 0$ for all x belonging to the invariant interval $[f_\lambda^2(1/2), f_\lambda(1/2)] \subset [0, 1]$. Therefore, for every $\lambda \in (3, \lambda^*)$ and $\nu > 0$ sufficiently small, equation (1) has a periodic solution $p_\nu(t)$ which is slowly oscillating (Theorem 6.1). Moreover, if $\lambda \in (3, 1 + \sqrt{6})$ (for this range of parameter values, the map f_λ has a globally attracting cycle of period 2) $p_\nu(t)$ converges to the function $p_0(t)$ on compact sets not containing integer points $t = n$, $n \in \mathbb{Z}$, as $\nu \to +0$. Here $p_0(t) = a_1$, $t \in [0, 1)$, $p_0(t) = a_2$, $t \in [1, 2)$ and $\{a_1, a_2\}$ is the cycle of period two of the map f_λ. The points a_1, a_2 are found as the real roots of the equation $f_\lambda^2(x) = x$, different from $x = 0$ and $x = 1 - 1/x$.

It is natural, however, to relate periodic solutions of equation (1) and cycles of the map f. This can be seen from the following heuristic arguments. Suppose $\beta = \{x_1, x_2, \cdots, x_n\}$ is an attracting cycle of the map f with components $U(x_i), i = 1, \cdots, n$, of domain of immediate attraction. Define subsets of the phase space $X = C([-1, 0], I)$ by setting $Y_i = \{\varphi \in X | \varphi(t) \in U(x_i) \forall t \in [-1, 0)\}$. Since β is an attracting cycle any $\varphi \in Y_i, i = 1, 2, \cdots, n$, gives rise to a solution $x_\varphi(t)$ of equation (2) converging uniformly on $[k, k + 1]$ as $k \to \infty$ to the steplike function $x^* = x_i$ for $t \in [i - 1, i), i = 1, 2, \cdots, n$. By virtue of the continuous dependence results (Chap. 3) which guarantee, for small ν, the closeness between solutions of the equations (1) and (2), it is natural to expect that, in some cases, a periodic solution of equation (1) with period close to n will correspond to the attracting cycle β. Generally speaking there may not be any such correspondence at all, as Example 4.3 and Theorem 5.1 show. Therefore some additional restrictions are needed to guarantee the correspondence. The idea is to use the continuous dependence results together with the existence of an attracting cycle of intervals, subjected to additional conditions. The conditions are roughly speaking, to ensure, the existence of an interval cycle with a large domain of immediate attraction.

Suppose the map f has an interval cycle $\{I_1, I_2, \cdots, I_n\}$. Consider the numbers $m(I_i)$ and $l(I_i), i = 1, 2, \cdots, n$, introduced in the previous chapter. Recall the notations $X_I = C([-1, 0], I)$, $X_k = C([-1, 0], I_k)$, $k = 1, 2, \cdots, n$.

Theorem 6.3. *If the conditions $m(I_i) > l(I_i), i = 1, 2, \cdots, n$, hold, then there exists a $\nu_0 > 0$ such that for every $0 < \nu \leq \nu_0$ equation (1) has a periodic solution $p(t)$ with the following properties:*

(i) $p(t)$ has period $T = n + O(\nu), \nu \to +0$;
(ii) there exists a sequence $0 < t_1 < t_2 < \cdots < t_n < T$ such that $p(t_k + t) \in X_k, t \in [-1, 0], 1 \leq k \leq n$.

We recall (see Remark 5.5) that the conditions $m(I_i) > l(I_i)$ imply the existence of an attracting cycle of intervals $\{I_1', \cdots, I_n'\}$ defined by $I_i' = \cap_{k \geq 0} f^{nk}(I_i)$. The set $I_1 \cup I_2 \cup \cdots \cup I_n$ is a part of its domain of immediate attraction.

Theorem 6.3 is a straightforward corollary of Theorem 5.2 and the Schauder fixed point theorem. Indeed, according to Theorem 5.2, for arbitrary $\varphi \in X_1$ there exists a sequence $0 \leq t_1 \leq t_2 \leq \cdots \leq t_k \leq \cdots \to \infty$ such that $t_{k+1} - t_k > 1$ for all $k \in \mathbb{N}$ and $x_\varphi^\nu(t_k + s) \in X_{k(\bmod n)}, s \in [-1, 0](0 \leq \nu \leq \nu_0, \nu_0$ is small enough) (see Remark 5.4). Define a map $G : X_1 \to X_1$ by setting: $(G\varphi)(t) = x_\varphi^\nu(t_n + t), t \in [-1, 0]$. More or less standard arguments show that X_1 is convex and bounded, and G is compact. Therefore, there exists a fixed point $\varphi_0 \in X_1$ of G which corresponds to a periodic solution of equation (1).

In the case when the cycle of intervals $\{I_1, I_2, \cdots, I_n\}$ contains a unique attracting cycle of the map f, the statement of Theorem 6.3 can be strengthened substantially. Let a finite set $\{A_1, A_2, \cdots, A_n\}$ of real numbers be given. We define a step function $p_0(t)$, $t \in \mathbb{R}$, by setting $p_0(t) = A_k$, $t \in [k-1, k)(\operatorname{mod} n)$.

Theorem 6.4. *Suppose the map f has a cycle of intervals $\{I_1, I_2, \cdots, I_n\}$ for which the inequalities $m(I_k) > l(I_k)$ hold for all $1 \leq k \leq n$. If the cycle of intervals contains a unique cycle $\{A_1, A_2, \cdots, A_n\}$ of the map f then the periodic solution $p(t)$, guaranteed to exist by Theorem 6.3, converges to the step function $p_0(t)$ as $\nu \to +0$. The convergence is uniform on every compact set not containing points $t = k$, $k \in \mathbb{Z}$.*

Remark. Under the conditions of Theorem 6.4 the convergence $p(t) \to p_0(t)$, $\nu \to +0$ holds but uniqueness of $p(t)$ is not claimed. In fact equation (1) may still have several or even countably many periodic solutions $p(t)$ [1, 3, 40]. All of them will be close to $p_0(t)$ (and therefore close to each other) and converge to $p_0(t)$ as $\nu \to +0$ in the following sense. Take a compact set $K \subset \mathbb{R}$ not containing points $t = i$, $i \in \mathbb{Z}$ and an arbitrary positive ε. Then there exists a positive ν_0 such that for every $0 < \nu \leq \nu_0$ one has $\sup\{|p(t) - p_0(t)|, \, t \in K\} \leq \varepsilon$ for any periodic solution $p(t)$ from Theorem 6.4. This result can be derived from the fine structure of periodic solution $p(t)$ obtained in [1, 3, 40] for the cases considered there. For our case it is proved below.

The proof of Theorem 6.4 is based on the properties of the shift operator $\mathcal{F}^t$ along solutions of equation (1) and on the continuous dependence results of Chap. 3 which we now adopt in Lemma 6.1.

Lemma 6.1 *Suppose $\varphi \in X_I$ and $[s_1, s_2]$ is a subinterval of $[-1, 0]$. For any positive ε, δ there exists a positive ν_0 such that $\sup\{|x_\varphi^\nu(t) - f(\varphi(t-1))|, \, t \in [s_1 + 1 + \delta, s_2 + 1]\} \leq \varepsilon$ for all $0 < \nu \leq \nu_0$.*

The lemma says that the iterate $f \circ \varphi$ of an initial function φ and the corresponding solution $x_\varphi^\nu(t)$ of equation (1) are as close on $[s_1 + 1 + \delta, s_2 + 1]$ as desired, provided ν is small enough.

Proof of the lemma. Since equation (1) is autonomous we may set $s_1 = -1$. For $t \in [0, s_2 + 1]$ the solution $x_\varphi^\nu(t)$ of equation (1) may be written in the form $x_\varphi^\nu(t) = \varphi(0)\exp(-t/\nu) + (1/\nu)\int_0^t \exp\{(s-t)/\nu\}f(\varphi(s-1))ds$. Using the identity $\exp(-t/\nu) + (1/\nu)\int_0^t \exp\{(s-t)/\nu\}ds = 1$ we have: $|x_\varphi^\nu(t) - f(\varphi(s-1))| \leq |\varphi(0) - f(\varphi(t-1))|\exp(-t/\nu) + (1/\nu)\int_0^t \exp\{(s-t)/\nu\}|f(\varphi(s-1)) - f(\varphi(t-1))|ds$, $t \in [0, s_2 + 1]$.

Since ε and δ are fixed there always exists ν_0' such that $\sup\{|\varphi(0) - f(\varphi(t-1))|\exp(-t/\nu), \, t \in [\delta, s_2 + 1]\} \leq \varepsilon/3$ for all $0 < \nu \leq \nu_0'$. This also implies $(1/\nu)\int_0^{t-\sigma} \exp\{(s-t)/\nu\}|f(\varphi(s-1)) - f(\varphi(t-1))|ds \leq M'(1/\nu)\int_0^{t-\sigma} \exp\{(s-t)/\nu\}ds \leq \varepsilon/3$, $t \in [0, s_2 + 1]$, for every $\sigma > 0$ and all $0 < \nu \leq \nu_0 = \nu_0(\sigma)$.

The function $f(\varphi(\cdot))$ is uniformly continuous since both $f(\cdot)$ and $\varphi(\cdot)$ are continuous. Therefore, for given $\varepsilon > 0$ there exists $\sigma > 0$ such that $|f(\varphi(t')) - f(\varphi(t''))| \leq \varepsilon/3$ provided $|t' - t''| \leq \sigma$. This implies $(1/\nu)\int_{t-\sigma}^{t} \exp\{(s - t)/\nu\}|f(\varphi(s-1)) - f(\varphi(t-1))|ds \leq \sup\{|f(\varphi(s-1)) - f(\varphi(t-1))|, \; s : |s-t| < \sigma\} \leq \varepsilon/3$.

Therefore $\sup\{|x_\varphi^\nu(t) - f(\varphi(t - 1))|, \; t \in [\delta, s_2 + 1]\} \leq |\varphi(0) - f(\varphi(t - 1))| \exp(-t/\nu) + (1/\nu)[\int_0^{t-\sigma} + \int_{t-\sigma]}^{t} \leq \varepsilon/3 + \varepsilon/3 + \varepsilon/3 = \varepsilon$ for every $0 < \nu \leq \min\{\nu_0', \nu_0''\}$. $\square$

Corollary 6.1. *Suppose $\varphi \in X_I$, $[s_1, s_2]$ is a subinterval of $[-1, 0]$. Then for any positive ε, δ and any positive integer N there exists a positive ν_0 such that $\sup\{|x_\varphi^\nu(t) - f^N(\varphi(t - N))|, \; t \in [s_1 + N + \delta, s_2 + N]\} \leq \varepsilon$ for all $0 < \nu \leq \nu_0$.*

The corollary is proved by induction using Lemma 6.1. Indeed $\varphi_1(t) = x_\varphi^\nu(t)$ and $\varphi_2(t) = f(\varphi(t-1))$ are close on $[s_1 + 1 + \delta/N, s_2 + 1]$ by the lemma. Consider φ_1 and φ_2 as elements of X_I and set $s_1' = s_1 + \delta/N$, $s_2' = s_2$. Then $x_{\varphi_1}^\nu(t)$ and $f(\varphi_1(t - 1))$ are close on $[s_1' + 1 + \delta/N, s_2' + 1]$ by Lemma 6.1. The functions $f(\varphi_1(t - 1))$ and $f(\varphi_2(t - 1))$ are close on $[s_1' + 1, s_2' + 1]$ since f is uniformly continuous on I. This implies that $x_\varphi^\nu(t)$ and $f^2(\varphi(t - 2))$ are close on the interval $[s_1 + 2 + 2\delta/N, s_2 + 2]$, and so on.

Proof of Theorem 6.4. Let $\{I_1, I_2, \cdots, I_n\}$ be a cycle of intervals of the map f for which the inequalities $m(I_k) > l(I_k), 1 \leq k \leq n$, hold. Let $\{A_1, \cdots, A_n\}$ be the only (point) cycle contained in the cycle of intervals $\{I_1, \cdots, I_n\}$. Then $\{A_1, \cdots, A_n\}$ is an attracting cycle of the map f and I_k is a proper subset of the component $U(A_k)$ of its domain of immediate attraction, $k = 1, 2, \cdots, n$. Therefore, for any positive ε there exists a positive integer k_0 such that $|f^{kn}(x) - A_k| \leq \varepsilon$ for every $k \geq k_0$ and all $x \in I_k$.

Let $X_k = C([-1, 0], I_k)$, $k = 1, \cdots, n$ be fixed (say $k = 1$; the case $k > 1$ is similar). Then for arbitrary $\varepsilon > 0$ and every $\varphi \in X_1$ there exists a positive integer $N_0 = n_0 \cdot n$ such that $\sup\{|f^{N_0}(\varphi(t - N_0)) - A_1|, t \in [N_0 - 1, N_0)\} \leq \varepsilon/2$. On the other hand according to Corollary 6.1 for any positive δ and given ε there exists a positive ν_0 such that $\sup\{x_\varphi^\nu(t) - f^{N_0}(\varphi(t - N_0))\}, \; t \in [N_0 - 1 + \delta, N_0]\} \leq \varepsilon/2$ (we apply the Corollary setting $s_1 = -1, s_2 = 0$). The latter inequality holds for every $\varphi \in X_1$ including those which give rise to periodic solutions. Use next Theorem 6.3. Take the particular $\varphi_0 \in X_1$ which generates the periodic solution $p_\nu(t)$ with period $T = n + O(\nu)$, $\nu \to +0$. To be definite we may always assume that $p_\nu(-1) = \inf I_1$ while considering $p_\nu(t)$ as an element of X_1. Denote by G the translation operator of time T along the periodic solution $p_\nu(t)$. We have $G^{ni}p_\nu(t) \in X_1$ for every integer i. Then $|p_\nu(t) - f^{N_0}(\varphi_0(t - N_0))| = |G^{ni}p_\nu(t) - f^{N_0}(\varphi_0(t - N_0))| = |x_{\varphi_0}^\nu(t) - f^{N_0}(\varphi_0(t-N_0))| \leq \varepsilon/2$ for all $t \in [N_0 - 1 + \delta, N_0]$, and small $\nu > 0$. Therefore, we have $|p_\nu(t) - A_1| = |G^{n_0}p_i(t) - f^{N_0}(\varphi_0(t - N_0)) + f^{N_0}(\varphi_0(t - N_0)) - A_1| \leq |G^{n_0}p_\nu(t) - f^{N_0}(\varphi_0(t - N_0))| + |f^{N_0}(\varphi_0(t - N_0)) - A_1| = |x_{\varphi_0}^\nu(t) - f^{N_0}(\varphi_0(t -$

$N_0))| + |f^{N_0}(\varphi_0(t - N)) - A_1| \leq \varepsilon$ for $t \in [N_0 - 1 + \delta, N_0 - \delta]$ and for every $0 < \nu \leq \nu_0$. This implies the convergence $p_\nu(t) \to p_0(t)$ as $\nu \to +0$ on the segments corresponding to A_1. For the other cases $k > 1$ arguments have to be repeated. This completes the proof. $\quad\square$

Finally, to illustrate Theorem 6.4 we give the following

Example 6.2. Consider equation (1) with a continuous nonlinearity $f(x)$ close to a step function which is constructed as follows.

Suppose $n \geq 2$ is fixed. Take two sets of real numbers $\{a_1, \cdots, a_{n-1}\}$ $\{A_1, \cdots, A_n\}$ satisfying $A_n < a_1 < A_1 < a_2 < A_2 < \cdots < a_{n-1} < A_{n-1}$. Let δ be positive and small (say $\delta = \delta_0$ where $\delta_0 = \min\{(a_1 - A_n)/2, (a_i - a_{i-1})/2, i = 1, 2, \cdots, n - 1\}$. Define $f(x)$ by setting: $f(x) = A_1$ for $x \leq a_1 - \delta$; $f(x) = A_k$ for $x \in [a_{k-1} + \delta, a_k - \delta]$, $k = 2, \cdots, n - 1$, $f(x) = A_n$ for $x \geq a_{n-1} + \delta$. Let $f(x)$ be an arbitrary monotone function on $[a_k - \delta, a_k + \delta]$, $k = 1, 2, \cdots, n - 1$ such that $f(x)$ is continuously differentiable everywhere.

It is easy to see that the map f has the invariant interval $I = [A_n, A_{n-1}]$ and a cycle of intervals $\{I_1, \cdots, I_n\}$ belonging to I. Here $I_1 = [A_n, a_1 - \delta]$, $I_2 = [a_1 + \delta, a_2 - \delta], \cdots, I_{n-1} = [a_{n-2} + \delta, a_{n-1} - \delta]$, $I_n = [a_{n-1} + \delta, A_{n-1}]$. Moreover, there exists the attracting cycle $\{A_1, A_2, \cdots, A_n\}$ of period n. Its domain of immediate attraction contains the cycle of intervals $\{I_1, \cdots, I_n\}$ as a proper subset.

By direct calculation one has $l_1(I_1) = (A_2 - a_2 + \delta)/(A_2 - A_1)$, $l_2(I_1) = 0, \cdots, l_1(I_{n-2}) = (A_{n-2} - a_{n-1} + \delta)/(A_{n-1} - A_{n-2})$, $l_2(_{n-2}) = 0$, $l_1(I_{n-1}) = 0$, $l_2(I_{n-1}) = (a_{n-1} + \delta - A_n)/(A_{n-1} - A_n)$, $l_1(I_n) = (A_{n-1} - a_1 + \delta)/(A_{n-1} - A_n)$, $l_2(I_n) = 0$, $m(I_k) = (A_k - a_k - \delta)/(A_k - a_k + \delta)$, $k = 1, 2, \cdots, n$.

Since $\lim_{\delta \to +0} l(I_k) < 1$ and $\lim_{\delta \to +0} m(I_k) = 1$ for all $1 \leq k \leq n$, there exists a positive δ_1 such that for every $0 < \delta \leq \delta_1$ the conditions of Theorem 6.4 are fulfilled. Therefore, equation (1) has a periodic solution $p_\nu(t)$ with period $n + O(\nu)$, $\nu \to +0$. Using the steplike form of $f(x)$, the solution $p_\nu(t)$ can be obtained explicitly. When $\nu \to +0$, the periodic solution $p_\nu(t)$ converges to a step function $p_0(t)$ on compact sets not containing integer points $t = i$, $i \in \mathbb{Z}$. Here $p_0(t) = A_{i(\bmod n)}$, $t \in [i - 1, i)$, $i \in \mathbb{Z}$.

Theorem 6.4 still holds true for small C^1 perturbations of the given steplike nonlinearity $f(x)$.

7. Concluding Remarks and Open Questions

The main problem we have discussed in this paper on the differential-delay equation

$$\nu\dot{x}(t) + x(t) = f(x(t - 1)) \tag{1}$$

with a small positive parameter ν concerns the relation between properties of its solutions and the dynamics given by the corrsponding one-dimensional

map $x \to f(x)$. The map f completely determines the properties of solutions
of the difference equation with continuous argument

$$x(t) = f(x(t-1)) \qquad (2)$$

obtained formally from (1) by setting $\nu = 0$. Thus, alternatively, we are concerned with the correspondence between solutions of equations (1) and (2),
when ν is small enough.

The natural question of closeness between solutions of equations (1) and
(2) arises. Two particular cases may be stated as follows:

(i) how are the solutions of equations (1) and (2) related within a finite time
interval?

(ii) to what extent does the one-dimensional map f define asymptotic properties of solutions for equation (1) as $t \to +\infty$?

The solution of problem (i) is natural and complete. When considered
within any finite time interval $[0, T]$, the solutions of equations (1) and (2)
are close provided the corresponding initial conditions are close and ν is small
enough. In particular, solutions of equation (1) follow, within a finite segment
of time solutions of equation (2), the behavior of which is studied in reasonable
generality [55].

The question about correspondence of asymptotic properties of the map f
and solutions of equation (1) is much more difficult. Except for some relatively
simple properties, this correspondence is not too direct. Two phenomena can
be observed from the results presented in this paper:

(iii) the dynamics given by the map f is simple while the asymptotic behavior
of solutions to equation (1) is complicated:

(iv) the dynamics given by the map f is complicated while the asymptotic
behavior of solutions of equation (1) is simple.

The first phenomenon was illustrated by an example for which the map f
has a globally attracting cycle of period two while the asymptotic behavior
of solutions to equation (1) (on a subject) is described by the induced one-
dimensional map which may exhibit very complex asymptotic properties. In
particular, the induced map may have an invariant measure which is absolutely
continuous with respect to the Lebesgue measure. It is worth noting that the
arising chaos is small, in a sense. For the example considered above all chaotic
solutions are close to a particular step function generated by the cycle of period
two. There are no results proved on the phenomenon for the case of a general
nonlinearity $f(x)$.

The second phenomenon occurs in the general case, and may be considered
as typical. Simplification occurs in that the dynamics of the map $f(x)$ on some
invariant subsets does not define any corresponding asymptotic properties of
the solutions to equation (1), at all. This can be explained by the existence of
attractors of the map f with "large" immediate basin. These large sets make

solutions to gradually damp out in amplitude in the long run, since every solution is continuous and spends a relatively large fraction of its transient time within large attractors. The phenomenon may be viewed, on the other hand, to be caused by the "damping" term $\nu\dot{x}(t)$.

Although there are many publications on equation (1) (see the List of References, for example), a series of natural and easily formulated questions about its dynamics have not been resolved in general so far. We would like to indicate some of these questions here.

1. Suppose the map f has an attracting cycle $\{a_1, a_2, \cdots, a_n\}$ of period n. Under what additional conditions does equation (1) possess an asymptotically stable periodic solution $p_\nu(t)$ with period $n + O(\nu)$, which converges to $p_0(t) = a_{k(\mod n)}$, $t \in [k-1, k)(\mod n)$ as $\nu \to +0$?

As was shown above (Theorem 5.1) attracting cycles of the map f need not give rise to nearby periodic solutions of equation (1). Some existence results on periodic solutions corresponding to cycles of intervals were given (Theorem 5.2.). No particular results on the stability of such solutions is known (except examples; see no. 4.2, 4.4).

A related question is the following. In what cases does a cycle $\{a_1, a_2, \cdots, a_n\}$ of the map f give rise to several nearby periodic solutions of equation (1)?

A particular variant of this first problem is the following.

2. Suppose the map f has an attracting cycle $\{a_1, a_2, \cdots, a_n\}$ which is a global attractor (this means that it attracts almost all trajectories, in a topological or measure sence). Does equation (1) have a periodic solution nearby this cycle? If so, under what additional conditions is the periodic solution asymptotically stable?

3. Supppose the map f has a so-called simple structure. That is, its topological entropy equals zero. This means that the map f has only cycles with periods given by powers of two. What additional conditions guarantee that the dynamics of equation (1) is also simple. That is, does equation (1) possess an asymptotically stable periodic solution which attracts almost all solutions? Almost all means that the attracted set is residual.

4. Suppose the map f has a complicated structure. For example, suppose there exists a cycle of period $(2k + 1)2^{i-1}$ for some positive integers k and i. This guarantees (see, e.g. [54]) the existence of a homoclinic trajectory for the map f, implying its chaotic dynamics.

What additional hypotheses are needed to produce complicated behavior of the solutions of equation (1)? When is it possible to prove the existence of a homoclinic solution for equation (1) which would imply complicated behavior?

Transversal homoclinic solutions with chaotic behavior for differential-delay equations were shown to exist in several examples [19, 23, 36, 61] (see remarks at the end of Chap. 4 also) and for an equation on the circle [63] in a general case.

5. A bifurcation problem

For some families f_λ of interval maps depending on a real parameter λ, a complication in the dynamics arises through period doubling bifurcations as λ varies (increases or decreases). In what cases is this complication followed by corresponding changes for equation (1)?

In the simplest case, the situation is as follows. There exists a sequence $\lambda_0 < \lambda_1 < \lambda_2 < \cdots < \lambda_n < \cdots$ of parameter values, convergent to some $\lambda_* < \infty$, such that the map f_λ has a globally attracting cycle of period 2^n for every $\lambda \in (\lambda_n, \lambda_{n+1}]$. For what families f_λ does the corresponding equation (1) possess an attracting periodic solution nearby the cycle of period 2^n, $n = 0, 1, 2, \cdots, \lambda \in (\lambda_n, \lambda_{n+1}]$?

Specifically we restate the problems for the familiy $f_\lambda(x) = \lambda x(1-x)$, $0 \leq \lambda \leq 4$, which map the interval $[0, 1]$ into itself.

It is well-known [54] that there exists a sequence of parameter values $\lambda_0 < \lambda_1 < \lambda_2 < \cdots < \lambda_n < \cdots \to \lambda_* \approx 3,569$ such that for every particular $\lambda \in (\lambda_n, \lambda_{n+1}]$ the map f_λ has cycles with periods $1, 2, 4, \cdots, 2^n$ only and the cycle of period 2^n is a global attractor (it does not attract only repelling cycles of periods $1, 2, 4, \cdots, 2^{n-1}$ and their preimages). For every $\lambda > \lambda_*$ the map f_λ has a cycle of period $(2k + 1)2^{i-1}$ for some $k, i \in N$. For an open set of parameter values λ, these cycles are global attractors. There exists a set Λ in the parameter space [0,4] of positive Lebesgue measure, such that for every particular $\lambda \in \Lambda$ the map f_λ has an invariant measure which is absolutely continuous with respect to the Lebesgue measure.

Considering equation (1) with $f(x) = f_\lambda(x) = \lambda x(1 - x)$, $0 \leq \lambda \leq 4$, the specific questions are:

1. Suppose f_λ has a globally attracting cycle of period n. Does equation (1) have a (asymptotically stable) periodic solution "close" to this cycle? If it does, what is the domain of attraction of the periodic solutions?

2. Suppose λ increases within the interval $1 < \lambda < \lambda_* \approx 3,569$ with f_λ going through period doubling bifurcations. Are these bifurcations followed by corresponding changes in the dynamics of equation (1)? That is: when $\lambda \in (\lambda_n, \lambda_{n+1}]$ does equation (1) have asymptotically stable periodic solution close to the particular cycle of period 2^n?

Some computer simulations for a different family [6] suggest this.

3. Do there exist values of the parameter λ for which the semiflow $\mathcal{F}^t$ defined by equation (1) admits the existence of an ergodic invariant measure in the phase space (or on a subset of the phase space)? If so, what is the measure of such λ's.

References

1. Aliev, S.Y.: Asymptotic properties of the solutions of a differential-difference equation. In: Differential-Difference Equations and Problems of Mathematical Physics. Institute of Mathematics of the Ukrainian Academy of Sciences, Kiev 1984, 126–130 (Russian)

2. Aliev, S.Y., Ivanov, A.F., Maistrenko, Y.L., Sharkovksy, A.N.: Singular perturbations of difference equations with continuous time. Preprint no. 84.33, Institute of Mathematics of the Ukrainian Academy of Sciences, 1984 (Russian)

3. Aliev, S.Y., Maistrenko, Y.L.: Chaotization of solutions for a differential-difference equation. In: Differential Functional Equations and Their Applications. Institute of Mathematics of the Ukrainian Academy of Sciences, Kiev 1985, 3–11 (Russian)

4. Blank, M.L.: Finite dimensional attractors in a certain model of turbulence. Differential equations **24**, no. 11, 1989, 1854–1862 (Russian)

5. Chow, S.N.: Existence of periodic solutions of autonomous functional differential equations. J. Diff. Eq. **15** (1974) 350–378

6. Chow, S.N., Green, D.: Some results on singular delay differential equations. Lecture Notes in Pure and Applied Mathematics **98** (1985), 161–182

7. Chow, S.N., Lin, X.-B., Mallet-Paret, J.: Transition layers for singularly perturbed delay differential equations with monotone nonlinearities. Journal of Dynamics and Differential Equations **1**, no. 1 (1989), 3–42

8. Chow, S.N., Mallet-Paret, J.: Singularly perturbed delay-differential equations. In: Coupled Nonlinear Oscillators. Chandra, J., Scott, A.C. (eds.), North Holland Math. Studies, Amsterdam 1983, 7–12

9. Chow, S.N., Walther, H.O.: Characteristic multipliers and stability of periodic solutions of $\dot{x}(t) = g(x(t-1))$. Trans. Amer. Math. Soc. **307**, no. 1 (1988), 127–142

10. Derstine, M.W., Gibbs, H.M., Hopf, F.A., Kaplan, D.L.: Alternate path to chaos in optical bistability. Phys. Rev. A. **27** (3) (1983), 3200-3208

11. Dmitriev, A.S., Starkov, S.O.: On a possibility of modeling some properties of developed turbulence using generators with delayed feedback. Radiotechnica and electronica 1988, Vol. XXXIII, no. 7, p. 1472–1481 (Russian)

12. Elsgoltz, L.E., Norkin, S.B.: Introduction to Theory of Differential Equations with Deviating Argument. Moskva, Nauka 1967 (Russian)

13. Farmer, J.D.: Chaotic attractors of an infinite dimensional dynamical system. Physica D, **4** (1982), 366–393

14. Fielder, B, Mallet-Paret, J.: Connections between Morse sets for delay-differential equations. J. Reine Angew. Math. **397** (1989), 23–41

15. Furumochi, T.: Existence of periodic solutions of one-dimensional differential-delay equations. Tôhoku Math. J. **30** (1978), 13–35

16. Hadeler, K.P., Tomiuk, J.: Periodic solutions of difference-differential equations. Arch. Ration. Mech. Anal. **65** (1977), 87–96

17. Hale, J.K: Theory of Functional-Differential Equations. Springer-Verlag 1977

18. Hale, J.K., Lin, X.-B: Examples of transverse homoclinic orbits in delay equations. Nonlinear Analysis, Theory, Methods, and Applications **10** (1986), 693–709

19. Heiden, U. an der: Periodic, aperiodic and stochastic behavior of differential-difference equations modeling biological and economical processes. In: Differential-Difference Equations: Applications and Numerical Problem Workshop, Basel e.a. 1983, 351–365

20. Heiden, U. an der, Mackey, M.C.: The dynamics of production and destruction: analytic insight into complex behaviour. J. Math. Biology **16** (1982), 75–101

21. Heiden, U. an der, Mackey, M.C., Walther, H.O.: Complex oscillations in a simple deterministic neuronal network. Mathematical Aspects in Physiology (F.C. Hoppenstedt (ed.), **19** (1981), 355–360

22. Heiden, U. an der, Walther, H.O.: Existence of chaos in control systems with delayed feedback. J. Diff. Eq. **47** (1983), 273–295

23. Heiden, U. an der, Walther, H.O: Existence of chaos in control systems with delayed feedback. Proc. IX Intern. Conf. Nonlinear Oscil., Kiev, Naukova dumka 1984, **2**, 88–91

24. Ikeda, K., Daido, H., Akimoto O: Optical turbulence: chaotic behavior of transmitted light from a ring cavity. Phys. Rev. Lett. **45** (1980), 709–712

25. Ikeda, K., Matsumoto, K.: High-dimensional chaotic behavior in systems with time-delayed feedback. Physica 29D (1987), 223–225

26. Ivanov, A.F.: On continuous dependence and asymptotic behavior of solutions for singular perturbed differential-difference equations. Preprint no. 85.64, Institute of Mathematics of the Ukrainian Academy of Sciences, 1985 (Russian)

27. Ivanov, A.F.: Asymptotically constant solutions of singularly perturbed differential-difference equations. Preprint no. 86.59, Institute of Mathematics of the Ukrainian Academy of Sciences, 1986 (Russian)

28. Ivanov, A.F.: Periodic solutions of singularly perturbed differential-difference equations. In: Differential Functional Equations and Their Applications to Nonlinear Boundary Value Problems. Institute of Mathematics of the Ukrainian Academy of Sciences, Kiev 1987, 11–17 (Russian)

29. Ivanov, A.F.: On periodic solutions of a nonlinear delay equation. Math. Phys. Nonl. Mech., Kiev: Naukova dumka **44** (1988), 18–20 (Russian)

30. Ivanov, A.F.: Attracting cycles of interval maps generating periodic solutions of a differential-difference equation. Ukrainian Math. Journal **41** (1989) no. 8, 1054–1058 (Russian)

31. Ivanov, A.F.: On a singular perturbed differential delay equation. Proc. XXVIII Semester on Dynamical Systems and Ergodic Theory, Banach Centrum Publications, Warszawa 1989

32. Jones, J.S.: The existence of periodic solutions of $f'(x) = -\alpha f(x-1)(1+f(x))$. J. Math. Anal. Appl. **5** (1962), 435–450

33. Kaplan, J.L., Yorke, J.A.: On the nonlinear differential delay equation $x'(t) = -f(x(t), x(t-1))$. J. Diff. Eq. **23** (1977), 293–314

34. Kolyada, S.F.: Interval maps with zero Schwarzian derivative. In: Differential Functional Equations and Their Applications, Institute of Mathematics of the Ukrainian Academy of Sciences, Kiev 1985, 47–57 (Russian)

35. Lin, X.-B: Exponential dichotomies and homoclinic orbits in functional differential equations. J. Differential Equations **63** (1986), 227–254

36. Mackey, M.C., Glass, L.: Oscillations and chaos in physiological control systems. Science **197** (1977), 287–289

37. Maistrenko, Y.L, Sharkovsky, A.N.: Turbulence and simple hyperbolic systems. Preprint no. 84.2, Institute of Mathematics of the Ukrainian Academy of Sciences, 1984 (Russian)

38. Mallet-Paret, J.: Morse decomposition and global continuation of periodic solutions for singularly perturbed delay equations. In: Systems of Nonlinear Partial Differential Equations. J.M. Ball (ed.), D. Reidel, Dordrecht 1983, 351–365

39. Mallet-Paret: Morse decomposition for delay-differential equations. J. Differential Equations **72** (1988), 270–315

40. Mallet-Paret, Nussbaum, R.D.: A bifurcation gap for a singularly perturbed delay equation. Chaotic Dynamics and Fractals. F.D. Barnsley, S.G. Demko (eds.), Academic Press, New York 1986, 263–286

41. Mallet-Paret, Nussbaum, R.D.: Global continuation and complicated trajectories for periodic solutions of a differential-delay equation. Proc. of Symposia in Pure Math. **45** (1986), Part 2, 155–167

42. Mallet-Paret, J., Nussbaum, R.D.: Global continuation and asymptotic behavior for periodic solutions of a differential-delay equation. Ann. Mat. Pura Appl. **145** (1986), 33–128

43. Martelli, M., Schmitt, K., Smith, H.: Periodic solutions of some nonlinear delay-differential equations. J. Math. Anal. Appl., **74** (1980), 494–503

44. Nussbaum, R.D.: A global bifurcation theorem with applications to functional differential equations. J. Funct. Anal. **19** (1975), 319–338

45. Pesin, Y.B.: On the behavior of solutions of a stronlgy nonlinear differential equation with delayed argument. Differential Equations **10** (1974), 1025–1036 (Russian)

46. Peters, H.: Comportement chaotique d'une équation différentielle retardée. C.R. Acad. Paris Ser. A, **280** (1980), 1119–1122

47. Rozanov, N.N.: Optical bistability – present state and prospects. Proceedings of the State Optical Institute, **59**, 193 (1985), 3–30 (Russian)

48. Siegberg, H.-W.: Chaotic behavior of a class of nonlinear differential delay equations. Annal. Mat. Pura Appl. **138** (1984), 15–33

49. Sharkovsky, A.N.: On cycles and the structure of continuous maps. Ukrainian Math. J. **17** (1965) no. 3, 104–111 (Russian)

50. Sharkovsky, A.N.: Oscillations of turbulent and relaxation types: differential-difference models. Proc. IX Intern. Conf. Nonlinear Oscil., Kiev Naukova dumka **2** (1984), 430–434 (Russian)

51. Sharkovsky, A.N.: On periodic solutions of nonlinear differential-difference equations. Uspechi Matemat, Nauk **40** (1985), no. 5 (245), 242 (Russian)

52. Sharkovsky, A.N., Ivanov, A.F.: Singular perturbations of attractors of differences equations. In: Abstracts of Conference on the Theory and Applications of Functional Differential Equations, Part 2, Dushanbe 1987, 151–152 (Russian)

53. Sharkovsky, A.N., Ivanov, A.F., Maistrenko, Y.L.: Relaxation type oscillations of singularly perturbed difference equations. Uspechi Matemat. Nauk **40** (1985), no. 5 (245), 239 (Russian)

54. Sharkovsky, A.N., Kolyada, S.F., Sivak, S.G., Fedorenko, V.V.: Dynamics of One-Dimensional Maps. Naukova Dumka, Kiev 1989 (Russian)

55. Sharkovsky, A.N., Maistrenko, Y.L., Romanenko, E.Y.: Difference Equations and Their Applications. Naukova Dumka, Kiev 1986 (Russian)

56. Sharkovsky, A.N., Maistrenko, Yu.L., Romanenko, E.Y.: Attactors of difference equations and turbulence. In: Plasma Theory and Nonlinear and Turbulent Processes in Physics (Proc. Internat. Workshop, Kiev 1987). V.G. Baryakhtar, V.M. Chernousenko, N.S. Erokhin, A.G. Sitenko, V.E. Zakharov (eds.), World Scientific 1988, **1**, 520–536

57. Sharkovsky, A.N., Romanenko, E.Y.: Asymptotic behavior of solutions for differential-difference equations. In: Qualitative Methods of Investigations of Nonlinear Differential Equations and Nonlinear Oscillations. Institute of Mathematics of the Ukrainian Academy of Sciences, Kiev 1981, 171–199 (Russian)

58. Walther, H.O.: Existence of non-constant periodic solution of a nonlinear autonomous functional differential equation representing the growth of a single species population. J. Math Biology **1** (1975), 227–240

59. Walther, H.O.: On instability, ω-limit sets and periodic solutions of nonlinear autonomous differential delay equations. In: Functional Differential Equations and Approximations of Fixed Points (H.O. Peitgen, H.O. Walther, eds.), Proceedings (Bonn 1978), 489–503. Lecture Notes in Mathematics 730. Springer-Verlag, 1979

60. Walther, H.O.: Density of slowly oscillating solutions of $x'(t) = -f(x(t-1))$. J. Math. Anal. Appl. **79** (1981), 127–140

61. Walther, H.O.: Homoclinic solution and chaos in $\dot{x}(t) = f(x(t-1))$. Nonl. Anal., Theory, Methods and Appl. **5** (1981), 775–788

62. Walther, H.O.: Bifurcation from periodic solutions in functional differential equations. Math. Z. **182** (1983), 269–289

63. Walther, H.O.: Hyperbolic periodic solutions, heteroclinic connections and transversal homoclinic points in autonomous differential delay equations. Memoirs of the Amer. Math. Soc. **79**, no. 402 (1989), 104 p.

64. Wright, E.M.: A nonlinear difference-differential equation. J. Reine Angew. Math. **194** (1955), 66–87

Topological Approach to Differential Inclusions on Closed Subset of $\mathbb{R}^n$

R. Bielawski, L. Górniewicz, S. Plaskacz

Introduction

The present paper is a survey of the current results concerning the existence problem, topological characterization of the set of solutions and periodic solutions of differential inclusions on subsets of euclidean spaces. First, based on [5, 15, 17, 19, 21], we give a topological approach to these questions on whole $\mathbb{R}^n$ or on balls in $\mathbb{R}^n$. It is presented in Sects. 5 and 6. Later, in Sects. 7, 8 and 9 we give some new results. Namely, we are trying to tackle the mentioned problems on compact subsets of euclidean spaces called by us sets with property p. Let us remark that in particular convex sets and smooth manifolds with boundary or without boundary have property p. Note that our results obtained in Sects. 7, 8 and 9 provide an application and generalization of respective results given in [3, 7, 13, 20, 21 and 25]. We would like to add that in our considerations, we use the topological degree methods only. Finally let us remark that instead of the topological degree the analytical methods in the theory of differential inclusions are well developed (cf. [3] and [30]).

The authors are very indebted to Professor Dr. K. Deimling for many valuable remarks concerning this paper.

1. Multivalued Mappings

In this paper all topological spaces are assumed to be metric. Let X and Y be two spaces and assume that for every point $x \in X$ a non-empty, compact subset $\varphi(x)$ of Y is given; in this case we say that $\varphi : X \to Y$ is a mulitvalued map. We associate with φ the diagram $X \leftarrow \Gamma_\varphi \to Y$, where

$\Gamma_\varphi = \{(x,y); y \in \varphi(x)\}$ is the *graph* of φ and the natural projections

$p_\varphi : \Gamma_\varphi \to X$, $q_\varphi : \Gamma_\varphi \to Y$ are given by $(x,y) \to x$, $(x,y) \to y$, respectively.

A multivalued map $\varphi : X \to Y$ is called *upper semi-continuous* (u.s.c) if for each open $U \subset Y$, the set

$$\varphi^{-1}(U) = \{x \in X; \; \varphi(x) \subset U\}$$

is an open subset of X; φ is called *lower semi-continuous* (l.s.c.), if for each open $U \subset Y$ the set

$$\varphi^{-1}(U) = \{x \in X; \; \varphi(x) \cap U \neq \emptyset\}$$

is an open subset of X.

By a standard calculation we get (cf. [3, 12, 17]):

Proposition (1.1). *Let* $\varphi : X \to Y$ *be a compact multivalued map. Then* φ *is u.s.c. if and only if the graph* Γ_φ *of* φ *is a closed subset of the product space* $X \times Y$ *of* X *and* Y.

If $\varphi : X \to Y$ and $\Psi : Y \to Z$ are two multivalued maps, then their *composition* is the map $\Psi \circ \varphi : X \to Z$ defined by

$$(\Psi \circ \varphi)(x) = \bigcup_{y \in \varphi(x)} \Psi(y) \, .$$

It is easy to see (cf. [17]) that the composition of two u.s.c. maps is an u.s.c. map.

In what follows the symbols φ, Ψ, χ are reserved for multivalued maps; we shall denote singlevalued maps by $f, g, h, \cdots, p, q, \cdots$

A (singlevalued) map $f : X \to Y$ is called a *selector* of $\varphi : X \to Y$ (written $f \subset \varphi$) if $f(x) \in \varphi(x)$ for each $x \in X$. Let A be a subset of X and let $\varphi : A \to X$ be a multivalued map. We let $\mathrm{Fix}(\varphi) = \{x \in A, \; x \in \varphi(x)\}$; then $\mathrm{Fix}(\varphi)$ is called the set of *fixed points* of φ.

We will need some terminology and results concerning the homology theory. By $H = \{H_n\}_{n \geq 0}$ we denote the Čech homology functor with compact carriers and coefficients in the field of rational number $\mathbb{Q}$ (for details see [17]). A non-empty compact space A is called *acyclic*, provided $H_0(A) = \mathbb{Q}$ and $H_n(A) = 0$, for every $n > 0$. For a continuous map $f : X \to Y$ we denote by $f_* = \{f_{*n}\} : H(X) \to H(Y)$ the induced linear map.

Consider the following diagram:

$$X \xrightarrow{f} \Gamma \xleftarrow{g} Y$$

then we define a space $X \otimes Y$ by setting:

$$X \otimes Y = \{(x, y) \in X \times Y; \quad f(x) = g(y)\}$$

and two maps $f_0 : X \otimes Y \to Y$, $g_0 : X \otimes Y \to X$ as follows $f_0(x, y) = y$, $g_0(x, y) = x$. In what follows the map g_0 is called the *pull-back* of g (with respect to f) and f_0 is called the *pull-back* of f (with respect to g).

A map $p : \Gamma \to X$ is called a *Vietoris map* (written $p : \Gamma \Rightarrow X$) provided the following conditions are satisfied:

(i) p is onto,

(ii) p is proper, i.e., for each compact $K \subset X$, the set $p^{-1}(K)$ is a compact subset of Γ,

(iii) for every point $x \in X$, the set $p^{-1}(x)$ is acyclic.

Some important properties of Vietoris maps are summarized in the following theorem:

Theorem (1.2). *(cf. [17, 18 or 25])*

(1.2.1) If $p : \Gamma \Rightarrow X$, then $p_* : H(\Gamma) \to H(X)$ is an isomorphism.

(1.2.2) If $p : \Gamma \Rightarrow X$ and $p' : X \Rightarrow X'$ are Vietoris maps, then so is the composite $p' \circ p : \Gamma \Rightarrow X'$.

(1.2.3) The pull-back of a Vietoris map (with respect to an arbitrary map) is also a Vietoris map.

(1.2.4) If $p : \Gamma \Rightarrow X$, then for any subset $A \subset X$ the map $p' : p^{-1}(A) \to A$, $p'(y) = p(y)$, is a Vietoris map, too.

(1.2.5) If $p : \Gamma \Rightarrow X$ and $p' : \Gamma' \Rightarrow X'$ are Vietoris maps, then so is the product map $p \times p' : \Gamma \times \Gamma' \Rightarrow X \times X'$.

An u.s.c. map $\varphi : X \to Y$ is called *acyclic*, provided for each $x \in X$ the set $\varphi(x)$ is acyclic.

Observe that if $\varphi : X \to Y$ is an acyclic map then we have:

(i) the natural projection $p_\varphi : \Gamma \Rightarrow X$ is a Vietoris map,

and

(ii) $\varphi(x) = q_\varphi[(p_\varphi)^{-1}(x)]$, for each $x \in X$.

This allows us to introduce the following definition (cf. [17]):

Definition (1.3). An u.s.c. map $\varphi : X \to Y$ is called *admissible* provided there exists a space Γ and two continuous (singlevalued) maps $p : \Gamma \to X$ and $q : \Gamma \to Y$ such that the following two conditions are satisfied:

(1.3.1) p is a Vietoris map ,

(1.3.2) $q(p^{-1}(x)) = \varphi(x)$,   for every $x \in X$;

then (p, q) is called a *selected pair* of φ (written $(p, q) \subset \varphi$).

We have already observed that any acyclic map is admissible. Let us remark that the class of admissible maps is quite large. One can show (cf. [17]) that φ is an admissible map if and only if it is composition of acyclic maps.

Some useful properties of admissible maps are summarized in the following (cf. [17]):

Proposition (1.4).

(1.4.1) If $\varphi : X \to Y$ and $\Psi : Y \to T$ are two admissible maps, then the composition $\Psi \circ \varphi : X \to T$ of φ and Ψ is an admissible map, too.

(1.4.2) If $\varphi : X \to Y$ and $\varphi' : X' \to Y'$ are two admissible maps, then the product map $\varphi \times \varphi' : X \times X' \to y \times Y'$ is admissible.

(1.4.3) If $\varphi, \Psi : X \to \mathbb{R}^n$ are two admissible maps, then the map $\chi : X \times [0,1] \to Y$ given by the following formula:

$$\chi(x,t) = t\varphi(x) + (1-t)\Psi(x) = \{tu + (1-t)v; \; u \in \varphi(x), \; v \in \Psi(x)\}$$

is an admissible map, where $\mathbb{R}^n$ denotes the n-dimensional euclidean space.

Proposition (1.4) is an easy consequence of Theorem (1.2).

2. Topological Degree of Admissible Mappings in $\mathbb{R}^n$

We will use the following notations:

$K^N(r) = \{x \in \mathbb{R}^n; \|x\| \leq r\}, \; r \in \mathbb{R}, \; r > 0, \; n \geq 2$,

$S^{n-1}(r) = \{x \in K^n(r); \|x\| = r\}$,

$K^n = K^n(1), \; S^{n-1} = S^{n-1}(1), \; P^n = \mathbb{R}^n \backslash \{0\}$,

$A(K^n(r), \mathbb{R}^n) = \{\varphi : K^n(r) \to \mathbb{R}^n; \; \varphi \text{ is admissible and } \varphi(S^{n-1}(r)) \subset P^n\}$,

$\mathbb{R}^n = K^n(r), \quad \text{if} \quad r = +\infty$.

We need the notion of homotopy in $A(K^n(r), \mathbb{R}^n)$. Let $\varphi, \Psi \in A(K^n(r), \mathbb{R}^n)$. We will say that φ and Ψ are homotopic (written $\varphi \times \Psi$), if there exists an admissible map $\chi : K^n(r) \times [0,1] \to \mathbb{R}^n$ such that the following conditions are satisfied:

(i) $\chi(S^{n-1}(r) \times [0,1]) \subset P^n$

(ii) $\chi(x,0) = \varphi(x)$ and $\chi(x,1) = \Psi(x)$, for every $x \in K^n(r)$.

It is well known that the topological degree theory can be extended from the case of singlevalued mappings to the case of admissible maps (cf. [17] and also [12, 16, 25, 27]). We shall formulate it in the following theorem ([17])

Theorem (2.1). *There exists a function* Deg $: A(K^n(r), \mathbb{R}^n) \to 2^Q \backslash \emptyset$, $r \in \mathbb{R}$, $r > 0$ *such that:*

(2.1.1) if Deg$(\varphi) \neq \{0\}$, *then there is a point* $x \in K^n(r)$ *such that* $0 \in \varphi(x)$;

(2.1.2) if φ and Ψ are homotopic, then Deg$(\varphi) \cap$ Deg$(\Psi) \neq \emptyset$;

(2.1.3) if φ is an acyclic map, then Deg$(\varphi) = \{\deg(\varphi)\}$ *is a singleton;*

(2.1.4) let $\varphi, \Psi \in A(K^n(r), \mathbb{R}^n)$ be two maps such that φ is acyclic; assume further that $\chi : K^n(r) \times [0,1] \to \mathbb{R}^n$,

$\chi(x,t) = t\varphi(x) + (1-t)\Psi(x)$, *is a homotopy joining* φ *and* Ψ; *then* $\mathrm{Deg}(\Psi) = \{\deg(\varphi)\}$ *is a singleton.*

Sketch of proof. First, we are going to define the topological degree $\mathrm{Deg}(\varphi)$ of an admissible map $\varphi \in A(K^n(r), \mathbb{R}^n)$. In order to do so assume that $(p,q) \subset \varphi$. Then we have the following diagram:

$$S^{n-1}(r) \xleftarrow{p'} \Gamma \xrightarrow{q'} P^n$$

in which $p'(y) = p(y)$ and $q'(y) = q(y)$.

It follows from (1.2.4) that p' is a Vietoris map. Consequently, in view of (1.2.1), we get the diagram:

$$\mathbb{Q} = H_{n-1}(S^{n-1}) \xleftarrow{(p')_*} H_{n-1}\Gamma) \xrightarrow{(q')_*} H_{n-1}(P^n) = \mathbb{Q}\,,$$

in which $(p')_*$ is an isomorphism.

We set

$$\deg(p,q) = ((q')_*[(p')_*]^{-1})(1)$$

and

$$\mathrm{Deg}(\varphi) = \{\deg(p,q);\ (p,q) \subset \varphi\}\ .$$

Now by a standard procedure (cf. [17]) we get (2.1.1), (2.1.2) and (2.1.3). □

It is well known (see [17]) that from the topological degree theory we are able to obtain the Lefschetz fixed point theorem.

We shall say that a metric space X is an ANR-space (absolute neighbourhood retract) if there exists an open subset U of a normed space E and two continuous maps $r : U \to X$, $s : X \to U$ such that $r \circ s = \mathrm{id}_X$; X is an AR-space (absolute retract), if we can take $U = E$.

In particular, any retract of an open subset in $\mathbb{R}^n$ (of $\mathbb{R}^n$) is an ANR-space (AR-space).

Recall that if X is a compact ANR-space then we define the *Euler characteristic* $\chi(X)$ of X as the Lefschetz number $\lambda(\mathrm{id}_X)$ of the identity map id_X over X. In particular, if X is a compact AR-space, then $\chi(X) = 1$.

Two admissible maps $\varphi, \Psi : X \to X$ are called homotopic (written $\varphi \sim \Psi$) if there exists an admissible map $\chi : X \times [0,1] \to X$ such that

$$\chi(x,0) = \varphi(x) \qquad \text{and} \qquad \chi(x,1) = \Psi(x), \qquad \text{for every} \quad x \in X\ .$$

We shall use the following special case of the Lefschetz fixed point theorem (cf. [17]):

Proposition (2.2). *Let X be a compact ANR-space such that $\chi(X) \neq 0$. If $\varphi : X \to X$ is an admissible map such that $\varphi \sim \mathrm{id}_X$ then $\mathrm{Fix}(\varphi) \neq \emptyset$.*

3. Aroszajn's Result

Recall that a compact non-empty space is called an R_δ-set (cf. [2, 3, 4, 19, 20, 21, 22, 25]) provided there exists a decreasing sequence $\{X_n\}$ of compact and contractible spaces such that $X = \cap X_n$. From the continuity of the Čech homology functor we deduce:

Proposition (3.1). *If X is an R_δ-set, then X is acyclic.*

Now, we shall generalize the notion of contractibility (cf. [19]):

Definition (3.2). A space X is called *acyclically contractible* if there exists an acyclic homotopy $\chi : X \times [0,1] \to X$ such that the following two conditions are satisfied

$$(3.2.1) \qquad\qquad x \in \chi(x,0) \text{ , for every } x \in X \text{ ,}$$

$$(3.2.2) \qquad\qquad x_0 \in \chi(x,1) \text{ , for every } x \in X \text{ and for some } x_0 \in X \text{ .}$$

Evidently, any contractible space is acyclically contractible. Observe that an arbitrary acyclic and compact space is acyclically contractible. Indeed, it is sufficient to put $\chi(x,t) = X$, for every $x \in X$ and $t \in [0,1]$. Moreover, one can prove the following (cf. [17] or [19]):

Proposition (3.3). *Any acyclically contractible space is acyclic.*

To formulate the Aronszajn result we need some additional notations. We shall start from the following:

Definition (3.4). Let $f : [0,1] \times K^n(2r) \to \mathbb{R}^n$ be a singlevalued map. We shall say that f belongs to the class **L** (written $f \in \mathbf{L}$), if the following three conditions are satisfied:

(3.4.1) $\exists 0 < \alpha < r \forall t \in [0,1] \forall x \in K^n(2r) : \|f(t,x)\| \leq \alpha,$
(3.4.2) $\forall x \in K^n(2r) : f(\cdot, x) : [0,1] \to \mathbb{R}^n$ is a Lebesgue measurable map,
(3.4.3) $\exists L > 0 \forall t \in [0,1] \forall x,y \in K^n(2,r) : \|f(t,x) - f(t,y)\| \leq L\|x - y\|;$

we shall say that f belongs to the class **C** (written $f \in \mathbf{C}$) if it satisfies (3.4.1), (3.4.2) and instead of (3.4.3) the following condition:

(3.4.4) $\forall t \in [0,1] : f(t, \cdot) : K^n(2r) \to \mathbb{R}^n$ is a continuous map.

Obviously, we have:

$$(3.5) \qquad\qquad\qquad \mathbf{L} \subset \mathbf{C}$$

For a given singlevalued map $f : [0,1] \times K^n(2r) \to \mathbb{R}^n$, a point $x_0 \in K^n(r)$ and $t_0 \in [0,1]$ we shall consider the following Cauchy problem (cf. [2, 11, 14]):

$$(3.6) \qquad \begin{cases} x'(t) = f(t, x(t)) \\ x(t_0) = x_0 \,, \end{cases}$$

where the solution $x : [0,1] \to K^n(2r)$ is understood in the sense of almost everywhere in $[0,1]$ (written a.e. in $[0,1]$).

We let

$$S(f, t_0, x_0) = \{ x : [0,1] \to \mathbb{R}^n; \quad x \text{ is a solution of } (3.6) \} \,.$$

The following theorem is well known (cf. [2, 11, 14] and also [18, 19, 22]):

Theorem (3.7).

(3.7.1) If $f \in \mathbf{L}$, then the set $S(f, t_0, x_0)$ is a singleton;
*(3.7.2) (**Aronszajn**) If $f \in \mathbf{C}$, then $S(f, t_0, x_0)$ is an R_δ-set;*
(3.7.3) If $f \in \mathbf{C}$ and $\hat{\varphi} : [0,1] \times K^n(r) \to C([0,1], \mathbb{R}^n)$, $\hat{\varphi}(t, x) = S(f, t, x)$, then $\hat{\varphi}$ is an acyclic map, where $C([0,1], \mathbb{R}^n)$ denotes the space of continuous maps with the supremum norm.

4. Selectionable and σ-Selectionable Multivalued Maps

Following ([3, 19, 20, 21]) we shall introduce the class of selectionable and the class of σ-selectionable multivalued maps which have interesting applications in the theory of differential inclusions. Note (cf. [19, 21], that selectionable and σ-selectionable maps can be constructed very easily.

Definition (4.1). A multivalued map $\varphi : [0,1] \times K^n(2r) \to \mathbb{R}^n$ is called **L-**selectionable (**C**-selectionable) provided the following two conditions are satisfied:

(4.1.1) $\exists 0 < \alpha < r \forall t \in [0,1] \forall x \in K^n(2r) \forall y \in (t,x) : \|y\| \le \alpha$,
(4.1.2) there is an **L**-map (**C**-map) $f : [0,1] \times K^n(2r) \to \mathbb{R}^n$ such that $f \subset \varphi$.
We let:

$$\mathbf{ML} = \{ \varphi : [0,1] \times K^n(2r) \to \mathbb{R}^n; \quad \varphi \text{ is } \mathbf{L}\text{-selectionable} \} \,,$$
$$\mathbf{MC} = \{ \varphi : [0,1] \times K^n(2r) \to \mathbb{R}^n; \quad \varphi \text{ is } \mathbf{C}\text{-selectionable} \} \,.$$

It is not difficult to see the following:

$$(4.2) \qquad\qquad\qquad \mathbf{ML} \subset \mathbf{MC} \,.$$

Let us observe that having a singlevalued map f (in **L** or **C**) we can construct many different maps in **ML** or in **MC** respectively.

From the Michael selection theorem (cf. [3]) we get:

Proposition (4.3). *If* $\varphi : [0,1] \times K^n(2r) \to \mathbb{R}^n$ *is an l.s.c. map with compact convex values, then* $\varphi \in$ **MC**.

Similarily, from the Cellina selection theorem (cf. [8] cf. also [1]) we obtain:

Proposition (4.4). *If* $\varphi : [0,1] \times K^n(2r) \to \mathbb{R}^n$ *is a bounded map with compact convex values, which is u.s.c. in* $t \in [0,1]$ *for every* $x \in K^n(2r)$ *and l.s.c. in* x *for every* t, *then* $\varphi \in$ **MC**.

Moreover, it is useful to define the following two classes of mutlivalued maps.

Definition (4.5). A multivalued map $\varphi : [0,1] \times K^n(2r) \to \mathbb{R}^n$ is called a σ-**MC**-*map* (written $\varphi \in \sigma$-**ML**, resp. $\varphi \in \sigma$-**MC**), if there exists a sequence $\{\varphi_n\}$ of multivalued maps from $[0,1] \times K^n(2r)$ into $\mathbb{R}^n$ such that the following three conditions are satisfied:

(4.5.1) $\forall n \in \mathbb{N} \forall t \in [0,1] \forall x \in K^n(2r) : \varphi_{n+1}(t,x) \subset \varphi_n(t,x)$,
(4.5.2) $\forall t \in [0,1] \forall x \in K^n(2r) : \varphi(t,x) = \cap \varphi_n(t,x)$,
(4.5.3) $\forall n \in \mathbb{N} : \varphi_n \in$ **ML**$(\varphi_n \in$ **MC**$)$.

Connections between the classes of multivalued mappings introduced above are described in the following diagram:

$$
\begin{array}{ccc}
\mathbf{ML} & \subset & \mathbf{MC} \\
\cap & & \cap \\
\sigma\text{-}\mathbf{ML} & \subset & \sigma\text{-}\mathbf{MC}
\end{array} \quad .
$$

Let us remark that for multivalued maps with compact values one can show that σ-**ML** $= \sigma$-**MC**. The class of σ-**ML** maps is quite rich, for instance we have (cf. [19, 20, 22, 25]):

Proposition (4.6). *If* $\varphi : [0,1] \times K^n(2^r) \to \mathbb{R}^n (r < +\infty)$ *is an u.s.c. map with convex values, then* $\varphi \in \sigma$-**ML**.

It is known (cf.[20] or [25]) that (4.6) can be formulated in the following stronger version:

Proposition (4.7). *Let* M *be a compact subset of* $\mathbb{R}^n$ *and* $\varphi : [0,1] \times M \to \mathbb{R}^n$ *be an u.s.c. convex compact valued map. Then there exists a sequence* $\{\varphi_n\}$ *of convex compact valued maps*

$\varphi_n : [0,1] \times M \to \mathbb{R}^n$ *satisfying the following conditions:*

(4.7.1) for every $(t,x) \in [0,1] \times M$ *and for every* $n \in N$ *:* $\varphi(t,x) \subset \varphi_n(t,x)$,
    $\varphi_{n+1}(t,x) \subset \varphi_n(t,x)$ *and* $\varphi(t,x) = \cap \varphi_n(t,x)$;
(4.7.2) φ_n *is l.s.c. and u.s.c. for every* $n \in \mathbb{N}$.

For some other examples of σ-**ML** and σ-**MC** maps see ([1, 3, 5, 15, 20]). We will use also selection theorems for l.s.c. mappings. First, we recall the special case of the Kuratowski and Ryll-Naordzewski theorem (cf. [3]):

Proposition (4.8). *Let* $\varphi : [0,1] \to \mathbb{R}^n$ *be a bounded multivalued map. If* φ *is u.s.c. or l.s.c., then* φ *has a Lebesgue integrable selector.*

Let $L_1([0,1], \mathbb{R}^n)$ denote the Banach space of all Lebesgue integrable functions and let A be a subset of $L_1([0,1], \mathbb{R}^n)$;

A is called *decomposable*, if for every two functions $x, y \in A$ and for every Lebesgue measurable set $J \subset [0,1]$ we have

$$(\chi_J x + \chi_{[0,1] \setminus J} y) \in A ,$$

where χ_I denotes the characteristic function of $I \subset [0,1]$.

The following selection theorem is proved in [6] (cf. also [5], [15]):

Theorem (4.9). *Let* K *be a separable space and let* $\varphi : K \to L_1([0,1], \mathbb{R}^n)$ *be an l.s.c. bounded map. If* φ *has closed and decomposable values, then there exists a continuous (singlevalued) selection* f *of* φ.

5. Differential Inclusions in $\mathbb{R}^n$

The Cauchy problem for differential inclusions was studied by many authors (cf. [1, 3, 4, 5, 7, 10, 12, 14, 18, 19, 20, 21, 22, 23, 25, 27, 29, 30]).

We shall present new results concerning: (i) the topological structure of the set of solutions in the case of u.s.c. maps and (ii) the existence problem in the case of l.s.c. maps. All results are formulated, for simplicity, on $\mathbb{R}^n$ but in fact we are able to obtain them on $K^n(2r)$, for an arbitrary $r < +\infty$ (cf. Sect. 4). First, we shall formulate the Cauchy problem for differential inclusions. Let $\varphi : [0,1] \times \mathbb{R}^n \to \mathbb{R}^n$ be an arbitrary multivalued map. We shall consider the following Cauchy problem:

$$(5.1) \qquad \begin{cases} x'(t) \in \varphi(t, x(t)) \\ x(0) = x_0 , \end{cases}$$

where the solution $x : [0,1] \to \mathbb{R}^n$ of (5.1) is an absolutely continuous function such that $x'(t) \in \varphi(t, x(t))$ a.e. in $[0,1]$.

By $S(\varphi, 0, x_0)$ we shall denote the set of all solutions of (5.1). In what follows, for simplicity, we shall consider the case when $x_0 = 0$ (the general case does not make any difference) and we let $S(\varphi) = S(\varphi, 0, 0)$.

We shall start from the following theorem:

Theorem (5.2). *If $\varphi \in$ ML, then $S(\varphi)$ is a contractible set.*

Proof. Let $f \subset \varphi$ be an L-map. Then, in view of (3.7.1), the set $S(f) = S(f, 0, 0)$ is a singleton and hence $S(f) \subset S(\varphi) \neq \emptyset$. Now we shall define a homotopy: $h : S(\varphi) \times [0, 1] \to S(\varphi)$ by putting

$$h(x, s) = y_{x,s} \,,$$

where $y_{x,s} : [0, 1] \to \mathbb{R}^n$ is a map given as follows:

$$y_{x,s}(t) = \begin{cases} x(t) \,, & \text{for } 0 \le t \le s \,, \\ S(f, s, x(s))(t) \,, & \text{for } s \le t \le 1 \,. \end{cases}$$

Evidently, $y_{x,s} \in S(\varphi)$. By using (3.7.3) we deduce that h is a continuous map. Moreover we have $h(x, 0) = S(f)$ and $h(x, 1) = x$ so the proof is completed.

$\square$

Theorem (5.3). *If $\varphi \in$ MC, then $S(\varphi)$ is an acyclically contractible set.*

Proof. Let $f \subset \varphi$ be a C-map. By (3.7.2) the set $S(f) = S(f, 0, 0)$ is an R_δ-set and hence $S(f) \subset S(\varphi) \neq \emptyset$. Now, we define a multivalued homotopy $\chi : S(\varphi) \times [0, 1] \to S(\varphi)$ as follows:

$$\chi(x, s) = \{y \in C([0, 1], \mathbb{R}^n) \; ; \; y(t) = \begin{cases} x(t), & 0 \le t \le s \\ z(t), & s \le t \le 1 \quad z \in S(f, s, x(s)) \end{cases} .$$

Then, in view of (3.7.3), χ is the required homotopy and the proof is completed.

$\square$

From the above theorem, in view of (4.3) and (4.4) respectively, we get:

Corollary (5.4).

(5.4.1) If φ is a l.s.c. convex valued and bounded map, then $S(\varphi)$ is an acyclically contractible set;

(5.4.2) If $\varphi : [0, 1] \times \mathbb{R}^n \to \mathbb{R}^n$ is an u.s.c. map for every fixed $x \in \mathbb{R}^n$ and an l.s.c. map for every fixed $t \in [0, 1]$, then $S(\varphi)$ is an acyclically contractible set.

Theorem (5.5). *If $\varphi \in \sigma$-ML, then $S(\varphi)$ is an intersection of a decreasing sequence of contractible sets.*

Proof. Let $\varphi_n : [0,1] \times \mathbb{R}^n \to \mathbb{R}^n$ be a sequence of **ML**-maps satisfying (4.5.1)–(4.5.3). Then for every $(t,x) \in [0,1] \times \mathbb{R}^n$ we have $\varphi(t,x) = \cap \varphi_n(t,x)$ and hence $S(\varphi) \subset \cap S(\varphi_n)$.

Now, let $x \in \cap S(\varphi_n)$ and let $A_n \subset [0,1]$ be a set of the Lebesgue measure zero such that $x'(t) \in \varphi_n(t, x(t))$ for every $t \notin A_n$.

Then the set $A = \cup A_n$ has the Lebesgue measure zero and evidently for each $t \notin A$ we get: $x'(t) \in \varphi(t, x(t))$. Hence $x \in S(\varphi)$ and the proof is completed. $\qquad\square$

Now, from (5.5) and (4.6) we are able to deduce (cf. [20, 22, 25] and also [10] for a different method):

Theorem (5.6). *If* $\varphi : [0,1] \times \mathbb{R}^n \to \mathbb{R}^n$ *is an u.s.c., convex valued and bounded map, then* $S(\varphi)$ *is an* R_δ-*set.*

Let us remark that Theorem (5.6) remains true if we assume only that φ is convex valued, bounded and satisfies the Caratheodory conditions (cf. [4]). Moreover, in the next section we shall use the following result proved in [3]:

Theorem (5.7). *Assume* φ *is the same as in (5.6) and let* $\hat\varphi : \mathbb{R}^n \to C([0,1], \mathbb{R}^n)$ *be the multivalued map defined by the following formula:* $\hat\varphi(x) = S(\varphi, 0, x)$, *for every* $x \in \mathbb{R}^n$. *Then* $\hat\varphi$ *is an acyclic (in particular u.s.c.) map.*

It is easy to see that similarly as (5.5) we are able to obtain the following theorem:

Theorem (5.8). *If* $\varphi \in \sigma$-**MC**, *then* $S(\varphi)$ *is an intersection of a decreasing sequence of acyclically contractible sets, in particular it is an acyclic set.*

Remark (5.9). Observe that the above characterization of the set of solutions depends only on a selection property of the map φ.

In the case of l.s.c. maps we don't know a general result concerning the topological characterization of the set of solutions for the Cauchy problem but then a very general existence result is true, which we shall prove below (for details concerning the l.s.c. case see [5, 7, 14, 15, 24, 27, 30]).

Theorem (5.10). *Let* $\varphi : [0,1] \times \mathbb{R}^n \to \mathbb{R}^n$ *be a l.s.c., bounded map with compact values. Then problem (5.1) has a solution.*

Proof. Assume that $\|y\| \le M$ for every $y \in \varphi(t,x)$ and for every $(t,x) \in [0,1] \times \mathbb{R}^n$. We let:
$K = \{x \in C([0,1], \mathbb{R}^n) ;\ x$ is absolutely continuous and $\|x'(t)\| \le M$, a.e. in $[0,1]\}$. It is easily shown that K is a compact and convex subset of $C([0,1], \mathbb{R}^n)$. Now, in view of (4.8), we can define a multivalued map $\eta : K \to L_1([0,1], \mathbb{R}^n)$ by putting:

$$\eta(x) = \{u \in L_1([0,1], \mathbb{R}^n \; ; \quad u(t) \in \varphi(t, x(t)) \,, \quad a.e. \text{ in } [0,1]\} \,.$$

Observe, that η satisfies the assumptions of (4.9) and therefore there exists a continuous selector $f \subset \eta$. We let

$$T : \eta(K) \to K \,, \qquad T(u)(t) = x_0 + \int_{[0,t]} u(\tau) d\tau \,.$$

Then we have a continuous map $g : K \to K$, $g = T \circ f$. Since K is a compact and convex set from the Schauder Fixed Point Theorem we get a point $x \in K$ such that $g(x) = x$. Now, it is easy to verify that x is a solution of (5.1) and the proof is completed. $\qquad\qquad\qquad\qquad\qquad\qquad\qquad\qquad\qquad\qquad\qquad\square$

We recommend [3, 23, 30] for some related results and other methods concerning problem (5.1) for l.s.c. maps.

6. Periodic Solutions of Differential Inclusions in $\mathbb{R}^n$

In this section using the topological degree of multivalued maps we shall get some existence results of periodic solutions for differential inclusions. Our approach is strictly connected with the method presented in [24] and [26] for ordinary differential equations. In this section we will assume that $\varphi : [0,1] \times \mathbb{R}^n \to \mathbb{R}^n$ is an u.s.c. convex valued and bounded map. For such a map φ we will consider the following differential inclusion

$$(6.1) \qquad\qquad\qquad\qquad x'(t) \in \varphi(t, x(t)) \,.$$

We let

$$e : C([0,1], \mathbb{R}^n) \times [0,1] \to \mathbb{R}^n, \; e(x,t) = x(t) - x(0) \,,$$
$$\text{for every } x \in C([0,1], \mathbb{R}^n) \quad \text{and} \quad t \in [0,1] \,,$$
$$e_t : C([0,1], \mathbb{R}^n) \to \mathbb{R}^n, \; e_t(x) = x(t) - x(0) \text{ for every } x \in C([0,1], \mathbb{R}^n) \,.$$

For given $t \in [0,1]$ we have the following diagram:

$$\mathbb{R}^n \xrightarrow{\hat{\varphi}} C([0,1], \mathbb{R}^n) \xrightarrow{e_t} \mathbb{R}^n$$

in which $\hat{\varphi}$ is the acyclic map given in (5.7). In view of (1.3.1) the map $\hat{\varphi}_t = e_t \circ \hat{\varphi} : \mathbb{R}^n \to \mathbb{R}^n$ is admissible; $\hat{\varphi}$ is called also the *Poincaré translation operator*. We let $i_r : K^n(r) \to \mathbb{R}^n, i_r(x) = x$ and $\hat{\varphi}_t^r = \hat{\varphi}_t \circ i_r$.

Remark (6.2).

(6.2.1) Observe that if $0 \in \hat{\varphi}_t(x)$ then there exists a solution $y \in \hat{\varphi}(x)$ such that $x = y(0) = y(t)$;

(6.2.2) If $0 \notin \hat{\varphi}_t(x)$ for every $x \in S^{n-1}(r)$ then $\hat{\varphi}_t^r \in A(K^n(r), \mathbb{R}^n)$.

We shall add one more assumption on φ. Namely, we shall assume that $\varphi : [0,1] \times \mathbb{R}^n \to \mathbb{R}^n$ is also an ω-periodic map with respect to the first variable, i.e.,

(6.3) $\exists 0 < \omega \leq 1 \forall (t,x) \in [0,1] \times \mathbb{R}^n : ((t+\omega) \in [0,1] \Rightarrow \varphi(t+\omega, x) = \varphi(t,x))$.

We prove the following:

Theorem (6.4). *Assume $\varphi : [0,1] \times \mathbb{R}^n \to \mathbb{R}^n$ satisfies the above assumptions. Assume further that there exists an $r > 0$ such that:*

$$\left\{ x \in S^{n-1}(r); 0 \in \hat{\varphi}_\omega(x) \right\} = \emptyset .$$

If $\mathrm{Deg}\hat{\varphi}_t^r \neq 0$ then there exists a periodic solution of (6.1).

Proof. From the assumptions it follows that there exists $x \in K^n(r)$ such that $0 \in \hat{\varphi}_t(x)$. Now, in view of (6.2.1), we get a solution $y \in \hat{\varphi}(x)$ such that $y(0) = y(\omega) = x$. We define $z : [0,1] \to \mathbb{R}^n$ by putting:

$$z(t + n\omega) = y(t), \quad \text{for} \quad t \in [0,\omega] \quad \text{and} \quad (t+n\omega) \in [0,1], \ n = 1,2,\cdots .$$

Obviously, z is an ω-periodic solution of (6.1) and the proof is completed. $\square$

We shall give an application of Theorem (6.4) to the method of guiding functions (cf. [24], [18] or [26]), which we will extend from the case of ordinary differential equations to the case of differential inclusions.

Definition (6.5). Let $V : \mathbb{R}^n \to \mathbb{R}^n$ be a C^1-function. We will say that V is a *guiding function* for the differential inclusion $x'(t) \in \varphi(t, x(t))$, if there exists $r_1 > 0$ such that the following conditions are satisfied:

(6.5.1) $\langle \nabla V(x), y \rangle > 0$, for every $x \in \mathbb{R}^n, \|x\| \geq r_1$, $t \in [0,1]$ and for every $y \in \varphi(t, x(t))$,

(6.5.2) $\langle y_1, y_2 \rangle > 0$, for every $x \in \mathbb{R}^n, \|x\| \geq r_1, t \in [0,1]$ and for every $y_1, y_2 \in \varphi(t, x(t))$,

where $\nabla V(x)$ denotes the gradient of V at x and $\langle .,. \rangle$ stands for the inner product in $\mathbb{R}^n$.

Let us observe (cf. (6.5)) that for any $r \geq r_1$ the topological degree $\deg \nabla V \circ i_r$ is well defined, so we are allowed to let:

(6.6) $\qquad\qquad \mathrm{Ind}(V) = \deg \nabla V \circ i_r, \ r \geq r_1$.

Then $\mathrm{Ind}(V)$ is called the *index of the guiding function V*. It is well known that, e.g. if $V : \mathbb{R}^n \to \mathbb{R}$ is a coercive map, i.e.,

$$\lim[V(x); \|x\| \to \infty] = +\infty , \qquad \text{then} \qquad \mathrm{Ind}(V) \neq 0 .$$

Below we will assume that $\varphi : [0,1] \times \mathbb{R}^n \to \mathbb{R}^n$ has also a guiding function
$V : \mathbb{R}^n \to \mathbb{R}^n$ such that:

(6.7) $\text{Ind}(V) \neq 0$.

To get the theorem on existence of periodic solutions for (6.1) we need some
lemmas.

Lemma (6.8). *For every* $r \geq r_1$ *there exists* $\delta > 0$ *such that for every* $t \in [0, \delta)$
we have
$$\{x \in S^{n-1}(r); x \in (s(x + \varphi(0,x)) + (1-s)\hat{\varphi}_t(x));$$
$$\text{for some} \quad s \in [0,1]\} = \emptyset .$$

Proof. Assume the contrary. Then there are sequences $x_n \in S^{n-1}(r_1), t_n \to$
0^+, $z_n \in \varphi(0, x_n)$, $s_n \in [0,1]$, $y_n \in \hat{\varphi}(x_n)$ such that $x_n = s_n(x_n + z_n) + (1 -$
$s_n)y_n(t_n)$, for each $n \geq 1$. From (6.5.1) it follows that $s_n \neq 1$ for each n, so we
get:
$$x_n - y_n(t_n) = \alpha_n z_n, \qquad \text{where} \qquad \alpha_n = s_n(1 - s_n)^{-1} \geq 0$$
and consequently $(y_n \in \hat{\varphi}(x_n))$ we obtain:
$$-\int_0^{t_n} u_n(\tau) d\tau = \alpha_n z_n ,$$
where $u_n(\tau) \in \varphi(\tau, y_n(\tau))$, a.e. in $[0, t_n]$. From the last equality we get:

(6.8.1) $\int_0^{t_n} \langle u_n(\tau), z_n \rangle d\tau \leq 0$,   for each $n \geq 1$.

To get a contradiction it is sufficient to show that there exists an m such that
$\langle u_m(\tau), z_m \rangle > 0$ a.e. in $[0, t_m]$. Since $\hat{\varphi} : \mathbb{R}^n \to C([0,1], \mathbb{R}^n)$ is u.s.c. we can
assume, without loss of generality, that $\lim_n x_n = x_0$ and $\lim_n y_n = y_0$. Let us
fix for the moment a natural number n. Then the map
$$\Psi_n : [0, t_n] \to \mathbb{R}^n , \qquad \Psi_n(\tau) = \varphi(\tau, y_n(\tau))$$
is u.s.c., so $\Psi_n([0, t_n])$ is a compact subset of $\mathbb{R}^n$. Therefore there is $\tau_n \in [0, t_n]$
and $v_n \in \varphi(\tau_n, y_n(\tau_n)) = \Psi_n(\tau_n)$ (depending on τ_n) such that: $\langle v_n, z_n \rangle =$
$\min \{\langle w, z_n \rangle; w \in \varphi(\tau, y_n(\tau))$ and $\tau \in [0, t_n]\}$.
Then we have

(6.8.2) $\langle u_n(\tau), z_n \rangle \geq \langle v_n, z_n \rangle$, for each $\tau \in [0, t_n]$ and for every n.

Now observe, that $n \to \infty$ implies that $\tau_n \to 0$ and $y_n(\tau_n) \to y_0(0) = x_0$.
So upper semicontinuity of φ implies: $\lim_n \langle v_n, z_n \rangle = \langle v_0, z_0 \rangle$ where $v_0, z_0 \in$
$\varphi(0, x_0)$ and hence, in view of (6.5.2) we get: $\lim_n \langle v_n, z_n \rangle = \langle v_0, z_0 \rangle > 0$. This
means (cf. (6.8.2)) that for large values of n the integral in (6.8.1) has to be
positive and the proof of lemma is completed. $\square$

Lemma (6.9). *There exists $r_2 \geq r_1$ such that for every $r \geq r_2$ and for every $t \in [0, \omega]$ we have:*

$$\{x \in S^{n-1}(r); \, 0 \in \hat{\varphi}_t(x)\} = \emptyset .$$

Proof. We let: $A = \{y \in C([0, \omega], \mathbb{R}^n); \exists t \in [0, \omega] \; \exists x \in K^n(r_1) : y \in S(\varphi; t, x)\}$. Since $y \in S(\varphi; t, x)$ if $y(s) = x + \int_t^s u(\tau)d\tau, u(\tau) \in \varphi(\tau, y(\tau))$, a.e. in $[0, \omega]$ and φ is bounded there exists a real $r_2 \geq r_1$ such that $\|y\| \leq r_2$, for every $y \in A$. Let $r \geq r_2$ and $t_0 \in (0, \omega]$. We are going to prove that $0 \notin \hat{\varphi}_{t_0}(x)$, whenever $x \in S^{n-1}(r)$. Assume the contrary. Let $x_0 \in S^{n-1}(r)$ be a point such that $0 \in \hat{\varphi}_{t_0}(x_0)$. This means that there exists $z \in S(\varphi; 0, x_0)(= \hat{\varphi}(x_0))$ such that: $z(0) = z(t_0) = x_0$. Then it follows that: $\|z(t)\| \geq r_1$, for each $t \in [0, t_0]$. Let $u : [0, t_0] \to \mathbb{R}$ be defined as follows: $u(t) = V(z(t))$, $t \in [0, t_0]$. Then $u'(t) = \langle \nabla V(z(t)), z'(t) \rangle$ and, in view of (6.5.1), we get $u'(t) > 0$, a.e. in $[0, t_0]$ but this contradicts the equality

$$u(0) = V(z(0)) = V(x_0) = V(z(t_0)) = u(t_0)$$

and the proof of Lemma (6.9) is completed. □

Remark (6.10). Let $t_0, t_1 \in [0, 1]$ and $r > r_1$. We would like to remark that $\hat{\varphi}_{t_0}^r$ and $\hat{\varphi}_{t_1}^r$ are homotopic. Indeed, let

$$\chi_r : K^n(r) \times [0, 1] \to C([0, 1], \mathbb{R}^n) \times [0, 1], \; \chi_r(x, s) = (\hat{\varphi}(x), s) ;$$
$$h : C([0, 1], \mathbb{R}^n) \times [0, 1] \to \mathbb{R}^n, \; h(y, s) = e(y, st_1 + (1 - s)t_0) .$$

Then $e \circ \chi_r$ is a homotopy joining $\hat{\varphi}_{t_0}^r$ and $\hat{\varphi}_{t_1}^r$.

Now, we will summarize our considerations in the following:

Theorem (6.11). *Assume that $\varphi : [0, 1] \times \mathbb{R}^n \to \mathbb{R}^n$ is an u.s.c. convex valued bounded map which satisfies (6.3) and (6.7). Then the differential inclusion:*

$$x'(t) \in \varphi(t, x(t))$$

has an ω-periodic solution.

Proof. In view of (6.3) it is sufficient to show that $\mathrm{Deg}\hat{\varphi}_\omega^r \neq 0$, for some $r > 0$. Take $r \geq r_2$, where r_2 is given in (6.9). Then from (6.5.1) we get

(6.11.1) $\qquad \mathrm{Deg}\varphi(0, .) \circ i_r = \mathrm{Ind}\, V \qquad$ or equivalently

$$\mathrm{Deg}(-\varphi(0, .) \circ i_r) = (-1)^n \, \mathrm{Ind}\, V .$$

Now, from (6.8), we deduce that

(6.11.2) $\qquad \mathrm{Deg}(-\varphi(0, .) \circ i_r) = \mathrm{Deg}\hat{\varphi}_t^r \qquad$ for sufficiently small $t > 0$.

Consequently, from (6.9) and (6.10), we deduce

(6.11.3) $\qquad\qquad\qquad \mathrm{Deg}\hat{\varphi}_t^r = \mathrm{Deg}\hat{\varphi}_\omega^r .$

Finally, from (6.11.1), (6.11.2) and (6.11.3) we deduce $\mathrm{Deg}\hat{\varphi}_\omega^r = (-1)^n \mathrm{Ind}\, V$ and since, in view of (6.7) ($\mathrm{Ind}\, V \neq 0$), we obtain $\mathrm{Deg}\hat{\varphi}_\omega^r \neq 0$; the proof of Theorem (6.11) is completed. $\qquad\qquad\square$

7. Sets with Property $\mathfrak{p}$

In the preceeding sections we have always assumed that the initial point x_0, in the considered Cauchy problem for a differential inclusion, is an inner point of the domain of φ. However, there are several basic problems (e.g. global existence, existence of periodic solutions) where one is interested in solutions through boundary points, in particular if the domain of φ has no inner points at all. In this section we introduce a class of subsets of $\mathbb{R}^n$, called by us sets with property $\mathfrak{p}$ (possibly with empty interior) for which we shall be able to get the same results as in sections 5 and 6.

We shall start from the following definition:

Definition (7.1). Let M be a compact subset of $\mathbb{R}^n$. We shall say that M has property $\mathfrak{p}$ (written $M \in \mathfrak{p}$) if and only if there exists an open neighbourhood U of M in $\mathbb{R}^n$ such that the following condition is satisfied:

(7.1.1) for each $y \in U$ there exists exactly one point $x = x(y) \in M$ such that $\|y - x\| = \mathrm{dist}(y, M)$, where $\mathrm{dist}(y, M) = \inf\{\|y - z\|;\ z \in M\}$.

As an easy observation we obtain:

Proposition (7.2). $M \in \mathfrak{p}$ if and only if there exists an open neighbourhood U of M in $\mathbb{R}^n$ and a retraction $r : U \to M$ such that:

(7.2.1) $\forall y \in U : \|r(y) - y\| = \mathrm{dist}(y, M)$.

In what follows the map $r : U \to M$ satisfying (7.2.1) is called *metric retraction*.

The class of sets with property $\mathfrak{p}$ is quite rich. It is well known that any compact and convex subset of $\mathbb{R}^n$ has property $\mathfrak{p}$. If $M \subset \mathbb{R}^n$ is a compact C^2-manifold then taking a tubular neighbourhood of M in $\mathbb{R}^n$ (cf. [16]) we are able to obtain that M has property $\mathfrak{p}$. Below we shall prove that any compact C^2-manifold with boundary has property $\mathfrak{p}$. So we assume $M \subset \mathbb{R}^n$ is a compact C^2-manifold with boundary. We shall denote by ∂M the boundary of M and we let $M^0 = M \backslash \partial M$.

We shall use the following lemma:

Lemma (7.3). *If $M \subset \mathbb{R}^n$ is a compact C^2-manifold with boundary, then there exists $\varepsilon > 0$ and an open neighbourhood U of M^0 in $\mathbb{R}^n$ such that (7.1.1) holds for M^0 and*

(7.3.1) $\forall y \in \mathbb{R}^n \quad ((\exists x \in M : \|y-x\| = \mathrm{dist}(y, M) \text{ and } \|y-x\| < \varepsilon) \Rightarrow y \in U)$.

The proof of Lemma (7.3) will be presented in Sect. 9.

Theorem (7.4). *If $M \subset \mathbb{R}^n$ is a compact C^2-manifold with boundary, then $M \in \mathfrak{p}$.*

Proof. Let U and ε be given as in (7.3). Since $\partial M \in \mathfrak{p}$, there exists W an open neighbbbourhood of ∂M in $\mathbb{R}^n$ satisfying (7.1.1) such that $W \subset O_\varepsilon(\partial M)$.

Let $t : U \to M$ and $s : W \to \partial M$ be metric retractions. We shall show that $r : U \cup W \to M$, given by:

$$r(y) = t(y) \qquad \text{for} \qquad y \in U \,,$$
$$r(y) = s(y) \qquad \text{for} \qquad y \in W \backslash U \,,$$

is a metric retraction. Let us consider a sequence $\{y_n\}$ of elements of U that converges to some $y \in W \backslash U$. Since M is compact there exists a subsequence (again denoted by $\{t(y_n)\}$) of $\{t(y_n)\}$ converging to some $z \in M$.

Then

$$\|y - z\| = \lim_n \|y_n - t(y_n)\| = \lim_n \text{dist}(y_n, M) = \text{dist}(y, M) \qquad \text{and}$$

$$\text{dist}(y, M^0) = \text{dist}(y, M) \le \text{dist}(y, \partial M) < \varepsilon \,.$$

From (7.3.1) we deduce that z does not belong to M^0. It follows that $\|y - z\| \le \text{dist}(y, \partial M)$, $z \in \partial M$ and $y \in W$, and finally $s(y) = z$. We have shown that $r : U \cup W \to M$ is a continuous map. Similarly we get (7.2.1) and the proof is completed. $\qquad \square$

In the next section we shall show that the assumption about the smoothness of M in (7.4) cannot be replaced by a weaker one (cf. Example (8.5)).

8. Contingent Cone Valued Maps

In this section we recall different concepts of contingent cones. We show that they coincide for sets with property $\mathfrak{p}$. We also examine the continuity of contingent cone valued maps for such sets.

Let M be a closed subset of $\mathbb{R}^n$. The *contingent cone* $T_M(x)$ to M at $x \in M$ is defined by:

$$T_M(x) = \left\{ y \in \mathbb{R}^n; \lim \inf[t^{-1}\text{dist}(x + ty, M); t \to 0^+] = 0 \right\} \,.$$

The above concept was introduced by Bouligand in the 1930's.

Following [9] we define *Clarke's cone of normals* $N_M^{\text{Cl}}(x)$ to M at $x \in M$

$$N_M^{\text{Cl}}(x) = \text{cl conv} \left\{ \lim[s_i(y_i - x_i); i \to \infty] \right\}$$

where $\{s_i\}, \{y_i\}, \{x_i\}$ stand for arbitrary sequences such that $s_i \ge 0$, $y_i \in \mathbb{R}^n$, $y_i \to x$ and $x_i \in M$ and $\|x_i - y_i\| = \text{dist}(y_i, M)$.

The polar cone $C^{\perp}$ to a cone C in $\mathbb{R}^n$ is defined by

$$C^{\perp} = \{y \in \mathbb{R}^n; \forall x \in C \quad \langle y, x \rangle \leq 0\} \ .$$

Following [9] we define *Clarke's contingent cone* $T_M^{\mathrm{Cl}}(x)$ to M at $x \in M$ by

$$T_M^{\mathrm{Cl}}(x) = (N_M^{\mathrm{Cl}}(x))^{\perp} \ .$$

It is known (cf. [9]) that $T_M^{\mathrm{Cl}}(x) \subset T_M(x)$ for every $x \in M$. For sets belonging to $\mathfrak{p}$ we define a normal cone in a different way. So, in what follows we shall assume that $M \in \mathfrak{p}$.

Let U be an open neighbourhood of M in $\mathbb{R}^n$ such that there exists a metric retraction $r : U \to M$. We define the *normal cone* $N_M(x)$ to M at $x \in M$ by

$$N_M(x) = \{y \in \mathbb{R}^n; \exists \alpha > 0 \qquad r(x + \alpha y) = x\} \ .$$

Let's observe that if $x \in M$ is the unique closest point in M to y then x is also the unique closest point in M to $\lambda x + (1 - \lambda)y$ for every $\lambda \in (0, 1)$.

So the definition of the normal cone to M at x is independent of the choice of U. By an easy calculation one can check that $N_M(x)$ is a convex cone for every $x \in M$. The basic property of normal cones is given in the following proposition proved in [28].

Proposition (8.1). *Suppose that $r : (M + \varepsilon B) \to M$ is the metric retraction. Then $r(x + y) = x$ for every $x \in M$ and $y \in N_M(x) \cap \varepsilon B$; where B is the unit open ball in $\mathbb{R}^n$ and $\varepsilon > 0$.*

As a consequence of (8.1) we get:

Corollary (8.2). *Let $M \in \mathfrak{p}$.*

(8.2.1) Then the normal cone valued map $N_M : M \to \mathbb{R}^n$ has a closed graph in $M \times \mathbb{R}^n$;

(8.2.2) Then $N_M(x) = N_M^{\mathrm{Cl}}(x)$ for every $x \in M$.

Moreover, we have the following (cf. [28]):

Proposition (8.3). *Let $M \in \mathfrak{p}$. Then $T_M(x) = N_M(x)^{\perp}$ for every $x \in M$.*

So, let's observe that Clarke's contingent cone equals Bouligand's contingent cone, under the assumption that $M \in \mathfrak{p}$.

We recall that if $N : M \to \mathbb{R}^n$ is a closed convex cone valued map with closed graph in $M \times \mathbb{R}^n$ then the map $T : M \to \mathbb{R}^n$ given by $T(x) = N(x)^{\perp}$ is l.s.c. (cf. [3]).

Now, from the above remark, (8.3) and (8.2.1), we obtain the main result of this section:

Theorem (8.4). *Let $M \in \mathfrak{p}$. Then the contingent cone valued map $T_M : M \to \mathbb{R}^n$ is l.s.c.*

Note that for closed convex subsets of $\mathbb{R}^n$ Theorem (8.4) is well known (cf. [3], [13]).

Now, we give an example showing that the assumption about the smoothness of M in (7.4) can not be replaced by a weaker one.

Example (8.5). Let the function $f : [0,1] \to \mathbb{R}^n$ be given by

$$f(x) = \begin{cases} |x|^{-1/2} \sin(1/x) & \text{for } x \neq 0 , \\ 0 & \text{for } x = 0 . \end{cases}$$

An elementary calculation shows that the function $h : [0,1] \to \mathbb{R}$ given by

$$h(x) = \begin{cases} \int_{[0,x]} f(t)\mathrm{d}t & \text{for } x \neq 0 , \\ 0 & \text{for } x = 0 ; \end{cases}$$

is differentiable on $(0,1)$ and $h'(x) = f(x)$ for every $x \in (0,1)$.

Finally, we set $g(x) = \int_{[0,x]} h(t)\mathrm{d}t$.

Obviously, we have $g''(x) = f(x)$ for every $x \in (0,1)$. We let $M = \Gamma_g$, where Γ_g denotes the graph of the function $g : [-1,1] \to \mathbb{R}$.

Recall that the radius of curvature $r(x)$ of M at $(x, g(x))$ is given by $r(x) = |g''(x)|^{-1}(1+g'(x)^2)^{3/2}$. So $\liminf[r(x); x \to 0] = 0$. Thus, there exist sequences $\{z_n\}, \{w_n\}, \{v_n\}$ such that: for every $n \in \mathbb{N}$ $w_n \in M$, $v_n \in M$, $w_n - z_n \in N_M(w_n)$, $v_n - z_n \in N_M(v_n)$ and $\lim[\|w_n - z_n\|; n \to \infty] = 0$, $\lim[\|v_n - z_n\|; n \to \infty] = 0$. By Proposition (8.1), M does not belong to $\mathfrak{p}$.

9. Differential Inclusions on Sets with Property $\mathfrak{p}$

The aim of this section is to show that all results of Sect. 5 can be obtained for differential inclusions when the right hand side φ is a map defined on a set with property $\mathfrak{p}$.

Assume that $\varphi : [0, \infty) \times M \to \mathbb{R}^n$ is a multivalued map such that $\varphi(t, x) \subset T_M(x)$ for every $(t, x) \in [0, \infty) \times M$. Let U be an open neighbourhood of M in $\mathbb{R}$ for which there exists a metric retraction $r : U \to M$. Let $\alpha : \mathbb{R}^n \to [0, 1]$ be an Urysohn function such that $\alpha(x) = 1$, for every $x \in M$ and $\alpha(x) = 0$, for every $x \notin U$. Then we define a multivalued map $\tilde{\varphi} : [0, \infty) \times \mathbb{R}^n \to \mathbb{R}^n$ by putting:

$$(9.1) \qquad \tilde{\varphi}(t,x) = \begin{cases} \alpha(x)\varphi(t,r(x)), & \text{for } x \in U \text{ and } t \in [0,\infty) \\ \{0\}, & \text{for } x \notin U \text{ and } t \in [0,\infty) \end{cases}$$

It is easy to verify that $\tilde{\varphi}$ is an extension of φ. We are going to prove that the existence problem and the characterization problem for the differential inclusion with right hand side φ may be reduced, very easily, to the case when the right hand side is $\tilde{\varphi}(\tilde{\varphi}$ is defined on all of $\mathbb{R}^n!$).

Proposition (9.2). *Let* $x : [0,\infty) \to \mathbb{R}^n$ *be an absolutely continuous function such that* $x(0) \in M$ *and* $x'(t) \in \tilde{\varphi}(t,x(t))$ *a.e. in* $[0,\infty)$. *Then* $x(t) \in M$ *for each* $t \in [0,\infty)$.

The proof of (9.2) is standard (cf. [13]), so we omit it.

Remark (9.3). Proposition (9.2) implies that

(9.3.1) $S(\varphi, 0, x_0) = S(\tilde{\varphi}, 0, x_0)$, provided $x_0 \in M$ and $\varphi(t,x) \subset T_M(x)$ for every $(t,x) \in [0,\infty) \times M$.

Moreover, the following properties of $\tilde{\varphi}$ are simple exercises and therefore we leave the proof to the reader.

Proposition (9.4).

(9.4.1) *If* φ *is an u.s.c. (l.s.c.) map, then* $\tilde{\varphi}$ *is also u.s.c. (l.s.c.).*
(9.4.2) *If* φ *has a continuous selector, then* $\tilde{\varphi}$ *has also a continuous selector.*
(9.4.3) *If* $\varphi \in \sigma\text{-}\mathbf{MC}$ *(on* M; *i.e., we have assumed that* $\varphi_n(t,x) \subset T_M(x)$, *for every* n*), then* $\tilde{\varphi} \in \sigma\text{-}\mathbf{MC}$.

Remark (9.5). In view of (9.2) and (9.4) we are able to reformulate the respective results presented in Sect. 5, for maps φ satisfying $\varphi(t,x) \subset T_M(x)$. In particular, theorems (5.6), (5.7), (5.8), (5.9) and (5.10) remain true in case when $M \in \mathfrak{p}$ and $\varphi : [0,\infty) \times M \to \mathbb{R}^n$ is a map satsifying the condition $\varphi(t,x) \subset T_M(x)$ for every $(t,x) \in [0,\infty) \times M$.

We apply methods developed above to the existence of periodic solutions. First, observe that if $M \in \mathfrak{p}$, then M is a compact absolute neighbourhood retract (cf. (7.2)).Therefore we can define the Euler characteristic $\chi(M)$ of M (cf. Sect. 2).

Now assume that $\varphi : [0,\infty) \times M \to \mathbb{R}^n$ is an u.s.c. map with compact convex values which satisfies the condition $\varphi(t,x) \subset T_M(x)$ for every $(t,x) \in [0,\infty) \times M$. Then the Poincaré translation operator:

$$\hat{\varphi}_\omega : M \to M$$

is an admissible map which is homotopic to Id_M (cf. Sect. 6).
Therefore in view of (6.4) and (2.2) we get:

Proposition (9.6). *If φ satisfies the above assumptions and $\chi(M) \neq 0$, then for any $\omega > 0$, the differential inclusion $x'(t) \in \varphi(t, x(t))$ has a solution $x :$ $[0, \infty) \to M$ such that $x(0) = x(\omega)$.*

Furthermore, if for some $\omega > 0$, φ satisfies

$$\varphi(t, x) \subset \varphi(t + \omega, x) \qquad \text{for any } (t, x) \in [0, \infty) \times M$$

then the differential inclusion $x'(t) \in \varphi(t, x(t))$ admits an ω-periodic solution.

The main result of this section is the following:

Theorem (9.7). *Suppose M belongs to $\mathfrak{p}$ and the Euler characteristic $\chi(M)$ is nonzero. Let $\varphi : [0, \infty) \times M \to \mathbb{R}^n$ be an u.s.c. map with convex compact values which is ω-periodic, $\omega > 0$, with respect to the first variable and satisfies*

$$\varphi(t, x) \cap T_M(x) \neq \emptyset \qquad \text{for every } (t, x) \in [0, \infty) \times M .$$

Then the differential inclusion $x'(t) \in \varphi(t, x(t))$ admits an ω-periodic solution.

Proof. By Proposition (4.7), there exists a sequence $\{\varphi_n\}$ of l.s.c. convex compact valued maps $\varphi_n : [0, \infty) \times M \to \mathbb{R}^n$ satisfying for each $(t, x) \in [0, \infty) \times M$: $\varphi(t, x) \subset \varphi_n(t, x)$, $\varphi_{n+1}(t, x) \subset \varphi_n(t, x)$, for every $\varepsilon > 0$ there exist $n_0 \in \mathbb{N}$ such that $\varphi_n(t, x) \subset \varphi(t, x) + \varepsilon B$ for each $n \geq n_0$. For every $n \in \mathbb{N}$, we define a nonempty convex compact valued map $H_n : [0, \infty) \times M \to \mathbb{R}^n$ by putting

$$H_n(t, x) = \mathrm{cl}((\varphi_n(t, x) + n^{-1}B) \cap T_M(x)) .$$

By Theorem (8.4), the map H_n is l.s.c. Thus, by the Michael selection theorem, there exists a continuous function $h_n : [0, \infty) \times M \to \mathbb{R}^n$ such that $h_n(t, x) \in H_n(t, x)$ for every $(t, x) \in [0, \infty) \times M$. Now, let us consider ordinary differential equations:

$$(9.8)_n \qquad\qquad x'(t) = h_n(t, x(t)) .$$

By Proposition (9.6), for every $n \in \mathbb{N}$ there is a solution $x_n : [0, \omega] \to M$ of $(9.8)_n$ such that $x_n(\omega) = x_n(0)$. Using the compactness theorem (cf. [3]) we can choose a subsequence (denoted again $\{x_n\}$) of $\{x_n\}$ such that x_n converges, for the corresponding topology of uniform convergence, to an absolutely continuous function: $x : [0, T] \to M$ and x'_n converges weakly in $L^1([0, T], \mathbb{R}^n)$ to x'. To end the proof, it suffices to prove that x is a solution of the differential inclusion $x'(t) \in \varphi(t, x(t))$. This is given by a standard argument, using Mazur's convexity theorem. $\qquad\qquad\square$

Now, we shall adopt the guiding function method to the multivalued case. To do this, we shall need the following:

Proposition (9.9). *Let $V : \mathbb{R}^n \to \mathbb{R}$ be a C^2-function such that there exists a real number β such that the following two conditions are satisfied:*

(9.9.1) the set $M = \{x \in \mathbb{R}^n; V(x) \leq \beta\}$ is nonempty;

(9.9.2) for every $x \in \mathbb{R}^n$, if $V(x) \geq \beta$, then $\nabla V(x) \neq 0$.

Then $M \in \mathfrak{p}$ and $\chi(M) \neq 0$.

Proof. For the proof it is sufficient to show that M is a retract of $\mathbb{R}^n$. Consider a C^1-map $g : \mathbb{R}^n \backslash M \to \mathbb{R}^n$ given as follows:

$$g(x) = -\nabla V(x) \|\nabla V(x)\|^{-2} \qquad \text{for} \qquad x \in \mathbb{R}^n \backslash M .$$

We define the required retraction $r : \mathbb{R}^n \to M$ by putting

$$r(x) = S(g, 0, x)(f(x) - \beta) , \text{ for } x \notin M ,$$
$$r(x) = x , \quad \text{for } x \in M ;$$

and the proof is completed.   □

Remark (9.10). Assume that $V : \mathbb{R}^n \to \mathbb{R}$ is a C^2-function and $M = V^{-1}(-\infty, a)$ is a nonempty set. If for some $x \in V^{-1}(a)$ and $v \in \mathbb{R}^n$ we have $\langle v, \nabla V(x) \rangle \leq 0$, then evidently $v \in T_M(x)$.

Summing up the above we get the following theorem (cf. Theorem (6.11) and Proposition VI.6 in [26] for singlevalued φ):

Theorem (9.11). *Assume that*

(9.11.1) $\varphi : [0, 1] \times \mathbb{R}^n \to \mathbb{R}^n$ is an u.s.c. with compact convex values which is ω-periodic with respect to the first variable map;

(9.11.2) $V : \mathbb{R}^n \to \mathbb{R}$ is a C^2-function such that there exists $\beta \in \mathbb{R}$ for which the following conditions are satisfied:

(i) the set $M = \{x \in \mathbb{R}^n; V(x) \leq \beta\}$ is compact and nonempty;

(ii) $\langle y, \nabla V(x) \rangle \leq 0$, whenever $x \in \mathbb{R}^n$, $V(x) = \beta$, $t \in [0, 1]$ and $y \in \varphi(t, x)$;

(iii) $\nabla V(x) \neq 0$, whenever $V(x) \geq \beta$.

Then the differential inclusion $x'(t) \in (t, x(t))$ has an ω-periodic solution $x : [0, 1] \to \mathbb{R}^n$ such that $V(x(t)) \leq \beta$, for every $t \in [0, 1]$.

We recommend [3, 24, 27, 29, 30] for some other problems (e.g., monotone solutions, control theory or differential inclusions on Banach spaces) concerning the subject considered in the present paper. Finally, let us remark that some existence-type results can be obtained without the assumption that $M \in \mathfrak{p}$ (cf. [7]).

10. Proof of Lemma (7.3)

Let $M \subset \mathbb{R}^n$ be a C^2-manifold and $x \in M$. By $T_x M$ we shall denote the tangent space to M at x and by $O_x M$ its orthogonal complement in $\mathbb{R}^n$, i.e., we have $\mathbb{R}^n = T_x M \oplus O_x M$. We let:

$\tau : M \to \mathbb{R}^n$, $\quad \tau(x) = O_x M$, $\quad$ for every $x \in M$;

$\beta_c : M \to \mathbb{R}^n$, $\quad \beta_c(x) = \{x + y; y \in \tau(x) \text{ and } \|y\| < c\}$, for every $x \in M$;

$\chi_c : M \to \mathbb{R}^n$, $\quad \chi_c(x) = \{x + y; y \in \tau(x) \text{ and } \|y\| < c\}$, for every $x \in M$;

$U(N, c) = \bigcup_{x \in M} \beta_c(x)$, where $N \subset M$ and c is a positive number .

For the proof of Lemma (7.3) we need three additional facts which are called by us Proposition (10.1), Proposition (10.2) and Proposition (10.3).

Proposition (10.1). *Assume that (X, d) is a compact metric space and $\{U_\alpha\}_{\alpha \in \Lambda}$ is an open covering of X. Then there exists a positive number ε such that*

$(10.1.1)$ $\qquad\qquad \forall x \in X \exists \alpha \in \Lambda : \operatorname{dist}(x, X \backslash U_\alpha) < \varepsilon$.

Proof. Assume the contrary. Then there exists a sequence $\{x_n\} \subset X$ such that $\operatorname{dist}(x_n, X \backslash U_\alpha) < n^{-1}$, for every $\alpha \in \Lambda$ and for every $n \in \mathbb{N}$.

Since X is a compact space we can assume without loss of generality that $\lim_n x_n = x_0$. Assume that $x_0 \in U_\alpha$ for some $\alpha \in \Lambda$. Then we deduce:

$$\operatorname{dist}(x_n, X \backslash U_\alpha) > \operatorname{dist}(x_0, X \backslash U_\alpha) - d(x_0, x_n)$$

and in view of our assumptions we get

$$n^{-1} \geq \operatorname{dist}(x_0, X \backslash U_\alpha) - d(x_0, x_n) , \quad \text{for every } n \in \mathbb{N} .$$

This implies that $\operatorname{dist}(x_0, X \backslash U_\alpha) = 0$ and we obtain a contradiction. The proof is completed. $\qquad\square$

Proposition (10.2). *If $\|y - x\| = \operatorname{dist}(y, M)$, for some $x \in M$ and $y \in \mathbb{R}^n$, then $(y - x) \in O_x M$.*

Proof. Suppose, to the contrary, that there exists $z \in T_x M$ such that $\langle y - z, z \rangle > 0$. Taking $\varepsilon = 2 \langle y - x, z \rangle \|z\|^{-2}$ we have $\|y - x - tz\| \leq \|y - x\|$, for every $t \in (0, \varepsilon)$. Let $S = \{v \in \mathbb{R}^n; \|y - v\| = \|y - x\|\}$, $K = \{v \in \mathbb{R}^n; \|y - v\| \leq \|y - x\|\}$. As $K \cap M = \emptyset$ and $(x + tz) \in K$ for $t \in (0, \varepsilon)$ we have $\operatorname{dist}(x + tz, M) \geq \operatorname{dist}(x + tz, S)$.

It follows that

$$\liminf [t^{-1} \operatorname{dist}(x + tz, M), \, t \to 0^+] \geq \liminf [t^{-1} \operatorname{dist}(x + tz, S), \, t \to 0^+] .$$

By an easy computation we obtain:

$$\liminf[t^{-1}\mathrm{dist}(x + tz, S), \, t \to 0^+] = \langle y - x, z \rangle \|y - x\| \, .$$

From our assumptions we infer:

$$\liminf[t^{-1}\mathrm{dist}(x + tz, M), \, t \to 0^+] = 0, \qquad \text{for every } z \in T_x M \, .$$

This contradics the fact that $\langle y - x, z \rangle > 0$ and the proof is completed. □

Proposition (10.3). *(cf. [16], p. 197) Suppose M is a C^2-manifold and $x \in M^\circ$. Then there exist an open neighbourhood N of x in M° and a positive number c such that the following conditions are satisfied:*

(10.3.1) $\forall x, y \in N : x \neq y \Rightarrow \chi_c(x) \cap \chi_c(y) = \emptyset$;
(10.3.2) $U(N, c)$ *is an open subset of* $\mathbb{R}^n$;
(10.3.3) the map $r : U(N, c) \to N$ *given by* $r(y) = x$ *whenever* $y \in \beta_c(x)$ *is continuous.*

Remark (10.4). Let N_1 be an open subset of N and assume that $c_1 = 2^{-1}\inf\{\mathrm{dist}(z, Fr\, U(N, c)); z \in N_1\}$ is positive. Then, it is easy to see that $U(N_1, c_1)$ satisfies (10.3.1), (10.3.2) and (10.3.3). Moreover the following condition holds:

(10.4.1) $\forall y \in U(N_1, c_1) : \|y - r(y)\| = \mathrm{dist}(y, N_1)$.

Now we are able to prove Lemma (7.3)

Proof. For a given $k \leq n$ we let $H_k = \{(x_1, x_2, \cdots, x_k) \in \mathbb{R}^n : x_k \geq 0\}$. Since M is a differential manifold inbedded in $\mathbb{R}^n$ for every $x \in M$ there exist: an open subset $U_x \subset \mathbb{R}^n$, an open neighbourhood W_x of x in $\mathbb{R}^n$ and a C^2-imbedding $\varphi_x : U_x \to W_x$ such that

$$V_x \cap M = \varphi_x(U_x), \quad \text{whenever } x \in (M^\circ) \, ;$$
$$V_x \cap M = \varphi_x(U_x \cap H_k), \quad \text{whenever} \quad x \in \partial M \, .$$

Let $M_x = \varphi_x(U_x)$. Then it is evident that $x \in M_x^\circ$. From (10.3) and (10.4) we obtain $N_x, c_x, r_x : U(N_x, c_x) \to N_x$. Applying Proposition (10.1) to the covering $\{N_x \cap M\}_{x \in M}$ of the compact set M we get a positive number ε such that (10.1.1) holds. So for each $x \in M$ we can fix a point $y(x) \in M$ such that $\mathrm{dist}(x, M \backslash N_{y(x)}) > \varepsilon$. Now for every $x \in M$ we choose an open subset $\tilde{U}_x$ of U_x such that $x \in \varphi_x(\tilde{U}_x)$ and $\mathrm{diam}(\varphi_x(\tilde{U}_x)) < 4^{-1}\varepsilon$. Let $\tilde{M}_x = \varphi_x(\tilde{U}_x)$. From (10.3) and (10.4) we obtain $\tilde{N}_x, \tilde{c}_x, \tilde{r}_x : U(\tilde{N}_x, \tilde{c}_x) \to \tilde{N}_x$. It is evident that $M \cap \tilde{N}_x \subset N_{y(x)}$ and

$$r_{y(x)}(z) = \tilde{r}_x(z), \quad \text{for every } z \in U(\tilde{N}_x \cap M, c) \text{ and for every } c \leq c_{y(x)} \, .$$

Since M is a compact space, we can choose $x_1, x_2, \cdots, x_m \in M$ such that $\left\{\tilde{N}_{x_i} \cap M\right\}_{i=1,2,\cdots,m}$ is a covering of M. We let $y_i = y(x_i)$, $c = \min(c_{y_1}, \cdots,$

$c_{y_m}, \tilde{c}_{x_1}, \cdots, \tilde{c}_{x_m}, 4^{-1}\varepsilon)$, $N_i = N_{y_i} \cap (M^\circ)$, $U_i = U(N_i, c)$, $r_i = r_{y_i}$, $\tilde{N}_i = \tilde{N}_{x_i} \cap M^\circ$, $\tilde{U}_i = U(\tilde{N}_i, c)$, $\tilde{r}_i = \tilde{r}_{x_i}$. Let us take $z \in \tilde{U}_i \cap \tilde{U}_j$. Then by an easy computation we get $\tilde{N}_i \subset N_j$ and hence $\tilde{r}_i(z) = r_j(z) = \tilde{r}_j(z)$. Finally, let $V = \cup \left\{ \tilde{U}_i : i = 1, 2, \cdots, n \right\}$ and let $r : V \to M^\circ$ be a map given as follows $r(z) = \tilde{r}_i(z)$, whenever $z \in \tilde{U}_i$. Then r satisfies conditions (7.2.1) and (7.3.1) and the proof of Lemma (7.3) is completed. $\qquad\square$

References

1. Antosiewicz, H.A., Cellina, A: Continuous selections and differential relations. J. Diff. Eq. **19** (1975) 386–398
2. Aronszajn, N.: Le correspondent topologique de l'unicit dans la théorie des équations différentielles. Ann. Math. **43** (1942) 730–738
3. Aubin, J.P., Cellina, A.: Differential inclusions. Springer-Verlag, Berlin Heidelberg New York 1982
4. Blasi, F.S. de, Myjak, J.: On the solution sets for differential inclusions. Bull. Acad. Polon. Sci. **33** (1985) 17–23
5. Bogatyrev, A.V.: Continuous branches of multivalued mappings and differential inclusions with nonconvex right-hand side. Mat. Sbornik **120** (1983) 339–348
6. Bressan, A., Colombo, G.: Extensions and selections of maps with decomposable values. Studia Math. **40** (1988) 69–86
7. Bressan, A.: Solutions of lower semicontinuous differential inclusions on closed sets. Rend. Sem. Mat. Univ. Padowa **69** (1983) 99–107
8. Cellina, A.: A selection theorem. Rend. Sem. Univ. Padowa **55** (1976) 143–149
9. Clarke, F.: Generalized gradients and applications. Trans. Amer. Math. Soc. **205** (1975) 247–262
10. Davy, J.L.: Properties of the solution set of a generalized differential equation. Bull. Austral. Math. Soc. **6** (1972) 379–398
11. Deimling, K.: Ordinary differential equations in Banach spaces. Lecture Notes in Math., 596, Springer-Verlag, Berlin Heidelberg New York 1977
12. Deimling, K.: Nonlinear functional analysis. Springer-Verlag, Berlin Heidelberg New York 1980
13. Deimling, K.: Multivalued maps and multivalued differential equations. Technical Report [#]233, RCAS of the University of Texas at Arlington (preprint), Arlington 1985
14. Filippov, A.F.: Differential equations with a discontinuous right-hand side. Nauka, Moscow 1975 (in Russian)
15. Fryszkowski, A.: Continuous selections for a class of non-convex multivalued maps. Studia Math. **76** (1983) 163–174
16. Fuks, D.B., Rohlin, W.A.: A beginning course in topology: geometrical chapters. Nauka, Moscow 1977 (in Russian)
17. Górniewicz, L.: Homological methods in fixed point theory of multivalued maps. Dissertationes Math. **129** (1976) 1–71
18. Górniewicz, L.: Topological degree of morphisms and its applications to differential inclusions. March-April 1983, 5, Raccolta di Sem. del Dip. di Mat., Univer. Degli Studi Della Calabria, pp. 1–48

19. Górniewicz, L.: On the solution sets of differential inclusions. J. of Math. Anal. and Appl. **113** (1986) 235–244

20. Haddad, G.: Topological properties of the set of solutions for functional differential equations. Nonlinear Anal. TMA **5** (1981) 1349–1366

21. Haddad, G., Lasry, J.M.: Periodic solutions of functional differential inclusions and fixed points of σ-selectionable correspondences. J. Math. Anal. and Appl. **110** (1983) 295–312

22. Himmelberg, C., Vleck, F. van: A note on the solution sets of differential inclusions. Rocky Mountain J. Math. **12** (1982) 621–625

23. Himmelberg, C., Vleck, F. van: Existence of solutions for generalized differential equations with unbounded right-hand side. J. of Diff. Eq. **61** (1986) 295–320

24. Krasnosel'skiĭ., M.A., Zabreĭko, P.P.: Geometrical Methods of Nonlinear Analysis. Springer-Verlag, Berlin Heidelberg New York 1984

25. Lasry, J.M., Robert, R.: Analyse non-linéaire multivoque. Centre de Recherche de Math., No. 7611, Paris-Dauphine, pp. 1–190

26. Mawhin, J.: Topological degree methods in nonlinear boundary value problems. Regional conference series in mathematics, no. 40, 1977

27. Pianigiani, G.: On the fundamental theory of multivalued differential equations. J. Diff. Eq. **25** (1977) 30–38

28. Plaskacz, S.: Periodic solutions of differential inclusions on compact subsets of $\mathbb{R}^n$. J. of Math. Anal. and Appl. (to appear)

29. Pruszko, T.: Some applications of the topological degree theory to multivalued boundary value problems. Dissertationes Math., 229 (1984) 1–48

30. Tolstogonov, A.A.: Differential inclusions in Banach spaces. Nauka, Moscow 1986 (in Russian)